Veblen's Century

Edited with an introduction by
Irving Louis Horowitz

Veblen's Century

A Collective Portrait

Transaction Publishers
New Brunswick (U.S.A.) and London (U.K.)

Third paperback printing 2009

New material this edition copyright © 2002 by Transaction Publishers, New Brunswick, New Jersey. All material originally published by Transaction Publishers.

This book is printed on acid-free paper that meets the American National Standard for Permanence of Paper for Printed Library Materials.

Library of Congress Catalog Number: 2001033299
ISBN: 978-0-7658-0099-2 (cloth); 978-0-7658-0882-0 (paper)
Printed in the United States of America

Library of Congress Cataloging-in-Publication Data

Veblen's century: a collective portrait / edited with an introduction by
      Irving Louis Horowitz
         p. cm.
      Includes bibliographical references.
      ISBN 0-7658-0099-3 (cloth: alk. paper) — ISBN 0-7658-0882-X
      (pbk: alk. paper)
         1. Veblen, Thorstein, 1857-1929. 2. Economics—United States.
      I. Horowitz, Irving Louis.

HB119. V4 V43 2001
330'.092—dc21   2001033299

Contents

Introduction

It may strike the reader as presumptuous for an editor to entitle this volume *Veblen's Century*. Every field of the sciences, humanities, and literature has its own heroes and icons. I have no wish to enter into an absurd contest as to whom is "better" or "more important" in the pantheon of scholars. Rather I have chosen this admittedly flamboyant title to illustrate the themes that played out over the course of time that are indelibly stamped with Thorstein Veblen's imprint, not who owned the twentieth century in intellectual terms.

In doing so, I make no judgment that Veblen was a sage or a prophet, or as right as rain on every issue. Indeed, my own remarks on Veblen's briefer essays, and many of the essays on Veblen contained in this special collection, call attention to the weakness of his formulations and even egregious mistakes in his predictions. That being the case, in what sense then can we define the twentieth century as Veblen's? Indeed, he is rarely placed on the same pedestal as, say, Albert Einstein, Sigmund Freud, or even his fellow economist, John Maynard Keynes. Thus, the task of introducing also becomes an obligation to justify.

I am, nonetheless, confident that those who persevere in reading this collection will find its title appropriate. The special place of honor reserved for truly important figures is deserved by Thorstein Veblen—iconoclastic economist, social critic, and moral judge of the American way of life. That Veblen has attracted such an unusually diverse and disparate group of commentators should in itself warrant close attention to him. People from every spectrum of political ideology and every branch of the social sciences have been drawn to his work—sometimes in praise, sometimes in criticism, but always with a sense of measuring what he said and how, or if, his position can be trumped.

Institutions of higher learning have drifted from a stodgy conservatism to a militant radicalism. The leisure class has turned out to be something other than the ruling class. People of means seem to prefer privacy to ostentation—and pay a great deal to achieve it. The power of wealth and assets is at least as apparent in our awareness as the conspicuous consumption that Veblen claimed guides us. One can continue in this vein in field after field: errors in the assessment of German intentions or capabilities, the role of corporate ownership vis-à-vis corporate management, and no less, a critique rather than celebration of American culture. Alienation from the mainstream has become more of a counterculture than Veblen ever imagined possible. But to fasten on such predictive shortcomings, as indeed we must at the sheer level of assessing truth, is to miss Veblen's unique contributions in sensitizing American intellectuals to the master strategies and issues of our time—his time and now ours.

It is hard to believe that Veblen died in August 1929, or one month before my own birth. He obviously missed, if that is the correct word, the Depression, World War II, nuclear weapons, the Nazi system and the Holocaust, the Stalinist phase of Soviet communism, the emergence of a Third World, a communications revolution far beyond anything he could imagine, the emergence of a post-industrial capitalism, and the collapse of the communist system worldwide. In purely domestic terms, he barely comprehended the enormous shift in racial relations in the larger society and gender relations in more intimate aspects of social life. This is not a matter of right or wrong prognostications, but simple shattering events that redefined the American landscape and the world system.

So what then are Veblen's contributions that have persisted through time? Each of the essays offers its own answer to such a question. My own assessment, and one to which others have also called attention, is not too hard to identify. First and foremost, is Veblen's keen linkage of psychology and economy, of mind and money as it were. For it remains a fact, or at least I would aver such, that at the end of the century, these two disciplines have most sharply characterized American life. Ours is not a political culture. Not that we do not have politics. Rather our politics are all bunched up precisely in some middle ground, one that seeks particularly a fusion of personal sentiments and economic goals.

Because of this, Veblen was ultimately a student—an anthropologist if you will—of the American culture. We share his emphasis, if not his alienation, his sense of the stranger within peering out at the complex foundation of behavior—whether such behavior is defined in terms of attitudes toward work and leisure, wealth and poverty, and finally war and peace. For better or worse, twentieth-century America showed the face of the proximate future to the world. Veblen knew this well, better than any other serious commentator. With all the emphasis on Veblen as an outsider, and even a foreigner within our midst, he probably was that thinker who most closely touched the inner core of what makes the American a different sort of person from, say, the European or the Asian. We have to look back to an Alexis de Tocqueville to come up with another student of American life who has looked so deeply into the soft underbelly of a culture formed in equal measure by psychological need and economical greed.

A casual look at the contributors to the Veblen literature serves to illustrate this point. Whatever their disciplinary background, whether they be David Riesman, Douglas Dowd, Max Lerner, E. Digby Baltzell, C. Wright Mills, Daniel Bell, or the other outstanding contributors, all share with Veblen a linkage between economic system, psychological propensity, and cultural formation. And that gets us to the amorphous world of "post-modernism" that in truth began with Veblen even if it may have ended with Foucault, Derrida, and Lacan. He caught a sense of the malleability of culture that broke the back of the nineteenth-century stranglehold on social analysis. He did so by simply seeing systems as volitional rather than deterministic in character, formed by human beings rather than by actors playing out preordained scripts.

Veblen was as close as America came in the twentieth century to producing a freewheeling intellectual; he was neither defined nor contained by a single university. He was not a product of an artifact such as the Chicago School, or any other departmental generated collectivity. For all his faith in socialism as a system, it was individualism that clearly made him stand apart as a man. Veblen was aware enough of this contradiction. He worked alone because only in this way could he emerge as a commentator to the social schools sciences but also a writer within the cultural setting of his age. It is little wonder that he stood closer to Theodore Dreiser than to Andrew Carnegie. He studied industrialists as a specimen, a literary type that merits scrutiny more than obedience. It was not that Veblen sought marginality, rather it was the combustion of native sentiment and natural resource that made the experience with nationhood so distinctive.

In an age that had just started to value specialization in its intellectual class, Veblen represented the reverse, the generalist who held the specialist in nonchalant contempt. Although trained in economics, Veblen's work is more likely to be found being taught in sociology and psychology classes. He was the father of the "soft" social sciences, the "marginal" social scientists. Veblen will forever remain their special saint. Concern for how personal behaviors and public morals shape our economic systems is hardly likely to send shivers down the spines of the "hard" social scientists—except, of course, when their prophecies go awry, and when crises take place that seem to defy easy categorization.

At times of crisis, Veblen will be drawn out of the closets. This will be so because he expresses the innermost suspicion of those who believe that all social science is "soft" because indeterminacy is a fact of all human life. At the end of the day, Veblen gave voice to a time in which culture and civilization have returned to dominate the discourse of the wise and the best among us. A hundred years from now, someone will again come along with the bright idea for a compendium (or an *e-book*) entitled once again *Veblen's Century*. Veblen endures.

Irving Louis Horowitz
January 31, 2001

Part I

1

Veblen in the Context of American Culture

David Riesman

> *Although Veblen was aloof, he was not isolated. Historians have emphasized his Norwegian inheritance, but Ole Rølvaag had a similar inheritance and was not flawed. The environment was more important—the Middle Border that produced in his generation Lester Ward and Frederick Turner, Vernon Parrington and Charles Beard, Simon Patten and John R. Commons, and so many others who broke through the neat patterns of thought which the wise men of the East had designed for them.*
> Henry Steele Commager, The American Mind

At least since the Romantic movement, the intellectuals of all the Western world have been prey to disaffection. On the Continent, they have not lacked place and power, but they have bemoaned the lack of stable class and symbolic identifications or have leaped into factitious identifications with "the workers" or "the State" or some similar abstraction. Everywhere, as an attempted banner of their own identity, they have elaborated a stance towards the machine, sometimes to rhapsodize but more commonly to denigrate. Occasionally, they have looked beyond the machine to the processes of social organization, viewed as machine-like—as in Max Weber's image of the West caught in an "iron cage" of overrationality and overcontrol, to be coped with only by stoic self-control. In the novels and aphorisms of Kafka these cumulated attitudes received perhaps their most profound expression.

We may remind ourselves of these attitudes by reference to what I regard as the most searching criticism that has been published on Veblen: T.W. Adorno's "Veblen's Attack on Culture," an article which makes the point that Veblen, for all his splenetic rage, was too much the prisoner of the norms of American culture, such as efficiency and hard-headed practicality, to render an adequate account of it.

Adorno writes (*Studies in Philosophy and Social Science,* vol. 9, 1941, pp. 392, 401):

> As the mass production of identical goods and their monopolistic distribution advances and as the framework of highly industrialized life permits less and less the genuine individuation of a *hic et nunc,* the pretension of the *hic et nunc* to escape universal fungibility becomes more illusory. It is as if each thing's claim to be something special were mocking at a situation in which everyone and everything is incessantly subject to a perennial sameness. Veblen cannot stand this mockery. His rebellion actually lies in his obstinate insistence that this world present itself with that abstract sameness of its commodities which is prescribed by its economical and technological condition.... To him, the false castle [modern Gothic and Baroque] is nothing but a reversion. He knows nothing of its intrinsic modernity and visualizes the illusionary images of uniqueness in the era of mass production as mere vestiges instead of "responses" to capitalistic mechanization which betrays something of the latter's essence.[1]

The wave of avant-garde pessimism about industrial (or "mass") society hit America late, and spottily. But, just as America had developed its own brand of economic interpretation of history prior to the importation of Marx—many of the Federalist papers are good examples—so a number of mid-nineteenth-century observers such as Hawthorne, Thoreau, Melville, had found their way to a pessimistic and sardonic view of their society—indeed, of human society in general. By the end of the century the native stream, with roots in seaboard provincialism, frontier loneliness, and, often, more or less secularized Calvinistic strains, had merged with the older and richer Continental tradition of pessimism and disenchantment. The nineties were not gay for Brooks and Henry Adams, for O. W. Holmes, Jr. (in his public role), Mark Twain, Henry James, the "new" Howells, Veblen. (Note that I do not include here the reformers and the muckrakers—such writers as Lloyd and Bellamy: these people were not deeply disaffected: for them the world was real; it made sense, or could readily do so provided such and such were done; their very protest related them to what was going on.)

Some of these men, it is true, were not so much impatient with the Western world as a whole as with the figure cut in that world by the United States. Brooks Adams much of the time was angry with his country for being crass, not strong and brave: he despised commerce and admired war. Henry Adams wavered between being cross with his country for not making more prominent use of him and his cadre and being in despair about the world of the dynamo where, as Walter Lippmann later put it, translating Aeschylus, "Whirl is king, having driven out Zeus." Henry James wanted to see America more cultured and civilized, an attitude common to many sensitive expatriates whether or not they left home; at the same time, like Brooks Adams, he had small hope even for the commercial culture of Britain.

In comparison with these men whose disenchantment with the world or with America was sophisticated, there is something jejune about Veblen, as also about the only literary man of stature who recognized him, namely Howells. Howells and Veblen, like Mark Twain, were Midwesterners and, though each in his way was educated in the East and in close touch with its thought and values, they were never socially secure enough to afford the kind of ennui-pessimism of the Eastern patricians. As a result, it is not surprising that avant-garde literary fashion in our day has left them pretty much out of account. And with a certain justice, I think. It is hard not to be impatient with Mark Twain when we read his remark about Henry James' *The Bostonians* (when it appeared in the same *Century* magazine with *Huckleberry Finn):* he'd "rather be damned to John Bunyan's heaven than read that"—a remark more in keeping with Paul Bunyan's America than John's heaven. If Veblen ever read *The Bostonians,* in this writer's judgment one of the finest novels ever written about America, his biographers give no sign of it, but they speak of his liking the verse of Edward Carpenter. Though himself one of the few social scientists to become a master of literary craft, he was incapable of identifying himself with the literary world—a not uncommon experience of American writers then and since. When he read Ibsen we can be pretty sure it was for the great Norwegian's iconoclasm rather than for his dramatic art.

By the same token, however, Veblen, Twain, and Howells partially escaped those currents of attitude towards America that engulfed men and women whose tastes were formed on European standards. In fact Veblen, like Mark Twain, was something of a Philistine, but he was not so provincial as to judge his country from the eyes of a foreign capital. He did not want anything for America that he did not also want for Europe. By making himself at home (true, with all the discomforts of home) in the international field of economics, he avoided petty transatlantic arguments. In his erudition, he is more cosmopolitan than Mark Twain or Henry Ford, both men with whom I wish now to compare him.

Veblen and Mark Twain

Veblen and Mark Twain have been linked in my own mind as men whose irony at once expressed and concealed a raging bitterness against all in the Gilded Age (Mark Twain's term) that was shoddy, effete, or pretentious. Both men grew less benign as they aged, and more willing to reveal their rancor. Both were instinctively on the side of the downtrodden—the Negroes, the ne'er-do-wells, the impious in the case of Mark Twain. Both viewed the Middle Ages in a similar Voltairean light, as a regimen of brutal lords and swindling priests. Indeed, *A Connecticut Yankee at King Arthur's Court* takes a view as rosy as Veblen's towards the machine process, and manifests as little nostalgia for the peasant and handicraft era. Both the *Connecticut Yankee* and *The Theory of the Leisure Class* have only ridicule for archaism, mystery and priestcraft: both are the books of freethinkers who keep hoping the better man, the matter-of-fact man with slide-rule, will win in the end. Bernard DeVoto writes (in *Mark Twain's America*, p. 274) that "The nineteenth century, which 'turns automata into men,' is vindicated and the Utopia of Mark's imagination is seen to be an affecting blend of Hannibal's small farms and the Colt's Arms culture of Hartford." Mark Twain urges the oppressed to take matters into their own hands but, like Veblen, he has little faith that they will: the book is full of pain at the way "this oppressed community had turned their cruel hands against their own class in the interest of a common oppressor." The book closes with the revolution defeated in a pool of blood.

What is striking in both men is that they believe in progress and yet doubt it. They are harbingers of doom and corruption while still sharing, with hardly an exception, the beliefs of the Enlightenment as transplanted to the American Midwest. They are against the corporations and against high tariffs, against chivalry and the genteel tradition, against all vested interests and for the common man. But they see the common man as easily duped; hence their despair. For one thing, both lack self-confidence: common men themselves, they feel vulnerable and pull or disguise their punches. Mark Twain submitted to editing by his refined wife and by refined editors such as Gilder and (to a degree) Howells, much as Veblen was persuaded to tone down *The Higher Learning.*

In Mark Twain the despair takes the form of seeing the pre-Gold Rush Midwest and pre-pubertal boyhood as idyllic: in his work as in his life, he could not come to terms with post-Civil War America, or with adults whom he tended to make either into saints like Joan of Arc or sinners like the corrupted men of Hadleyburg. Veblen describes his own similar difficulties projectively when, in *The Theory of the Leisure Class,* he discusses the character and aptitudes of his concededly somewhat mythical savage (pp. 223-224):

> As seen from the point of view of life under modern civilised conditions in an enlightened community of the Western culture, the primitive, ante-predatory savage…was not a great success. Even for the purposes of that hypothetical culture to which his type of human nature owes what stability it has even for the ends of the peaceable savage group—this primitive man has quite as many and as conspicuous economic failings as he has economic virtues,—as should be plain to any one whose sense of the case is not biased by leniency born of a fellow-feeling. At his best he is "a clever, good-for-nothing fellow." The shortcomings of this presumptively primitive type of character are weakness, inefficiency, lack of initiative and ingenuity and a yielding and indolent amiability, together with a lively but inconsequential animistic sense. Along with these traits go certain others which have some value for the collective life process, in the sense that they further the facility of life in the group. These traits are truthfulness, peaceableness, good-will, and a non-emulative, non-invidious interest in men and things.

Even if his fellow-men had followed Veblen's injunction not to write any biographies of him, this passage would serve as an amiable, non-invidious description of him. He might cavil only at the statement that he possessed an animistic sense, since so much of his life was spent attacking animism, but I am inclined to think (and can find supporting passages in Veblen himself) that hardly anyone gets through life without some animism—certainly, few scientists do. However that may be, the passage expresses Veblen's lack of self-confidence and his feeling, which he shared with Mark Twain, of vulnerability in the modern market-place. While Veblen disguised his feelings of inadequacy by silence and withdrawal in company, Mark Twain disguised his by joking and occasional truculence, but when this was ill-received as in the famous dinner for the elder Holmes, Twain would beg apologies abjectly. This is not unlike Veblen's method of repeated disclaimer that he means no ill in his books, and we must recall in this connection his abject reply to Cummings.

These similarities led me to wonder whether Mark Twain, like Veblen, had suffered from an intimidating father coupled with a weak but whimsical mother. Dixon Wecter's book, *Sam Clemens of Hannibal,* offers some fairly convincing evidence on this. Mark Twain described his father as "a stern, unsmiling man"—"My father and I were always on the most distant terms when I was a boy—a sort of armed neutrality, so to speak" (Wecter, p. 67). The father "never demonstrated affection for wife or child." Sam Clemens, like Veblen, was a silent rebel, a prankish nonconformist. Wecter quotes an autobiographical note: "Campbellite revival. All converted but me. All sinners again in a week" (p. 88). Mark Twain's mother, like Veblen's, was more whimsical than the father and less orderly, given to fairy tales and fond of the Bible.

Mark Twain's *Mysterious Stranger,* in an unpublished version, "thinks well of the cat because she is the only independent; says there is no such thing as an independent human being—all are slaves...." The Stranger "often said he would not give a penny for human company when he could get better.... He said that the natural man, the savage, had no prejudices about smells, and no shame for his God-made nakedness.... The wild creatures trooped in from everywhere, and climbed all over Satan, and sat on his shoulder and his head; and rummaged his pockets and made themselves at home...."

This mood vis-à-vis the animal kingdom, it seems to me, strikingly resembles Veblen's—recall his defense of cats whom he praised as against the servility of dogs in *The Theory of the Leisure Class.* Duffus describes Veblen at Cedro as getting on better with animals than with men. A skunk would brush against him, and animals would wander in and out of his house without Veblen moving a muscle. "He had no sentimental love for nature," Duffus writes; "What he had was a kind of amused tolerance."

Shortly before he died, Veblen wrote a characteristically self-effacing note (quoted by Dorfman, p. 504):

> It is also my wish, in case of death, to be cremated, if it can conveniently be done, as expeditiously and inexpensively as may be, without ritual or ceremony of any kind; that my ashes be thrown loose into the sea [he was in Stanford at the time], or into some sizable stream running to the sea; that no tombstone, slab, epitaph, effigy, tablet, inscription, or monument of any name or nature, be set up in my memory or name in any place or at any time; that no obituary, memorial, portrait, or biography of me, nor any letters written to or by me be printed or published, or in any way reproduced, copied or circulated.

There are of course many ironies in Veblen's use here (as in other writings) of the language of legal chicane that had cost his father so dear—as if to prove he could handle the English language as badly as any man of native stock. But what is more striking is how closely

Veblen's attitude here, too, resembles that of Mark Twain who wrote to a friend (Wecter, p. 119):

> If Henry and my father feel as I would feel under their circumstances, they want no prominent or expensive lot, or luxurious entertainment in the new cemetery. As for a monument—well, if you remember my father, you are aware that he would rise up and demolish it the first night. He was a modest man and would not be able to sleep under a monument.

Yet, concealed in such casual attitudes towards the bodies of the dead, are bitter aggressions against the sentiments of the living. To be sure, Mark Twain, who ended up an unhappy celebrity, did not order his papers destroyed; he handled the problem of post-mortem scrutiny quite differently. Life forced and aided him to overcome his tendencies to withdrawal; although like Veblen he seems never to have come to terms with his own sexuality either in his life or in his work, he himself became something of a businessman and promoter, following in this in the footsteps of Tom Sawyer. Veblen's picture of the American businessman was much more steadily relentless, and his critique of course far more searching. What nevertheless links the two men beyond the details of biography and theme are the courage and the limitations of their satire. For both, satire served as a mask of detachment from the world's brutalities. Neither, however, could maintain a consistent tone: in both, irony sometimes barely rises above mere description, sometimes verges on burlesque. Even their best books proceed by association from one thing to another: both were too much, for good and ill, at the mercy of their material to impose plot and ordered structure upon it. Both repeat themselves endlessly—possibly, satire cannot escape monotone since it compels only a one-eyed view of its subject, and Gulliverts voyages fade into one another as do Mark Twain's and as do Veblen's sallies against the sporting men and the "kept classes," the Yahoos of his day. But every limitation for a writer is also an opportunity, and in both Veblen and Mark Twain it is satire that saves them from the dreariness of muckraking and the pieties of the genteel tradition in literature and scholarship.

If Veblen as an artist bears comparison with Mark Twain, Veblenism as a set of attitudes bears comparison with Fordism. When my colleague, Reuel Denney, called the Model-T, and its successors among the hot-rods, "Veblenian vehicles," he meant that the stripped-down, matter-of-fact car could be taken as representing a protest against the plushy, yacht-like cars of 1915 and the chrome-spangled parlor sofa which has become the Detroit merchandising staple today. Staughton Lynd, who assisted me in this book, has pointed out the personal and ideological resemblances of Ford and Veblen. Ford, indeed, may be seen as the archetype of the Veblenian engineer, waging relentless war on behalf of industry against business (with its subsidiary chicaneries of banking, law, and politics), and against conspicuous consumption and leisure-class values generally.

Garet Garrett says of Ford in *The Wild Wheel* that he "discovered familiar things with the innocence of first-seeing" (p. 19). Money, he never wearied of pointing out, had not built the Ford Motor Company but hard work, coupled with the skills embodied in machinery. Like Veblen, Ford did not believe that work went on in the office. It is a twice-told tale how he was always either firing white-collar workers or forcing them into overalls—he himself never used his office in the Administration Building which had somehow risen in spite of him, and he was happiest on the factory floor. Once he discovered a group of men who told him they comprised the Statistical Department. He told his production boss Sorensen he could have the space, and the latter moved in with crowbars and demolished the department.

Fearing constraint and formal rules much as Veblen and Mark Twain did, Ford refused to allow any titles to develop in his organization. Hating absentee ownership and the "money power," it is well known how he chivvied his stockholders, refusing to pay them more than trivial dividends until compelled by a court order, and finally managing by a series of ruses to buy them out. It is ironical that the freedom from Wall Street and stockholder control that he fought for so bitterly is now available to most large corporations, quite differently managed, because they have disfranchised their stockholders by wide ownership dispersion and have consequently been able to retain profits (and heavy depreciation reserves) as a source of expansion without the need periodically to consult the money market. All his life, Ford inveighed against the profit motive and was in favor of the industrial motive of "providing goods for all" *(The Wild Wheel,* pp. 17-18); in the stockholder suit he testified *(ibid.,* p. 117):

> The money is not mine to do with as I please. The men who work with me have helped to create it. After they have had their wages and a share of the profits, it is my duty to take what remains and put it back into the industry to create more work for more men at higher wages.

When he set up his tractor business he proclaimed there would be "no stockholders, no directors, no absentee owners" and no more "parasites" (Keith Sward, *The Legend of Henry Ford, p.* 69). At the same time, he insisted no less emphatically than Veblen that he was "not a reformer" (*ibid.*, p. 79), and he refused to commit himself permanently to any party or group inside or outside his plant.

On the side of production, then, Ford shared Veblen's awareness of the enormous productive possibilities of American industry, though the latter seems to have lacked Ford's recognition that mass production depends on mass consumption. The sense they had in the early 1900s of what "miracles" technology could accomplish was prophetic, and their belief that it was the business-law-banking fetters that held engineering genius down, though an oversimplification, receives some measure of support from Ford's own struggle to expand and lower costs rather than pay dividends. For Ford and for Veblen, price policy was no problem: the problem was to get rid of the legalistic stratagems which hampered and obfuscated the "obvious" engineering solutions to the tasks at hand. (In Ford's case, literally at hand: according to Garrett, he thought with his fingers.) It is a grand Veblenian irony that Ford was finally defeated by consumption tastes of the leisure class rather than by the wiles of bankers. He nearly bankrupted the company (and did bankrupt many dealers and employees) before he consented to abandon the workmanlike Model-T for a model more suited to genteel suburban life. Partly, he gave in to the insistence of his son Edsel, whose moving to Grosse Point, the Detroit "society" suburb, seemed to his father an invitation to betrayal and ruin at the hands of dilettantes, wastrels, and snobs.

For all the polite, smooth ways of modern business enterprise and modern social intercourse both Ford and Veblen had nothing but contempt. True, Veblen did not say as Ford did that "history is bunk," but much else of the classical, gentlemanly culture he did think to be bunk; like Ford and Mark Twain, he regarded religion as bunk;[2] and certainly he rated any pre-Darwinian science not much higher. Both Ford and Veblen distrusted the received realities, though of course Veblen went about his subversion in a more roundabout way. The War had a similarly up-rooting effect on both, leading Veblen into the Washington adventures already discussed and Ford into the fabulous foray of the Peace Ship.

No less striking than these similarities are the more deeply personal ones. Both men had a romantic sympathy for the insubordinate underdog—in fact, their attack on the received realities may be viewed as a defense of the unreceived ones. Veblen admired the Wobblies and their precursors throughout history—he admired the Vikings while regarding them as a bunch of crooks—whereas Ford (see Harry Bennett's *We Never Called Him Henry*) was drawn to criminals and the underworld. Even Ford's anti-Semitism had pro-underdog roots; he was going to be for Hitler and Gerald K. Smith since all the good people in his circle seemed to be down on them (Veblen, the friend of Jacques Loeb and admirer of Marx, never made the fatal Populist identification of Jews with Wall Street bankers and Washington financiers). Stories of Ford's dress—his insistence on wearing cheap socks despite his wife's entreaties—could easily be matched by Veblen's economies in dress.

Both men, moreover, were shy, sly and evasive. Ford enjoyed slipping out the back door of Harry Bennett's office to avoid a distinguished visitor much as Veblen slipped out of the paperwork requirements of academic administration. Harry Bennett tells the story of how Ford, walking one day on the roadbed of his Detroit, Toledo and fronton Railway, saw slag from the Rouge plant being dumped which contained visible traces of iron ore; he ordered it to be sent back and re-smelted—a costly procedure for an infinitesimal return. To avoid this, Sorensen improved his recovery of ore, but was curious why Ford had not told him directly to do so; apparently, it was Ford's ironical way of controlling waste, which he hated with a passion akin to Veblen's. Ford's irony, of course, was not literary, but it sprang from a similar delight in indirection, a country boy's way of being sharp.

Ford, like Veblen, grew up hating farm work; as he wrote (Garrett, p. 192):

> What a waste it is for a human being to spend hours and days behind a slowly moving team of horses when in the same time a tractor could do six times as much work!

When he went back to the farm as a rich man, it was with tractors; he boasted: "Our dairy farm is managed exactly like a factory." Yet, like Veblen with his sagas, foot-races with Icelandic friends, and Baltic antiquities, he was prey to fabulously inconsistent nostalgias, going in late in life for folk-dances, fiddlers and American antiques—and foot-races.

Needless to say, there were great differences as well as similarities between Ford and Veblen. Ford, active and successful man that he was, dominated his son and the men around him in ways utterly alien to Veblen's softer and more resigned temperament. Moreover, one can hardly emphasize enough Veblen's marginality as a second-generation Norwegian, put off and alienated from the parents' parochial culture but without the ability fully to assimilate and accept the available forms of Americanism—indeed, already anticipating in his loving translation of the Laxdaela Saga the third-generation nostalgia (to whose literary forms Marcus Hansen has called attention). This marginality drove Veblen into the Bohemian fringes of society, as it also drove there many other second-generation internal exiles in the period from 1890 to 1930; Ford, by contrast, while eccentric, was never in the least Bohemian.

Thus, rather than pushing too far the similarities in outlook and disposition between Veblen and Ford, it is important to study Ford as a living embodiment of Veblen's ideal engineer, whose eye was on the industrial arts, not the business ones, and who, far from despoiling industry for the sake of his own emulative consumption, lived sparely and simply, using technological advance and a widening market to cut production costs (not only in his own plants but also, by enforced economies, in his suppliers' and the railroads that served him), raise wages, and rebuild obsolescent plants. To be sure, Veblen never mentions Ford by name, but then he seldom cited his sources, either of person or print. And in *The Engineers and the Price System,* written after Ford had gained national celebrity, Veblen makes what is for him an unusual admission. After once more setting forth his shibboleth of the conflict between engineer and financier, he declares that there exist (p. 10):

> exceptional, sporadic, and spectacular episodes in business where business men have now and again successfully gone out of the safe and sane highway of conservative business enterprise that is hedged about by conscientious withdrawal of efficiency, and have endeavored to regulate the output by increasing the productive capacity of the industrial system at one point or another.

Later on, he makes the even more startling admission, inconceivable to Marx or the earlier Veblen, that business could actually make more profit by quantity production at low prices than by restricted production at high prices. Scattered throughout the book, moreover, one encounters types intermediate between the angelic engineer and

Satanic financier: the investment banker less speculative than the old corporate financier because more bureaucratic in his procedure and more closely in touch with the technological experts; the "consulting engineer" who advises the investment banker not only as to the commercial but also as to the industrial soundness of any enterprise that is to be underwritten; the captain of industry who, even in this later day, is more interested in production than the absentee owner and comes into conflict with the latter.

These, however, are mere hints, which are undeveloped in the book; they are quite lost amid the usual raillery at "one-eyed captains of industry," and the "unearned increment" gained by chicane-minded men capable only of sitting tight at the expense of the gullible common man. For Veblen, such men as Ford were relics of a more heroic age, not—short of revolution sparked by the aroused engineers—part of the American future.

Yet Ford marches on around the world. His impatience with the human, non-economic costs of the machine process is duplicated by the Soviets and their satellites for whom Ford was becoming a hero just about the time Americans were taking a more critical look at him. American emissaries, no longer welcome at home with their gospel of hard work and industrial progress, compete with Communist intellectuals in bringing Fordism to "backward" countries. Meanwhile advertising men, sharing Veblen's belief that they belong to the kept classes and Ford's belief that cars aren't built with words, seek to expiate their guilts by government service, work with their hands on their country places, and the use of their media to sell intangible values like tolerance and the American Way. It would, in fact, take an ironist of Veblen's skeptical and disenchanted power to crack open the deadly seriousness with which all these activities, influenced by attitudes to which he gave currency, are conducted. We will not find this in the heavy portentousness or hardly less heavy humor characteristic of most American talk and writing in our own day no less than in his.

Whatever our debt to the theories Veblen developed, I think we are all in his debt for his way of seeing. Irreverent and catty to the very end, he avoided becoming a substantial citizen, which he defined as one who owns much property. He died insolvent. But the intangible assets that have come down to us, his books and his personal style, have still the power over us that Veblen was all too inclined to disparage: the power of ideas and of personality.

Notes

1. These excerpts should of course not be taken as representing the total animus of the Adorno essay, with its intense and ramified scrutiny of *The Theory of the Leisure Class.* For instance, Adorno has a sense of the mindlessness implicit in Veblen's debunking attitude—Veblen blaming angels for the "industrially unproductive rehearsal" which occupies them is an example of his hatred for all mediation, whether that of the priest, the decorator, the trader, or at times even the thinker. Adorno relates this outlook to "the zealotry of Scandinavian Protestantism which does not tolerate any intermediary between God and inwardness."

2. Persons close to Ford have told me that late in life he became interested in the cult of the "Pyramid Inch," a pseudo-religion and pseudo-key to history.

2

The Strengths and Weaknesses of Veblen

Douglas F. Dowd

Thorstein Veblen presumed to be neither judge nor prophet, despite his many judgments and prophecies. Notwithstanding his view of himself, Veblen's readers seldom fail to be impressed by the telling ring of his judgments, the deadly accuracy of his expectations, the degree to which he caught the quality of the twentieth century.

We naturally admire those who see through their present to the future; but we measure the worth of a social scientist by something more enduring than his vision; and this leads us to ask several questions of Veblen. Did he develop procedures, hypotheses, theories, which can be used by others? Did he furnish an analytical framework adequate to the problems he tackled? Was his vision dependent upon scattered insights, or was it a product of a theoretical framework that can be used, and improved upon, by others with similar, or even different, values? When he was right, was he right for good reasons?[1]

It is not possible here—perhaps not at all—to give a definitive answer to these questions for Veblen. His work traversed a vast array of issues and problems, and his procedures were often left obscure. But before we go on to evaluate the usefulness of Veblen for contemporary social science let us first digress to examine the important question of "similar values."

Veblen well understood the close relationship between the preconceptions and values of social scientists and the theories they construct. But, as noted earlier, Veblen regularly denied any involvement in the issues he analyzed. It was his style, after a trenchant criticism, to assert that he was not criticizing, which would have implied evaluation; that he was merely describing the "facts"—e.g., when, in the course of a devastating critique of American college education, he says, "it is by no means here assumed that learning is substantially more to be desired than proficiency in genteel dissipation" (VI, 89). If Veblen deluded others with this device, he surely did not fool himself. He often stated, for example, that "the reason for a denial"—such as the one above—"is the need for it" (e.g., IV, 258n). Veblen's style was a persistent, consummate irony. We must deduce the values of Veblen not from what he said of them, but from what he praised and attacked; we must ignore his disclaimers.

Veblen despised war, hypocrisy, waste, tyranny, conformity, patriotism, supernaturalism, privilege—"force and fraud." For him, the good society would be at once democratic, peaceable, efficient, just, and scientific. Such a society he described by the term "industrial democracy," and he placed emphasis on both the adjective and the noun. He believed that industrial democracy could emerge only if the institutions supporting and resting upon patriotism, religion, and money-making receded and disappeared. This was asking a lot, and because that is so there are not many who fully share Veblen's values. Veblen would say that our notions of what is good and right are derived from the institutions within which we have lived. Since we have all lived in large part within those institutions that Veblen looked upon as obstacles to human progress, few of us can survive Veblen's slashing critiques without at least an occasional sense of outrage.

But there are some. And there are others who, reading Veblen, "take thought," or have second thoughts, on matters they have taken for granted, matters challenged so incisively by Veblen. In this respect, Veblen has value apart from the theories he built, or apart from those he made possible. That value inheres in his exposure of the pervasiveness, the meaning, and the danger of the violent and the irrational in the world about us. It inheres in Veblen's delineation and explanation of what constitutes irrational behavior. In short, Veblen is useful for the process of unlearning, always an integral part of the process of learning.

Veblen never actively espoused the things he believed in, as we have seen. It was his life's work to attack those institutions[2] he saw as menacing to a healthy society. It was his assumption that the removal of "imbecile institutions" would allow the emergence of an industrial democracy. This happy development would signify and result from the triumph of the constructive instincts of man—the parental bent and the instincts of workmanship and idle curiosity. Had Veblen expected these developments—and he did not—he, no less than those he criticized, could be accused of being "teleological" in his analysis. But what Veblen thought desirable, he seldom expected to occur. Not expecting any substantial improvement in the condition of man—indeed, despairing of it—Veblen constructed no program of reform or action to bring it about. Like Marx, he did not "concoct kitchen recipes for the future."[3] Marx did not do so (except in general statements concerning socialism) because he appreciated the difficulties of institutional prescriptions for a future situation that could be dimly apprehended at best. But Marx, if with excessive optimism, did specify the process by which change could (and, he thought, would) be brought about, and Marx participated in the political process moving along those lines. It may be offered that Marx's optimism was one factor leading him to take pains in systematizing his theory.

Veblen's gloomier position, apart from any more personal factors, led him to neglect serious discussion of the process by which desirable change might be brought about. But Veblen was gloomy not only in his social analysis. Pessimism pervaded his entire existence, coloring his marriages, his career, and his daily associations. Veblen was a recluse who, if he found satisfaction in attacking society and its stuffed shirts, found joy only "outside" society: he loved animals, he loved making things with his hands, he loved books. His writings reveal this quality of the recluse, of the outsider; and this quality gave to Veblen's works their chief merit as well as their chief defect. This point will bear more detailed examination.

Veblen was a teacher of economics for much of his life. His teaching had at least two qualities in common with his writings: (1) he was a source of life-long inspiration for a small group of devoted students; (2) he was virtually unintelligible, at times even inaudible, in the classroom. When Veblen taught, he mumbled, and in a low voice. It may be said of his writings that they, too, often "mumble, and in a low voice."

Veblen's performance as a teacher and writer was integrally connected to his general outlook. That outlook informed him that it is not only virtually hopeless to seek progressive change; it is also personally foolhardy. Veblen may have been correct to some degree in both these assumptions; but he acted on them at times in an extreme, self-defeating, manner.[4] His professional career was unavoidably turbulent, given his unconventional ideas and his unconventional personal life. But a reading of Veblen's life reveals some moments, at least, when he effectually encouraged an unsatisfactory situation to persist or to develop; instances occur, as a sociologist might put it, of "the self-fulfilling prophecy."

Veblen's personal life is revealing, but of greater importance here are his writings. Taken together, they illuminate contradictions which Veblen never resolved, and which weakened his contribution to understanding. On the one hand, Veblen is one of the wordiest and most repetitive of writers. His meaning is frequently unclear; his sentences are often long, rambling, involute; he is often vague to the point of cloudiness. Also, as we have seen, he presumed himself to be aloof from the social maelstrom. On the other hand, Veblen was witty. He could with a succinct phrase rip away what had been in others' hands a tangled mat of confusion. When he was clear, his words snapped and sparkled. And his writings are almost entirely occupied with the origins, the nature, and the meaning of the social problems concerning which he pretended insouciance.

In the face of these considerations, one may presume that when Veblen was unclear, he had allowed himself—or had chosen—to be. Social indifference does not easily square with the prodigious effort supporting Veblen's analyses of social issues. One need not be psychiatrically inclined to infer that Veblen's protestations of indifference were a form of camouflage. But camouflage that can confuse one's enemies can to the same degree confuse one's friends. Unfortunately, Veblen probably confused his followers more than those he despised, if only because the former were the more likely to read him.

Veblen was against waste, but his own writings were generally as inefficient as the business system he attacked. He was merciless in his analyses of "devout observances" and "ceremonial ritual," but he played these games himself; even though he did so ironically, the result was that he "threw sand in his own gears." To all this, Veblen might respond that the possibilities for social improvement, and for finding a serious and influential audience, were so dim as to make care and seriousness inappropriate. However, it is difficult to believe that Veblen's impressive contributions were made without some hope that his efforts might have meaning. That they did have meaning is indicated by the economists and sociologists (among others) who have acknowledged their indebtedness to Veblen, and by the even greater number of those who have unknowingly been influenced by him. That his camouflage and lack of clarity worked against his own purposes, on the other hand, is indicated by the feckless works of some of those who have attempted to follow his leads.

The preceding interpretation raises the suspicion that much of what is obscure in Veblen was calculated to be so. Much else seemingly reflects a casual attitude toward important questions, as a result of Veblen's deeply if not consistently held conviction that there was nothing much that could be done; even, as David Riesman has argued, that "nobody was listening."

Veblen's contribution towers above that of any other American economist, however much he has left to be done, and however difficult it is to work with what he left us. It is saying a great deal of Veblen to point out that the structure he built is strongest in its foundations and weakest in its superstructure. For those who share his values, those foundations provide a substantial and enduring base on which to build. But, as with other great economists, such as Keynes and Marx, one need not fully share Veblen's values to find his approach useful. This is true to the degree that Veblen illuminated particular strategic relationships in the functioning of society. One need not find Veblen congenial to find him helpful.

Having digressed to assess the sources of Veblen's weaknesses, let us now attempt to distinguish between the solid and the insubstantial in his writings, appreciating at the outset that in Veblen's work his strengths and his weaknesses intermingle in a complex, often inextricable manner. Veblen's method is the appropriate starting point for such an appraisal; it is there we are most likely to find an answer to the questions posed earlier: in brief, "when Veblen was right, was he right for good reasons?" Veblen was "right" about so much, in his own day, and down to the present, that it seems implausible to credit "luck" as the explanation.[5]

Veblen's approach may be seen as having two major components: (1) his emphasis on genetic analysis—i.e., his concern with the origins, the present functioning, and the future probabilities associated with a given situation; (2) his assumptions and key variables. These two aspects of Veblen's approach were not separated, of course; but in general it may be said that Veblen's superiority to the neo-classical economists—for those currently interested in economic processes and problems—is primarily due to the first of these; the greater accuracy of Veblen's predictions over those of Marx results from his assumptions and key variables. In pursuing these points in more detail, one should also indicate the areas in which the objects of Veblen's criticisms of economics had strengths he lacked.

It is generally agreed that neo-classical economics is "welfare economics." The concern of the value and distribution theories that comprise this school of economics is the question: "What are the principles of optimal choice?" Or, more specifically, "under assumed institutional and technological conditions, and irrespective of time and place, what will maximize welfare?"[6] This is another way of stating the question: "Assuming no institutional constraints, what constitutes completely 'rational' behavior?" Here "rational" means that the sole problem is one of making the most of scarce resources, and that the actors are motivated only by rational considerations.

The criticisms of the neo-classical approach made by Veblen and other institutionalists have not caused the neoclassicists to abandon their assumptions and theories; but such criticisms have influenced some neo-classicists to make their assumptions more explicit, to become more conscious of the limitations of the analyses, and (for all but the "purists") to abandon earlier pretenses that the world they discuss in fact exists. Consequently, if some of Veblen's criticisms no longer ring true, a major reason is that his arguments had a reforming effect on economics.

In earlier pages the assumptions of neo-classical economics were subjected to Veblen's critique; here several things will be said of the analysis from a contemporary standpoint. By assumption and by focus, the neo-classical economist is led to ignore (1) the persistent clash of interests in society, as reflected in the realm of politics and social movements, and (2) the fundamental and unsettling force of technology and technological change. In taking institutions as given, the neo-classical economist (3) is led to define as an improvement in welfare only those changes that involve neither social conflict nor institutional change, and (4) is inhibited from examining the social process at all, except as something "outside" the theory.[7]

In these and other respects, such an economics, whatever else it may achieve, serves to deflect attention from social relationships and processes that tend to upset the status quo. Such analysis does not tend to *maintain* the status quo, for that *cannot* be maintained. But it does absorb energies in the pursuit of universal principles of rational economic conduct—energies that might, with different training, be spent in attempting to understand how the ever-changing "status quo" can be led to change in ways more beneficial than detrimental to mankind. It should be clear that theory concerned directly with the factors making for change in society can serve conservative, liberal, or radical ideologies—of course, in different measure and with different emphases. But when the social process is abstracted from by economists to the point where only those on the fringes of the discipline are concerned with the problems of change, all of society is the worse for it.[8]

The material welfare of society is determined most importantly by changes taking place over time; consequently, the focus of the neoclassical economist on the "short-run" (defined so as to preclude both technological and institutional change) renders him incapable of examining the very question he takes up and that society expects him to take up. It may be argued with some justice that it is not the economist's function to seek answers to questions predicated by laymen. With equal justice it may be asked, if the economist does not occupy himself with the moving economic questions of his day—even if that leads him into the muddy fields where economic, social, and political institutions are stirred by technological change and human aspirations—who will? We need not search long or far for an answer. The economist alone has the professional function to examine and understand the economic interests of society as a whole; when he abdicates that function, whether by conscious choice or by the focus and method of his analysis, he leaves the public unarmed to face the continuing and self-seeking thrusts of "the vested interests"—in business, in labor, in agriculture, in politics, or wherever they may exist.

Neo-classical economics, whether in the past or the present, has contributed to our understanding of certain basic, "purely economic," questions. These are questions of enduring interest—irrespective of time, place, ideology, or technology. They are questions that revolve around the problem of scarce resources and rational choice between competing uses of such resources—a problem for societies institutionally and technologically so diverse as eighteenth-century England, nineteenth-century America, and twentieth-century China. The analysis of such problems legitimately and necessarily entails a high level of abstraction. Veblen rejected such analysis peremptorily, perhaps too much so. If they are to be approached wisely, even in the "affluent society" of the United States, there are problems of choice that require the kind of "rational" economics developed in neoclassical theory.

The question, therefore, is not whether neo-classical economics has *any* usefulness or meaning; it surely has some.[9] The more serious question is concerned with balance. Is the training, the time, the energy, the output of economists devoted to refining neo-classical analysis proportionate to the range of economic problems confronting society? The question is not, should the principles of rational choice be clarified? Of course they should. But, with so much else demanding clarification by economists, it would appear that Veblen's out-of-hand rejection of this economics comes closer to a correct judgment of how economists should use their skills—and what skills they should develop—than does the present bias of the discipline. This position is given added weight when it is understood that all too frequently the neoclassical analysis is applied to problems to which it is wildly inappropriate—problems centering on change and institutional conflict—by economists whose narrow training prevents them from recognizing the relevant "institutional variables"—the relevant "facts."[10]

This question may be put differently. Of what value are the principles of rational choice when the institutions of society prevent rational choices from being made? Of what use is an economics concerned with scarcity when society finds itself plagued by its inability to utilize already existing resources—natural, human, and man-made? The answer is not, "of no use." Celestial navigation, for example, may be a useful art even to those on a sinking ship; perhaps, even, on a cloudy night. But other kinds of knowledge are at such times considerably more important. These other kinds of knowledge (e.g., what it is that prevents rational choices from being made) Veblen emphasized; although in attempting to redress the balance, he may have swung back too far.

In contrast to the neo-classical economists—and many conventional economists still today—Veblen took as the central problem of the economist, (1) the restlessness and imperatives of technology, (2) the institutions shaping human behavior, (3) the social psychology of man, and (4) the interaction of all these as determining the quality of a society at any time and as giving rise to social change and conflict.

Veblen said of the neo-classicists that "their arguments have been as good as the premises on which they proceed" (VII, 86). Veblen's own arguments—concerning the structure and functioning of the economy, and related social and political processes—have been largely validated by subsequent events, and we may credit his "premises" as the explanation. The choice of premises, or assumptions, is a matter of judgment; it is a resultant of some combination of values, knowledge, and insight. In the mind of a careful thinker, such judgments become hypotheses, the validity of which is tested against events. The economist assumes that "events"—i.e., the real world—are the matters directly concerning the theorist. Unlike the neo-classical economists, Veblen saw the real world as the only legitimate concern of the economist; anything else amounted to exercises in logic, or versions of what he called "homiletical exegesis."

The kind of world Veblen saw about him was one in which efforts to develop a refined calculus of choice were a form of conspicuous waste at best; a dangerous luxury, at worst. The world's problem was to prevent retrogression into barbarism. The many dimensions of that problem require for its understanding the greatest diligence, the greatest cooperation, the greatest good sense that social scientists can muster. For Veblen, the world was not steadily climbing a mountain at whose peak it would find Utopia; it was a world constantly poised on the edge of a frightful abyss. If it was not to fall into that abyss, it must move away from it; and that, even for Veblen, meant climbing the happy mountain. But Veblen was more concerned with the abyss than with the mountain. He was a pessimist; not least because he thought that man could be led to confuse abyss with mountain; to accept, even to cherish, a social process that meant deprivation of spirit, of material comfort, and of life itself. Whether Veblen's theory made him a pessimist, or his pessimism shaped his theory, and how these may have interacted, is an interesting question, but not a vital one. We should be interested in the validity and usefulness of theory rather more than with its psychiatric origins.

Adequate social theory is not of course a sufficient condition for preventing social disaster or for bringing about social improvement. Theory must be matched with action. But adequate theory is necessary if social action is to be sufficient. Without understanding the process of social change, socially active groups will move only by chance and good fortune in persistently and enduringly beneficial directions. History is strewn with the wreckage left by well-motivated individuals and groups, shattered by forces they did not comprehend and could not control.

We do not possess an adequate theory of society or of social change. Marx, it may be said, attempted one. With all the limitations of Marxian theory, it has proved to be more influential than Veblenian theory. Among other reasons, Veblenian "theory" is so unsystematic; it is, in an important sense, implicit rather than explicit. It is also riddled with gaps and marred by unsupported, at times unsupportable, generalizations.

Veblen's contribution suffers both because of Veblen's personality and temperament, and because of factors outside and beyond him. Pessimism and caution interacted to deprive Veblen of both the morale and the courage required to develop a forthright, systematic body of theory. His role as a radical social critic, in addition, placed him at a disadvantage he could not overcome.

The radical social critic is fated to work at a disadvantage that affects his ability to develop a rounded body of adequately supported conclusions; for some, the will to make the effort is finally weakened. *Because* he is radical, the radical critic early finds himself concerned with an immense range of issues, however narrow his initial focus may have been. The study of leaves is complicated; but to trace the leaf to the twig, the twig to the branch, the branch to the trunk, and the trunk to its roots and the soil in which it grows; and to understand each aspect and the processes and relationships tying each to the other is much more difficult. To drop the metaphor, to attempt this for society is an infinitely more complex study of another and much greater magnitude. It was this latter study that Veblen attempted. The analytical and empirical challenges involved in such an enormous task are themselves forbidding; to attempt them single-handedly is impossible.

Like other radicals before and since his time, Veblen found himself working almost alone. In the nature of things, and for reasons Veblen himself described, the unconventional analyst is bound to be surrounded by those who accept things as they are. Veblen lived in a society that seemed almost eager to accord with his gloomiest observations. He associated with colleagues who viewed him with some combination of tolerant amusement, hostility, and almost determined obliviousness to the facts of life and the imperatives of social theory. It is little wonder that his theory was less than completely worked out. It is little wonder, too, that as the years passed, Veblen became increasingly intemperate, and even shrill, in his judgments. Veblen was scarcely a genial observer of the social scene as a young man; he began as a bemused skeptic. But he ended his life in bitterness—secluded, alone, a virtual anchorite.

In the nature of things, one may suppose, a critic such as Veblen will be judged by his defects more than by his virtues, if only because a full recognition of such virtues might produce discomfort in the judges. Veblen's defects are undeniable. Some of these have been suggested earlier; more will be touched on now, although there will be no attempt to reproduce them in full catalogue. It will be useful to indicate the weaknesses in Veblen's areas of greatest strength, for here the most fruitful use may be made of his work. Thus it will appear that the few moments of optimism in Veblen were no more and no less justified than the pervasive optimism of Karl Marx; it will appear, also, that society is even more complicated than Veblen proposed. If some of these complications add to the problems that Veblen saw, others may provide a basis for hopeful developments that he overlooked. Thus a brief re-examination of (1) Veblen's theories of the leisure class and conspicuous consumption, (2) his theory of instincts, (3) his distinction between "business" and "industry," and (4) his treatment of nationalism will indicate the manner in which Veblen's ideas may still be put to use. For the sake of convenience, these four aspects of his thought will be intermingled in the following discussion.

Veblen's *Theory of the Leisure Class* made its mark as a witty, skeptical view of the foibles of mankind, but it is more importantly the foundation for a theory of power and prestige. It is generally accepted that a theory of social change must include a theory of the state—i.e., an explanation of the sources and uses of power. In Marx, the theory of the state rests upon his concept of "the ruling class," whose power derives from the ownership and control of the means of production. Given the ruling class, and the opposed interests of the working class, social change centers on the class struggle motivated by clashing economic interests.

The closest thing to a ruling class in Veblen is "the vested interests." Veblen's theory of the leisure class provides an explanation of how and why the vested interests gain, hold, and use power; and, through his concept of "emulation," Veblen shows how and why the "common man" seeks to be like, rather than to overthrow, the vested interests. The root of Veblen's difference with Marx dies in Veblen's having added "prestige" to "power." This is to say that Veblen integrated social psychology—if inadequately—with the economics and politics analyzed by Marx.[11]

Power in America, for Veblen, is gained and held through the ownership and control of wealth (whereas in Veblen's Germany, increasing economic power combined with traditional military and political strength). State power is the expression of the interests of dominant business groups. Politics is the manifestation of this relationship. Should military power grow, it is at the behest, or with the acquiescence, of business rulers. The latter comprise but a tiny percentage of the total population. They wield authority without overt coercion and without challenge because of supportive social institutions and the emulative propensities of the underlying population. These propensities have two major outlets: patriotism and conspicuous consumption. In turn, patriotism and conspicuous consumption (and patterns of behavior related to them) are maintained and encouraged (1) by the steady support given to the aims and values and interests of the "vested interests" by the institutional framework of a business enterprise society—not least by its educational system, the media of communication, and the courts —and (2) by the predatory instincts of man. The process of social change resulting from these relationships is compounded of economic inefficiency and waste, a *de facto* political oligarchy, and intermittent warfare, the last acting as a solvent of economic depression and social unrest. Working against this unhappy process, but without substantial effect, are the constructive instincts of man: the parental bent, the instinct of workmanship, and the instinct of idle curiosity.[12]

In its main outlines, Veblen's theory of the state, which rests upon the nature, functioning, and maintenance of the "vested interests," appears to have considerable validity. Businessmen and business values dominate the thinking of most Americans, so much so that they are accepted "unthinkingly." There are, however, divisions of opinion within the business community. Even more to the point, there are divisions of opinion between business groups as a whole and those whom Veblen would take as their kept creatures—in government, in organized religion, in labor, in the schools and universities, and in the media of communication; there is conflict between the values and pressures of business society and the broader values Americans (including some businessmen) choose to think they hold. These broader values are quite compatible with Veblen's expectations concerning the "constructive instincts," but they go beyond the implications of that concept.

As the entire world shivers with the fear of a thermonuclear war and seems unable to come to grips with it, it would not be seemly to make too much of the cracks in the solid front of what Veblen called "predators"; but that nuclear war has been skirted for this long suggests that considerations other than those dealt with by Veblen may have intruded for a while. Veblen contended that the longer that "while" could be extended, the greater the reasons for expecting beneficial social change. Whether we agree or disagree with Veblen, it becomes necessary to explore the nature of, reasons for, and means of enhancing existing complexities in "the structure of social forces."

The world has changed swiftly and dramatically since Veblen died. If much of that change has been disastrous, and much of it along the lines he expected, some of it contains hopeful possibilities. In recent years the American people have participated in a process of mounting xenophobia which is more substantial, more pervasive, and more lasting than that dissected by Veblen in his "Dementia Praecox" in 1922, when he wrote that "a Practicable Power has to rest its case on a nerve-shattering popular fear of aggression from without" (XI, 424). The conformity and patriotism marking the present, embedded in and supporting the Cold War, come uncomfortably close to the kind of thing envisaged by Veblen in the last pages of *The Theory of Business Enterprise*—down to and including the rapidly increasing influence of military criteria, and the manner in which the latter tend increasingly to take priority over "businesslike" criteria.

Both the technology of warfare and the rhetoric of the Cold War must be taken into consideration in assessing the long-run prospects for peace and war. Veblen, who dwelt so much on technology, recognized that technology had transformed warfare and diplomacy; but he did not and could not take account of a military technology that would, if used, annihilate both victor and vanquished. Whether or not the fear of mutual annihilation will cause the world's leaders to avoid nuclear war in the future cannot be more than guessed at; but that this element of the contemporary situation requires modification of Veblen's analysis may be stated firmly.

At present the hopes introduced by military technology are somewhat less commanding than the fears; but there is another, less obvious element, one which Veblen did not directly confront and which must also be considered.[13] It has to do with the rhetoric of national and international politics today. That rhetoric strongly emphasizes notions of democracy and material well-being for all. Its economic manifestations emphasize consumer well-being and economic security. Whether and to what degree such rhetoric is honored in fact is of course important; but the rhetoric has an importance of its own, the more so the longer the world persists without war. Today, the major powers of the world—East and West—are under pressure to "produce," economically and politically, to a degree not approximated when Veblen wrote. It is easy to show that the most important product of these new factors is an endless "improvement" in the art of public relations, designed to create a "decorous" national appearance. Again, there is more to the matter than public relations; how much more is a matter for investigation. The astounding productivity of modern technology creates the possibility—and, it can be argued, the necessity—that rhetoric and reality, with appropriate pressure and direction, will move closer together than Veblen thought possible. On the other hand, we shall have missed what Veblen taught if we ignore the possibility that the rhetoric itself can continue to be altered to suit a garrison state society along the lines suggested in Orwell's *1984*. The tension between the hopeful and the dreadful possibilities constitutes the drama of this century.

An energetic, updated, systematic adaptation and use of Veblen's approach today would imply a substantial rehabilitation of the social sciences, as well as a cogent and clear-eyed appraisal of the nature of existing social problems. Problems of structure and ideology, cutting across disciplines, caught up in process, and centering upon the relationships between institutions and technology grip us today. They are problems that cannot be comprehended, let alone resolved, by analyses that take institutions as given and ignore the problems and possibilities posed by today's technology.

In the domestic realm, we need not speculate for long on the problems of most concern. They include persistent high-level unemployment, an inadequate rate of economic growth, a developing educational crisis, a spreading pall of conformity, urban blight, and a substantial and enlarging hard core of poverty—all this and more in the "affluent society." Internationally, we are confronted with the already great and growing strength of the Communist world, the "urge to industrialize" and widespread unrest in the underdeveloped areas, and the politics and economics of the European Common Market.

One need not be a Veblenian to recognize these problems or to see that, at home and abroad, they are significantly related to each other, both in their origin and in their potential resolution. But, even when the conventional social scientist possesses such recognition, he nonetheless allows a broad chasm to stand between what he appreciates and what, as a specialized professional, he studies. Specialization is of course necessary, in the social sciences as elsewhere, when specialization is the opposite of dilettantism. But specialization and trivialization are not the same thing.

Specialization in Veblen's time was just beginning to emerge in the social sciences; today it approaches the limits of credibility. More to the point, specializations are steadily separated from the main trunk of thought and problems of which they are presumed to be branches. Today, specialization—and its natural offspring, quantification—takes on a life of its own that increasingly makes technique competitive with perspective, rather than complementary. To the degree that unwitting specialization characterizes the social sciences, they accumulate more "knowledge" while simultaneously reducing their ability to use that knowledge to understand the nature of social problems.

Today's problems lend themselves appropriately to a Veblenian analytical framework. Emphasis must be placed on the nature, the functioning, and the interaction of social institutions, which are always in some degree anachronistic and anomalous. The degree to which institutions are "senile" or "imbecilic" today, it may be asserted, is critical. The institutions most commanding attention in this respect are those clustering around the system of business enterprise and the national state.

Institutions come into being—consciously or unconsciously—as the means by which men as individuals and in groups, conflicting and cooperating, for better or for worse, organize and control social behavior. Institutions may emerge from an unspoken consensus, as a matter of custom; they may be created in the process of conscious struggle, as was true, for example, of our Constitution. Institutions emerge in many ways that lie between the extremes of accepted custom and revolutionary change. However they may arise, institutions tend over time to become a part and an expression of an ideology, a set of beliefs and principles supporting a way of life. Paradoxically, when institutions function effectively, the setting in which they exist is changed. As time goes on, therefore, institutions necessarily serve functions at least in part different from those for which they were initially suited. As time goes on, also, institutions become shelters for vested interests which, attempting to make the most of what they have, attempt also to prevent institutional change, and do so with power, habit, and law behind them. All this activity is recognized widely—e.g., in concepts such as "the social lag," and in the continuous re-interpretation of the Constitution provided by the courts.

The institutions providing the foundation of American capitalism (and, as we shall see, modern nationalism) are no exception to the foregoing generalizations. The historical and legal foundations of our economic institutions developed in an era of expanding agriculture, spreading trade, and early industrialism. In fact and in law our economic institutions have changed much as we have become an industrial society; but we incline still to evaluate proposals for institutional change in a mood appropriate to that world long past. A striking symbol of this inclination is the legal fiction of the corporation as a "person"; no less striking, but of greater importance, is the pervasive belief that the spirit of business enterprise is the only proper approach to the problems of an advanced industrial society.

Unemployment, low growth rates, hard-core poverty, and related "social" problems of urban congestion and inadequate educational and health facilities are domestic problems which the system of American business enterprise is unable or unwilling to tackle directly. As Veblen was quoted as saying earlier, "it is a question of what businessmen may be expected to do for cultural growth on the motive of profits." It is not the function of businessmen to deal with national economic problems such as unemployment; nor would we wish them to deal with, say, health problems, on the basis of expected profits.

The easy answer that the market system *can* handle these matters is made doubtful by pointing out that it *hasn't*. Indeed, these problems have emerged from an economy dominated by a market system—and have emerged both despite and because of that dominance. The subtler suggestion that the market system has been hampered and interfered with by taxes, labor unions, regulation, and the whole apparatus of modern society may be answered by asking a question: Who will or can turn the clock back, how, and how far, and m doing so explain the origins of these "intrusive institutions" apart from the evolution of an industrial society? For in no highly developed industrial society do we find this "apparatus" missing in any important degree.

In recent decades, and particularly since the depression of the thirties, many explicit departures have been made from the institutions of a free private enterprise system. But it is important to note two characteristics of that process of change: (1) it has taken place in a piecemeal fashion, usually on the assumption that it was a reaction to aberrations or emergencies; (2) it has been apologetic in spirit and halting in application. These characteristics have been due in part to the hold of the past over men's minds, including even those pressing for change; in part they have resulted from the continuing power of "the vested interests" to hold back change.

Veblen's analysis of the nature and meaning of business enterprise stemmed from a deep aversion to both business principles and businessmen; he formed his ideas about business in the midst of its most buccaneering period, and the illustrations he used, e.g., in *The Theory of Business Enterprise*, are most frequently drawn from the spectacular revelations of governmental investigations of the time. Writing in such a period, when businessmen were on their worst behavior, and regarding businessmen with skepticism even when at their best, Veblen not surprisingly failed to give credit where credit was due and attributed some evil where it was not deserved.

The "credit" due belongs not to businessmen as such, but to the function of competition within a business-enterprise system. Veblen was doubtless correct in assuming that businessmen had a mortal fear of competition; but he was just as surely incorrect in assuming that competition served no beneficial function whatsoever, that it was a mere multiplication of money-seekers. Veblen acknowledged the benefits of competition for an earlier period, but he failed to give it credit for the period in which he wrote.

The foregoing defect is relevant to Veblen's critical distinction between "business" and "industry." The virtues of the American economy Veblen attributed to industrialism as such; the defects he attributed to the aims and techniques of the business community. It seems more accurate to think that there are *some* virtues arising out of business self-seeking, and *some* problems arising out of industrialism. Veblen was generally correct; but for purposes of formulating sensible and feasible policies, finer distinctions are required. These in turn require investigations going beyond anything Veblen accomplished or contemplated.

It is not difficult to find grounds for accepting Veblen's notions that business aims and methods are basic to the waste, inefficiency, and general foolishness of much of contemporary economic life. After all, businessmen have made most of the relevant decisions. But matters would be even less desirable if the process of competition in the market were abandoned where it exists—keeping in mind

that market competition that cuts costs is considerably less pervasive than the "competition" that, while maintaining prices through
collusion, acts through advertising expenditures and trivial product
differentiation. Still, Veblen's now widely accepted contention that
modern technology will not support a beneficially competitive market structure (because it will efficiently support only a few firms)
except in the early phases of growth in an industry has considerable
validity. This contention would not seem a novel idea to conventional economists today; however, their time might usefully be spent
pondering the institutional and legal implications of this approach
rather than in spinning out the niceties of a perfectly competitive
market in long-run equilibrium.

If Veblen was eager to find fault with business, he was disinclined
to do the same with industry. Industrialism has grown up in many
different institutional patterns, as different as those characterizing
Great Britain, the United States, Germany, Japan, and the Soviet
Union. In no case has industrialism emerged in what might be thought
of as its "pure" terms: namely, under the guidance of "engineering
criteria." Nor, one may say firmly, could it ever, as Veblen well knew.
There have always been some problems associated with industrialism
that seem independent of the *type* of institutional framework. They
are problems having to do with morale, discipline, quality, efficiency,
with the organization of large-scale activities. Conceivably one could
specify institutions to meet such problems with perfection; but on the
whole such an approach would be no less "make-believe," to use
Veblen's phrase, than the make-believe idealizations of private enterprise and neo-classical economics. This is not to say that such problems are insoluble. Nor does it mean that some situations are not worse
than others. It is to say rather than Veblen did not take such problems into account, that he attributed all evils of industrial operation
to business control, and that such problems *are* important.

But if it is clear that Veblen was sometimes careless, it is not at all
clear that he was mistaken in his main proposition which states that
the aims and methods of business enterprise become increasingly
unsuited to the needs of a developing industrial society. The heart of
this conception is the interdependence of the modern economy,
caused by an industrial technology. If that is the heart, the circula-
tory system is the flow of goods and services that is increasingly
subject to arteriosclerosis as the structure of production, and the institutions that guide its use become both unbalanced and inadequate.

Today's persisting unemployment, low growth rates, and hard-core poverty are the outcome of some combination of a technology that requires rapidly decreasing amounts of labor per unit of output, a structure of production critically dependent upon the market for durable goods (including weapons), a long period of high levels of income and associated satiation of consumer wants for manufactures (given the distribution of income), a pattern of market controls that prevents both price and wage reductions, and, most generally, the fact that we are a highly developed industrial capitalist society.

America enjoyed its greatest buoyancy during periods of rapid institutional and/or technological change (in both product and technique); they were periods of innovation. The day will never come when innovations are exhausted, but the impact of any particular product or technique innovation today, given the fact that it is taking place in a "larger" economy, is less than the same development would have been at an earlier day. Moreover, the "innovations" most needed today are in areas traditionally kept at arm's length from the market: they are in the realm of *social*, not individual, needs, and for their implementation *institutional* innovation is required. Since our educational system is inadequate, our medical facilities costly and scarce, our cities congested and blighted, our transportation system verging on paralysis, there is much obviously to be done. Doubtless it would stimulate the entire economy, relieve unemployment, increase our rate of growth, and lessen poverty, if needed changes were made.

Economists are of course aware of these problems, but their *theoretical* apparatus does not meet them. Economic analysis, as such, focuses upon the immediate past, the present, and the immediate future. The changes in ("micro-" and "macro-") economics since Veblen wrote are modifications of the neo-classical framework. Modern economists typically view neo-classical economics with healthy skepticism; but that economics remains their starting-point, both in their training and in their analyses. An economics built on assumptions of given institutions and technology, and of perfect mobility of capital and labor, is not suited to problems emerging from and requiring institutional and technological change, and rigidities in capital and labor markets. It is as if modern astrophysicists were to work with Ptolemaic astronomy and Aristotelian physics, much modified. Such an approach would not only be cumbersome; its initial perspective would be crippling.

Conventional economists characteristically limit their recommendations in the realm of public policy to a narrow range: more competition, for "micro" problems; monetary and fiscal policies for "macro" problems. There are difficulties in implementing "more competition" in industries where such a policy is neither politically feasible nor economically workable; apart from that, however, competition within an *industry* does not relieve structural imbalance in the *economy*. Competition, whatever its virtues, does not cause excess productive capacity to flow to areas of inadequate productive capacity, not just because there are rigidities in the market system, but because the areas of shortage are areas of public need and do not appear in the marketplace.

Nor do monetary and fiscal policies, however important they may be for short-run problems, act to promote long-run economic growth. It is not that there is no effect; for the short-run and the long-run growth are of course interrelated. When structural problems exist—unused capacity in coal, in machinery, in automobiles, in steel; and increasing groups of technologically unemployed labor, and new entrants to the labor market who are unable to find jobs at all—they can be resolved only by structural change, and monetary and fiscal policies do not achieve structural change, at least not by design. "Not by design." That is perhaps the problem.

Economists are often pleased to see themselves as objective scientists, as highly trained thinkers dispassionately examining the implications of assorted economic relationships. Economists *should* be objective, but they *are* not dispassionate—although many assume that by taking basic institutions as given and conducting abstract analyses they have combined objectivity and neutrality. Veblen adopted a neutral pose; but the pose was a matter of words, not of focus. In his teaching and writing, unlike most other economists, Veblen examined, he did not take as given, "the principles of action which underlie the current, businesslike scheme of economic life..."; Veblen questioned "the existing law and order" (VIII, 239). To achieve desirable structural change in the economy requires just such a questioning process, and it requires achieving structural change by design.

If economists are to move in this direction, it is frequently argued, they must sacrifice objectivity. More to the point, they must sacrifice a spurious neutrality. A doctor does not sacrifice his objectivity when he recommends that his patient give up smoking, change his diet, or undergo an operation. The economist is more like a doctor than a physicist, as is often presumed. To remain objective an economist must make his procedures specific, regard the relevant evidence honestly, and specify his values. He need not, and he cannot, give up his values, as though he were apart from the society he analyzes. Whatever his political or social views, no economist accepts *all* economic institutions in existence. The question is not whether economists should evaluate institutions or seek change; the question is the *degree* of institutional change required, why, in what combinations, and how it can be achieved most satisfactorily. It involves values, theory, and fact; it is a question not likely to be treated adequately if its legitimacy is denied. Consciously or not, by proposal or by default, economists are "in the business" of accepting or rejecting particular institutions. The "business" will be done better when it is carried on by those who know what they are about.

The approach implied above, the approach pursued by Veblen, requires not only that economics shed much of its synthetic purity; it requires that economics more consciously relate itself to the other social sciences. Institutions are social phenomena, caught up in and affecting history. An increased emphasis upon institutions in economics implies an increased emphasis on politics, sociology, psychology, and history. Sociologists and historians are not interested in Veblen by accident; nor is it surprising that social scientists find Veblen too general. He could not succeed in the task he set himself. What Veblen could not do alone, cooperating social scientists may be able to do. The attempt has not yet been made.

The necessity for broadening the analytical framework of the economist is all the more obvious when we turn to international economic problems. Questions of nationalism then intrude; but in the underdeveloped areas it is also clear that economic institutions appropriate to industrialization cannot be "created" without substantial and pervasive change in the politics and the culture of such societies—and in their relationships with the already industrialized societies. Secondly, when we examine the probabilities associated with the European Common Market, it is clear that political and economic issues inextricably intertwine. Thirdly, one need merely mention the problems raised by the Communist Bloc, to indicate the necessity for an analysis that combines "economic" considerations with those of nationalism and ideology. If economists have done much fruitful work regarding these problems, most of it has been done outside the mainstream of conventional analysis. Veblen's approach, used consciously, could increase the fruitfulness of such work in the future.

Notes

1. As will be touched upon below, a sharp line cannot be drawn between "hunch," insight, hypothesis, and theory. A "hunch" that leads to a systematic insight, taken together with experience and training, furnishes the basis for a hypothesis which, if validated, can become part of a theory, part of a *system* of explanation.
2. One noted critic of Veblen, whom politeness suggests be left nameless, has claimed that Veblen was "against institutions." This absurd idea, if it means anything, is tantamount to saying that a doctor who prescribes preventive medical care, or who advises surgery, is "against bodies."
3. The widespread belief that Veblen did so, in his "Memorandum on a Practicable Soviet of Technicians" (IX, 138ff.), will be examined in later pages.
4. For example, on the personal level, in 1925 Veblen was in effect offered the presidency of the American Economic Association (of which he was not a member), the highest honor that can be accorded to an economist. He turned the offer down, essentially out of bitterness. (Interestingly enough, the move to gain this office for Veblen was begun by Professor Paul Douglas, later to be Senator from Illinois.)
5. It is seemingly less implausible to argue that, because Veblen's predictions were almost all on the gloomy side, and the world is a vale of tears, he was bound to be "right" more often than not. Apart from the fact this is in itself a "theory" of sorts, the contention may be answered by pointing out that Veblen was not merely gloomy; he specified the *manner* in which relevant processes would work out, with what he would can "a cause and effect. genetic analysis." That Veblen also left unexamined much that is important for understanding the problems he deemed vital will be taken up subsequently.
6. It is this aspect of such economics that has led it to be called "Robinson Crusoe economics": that is, an economics that is as meaningful in the simple setting of a desert island as in modern England—or as meaningless. It must be pointed out that neo-classical economics is not as "institutionally neutral" as our characterization may suggest, or as some of its adherents would believe. It assumes private property in the means of production, takes a profit-maximizing businessman as its decision-making focus, assumes away market restraints from either the business or the labor side, and posits the absence of social intervention. It frequently concludes by opposing the real development of the constraints assumed away in the model. Thus, "laissez-faire" economics. The few "pure" adherents of this school today oppose any and all departures from the free and unfettered operation of markets for all goods and services—to an extent that goes so far as to decry public education. It is fair to say that such an economics does more to attract its adherents than it does to produce them. It also has a hand in turning many away from economics.
7. The practical meaning of the neo-classical approach is underlined when it is recognized that "welfare economics," not only provides no guidelines for those involved or interested in constructing "the welfare state," it is a body of theory that—given its assumptions—stands in opposition to any such developments. To one degree or another, "welfare" developments are taking place; but they are taking place with little or no *theoretical* basis in economics.
8. Unless, of course, one holds to the view that the scientific analysis of society is neither possible nor desirable nor necessary. But that view is seldom taken today; least of all by social scientists.

9. Paradoxically, it is probably correct to say that the economics of choice developed by the bourgeois economists of Western capitalist societies has much greater usefulness in planned socialist economies than in the economies for which it was developed. If this is so, it is because the matters taken as "given" in neo-classical economics are under much more, if not by any means complete, control in socialist than in capitalist economies; also, there is presently a greater "scarcity problem" in, say, the Soviet Union than in, say, the United States. (The same comment would be true of mathematical economics and econometrics.)

10. The excessive degree to which refinements of neo-classicism have been carried is suggested by a highly placed and highly trained theoretical economist now in government circles who has remarked that all that is useful in neo-classical theory in his own work (which involves, among other things, the avocation of scarce resources to competing ends) is taught on the sophomore level in college economic courses. See *Business Week*, January 5, 1963, p. 19.

11. The late C. Wright Mills, in his *Power Elite* (1956) and other writings, combined Veblen and Marx (and others) in his own analysis, which he developed a generation after Veblen's death. Mills's "elite" is composed of three basic groups—business, political, and military—which interact in a manner compatible with, but more complicated than that posited by Veblen. The degree of additional complication revolves around the problems and possibilities posed by contemporary technology, taken in the context of the Cold War.

12. No attempt can be made here to view Veblen's instinct theories against contemporary psychological theories; it is clear that such an attempt would find many areas both of congruence and of conflict.

13. A sense in which Veblen did confront the question now to be discussed will be examined in our concluding pages.

3

The Place of Veblen in the History of Ideas

Wesley Clair Mitchell

The son of Norwegian immigrants, Veblen was born on a Wisconsin farm, July 30, 1857. When he was eight years old, his parents moved to a larger farm in Minnesota. There he grew up in a frontier settlement with eight brothers and sisters who continued to speak Norwegian at home while they learned English in school. The Veblens prospered as efficient farmers may, and gave their children better educational opportunities than most native American farmers have thought worthwhile. An intellectual drive seems to characterize the family. An elder brother of Thorstein's became a professor of physics and one of his nephews is a distinguished mathematician.

At seventeen Veblen entered the academy of Carleton College; at twenty he entered the college, and at twenty-three he graduated with the class of 1880. Carleton was then a small Congregational school that gave a youth predisposed to skepticism abundant provocation to amuse himself with the infirmities of traditional wisdom. By all accounts, the undergraduate impressed his college circle much as the adult was to impress the reading public. But however gravely folk might reprobate his views, everyone acknowledged his extraordinary capacity for assimilating knowledge and putting it to strange uses.

John Bates Clark, later to win fame as one of the foremost economic theoreticians of his generation, was teaching in Carleton in the late seventies. Thus Veblen was introduced early to the subject about which he finally organized his interests. But for the time being he was engrossed by classical philology, natural history, and philosophy. When he went to Johns Hopkins University in 1881, philosophy was his major subject and economics his minor. Not finding what he wanted, Veblen transferred to Yale, where he took a doctor's degree in philosophy in 1884, with a dissertation entitled "Ethical Grounds of a Doctrine of Retribution." In that same year he published a paper on "Kant's Critique of Judgment"[1] in the *Journal of Speculative Philosophy*.

All this looked like the fair beginning of an academic career. But in those days there were not many openings for young philosophers whose preconceptions resembled Hume's. Veblen was never one who could "sell himself," as advertisers have taught us to say. So he returned to Minnesota, presently married a classmate of literary gifts, and entered on a desultory course of life with wide reading, some writing, and a bit of nondescript office work. This period of incubation lasted some six or seven years. Doubtless the difficulty of obtaining an academic appointment reinforced Veblen's critical attitude toward American "seminaries of the higher learning." Hope deferred is a bitter diet. But the lack of regular occupation and of intellectual companions other than his wife gave Veblen long hours to follow his own thoughts wherever they led. He became more detached than ever from conventional viewpoints and more firmly rooted in his own habit of mind.

A new phase of Veblen's life began in 1891, when he entered Cornell as a graduate student of the social sciences. While there he published a paper called "Some Neglected Points in the Theory of Socialism."[2] It was "offered in the spirit of the disciple" to Herbert Spencer—in the spirit of the disciple who demonstrated that his master misconceived the grounds of popular dissatisfaction with economic "freedom." Professor J. Laurence Laughlin, then at Cornell, appreciated the quality of this essay. When asked to take charge of the department of economics at the newly founded University of Chicago, Laughlin invited Veblen to go with him. Thus Veblen became one of that extraordinary faculty which President Harper gathered about him—perhaps the most stimulating group of scholars in the country, certainly the group with the most varied traditions.

Teaching courses on agricultural economics, socialism, and the history of economic theory, plus managing the *Journal of Political Economy,* was a heavy load for one of Veblen's physique and temperament. But he seems to have worked best under pressure. In 1898 he published his first critique of economic theory, "Why Is Economics Not an Evolutionary Science ?"[3] and in 1899 brought out his first

book, *The Theory of the Leisure* Class. From that year he was a man
of mark, known as widely to the intelligentsia as to his professional
brethren.[4]

II

The essence of Veblen's critical work and the type of his constructive efforts, as we have known them since, are revealed in the
article of 1898 (which was elaborated in "The Preconceptions of
Economic Science," 1899–1900) and the book of 1899. It is time to
see what account we can make his writings yield of their author's
viewpoint.

In that effort my bald sketch of his early life gives a hint. It sug-
gests that as an observer of social behavior in the American field,
Veblen had the initial advantage of coming from a different culture.
In his essay on "The Intellectual Pre-eminence of Jews in Modern
Europe,"[5] Veblen explains how such an experience fits a youth for
scientific inquiry:

> The first requisite for constructive work in modern science, and indeed for any work of
> inquiry that shall bring enduring results, is a skeptical frame of mind....
>
> The young Jew who is at all gifted with a taste for knowledge will unavoidably go
> afield into that domain of learning where the gentile interests dominate and the gentile
> orientation gives the outcome. There is nowhere else to go on this quest....
>
> Now it happens that the home-bred Jewish scheme of things, human and divine...all
> bears the datemark, "B.C."...it runs on a logic of personal and spiritual traits, qualities
> and relations, a class of imponderables which are no longer of the substance of those
> things that are inquired into by men to whom the ever increasingly mechanistic orienta-
> tion of the modern times becomes habitual.
>
> When the gifted young Jew, still flexible in respect of his mental habits, is set loose
> among the iron pots of this mechanistic orientation, the clay vessel of Jewish archaism
> suffers that fortune which is due and coming to clay vessels among the iron pots.... He
> is divested of those archaic conventional preconceptions which will not comport with
> the intellectual environment in which he finds himself. But he is not thereby invested
> with the gentile's peculiar heritage of conventional preconceptions which have stood
> over, by inertia of habit, out of the gentile past, which go, on the one hand, to make the
> safe and sane gentile conservative and complacent, and which conduce also, on the
> other hand, to blur the safe and sane gentile's intellectual vision, and to leave him
> intellectually sessile....

By consequence [the young Jew] is in a peculiar degree exposed
to the unmediated facts of the current situation; and in a peculiar
degree, therefore, he takes his orientation from the run of the facts

as he finds them, rather than from the traditional interpretation of analogous facts in the past. In short, he is a skeptic by force of circumstances over which he has no control. Which comes to saying that he is in line to become a guide and leader of men in that intellectual enterprise out of which comes the increase and diffusion of knowledge among men, provided always that he is by native gift endowed with that net modicum of intelligence which takes effect in the play of the idle curiosity.

Now, a Norwegian family of farmer folk is like an orthodox Jewish family at least in one respect: it also has a culture that differs widely from the culture of modern America. The Norwegian brand is not date-marked "B.C.," but it savors of the sagas. There is less of business in the Norwegian than in the Jewish heritage, and the former is by so much the more remote in spirit from today. A boy brought up in such a family, largely sufficient unto itself, acquires an outlook upon life unlike that of the son of thoroughly acclimated parents. As he ventures into the world, he finds much strange which those to the manner born take for granted. If endowed with curiosity, he wonders both about the notions that his parents cherish and about the notions that his mates accept. That was Thorstein Veblen's case. And he was insatiably curious about everything he encountered—minerals, plants, and animals, the tongues men speak, the arts they practice, the faiths they venerate, and the proofs they find convincing. He had no collection of established truths to check his questioning; for the truths taken for granted at home and the truths taken for granted in school raised doubts about one another. Thus he, like the Jewish boy of his analysis, became "a skeptic by force of circumstances over which he had no control." On some such lines, the creature of these circumstances might explain his own preparation for scientific inquiry.

But scientific inquiry does not exhaust itself in asking questions; it seeks also to find answers. Veblen's constructive bent is not less marked than his skepticism, though of course it is more specialized. An inquisitive youth may come to doubt all things on principle; but when he begins to contrive explanations, he must limit himself within a range that he can study intensively. What fixed Veblen's choice of problems ?

All I can say in answer is that, given his temperament, Veblen's final choice seems a natural outcome of his circumstances. A son of immigrant farmers must wonder about differences among people.

That theme is both obvious and subtle; it is beset by prejudices, difficult to treat objectively, fascinating, and slippery. Veblen found its dangers, open and concealed, alluring; for in the realm of thought he was bold as a Viking, and as fond of wiles. Yet differences among people are manifold; no one can explore and explain them all. Veblen might have held fast to his early philological interest, fed by his bilingual upbringing. He might have stuck to his first "major," philosophy. Perhaps he would have done so, had he secured a position in that department of learning. He might have pushed deeper into biology, which in the days of Darwinian speculation seemed neatly fitted to his talents. In the end he found for himself a field more attractive than any one of these. He could fuse his leading interests by studying human cultures. That large venture gave scope to his double heritage from home and school, to his linguistic equipment and facility, to his inveterate skepticism, to his liking for organized systems of thought, to his interest in biology. Also it gave free play to another set of impulses that were as much a part of him as curiosity.

Veblen loved to play with the feelings of people not less than he loved to play with ideas. Now, there are few objects of scientific scrutiny more exciting to our feelings than cultural differences. These differences touch our dear selves. Recall how fond we are of making invidious comparisons between people of our own kind and others. We feel magnanimous if we let the comparisons turn to our disadvantage; we feel resentful if others point out inferiorities in us. However objectively our traits are analyzed, we react emotionally. The delicate nature of this subject must repel men who dislike complex and ambiguous situations; it attracted Veblen. He usually wrote with one eye on the scientific merits of his analysis, and his other eye fixed on the squirming reader. To him, this reader is the creature of cultural circumstances that have produced standard habits of feeling as well as norms of thinking. Veblen practices vivisection upon his contemporaries; he uses no anaesthetic; he has his notions about what emotional reactions each type will exhibit. Instead of seeking to facilitate the reception of his analysis by minimizing the reader's emotions, he artfully stimulates them for his own delectation.

Of course, most critics of modern culture have strong feelings of their own, which they strive to impart to their readers. Moral indignation is the commonest note, and the one to which we respond most readily. We get a certain satisfaction from being preached at; even when we think the preacher bears down rather hard upon our amiable weaknesses, we respect his zeal. Also we are used to the open satirist who seeks to laugh us out of our follies. Veblen repudiates preaching. As an evolutionist, his office is to understand, not to praise, or blame, or lead us into righteousness. From his point of view, any notions he may entertain concerning what is right and wrong are vestiges of the cultural environment to which he has been exposed. They have no authority, and it would be a futile impertinence to try to impose them upon others. There is much of the satirist in him; but it is satire of an unfamiliar and a disconcerting kind. Professedly, he seeks merely to describe and to explain our cultural traits in plain terms. But he likes to put his explanations in a form that will make the commonplaces of our daily lives startling and ridiculous to us. It is this his bionic foible which gives his writing its peculiar flavor.

Veblen is an inveterate phrasemaker, and he designs his phrases to get under our skins. "Conspicuous waste" fits our habits of consumption like a whiplash. Our philanthropies are "essays in pragmatic romance." Modern industry is so "inordinately productive" that prosperity requires "a conscientious withdrawal of efficiency" by the businessmen in control—their chief service to production is to practice "capitalistic sabotage." The common stock of trusts formed by combining companies that had competed with one another represents "defunct good-will." As individuals, we find our places either in the "kept classes" or among the "underlying population"— and either ranking makes us wince. His wit spares nothing and no one. If the pulpit is "the accredited vent for the exudation of effete matter from the cultural organism," the scientist is a "finikin skeptic," an "animated slide-rule," "machine made."

To explain this quirk in Veblen's humor would require the assurance of an amateur psychoanalyst. One who lacks that qualification must take the trait for granted, and merely register its consequences. I think Veblen's fondness for quizzing folk helped to determine his choice of problems and to shape the course of his analysis. I am sure it has been largely responsible for the reactions of readers, both professional and lay, to his work. One must be highly sophisticated to enjoy his books.

Within the field of human culture, an investigator must make a more definite choice of themes. Anthropology, history, sociology, economics, political science, social psychology, all deal with culture. A worker in that field must know something of all these disciplines, and Veblen knew much. In the end he organized his inquiries about economics. Perhaps his early contact with an original, though widely different, thinker in that line had some influence upon his choice. But there is an explanation in terms of logic that carries more conviction than psychological conjectures.

Darwin tells what stimulation he received from reflecting upon Malthus's theory of population when he was groping after his own theory of natural selection. An installment upon this debt of biology to economics was paid by the stimulation that Darwin's doctrines gave to Veblen's theory of cultures. Cultures are complexes of "prevalent habits of thought with respect to particular relations and particular functions of the individual and of the community."[6] The significant question about these habits is the question that Darwin asked about animal species: How did they develop into the forms that we observe?

The biological view of man's evolution suggests that habits of thought are formed by the activities in which individuals engage. The activities that occupy most hours are likely to exercise most influence in making the mind. The task of getting a living has busied incomparably more men and women for more time than any other task. Hence, economic factors have had and still have a major share in shaping mass habits of thought; that is, in making human culture what it has been under varying circumstances in the past, and what it is today. Other types of activity get whatever time and attention the peremptory job of finding food and shelter leaves free. Where the economic activities themselves are efficient, this margin for indulging such human propensities as emulation, propitiation, predation, and idle curiosity becomes appreciable. A good many individuals can spend most of their time in other tasks than making a living, and so can build up a considerable body of habits not drilled in by the exigencies of humdrum work. Yet there is perforce a certain congruence among all the mental habits formed in any single brain, and even among the habits prevalent in any community at a given time. So the emancipation even of our religious, aesthetic, and scientific notions from economic determination is but partial.

Only one other factor can conceivably rival the influence of getting a living in shaping culture. That is the strictly biological factor of breeding. Veblen thinks, however, that the evidence is all against supposing that *homo sapiens* has undergone any substantial change in anatomy or physiology for thousands of years. Our brains are about as efficient organs as were the brains of neolithic men. Selective breeding under stress of changing circumstances doubtless tends to lower the reproduction rate of individuals whose propensities run toward violence in exceptional degree. Perhaps other generalizations of that type may be made. But the effects of the breeding factor are slight and dubious in comparison with the effects of cumulative changes in habits of thinking under the discipline of cumulative changes in modes of getting a living. That the lives we live today are so vastly different from the lives lived by our ancestors who left their sketches on the walls of caves and lost their stone implements in the kitchen middens is due in but minor measure to bodily modifications. The theory of evolution begun by biologists must be continued by students of culture, and primarily by economists.

III

Needless to say, economists found this a novel conception of their office when Veblen began writing. The "science of wealth," as they commonly defined their subject, dealt with production, exchange, and distribution, as these processes run in modern times. About the way in which the modern scheme of institutions has evolved, the professed theorists knew little and cared little, for they did not see that such knowledge would help to solve what they took to be their central problem—how prices are determined now, particularly the prices that effect the distribution of income.

Veblen does not claim that genetic studies will answer the questions that economists have posed in the form they have chosen. His fundamental criticism is that economists have asked the wrong questions. Their conception of science and its problems is antiquated, pre-Darwinian.

> The sciences which are in any peculiar sense modern take as an (unavowed) postulate the fact of consecutive change. Their inquiry always centers upon some manner of process. This notion of process about which the researches of modern science cluster, is a notion of a sequence, or complex, of consecutive change in which the nexus of the sequence, that by virtue of which the change inquired into is consecutive, is the relation of cause and effect.[7]

Neither the theory of value and distribution as worked out by Ricardo nor the refined form of this theory presented by Veblen's teacher, J. B. Clark, deals with consecutive change in any sustained fashion. The more classical political economy was purified, the more strictly was it limited to what happens in an imaginary "static state." Hence, orthodox economics belongs to the "taxonomic" stage of inquiry represented, say, by the pre-Darwinian botany of Asa Gray. Therefore, it possesses but meager scientific interest. If political economy is to modernize itself, it must become "an evolutionary science," and it can become an evolutionary science only by addressing itself to the problem: How do economic institutions evolve ?

> In so far as modern science inquires into the phenomena of life, whether inanimate, brute, or human, it is occupied about questions of genesis and cumulative change, and it converges upon a theoretical formulation in the shape of a life-history drawn in causal terms. In so far as it is a science in the current sense of the term, any science, such as economics, which has to do with human conduct, becomes a genetic inquiry into the human scheme of life; and where, as in economics, the subject of inquiry is the conduct of man in his dealings with the material means of life, the science is necessarily an inquiry into the life-history of material civilization, on a more or less extended or restricted plan.... Like all human culture this material civilization is a scheme of institutions—institutional fabric and institutional growth.[8]

Associated with this fundamental charge, that economists have mistaken their chief problem, is a second criticism, that they have worked with an antiquated conception of human nature.

> In all the received formulations of economic theory...the human material with which the inquiry is concerned is conceived in hedonistic terms; that is to say, in terms of a passive and substantially inert and immutably given human nature. The psychological and anthropological preconceptions of the economists have been those which were accepted by the psychological and social sciences some generations ago. The hedonistic conception of man is that of a lightning calculator of pleasures and pains, who oscillates like a homogeneous globule of desire of happiness under the impulse of stimuli that shift him about the area, but leave him intact.[9]

Veblen molded his own notions of human nature on Darwin, William James, and anthropological records. To the biologist and the open-eyed observer, man is essentially active. He is not placed "under the governance of two sovereign masters, pain and pleasure," as Jeremy Bentham held; on the contrary, he is forever doing something on his own initiative. Instead of studying pleasures and pains, or satisfactions and sacrifices, on the supposition that these "real forces" determine what men do, economists should study the processes of human behavior at firsthand. For this purpose, the important psychological categories are not the felicific calculus and the association of ideas, but propensities and habits. The human individual is born with a vaguely known equipment of tropisms and instincts. Instincts differ from tropisms in that they involve an element of intelligence; in other words, they are susceptible of modification by experience. What modifications instincts will undergo, into what habits they will develop, depends upon the nature of the experience encountered, and that depends in turn upon the environment, especially the human environment, in which the individual grows up. The human environment is of critical importance because through tradition, training, and education "the young acquire what the old have learned."

> Cumulatively, therefore, habit creates usages, customs, conventions, pre-conceptions, composite principles of conduct that run back only indirectly to the native predispositions of the race, but that may affect the working out of any given line of endeavor in much the same way as if these habitual elements were of the nature of a native bias. Along with this body of derivative standards and canons of conduct, and handed on by the same discipline of habituation, goes a cumulative body of knowledge, made up in part of matter-of-fact acquaintance with phenomena and in greater part of conventional wisdom embodying certain acquired predilections and pre-conceptions current in the community.[10]

This emphasis upon the cumulative character of cultural changes takes us back to Veblen's conception of what constitutes the problems of science and to his fundamental criticism of economics. The distinctively modern sciences, we have found him contending, deal with consecutive change. He might have added, though I do not recall his doing so, that the consecutive changes studied by different sciences appear to be cumulative in varying degree. Even physics and chemistry, when applied to the history of the cosmos, are concerned with a situation that develops from millennium to millennium. Biology has its branches that deal with processes conceived to repeat themselves over and over without marked alteration in the total situation to be accounted for; but the problems in which cumulative change is prominent bulk larger in biological than in physico-chemical theory. Cumulation rises to its highest pitch, however, in the social sciences, because the behavior of men changes in the course of experience far more rapidly than does the behavior of stars and infra-human species. For that reason, the major explanation of human behavior at any point in the life-history of our race must be sought in the preceding installments of the story. As Veblen put it: "Each new situation is a variation of what has gone before it and embodies as causal factors all that has been effected by what went before."[11] To take economic institutions as they stand at a given moment for granted, and merely to inquire into their working, cuts out of economics that behavior trait which differentiates human activities most clearly from all other subjects of scientific inquiry.

Yet Veblen might have admitted that the quasi-mechanical economics, which takes existing institutions for granted and inquires how they work, has a certain value. This type of inquiry may be regarded as elaborating the logic implicit in the institutions of which it takes cognizance, usually without recognizing their transient character in the life-history of mankind. For example, pecuniary institutions are a prominent feature of current life in the Western world. Most of us make money incomes and buy what we want at money prices. To some extent all of us are drilled by experience into the habit of thinking in dollars; all of us acquire some skill in "the exact science of making change"; all of us accept in part "the private and acquisitive point of view." Now, a theory such as Veblen's warm admirer, Herbert J. Davenport, developed on the express assumption that all men are animated by the desire for gain throws light on our economic behavior just to the extent that men are perfect products of the countinghouse. The logician who excogitates this mechanical system is prone to exaggerate its adequacy as an account of contemporary behavior. But Veblen would be the last to deny the importance of pecuniary institutions in modern culture. He does not, in fact, hold that work such as Davenport has done is wrong, or wholly futile. Yet he inclines to take what is valuable in it for granted, much as Davenport takes for granted the existing scheme of institutions. For Veblen is impatient of the well known and eager to develop aspects of the modern situation about which more orthodox types of economic theory have little to say. Men whose conception of what is "scientific" has been molded by mechanics, criticize his precipitate neglect of their problems, much as Veblen, who builds upon Darwinian biology, criticizes them for their precipitate neglect of evolutionary problems.

One more characteristic of Veblen's procedure must be noted. Representatives of the "exact" sciences stress the importance of measurement. There are those, indeed, who go so far as to claim that the outstanding characteristic of scientific thought is its quantitative precision. Now, Darwinian biology was not an exact science; it made but slight use of measurements in any form; it confined itself mainly to "qualitative analysis," supplemented by a recognition that certain factors have played major and other factors minor roles in the development of species. In comparison with Darwin's method, Mendel's experiments in heredity seem precise, and we all know what an impetus the rediscovery of Mendel's work gave to biological research.[12]

Veblen was a good Darwinian in this respect also. His native bent was toward speculation of a philosophical sort. No one had keener insight or nicer subtlety in dealing with ideas, and like all efficient inquirers, he used the tools of which he was master. Further, the statistical invasion of the biological and social sciences was but just starting in Veblen's youth. Galton was not then recognized as a figure of the first magnitude; Pearson's and Edgeworth's work on quantitative methods lay in the future. It was easy for one who had little liking for mathematical procedures to overlook the promise of statistics. Finally and most important, problems of cumulative change in "life-history" are exceedingly difficult to treat by any method of measurement. Each change is by hypothesis a unique event, begotten by an indefinite number of causes. To disentangle the tangled skein is impossible. Without the aid of an elaborate technique it is hard to do more with such problems than what Darwin and Veblen have done—that is, to study the evidence and select for particular attention what seem to be the salient factors. That might go without saying concerning all parts of man's history before social statistics were collected on a liberal scale and preserved for analysis. It is only when he comes to recent changes that an investigator has tolerably accurate data. These materials Veblen did not reject; but he made no great effort to exploit them. In this respect, at least, his practice resembled that of most orthodox economists.

While not addicted to the quantitative method, Veblen was a keen observer. Having climbed to Darwin's mountain peak, his eyes ranged over a vast stretch of human experience. About many matters quite invisible to economists immersed in the nineteenth century he thought intensively. The Neolithic age in Europe, the feudal system in Japan, the lives of the Australian blackfellows, and a thousand things equally remote in time or space from present-day America seemed strictly pertinent to his problem. Even what he saw of his immediate surroundings differed from what was patent to his contemporaries.

"All perception," said William James, "is apperception." Every scientific inquirer sees what his mind is prepared to see, and preparation of the mind is a compound of previous experiences and the thoughts to which they have given rise. Recall how Darwin's vision was clarified when, after long fumbling with a mass of observations, he hit upon the idea of natural selection.

What Veblen saw when he looked at man's activities differed from what other economists saw because his mind was equipped with later psychological notions. How widely Veblen's conception of human nature departed from that which he imputed to his predecessors has been remarked. It remains to show how his ideas upon "original nature" and "culture" controlled the larger issues of his theorizing, just as notions concerning man's substantial rationality controlled the larger issues of earlier speculation.

There are two ways of studying behavior. One may observe men "objectively," as an experimental psychologist observes animals, and try to form generalizations concerning their activities without pretending to know what goes on inside their heads. Or one may take his stand inside human consciousness and think how that organ works. If the latter method is chosen, the results arrived at depend upon the thinker's notions about consciousness. Logically, these notions form one premise—usually tacit—in a syllogism. The procedure at this stage is "deductive," though it may have been preceded by an "inductive" derivation of the psychological premise, and it may be followed by an "inductive" testing of the conclusions.

Veblen adhered to the standard practice of the classical masters— he chose to reason out human behavior. But he sought to explain actual behavior, not what men will "normally" do; his conclusions are supposed to conform to "facts" and to be open to testing by observation in a directer fashion than are most expositions of "economic laws." Also Veblen gave closer attention than his predecessors to the character of his psychological premise and made it explicit. Profiting by two generations of active research in biology and anthropology as well as in psychology, he could reach what is certainly a later, and presumably a juster, conception of human nature. In so far as his economic theories rest upon psychological premises, they may be rated a more "scientific" account of human behavior than theories which rest upon what latter day writers call the "intellectualist fallacy of the nineteenth century." Yet in so far as any theories of behavior are conclusions deduced from some conception of human nature, they must be subject to change as knowledge of human nature grows.

Veblen's dealings with psychology, however, are not confined to borrowing ideas from other sciences for use as premises in economics. Anyone who gives an enlightening account of any phase of human behavior is himself contributing toward our understanding of ourselves. By working with psychological conceptions, he develops them and makes their value and limitations clearer. Thus Jevons contributed to the breakdown of hedonism by applying Bentham's felicific calculus in good faith to explain how exchange value is determined. His literal exposition helped economists to realize the artificiality of ideas which seem plausible so long as they remain vague. The more clearly a social scientist sees that he is dealing with human behavior, and the more explicit he is about the conceptions of human nature with which he works, the larger the service which he can render to our self-knowledge. Veblen's service in this direction is that he has applied the instinct-habit psychology of Darwin and William James to explain a wide range of human activities. The nascent science of social psychology owes him a heavy debt of gratitude for this accomplishment—a debt which will be all the heavier if his work helps future investigators to do something better than he accomplished.

One of the ways to press forward along Veblen's path is to turn back and test for conformity to "fact" our plausible reasonings about how men behave—that is, to see how our theories about what men do agree with what we can observe. Of course, what we can observe is not wholly objective. As recalled above, it depends upon what we are mentally prepared to see, and also upon our techniques. Yet when we can apply them, factual tests of ideas are one of our most effective ways of promoting knowledge. The men who laid the foundations of economics recognized this point, and in their writings upon method admitted the desirability of "inductive verification." But in practice they spent little effort upon this desideratum—it seemed too hopeless a task as matters stood. The notion that inquiries should be framed from the start in such a way as to permit of testing the hypothetical conclusions was not common property in their time. Unless such plans are laid in advance, and laid with skill, it is more than likely that the results attained by reasoning will be in such form that no inquirer can either confirm or refute them by an appeal to facts. Observing this run of affairs, the classical methodologists spoke disparagingly of induction in general and of statistical induction in particular: it seemed to them a tool limited to a narrow range of uses in economics.

Veblen's case is not so very different, except that he deals with actual as distinguished from "normal" behavior. He does not plan in advance for testing his conclusions. Of course, he is bound to be skeptical about them—that attitude is not merely logical in him, but also congenial to his temperament. There is always an aura of playfulness about his attitude toward his own work in marked contrast to the deadly seriousness of most economists. Yet, when the opportunity offers, he will cite evidence to support a contention. Usually it is evidence of a sweeping sort which those who do not agree with his viewpoint can interpret in a different sense. Sometimes the evidence is an illustrative case, and the question remains open how representative the case may be. Rarely does he undertake a factual survey. Many of his propositions are not of the type that can be tested objectively with the means now at our disposal. His work as a whole is like Darwin's—a speculative system uniting a vast range of observations in a highly organized whole, extraordinarily stimulating both to the layman and to the investigator, but waiting for its ultimate validation upon more intensive and tamer inquiries.

IV

All this about the man, his problems, his viewpoint, and his methods of work. What constructive results did he reach ?

Veblen's studies in the life-history of mankind range over the whole interval between "the origin of the blond type" and the future prospects of business enterprise. Into this range he has dipped at will, preferring always the little-known features of the story. He has never written a systematic treatise upon economics; instead, he has produced numerous essays and ten monographs. An adequate summary of the ideas he has contributed to the social sciences would fill another volume as large as *Absentee Ownership*. All that is feasible here is to select topics illustrative of his conclusions. The whole body of writing is so much of one piece that almost any of his disquisitions would serve as an introduction to the whole. Doubtless it is best to take discussions of matters with which everyone is familiar.

Looking over the modern world, Veblen marked a difference between industrial and pecuniary employments; that is, between the work of making goods and the work of making money; in still other terms, between the machine process and business enterprise. No fact of daily life is more commonplace than this difference; neither men on the street nor economic theorists see in it anything exciting or novel. What comments it seems to call for have been made long since. Adam Smith pointed out in the *Wealth of Nations* that division of labor requires exchange of products and that exchange is greatly facilitated by money. But money is merely an intermediary; we must not exaggerate its importance, as the mercantilists did. Bentham's psychology reinforced this view. Pleasures and pains are the only things that really matter to men; commodities and services are important as instruments of pleasures and pains; money stands at a further remove—it is a means of getting commodities and services. The prevalent common sense on the subject was summed up by John Stuart Mill in a famous passage:

> There cannot, in short, be intrinsically a more insignificant thing in the economy of society, than money; except in the character of a contrivance for sparing time and labor. It is a machine for doing quickly and commodiously, what would be done, though less quickly and commodiously, without it; and like many other kinds of machinery, it only exerts a distinct and independent influence of its own when it gets out of order.[13]

Acting on this conviction, economists have paid a great deal of attention to the monetary mechanism—the best ways of designing it and of keeping it in order. But they treat this problem as a specialty that has little to do with general economic theory. In discussing value and distribution they take money as a tool for investigating more important matters. Thus Alfred Marshall declares that money

> is the center around which economic science clusters...not because money or material wealth is regarded as the main aim of human effort, nor even as affording the main subject-matter for the study of the economist, but because in this world of ours it is the one convenient means of measuring human motive on a large scale.[14]

The "real forces" that control behavior, on Marshall's showing, are satisfactions and sacrifices. It is these real forces, and the balancing of one set of them against the other set, that require analysis. Money is an indispensable tool for measuring the force of opposing motives; but it remains merely a tool so far as the fundamental principles of economics are concerned.

This view of the place of money in economic theory is perfectly consistent with the conception of human nature entertained by Marshall. Despite his substitution of less colorful terms for "pleasure" and "pain," he thought after Bentham's fashion. Men practice a sort of double-entry bookkeeping, satisfactions on the credit and sacrifices on the debit side of the account; they discount for futurity and for uncertainty; they are ready reckoners. To tell what they will do, one needs to know the motive force of the satisfactions and sacrifices promised by alternative lines of action. That force can best be expressed in terms of money; but the use of money does not alter the substantial character of economic behavior.[15]

Shift from Marshall's psychological notions to Veblen's, and the whole picture changes. Money becomes a most significant thing in the economy of society, because it shapes the habits of thought into which our native propensities grow. Instead of being "a machine for doing quickly and commodiously what would be done, though less quickly and commodiously, without it," the use of money "exerts a distinct and independent influence of its own" upon our wants as consumers, upon our skill as planners, upon our methods as producers, and upon our ideals as citizens. And since the discipline that the use of money imposes upon our minds affects some classes far more than it does others, this institution produces social stresses— stresses that may disrupt the present polity.

To begin where Veblen began: In a society where moneymaking is the commonly accepted test of success in life, our native propensity toward emulation takes on a pecuniary twist. We wish to seem well-to-do, and to attain that agreeable rating we cultivate an air of careless affluence as much as our means permit. We like goods that look expensive, we keep up with the changing styles however uncomfortable they may be, we subject ourselves to inane and fatiguing social frivolities, we teach our children accomplishments that are elegant because they are costly. Our sense of beauty is stamped with the dollar sign. We stand in awe of the very rich, and approach as close to their reputed manner of life as we can. Though born with an instinct of workmanship that makes futility disagreeable, we get satisfaction from conspicuous waste. Though active creatures, we practice conspicuous leisure, or make our wives and menials do it for us. The higher modern technology raises our standards of living above the "minimum of subsistence," the wider the scope of our invidious consumption. Money cannot be intrinsically insignificant in the economy of a society whose inner cravings bear so deep an impress of pecuniary standards. All this and much more was set forth in Veblen's first volume, *The Theory of the Leisure Class.*

Secondly, money-making drills into us a certain type of rationality—the type that reaches its flower in modern accounting. The monetary unit provides us with a common denominator in terms of which the best drilled among us can express all values, not excepting the value of human lives. However vagrant our fancies, we are all forced by the environment of prices to be somewhat systematic in planning. We learn to reckon costs and income, to make change, to compare the advantages of different types of expenditure. It is the habit of mind begotten by the use of money that makes the pleasure pain calculus plausible as an account of our own functioning. Thus the use of money lays the psychological basis for that philosophy of human behavior which Bentham and Mill, Marshall and Clark, represent—a philosophy which, ignorant of its origins, treats money as a thing of slight moment except in facilitating trade and research. As pointed out above, economic theory written from the private and acquisitive viewpoint becomes a system of pecuniary logic that exaggerates the importance of one institutional factor in behavior to the neglect of others.

Thirdly, money-making both promotes and obstructs the fundamental task of getting a living. Veblen pictures two sets of economic activities running side by side through the life of a modern community. One set is concerned with producing raw materials, working them up into serviceable goods, transporting and distributing the things men desire to use. The other set is the endless series of concatenated bargains by which men determine how much each individual can take to himself of what others have made. The material welfare of the community as a whole depends solely upon the quantity and quality of the goods brought to consumers by the first set of activities. Money-making conduces to material well-being just in so far as it enlarges the quantity or improves the quality of the serviceable goods obtained from a given expenditure of energy. From a common-sense viewpoint, therefore, money-making is a means to getting goods. But in practice we reverse the relation. We make goods in order to make money. Veblen never wearies of expounding that central paradox and of developing its consequences.

He grants the commonplaces about the economic advantages of this scheme of organization. Adam Smith was right: industrial efficiency requires division of labor, division of labor requires exchange, and exchange requires money. No other scheme of organization that men have tried out in practice yields so large a per capita flow of goods to consumers as the current scheme of making goods for profit. Business accounting is a marvelous device for controlling complicated undertakings. Industry requires capital and credit, and, as matters now stand, who can supply capital and credit but the capitalist and the banker? The businessman is the central figure in modern economic life, the prime mover, what you will. There is no call to quarrel with encomiums of this sort which anyone is moved to pronounce upon the present order. But it is interesting to reflect upon certain features of the situation that are less obvious to business-trained eyes.

One is that the recurrent crises and depressions which ever and again reduce the flow of goods to consumers are due to business, not to industry. There is no technological reason why every few years we should have idle factories and unemployed men walking the streets, while thousands lack the goods employers and men would like to supply. The trouble is that business enterprises are run for profit, not to meet human needs. When times are good, prices rise, profits are high, businessmen borrow freely and enlarge their output. But such prosperity works its own undoing. The substantial security behind the loans is prospective net earnings capitalized at the current rate of interest. When the rate of interest rises, as it does during prosperity, the capitalized value of a given net income declines, and the loans become less safe. More than that, net earnings in many cases prove less than had been expected in the optimistic days of the nascent boom. Prices cannot be pushed up indefinitely; the costs of doing business rise and encroach upon profits; bank reserves fall and it becomes difficult to get additional credit. When fading profits are added to high interest, creditors become nervous. In such a strained situation, the embarrassment of a few conspicuous concerns will bring down the unstable structure which had seemed so imposing. A demand for liquidation starts and spreads rapidly, for the enterprises pressed for payment put pressure upon their debtors to pay up. So prosperity ends in a crisis, followed by depression. In short, business enterprises cannot prosper without committing business errors that bring on a crisis, and from these errors the whole community suffers.

More serious in the long run than these acute fits of indigestion is a chronic malady of the present order. Businessmen seek to fix their selling prices at the maximum net-revenue point. There is always danger that an oversupply of products will reduce prices more than the increased turnover will compensate for. This danger is peculiarly great because of the "inordinate" productivity of the modern machine process. Give the engineers their heads and the markets might be swamped by a flood of goods. Businessmen are constantly on their guard against this peril. It is their office to adjust supply to demand; that is, to prevent an unprofitable rate of output; that is, to keep industrial efficiency "subnormal"; that is, to practice "capital-istic sabotage."

Indeed, by their very training, businessmen are incompetent to serve as captains of industry. Technology is becoming more and more an affair of applied science. We have elaborate schools for engineers in which mathematics, physics, chemistry, and electrical theory are the basic subjects of instruction. The graduates from these schools are the men who know how to make goods. If permitted to organize production on a continental scale, they might, with their present knowledge, double or triple the current output of industry. That they will not be suffered to do, so long as they are subject to the higher authority of businessmen, who do not understand technol-ogy and who distrust the vaulting plans of their own engineers. And this distrust is well founded, so long as business enterprise is orga-nized in many units. To set engineering science free from business shackles would smash the independent enterprises of today, and lay out the process of making goods on much broader lines. In the early days of the industrial revolution, the businessman was an industrial leader; in these later days the development of technology has turned him into an industrial incubus.

Yet the situation of business enterprise which seems so firmly entrenched is becoming precarious, because the habits of thinking engendered in men by modern life are undermining the habits of thinking on which business traffic rests. If businessmen do not speak the same language as engineers, or enter into their thoughts, neither do engineers speak the language or share the ideas of businessmen. The one group talks in terms of physical science, the other talks in terms of natural rights, particularly the right of ownership. It is in-creasingly difficult for the engineer to see why he should not be allowed to develop his plans for increasing output to the limit. He asks why the pecuniary interests of a handful of families should stand in the way of a doubled per capita income for the community as a whole. Demonstrations that absentee owners have a perfect right to draw dividends from industry without contributing personal ser-vice leave him cold. What is more threatening than this doubting mood of the technologists is a growing disaffection among the masses of factory hands. Though not schooled in physical science, these people fall into a somewhat similar habit of thought. Their daily work with materials and machines teaches them to seek an explana-tion of all things in terms of cause and effect. They tend to become skeptical, matter of fact, materialistic, unmoral, unpatriotic, undevout, blind to the metaphysical niceties of natural rights. And nothing effective can be done to check the spread of these subversive habits of thought so long as the workers must be kept at their machines. So it appears that the time is coming when the present order of society, dominated by business enterprise in the interests of absentee ownership, will no longer seem right and good to the mass of mankind.

Veblen has no definite specifications for the new structure of institutions that will grow up in place of the present one, beyond an expectation that technically qualified engineers will have a larger share in managing industry. His evolutionary theory forbids him to anticipate a cataclysm, or to forecast a millennium. What will happen in the inscrutable future is what has been happening since the origin of man. As ways of working shift, they will engender new habits of thinking, which will crystallize into new institutions, which will form the cultural setting for further cumulative changes in ways of working, world without end.

V

If Veblen has descried aright the trend of cultural change, his economic theories will commend themselves to a wider circle in the next generation than in his own. For on his showing, science, like all other cultural excrescences, is a by product of the kind of work folk do. Circumstances made a certain Thorstein Veblen one of the early recruits in the growing army of men who will look at all social conventions with skeptical, matter-of-fact eyes. Just before his time the German historical school had perceived the relativity of orthodox economics; but they had not produced a scientific substitute for the doctrine they belittled or discarded. Karl Marx had been more constructive. In Veblen's view, Marx had made a brave beginning in cultural analysis, though handicapped by a superficial psychology derived from Bentham and by a romantic metaphysics derived from Hegel. Bentham's influence led Marx to develop a commonplace theory of class interests that overlooked the way in which certain habits of thought are drilled into businessmen by their pecuniary occupations and quite different habits of thought are drilled into wage earners by the machine process in which they are caught. Hegel's influence made the Marxian theory of social evolution essentially an intellectual sequence that tends to a goal, "the classless economic structure of the socialistic final term," whereas the Darwinian scheme of thought envisages a "blindly cumulative causation, in which there is no trend, no final term, no consummation." Hence, Marx strayed from the narrow trail of scientific analysis appropriate to a mechanistic age and attained an optimistic vision of the future that fulfilled his wish for a socialist revolution.[16] The Darwinian viewpoint, which supplies the needed working program, will spread among social scientists, not because it is less metaphysical than its predecessors or nearer the truth (whatever that may mean), but because it harmonizes better with the thoughts begotten by daily work in the twentieth century. That the majority of economists still cling to their traditional analysis is to Veblen merely the latest illustration of the cultural lag in social theory—a lag readily accounted for by the institutional approach.

Yet Veblen remains an inveterate doubter even of his own work. The Darwinian viewpoint is due to be superseded in men's minds; the instinct-habit psychology will yield to some other conception of human nature. The body of factual knowledge will continue its cumulative growth, and idle curiosity will find new ways of organizing the data. His own view of the world is date-marked "A.D. 1880–1930," as definitely as Jewish culture is date-marked "B.C."

A heretic needs a high heart, though sustained by faith that he is everlastingly right and sure of his reward hereafter. The heretic who views his own ideas as but tomorrow's fashion in thought needs still firmer courage. Such courage Veblen had. All his uneasy life he faced outer hostility and inner doubt with a quizzical smile. Uncertain what the future has in store, he did the day's work as best he might, getting a philosopher's pleasures from playing with ideas and exercising "his swift wit and his slow irony" upon his fellows. However matters went with him, and often they went ill, he made no intellectual compromises. In his retreat among the lovely coast hills of California, he died on August 3, 1929, a "placid unbeliever" to the end.

Notes

1.   Reprinted in *Essays in Our Changing Order,* New York, 1934.
2.   *The Annals of the American Academy of Political and Social Science,* November 1891; reprinted in *The Place of Science in Modern Civilisation,* New York, 1919.
3.   *The Quarterly Journal of Economics;* reprinted in *The Place of Science in Modern Civilisation,* New York, 1919.
4.   Dr. Joseph Dorfman has given a full account of Veblen's life and an admirable analysis of his work in *Thorstein Veblen and His America*, New York, 1934.

5. *Political Science Quarterly,* vol. XXXIV, March, 1919; reprinted in *Essays in Our Changing Order,* pp. 226–230, New York, 1934.

6. *The Theory of the Leisure Class,* p. 190, New York, 1899.

7. The Evolution of the Scientific Point of View." Read before the Kosmos Club, at the University of California, May 4, 1908; first published in *University of California Chronicle,* vol. X, no. 4; reprinted in *The Place of Science in Modern Civilisation,* p. 32, New York, 1919.

8. "The Limitations of Marginal Utility," 1909. Reprinted in *The Place of Science in Modern Civilisation,* pp. 240–241, New York, 1919.

9. "Why Is Economics Not an Evolutionary Science?" 1898. Reprinted in *The Place of Science in Modern Civilisation,* p. 73, New York, 1919.

10. *The Instinct of Workmanship,* p. 39, New York, 1914.

11. "The Limitations of Marginal Utility," 1909. Reprinted in *The Place of Science in Modern Civilisation,* p. 4, New York, 1919.

12. That Veblen grasped the significance of Mendel's work and of the experiments to which it led is shown by his paper on "The Mutation Theory and the Blond Race," reprinted in *The Place of Science in Modern Civilisation,* pp. 457–476, New York, 1919. See also his references to "the Mendelian rules of hybridization" in *The Instinct of Workmanship,* pp. 21-25, New York, 1914, and in *Imperial Germany and the Industrial Resolution,* pp. 277-278, New York, 1915. But this appreciation, supplemented by his admiration for the experiments of Jacques Loeb, did not induce him to attempt close quantitative work of his own. Two early articles on the price of wheat and "A Schedule of Prices for the Staple Foodstuffs" drawn up for the Food Administration in 1918 are the only papers I recall in which Veblen made detailed statistical inquiries. The articles appeared in *Journal of Political Economy,* vol. I, pp. 68–103, 156–161, December, 1892, and 365–379, June, 1893; the memorandum for the Food Administration was unearthed by Dr. Dorfman and may be found, minus the statistics, in *Essays in Our Changing Order,* pp. 347–354, New York, 1934.

13. *Principles of Political Economy,* Ashley's ed., p. 488, London and New York, 1909.

14. *Principles of Economics,* 6th ed., p. 22, London and New York, 1910.

15. In fairness it should be noted that Marshall's discussions of economic behavior are far more realistic than this schematic framework seems to promise.

16. See Veblen's two papers on "The Socialist Economics of Karl Marx and his Followers," originally published in *Quarterly Journal of Economics,* August, 1906, and February, 1907; reprinted in *The Place of Science in Modern Civilisation,* pp. 409-456, New York, 1919. The phrases quoted are from pp. 417, 436.

     After dilating upon the "disparity between Marxism and Darwinism," Veblen points out that "the socialists of today" have shifted from "the Marxism of Marx" to "the materialism of Darwin," though "of course" without admitting that "any substantial change or departure from the original position has taken place." See pp. 417, 432, 433.

4

Thorstein Veblen: Recipe for an American Genius[1]

Max Lerner

THORSTEIN VEBLEN came of Norwegian ancestry, of a land-hungry and land-tenacious tradition, with an intensely agrarian view of life. His parents had emigrated from Norway in 1847 and had settled on the Wisconsin frontier under conditions of enormous hardship. There Veblen was born in 1857. When he was eight the family moved to Minnesota, where his father took up a middling farm tract. The boy grew up in a clannish and culturally tight Norwegian community, well insulated against the more mobile life of the Americans around. He learned more of Norwegian speech than English. He was a queer precocious boy, prematurely skeptical and unpleasantly witty. At seventeen, because of his father's zeal for education, the boy was packed into a buggy and deposited at Carleton College, in Northfield, Minnesota, where he spent three years in the preparatory department, and finished the college course in three more, graduating in 1880. He suffered a good deal—a strange "Norskie" boy among Americans, with a scanty knowledge of English, lacking money and social standing, uneasy in the theological atmosphere in which the college was drenched. He had a lazy manner and a biting tongue that infuriated students and faculty alike; the only teacher who saw his promise and whom Veblen liked was John Bates Clark, at whose theory of distribution he was to aim his sharpest shafts years afterward.

But no college, however uncongenial, and no artificial textbook learning could keep Veblen's mind from developing. He read English literature, dabbled in poetry, delivered ironical orations, studied philosophy and economics, trifled with some of the radical doctrines then current, fell in love. After graduation he taught for a year and then, lured by the growing, reputation of Johns Hopkins, he left for Baltimore to do graduate work. But the eastern university did not put itself out to welcome the gawky penniless Norwegian boy.

When he failed to get a fellowship at Johns Hopkins, he left before the end of the term to study philosophy at Yale with President Noah Porter, and social theory with William Graham Sumner. Both men were impressed with him, and both his essay on "Kant's *Critique of Judgment*" and his history of the surplus revenue of 1837 (awarded the John Addison Porter prize in 1884) marked him as a distinctive mind. And yet his stay at Yale seems to have been unfruitful and frustrating. He had to struggle along, lonely, always in debt, earning his board by teaching in a military academy, regarded as a foreigner and an agnostic. When he took his Ph.D. degree in philosophy in 1884, he found that teaching posts were available only to the orthodox and acceptable young men with a divinity training. Disheartened, he took his useless Ph.D. degree back with him to his Minnesota farm.

The next seven years were probably the most miserable in Veblen's life. His education among Americans had unfitted him for the narrow life of a Midwestern Norwegian farmer, yet it had not placed any other way of life within his grasp. He seemed to disintegrate. While he read aimlessly and without stint he kept complaining of his health, railing at the parasitism of businessmen, mocking the sanctities of a conventional Lutheran community. He tried repeatedly for a teaching position, but always without success. In 1888, largely as a way out of a blind alley, he married Ellen May Rolfe, with whom he had once had a college romance and whose connections with a prominent business family held out some hope of employment. But an untoward turn of events shattered even that hope, and Veblen and his wife settled down on a farm in Stacyville, Iowa, waiting for something to turn up. Nothing did. Each year it became increasingly difficult to get a teaching job because of the embarrassment Veblen had in explaining his long absence from academic life. He finally decided to get back to some institution of learning as a graduate student and use that as a fresh point of departure.

In 1891, at the age of thirty-four, he turned up at Cornell, rustic, anemic, strange-looking in his corduroys and coonskin cap.

J. Laurence Laughlin, who was worlds apart from Veblen and yet saw some of his quality, managed to obtain a special fellowship for him. Veblen's first essay, "Some Neglected Points in the Theory of Socialism" *(Annals of the American Academy of Political and Social Science,* Nov. 1891), contained many of the germs of his later theories. He seemed to spring into sudden maturity. And when Laughlin, called to be the head of the economics department at President Harper's new University of Chicago, took Veblen with him and secured him a teaching fellowship there (1892-93) at $520 a year, Veblen's long quest for some niche in the academic world seemed at last realized. Although he was never regarded with favor by the ruling powers at the Rockefeller-endowed university, the next year he became a reader in political economy, then an associate, in 1896 an instructor, and in 1900 an assistant professor.

Veblen dug down into anthropology and psychology and used them to focus a sharp new light upon economic theory. His mind had not brooded all those years to no purpose: it was crammed full of daring hypotheses and of significant detail quarried from a vast field of reading. Each essay he now wrote opened up whole areas for later exploration. The titles of his essays, generally published in learned journals, reveal the turn of his mind: "The Economic Theory of Woman's Dress," "The Instinct of Workmanship and the Irksomeness of Labor," "The Beginnings of Ownership," "The Barbarian Status of Women," "Why Is Economics Not an Evolutionary Science?" "The Preconceptions of Economic Science," "Industrial and Pecuniary Employments." His work as managing editor of the university's *Journal of Political Economy* (1896-1905, and in effect earlier) gave his thinking further range and depth. He met, either in the university or near by, a group of mature minds with which he could match his own: Jacques Loeb, Franz Boas, James H. Tufts, John Dewey, William I. Thomas, Lester F. Ward, Albion W. Small. At thirty-nine he began planning his first book.

The book that finally emerged was *The Theory of the Leisure* Class, published in 1899 when Veblen was forty-two. It gave him prominence overnight. Into it he poured all the acidulous ideas and fantastic terminology that had been simmering in his mind for years. It was a savage attack upon the business class and their pecuniary values, half concealed behind an elaborate screenwork of irony, mystification, and polysyllabic learning. The academic world received it with hostility. "It fluttered the dovecotes in the East," wrote a contemporary. "All the reviews…are shocked and angry. Clearly their household gods have been assailed by this iconoclast." The literary men, led by William Dean Howells, were delighted with its merciless exposure of aristocratic attitudes but missed its attack on the businessmen and the middle class.

Veblen now proceeded to a more direct analysis of business, and five years later, in 1904, he published his second book, *The Theory of Business Enterprise,* based on the material turned up in the nineteen-volume *Report of the Industrial Commission* (1900-02). It contains Veblen's basic economic theory—dealing with the effects of the machine process, the nature of corporate promoting, the use of credit, the distinction between industry and business, and the influence of business ideas and pressures upon law and politics.

It was almost a decade before Veblen published another book. In the interim he wrote essays on the methodology of economics for the professional journals. His life was disturbed by marital difficulties, and when, in 1904, his wife reported one of his relationships to the university authorities it became impossible for him to remain at Chicago. In 1906 he went as an associate professor to Leland Stanford University at the invitation of President David Starr Jordan. For a time he was reunited with his wife at Palo Alto, but soon the difficulties between them began again, and the two were finally separated. Veblen was relatively happy at Stanford. He spent part of his time in a mountain cabin, with a little farm around him. He made friends, had the esteem of the faculty, went his own way. But once more an unconventional relationship with a woman violated the academic *mores,* and he was forced to leave. He sought a Carnegie grant for an archaeological expedition to the Baltic and Cretan regions, and dug deep into the literature of the subject. But the grant was not forthcoming. Finally through the efforts of Herbert J. Davenport he was invited to the University of Missouri as lecturer and began his teaching there in 1911. About that time he secured a divorce, and on June 17, 1914, he was married to Anne Fessenden Bradley, who also had been divorced and had two daughters.

Veblen stayed at Missouri for seven years. It was there that his most famous course, which he had already begun to teach at Chicago—"Economic Factors in Civilization"—reached its classic form. It was rambling, erudite, omniscient; it swept all history and all cultures. His classroom manner was casual and inarticulate to the point of despair. He cared little about teaching itself, and had no talent for it. But while he was never popular with the run of students he had many disciples and won their unstinted affection. He used all his courses as the basis for his writings, but the book which most nearly approximates the content of his principal course is his third, *The Instinct of Workmanship* (1914), which Veblen himself later called his most important book.

After 1914 the sequence of war, peace, revolution, and industrial collapse turned Veblen's interests from topics of professional concern to current issues. His writing took on a faster tempo and a more strident tone. His tenure at Missouri also became precarious, and finally in 1918 he burned his academic bridges and moved to New York, where he became first an editor of the *Dial* and then, in 1919 a member of the faculty of the New School for Social Research.

To this period belong his more revolutionary writings. Much of Veblen's appeal up to that time had lain in the fact that his most savage attacks on the social system had been made in the blandest manner. He had combined his uncompromising idol-smashing with all the intellectual qualities of the liberal mind—detachment subtlety, complexity, understatement, irony. Now the urgency of Veblen's interests produced a progressive departure from this manner. His *Imperial Germany and the Industrial Revolution* (1915) has a bareness of structure not found in his earlier books, although it was still ambiguous enough to suffer the supreme irony of having George Creel's Committee on Information use it as grist for the propaganda mills while the Post Office Department held it up as subversive doctrine. Its thesis was that Germany's strength lay in the fact that she borrowed the industrial techniques from England but instead of borrowing the English democratic procedure along with them she combined them with the unqualified feudal-militaristic institutions congenial to business. In An *inquiry into the Nature of Peace* (1917*)* Veblen made his meaning clearer by describing patriotism and business enterprise as having the common trait of being useless to the community at large, and analyzing them as the principal obstructions to a lasting peace. In *The Higher Learning in America* (1918) he leveled so bitter and direct an attack on the "conduct of universities by businessmen" that on reading an earlier draft friends had advised him to withhold it from publication.

Whatever its immediate subject matter, every one of Veblen's books was in reality directed at an analysis of business enterprise. In *The Vested Interests and the State of the Industrial Arts* (1919) he came closer to his subject, with a savageness of tone that repelled many of his disciples who had been accustomed to his subtler manner. He defined a vested interest as "a marketable right to get something for nothing," pointed out that the aim of business was to maximize profits by restricting or "sabotaging" production, and sharpened his now familiar antithesis between business and industry. During the "red hysteria" of 1919-20, Veblen, writing editorials for the *Dial,* described the passions aroused by the concern for the safety of capitalist institutions as a form of dementia praecox, contrasted the aims of Bolshevism with those of the guardians of the "vested interests" without discrediting the former, and wrote openly of the possibilities of a revolutionary overturn. In his papers collected in *The Engineers and the Price System* (1921) he sketched out a technique of revolution through the organization of a soviet of technicians who would be in a position to take over and carry on the productive processes of the nation. Veblen was no longer hiding his meaning.

Veblen's last years were lonely and his life tapered off. For a while he had plans, as the head of a group of technicians, for pushing further the investigation of the revolutionary role of engineers. But as with his other plans, nothing came of it: he had no talent for promotion or organization. His investigations for the Food Administration among the IWW for five months in 1918 had met with no official response. His attempts to become part of President Wilson's peace-conference mission had come to nothing. No one would furnish money for a trip to England to study British imperialism. In 1920 his second wife died. He felt tired, ill, rootless. Finally some ladies, solicitous for his health and admirers of his genius, took him into their home and watched over him. He had reached the stage of being greatly lionized and little understood. He moved about like a ghost among groups of liberal intellectuals, with his pale sick face, his sharp Vandyke, his loose-fitting clothes, his shambly gait, his weak voice so infrequently used, his desperate shyness.

His last book, *Absentee Ownership and Business Enterprise in Recent Times* (1923), was in a sense a summary of his doctrine. In 1925 an offer of the presidency of the American Economic Association, made after considerable opposition from within the organization, was rejected by Veblen because, as he said, "they didn't offer it to me when I needed it." In May 1926 Ellen Rolfe died, and Veblen returned to his cabin near Palo Alto.

Here he lived with his stepdaughter until his death in 1929 amidst furniture he made with his own hands, wearing rough clothes purchased through the mail-order houses, reading aimlessly, worrying incessantly about his losses through investment, watching the movement of events with a dull ache of bitterness and resignation. Six months before his death he said: "Naturally there will be other developments right along, but just now communism offers the best course that I can see." He died, presumably of heart disease in Palo Alto, leaving instructions that his body be cremated and the ashes thrown into the sea, and that no memorial of any kind be raised for him and no biography written.

1937

Veblen and the Wasteland

By some strange mutation there emerged out of the arrested energies of the nineties the most considerable and creative mind American social thought has yet produced. *It* belonged to Thorstein Veblen, whose paradox it was that, himself a product of Scandinavian stock which had for generations fought with the soil for life, he became absorbed with the surpluses of a leisure class civilization; that, starting to reform professional economic theory, he made Americans aware of the wasteland of their contemporary social institutions.

After some *Wanderjahre* as a student and further years spent in desultory callings, Veblen come finally in 1892 to the glittering new University of Chicago as an instructor in economics. Into the group there—the first body if autonomous economic teaching in America— Veblen threw his startling generalizations about society, quarried from ethnological writings dusted off in the dark corners of the university library, or fashioned from a hint derived from conversations with John Dewey about philosophy or with Jacques Loeb about tropisms. But always, more coercive of his thought than anything else, there was Chicago itself, pressing its bulk and growth and tinsel wealth into his consciousness. Scarcely mentioned in his writings, it nevertheless polarized his thought and became a symbol of the society toward which his curious indirections were directed. And when on a battered Blickensderfer he had pounded out night after night the amazing pages of *The Theory of the Leisure Class* that society was for the first time made disquietingly aware of itself.

Veblen took as his threat the unproductiveness and inutility which become the ideals of a leisure class, and their psychological effects upon the whole of a society. He showed how, in such a society, prestige depends upon the flaunting of superfluous wealth through "conspicuous consumption" and "conspicuous waste," and through the "vicarious consumption" and "vicarious leisure" of the lady of the house and the corps of servants. He showed how the pecuniary values that dominated such a social structure informed every phase of life—religion, art, government, education; and in the tracing of the ramifications of leisure-class ideals through the whole of bourgeois culture lie fulfilled the subtitle of the book—"An Economic Study of Institutions." Although his argument was unlocalized, we applied the moral to ourselves—to our *parvenu* millionaires and the ostentations of the gilded age—to the "common man" whom the previous decades had discovered and made a symbol of, and whom Veblen now showed to be exploited, accepting his status clingingly, subservient to those in whose pecuniary glory he hoped some day to participate.

With the writing of the *Leisure Class,* Veblen's energies were liberated and his thought flowed strongly into the channels of significance that he found in modern life. He had waited for maturity to write his first book (he was forty-two when it appeared) and had in the interim crammed his mind full of hypothesis and conjecture about social institutions. Now in ten books, in the space of two decades, he poured forth this stream of ideas, spilling over each theme he treated; for he could never prune his thought or narrow his emotion to his specific subject. The argument is considerably repetitive and far from clear-cut. Veblen's writing is obscure, mannered, baffling; as Mr. H. L. Mencken has pointed out in one of his wittiest and least sympathetic essays, it wastes much effort in labored explanation of the obvious. But it encompasses the most important body of social analysis in modern American thought.

Veblen's principal motivation lay probably in making economic thought congruous with the conditions and spirit of latter-day economic activity. His brilliant series of essays on method, "The Preconceptions of Economic Science," in a manner which exasperated because it was at once summary and elegiac, rejected not only the prevailing economic doctrines but the unconscious premises behind them. These premises had emerged from the intellectual temper of their day, but they were out of accord with ours. Their world had vanished. In its place there was a new world whose principal economic outlines Veblen sought to sketch in *The Theory of Business Enterprise.* The small-scale entrepreneur had been replaced by an absentee-owned corporation, the thrifty captain of industry by the financier, the isolated machine by a well-knit and exacting machine process, the higgling of the market by an all-pervading price system, and competition by a set of refined and ingenious devices for price control.

But the most important change of all was the broadening cleavage, in economic activity, between industry and business. Industry was the thing-technique; it worked with things to produce things. But at the helm, directing industry to its own purposes, was business, which worked with intangibles to produce money-values. This dichotomy fascinated Veblen. It became for him something closely symbolic of Balder and Loki—a dualism which in spite of his detestation of moral valuations he could not help viewing morally. His quest for the springs of human motive behind these two strains led him to write *The Instinct of Workmanship,* at once the most searching and perplexing of his books. It is an ambitious affair, full of provocative blind alleys, and at least half a splendid failure. Plunging morass-deep into "instinct" psychology, it emerges with the thesis that the "instinct of workmanship," deeply ingrained in man since savage times, has impelled him always not to waste his resources on alien and irrelevant purposes, but that it has been thwarted throughout human history by the piling-up of institutions which have run counter to it.

Veblen tended more and more to dwell on this monstrous conflict. As the steady pressure of science and technological advance beats the conditions of life mercilessly onward, and keeps forever changing the economic landscape and with it the contours of society, man finds himself ever farther away from the sense of economy and workmanship and social order that his primitive instincts called for. And as if to deepen the irony of his position, every attempt that he makes to adjust himself rationally to the new conditions of life is doomed by the nature of his own institutions. For an institution, while Veblen often thought of it merely as a pattern of social life—an organized way of doing things—was much more essentially for him the common way of thinking implied by it and growing out of it. And these ways of thinking—the belief, for example, in the "natural rights" of the individual—exercise their most tyrannical power when

the patterns of life to which they were attached have been superseded. Out of their phantasmal world they reach the "dead hand of
the past" to paralyze any attempt man might make to come to terms
with his new world.

Inducted into a group of academic theorists who had exhausted
themselves in warfare between rival camps, such an economics as
this, with its airy rejection of all the stakes of conflict and its amazing vitality of thought, had an element of the grotesque, as if it were
some exotic growth transplanted into dour and barren ground. Like
all new doctrine, it had its trials at first. It was not even dignified by
being called a heresy, but was dismissed as, whatever its merits,
something other than economics—sociology, perhaps. But rapidly
the younger scholars, those with energy and eagerness and a glim-
mer of daring, clustered around it. They became a school—the "institutionalists," from the conspicuous place in economic study that
they give to the institutional patterns. And so Veblen's doctrine had
its triumphs as well; and if it has not yet become orthodox, it ranks at
least as a respectable heresy.

The generation which thus welcomed Veblen had been nurtured
on a body of thought whose informing principle was that of a neatly
arranged universe. In economics, physics, psychology, in art, morality, religion, political and legal theory, the prevailing attempt was
to cling to a rapidly slipping sense of order. Veblen's principal achievement lay in his summary rejection of these dreams of social order.
He saw a world in which the accumulated technical knowledge of
generations of scientists and craftsmen—the current "state of the
industrial arts"—was turned to the uses of an indifferent and even
hostile system of business enterprise; a world in which there was a
continuous "sabotaging" of industry by business whenever the aims
of production threatened to clash with those of profit-making; and
in which the natural resources of a country such as America had
been squandered and exploited because, by our system of economic
individualism, haste is especially profitable when it is accompanied
by waste. In the realm of business he saw the growth of huge corporations under an "absentee ownership," where the most valuable arts
were the refinements in manipulating items on a balance-sheet. He
saw the incrustation of the "haves" into "vested interests" with a
heavy stake in the maintenance of things as they are; and, exploited
by them and subservient to them, an "underlying population" whose
function as producers was to feed the "machine process," and as

consumers to pay for their commodities a price of which the larger part went to items such as advertising and salesmanship and marketing. He saw in religion that the churches had become infected with commercialism, and in education that men had almost given up their strange task of domiciling the ideals of a disinterested "higher learning" in a society at the mercy of pecuniary values.

From what obscure impulsions in his brain Veblen's chugging polysyllables took their perverse direction can be left only to conjecture. But we do know that the advancing *Zeitgeist* was on his side. His thought, judged cynical and pessimistic by the generation that saw the publication of the *Leisure Class,* struck an accord with the mood of the generation that read T.S. Eliot. In its essential symbols Veblen's wasteland of social institutions corresponded with the world as it revealed itself to the more sensitive post-War poets and novelists. If Veblen in some respects anticipated their notation of the modern spirit it was because, while they had needed the personal experience of War to impress upon them the plight of the individual in a disintegrating society, Veblen had sensed this plight more easily because his mind was not turned in upon itself, but was always directed toward the volcanic play of social energies. His greatest appeal was to those for whom the neat garden-walks and trim hedges of contemporary social thought contained fictitious patterns, clipped of all emotional evocation and unfruitful of any satisfying analyses.

In a sense Veblen helped tide American social thought over a period of desperate transition. The optimistic world of the early stages of industrialism, in which the machine had been accepted as an absolute boon, was behind us. A not impossible world in which we shall have learned what to do with the things that the machine has put within our reach is still to come. In the confusion between these two certitudes it was Veblen's achievement to make articulate the desolateness of our position. He has shown us by what impalpable puppet-strings we are tied to our racial and cultural past, and yet how uniquely our economic institutions differ from any the world has seen. The fierceness of his intellectual processes was combined paradoxically with an unimpassioned appraisal of all our bigness and shrillness and showiness. By insisting on a realistic picture of our economic society, by himself isolating and analyzing the economic changes which were cutting away the ground under established ways of living and orderly habits of thought, he revealed transitional America to itself.

How effectively he did this is attested by the rapidity with which his analyses have become the customary and slightly worn currency of our thinking. Walton Hamilton has remarked that practically every vein of importance that is being explored today in economic thought may be traced back to Veblen. Not alone in the technical literature of economics but in so influential a lay theorist as Stuart Chase and so appreciable a figure in fictional social criticism as Sinclair Lewis, the influence is unmistakable. Known first as an eccentric who spun out labored ironies on what the reviewers were pleased to call our "social foibles," Veblen has suffered the most consummate compliment that can be paid to any thinker: in a few decades his ironies have become the basic material of economic discussion.

1931

What Is Usable in Veblen?

JOSEPH DORFMAN'S important recent biography of Veblen,[2] with all its material on his life and writing and the America that he lived and wrote in, gives us at least the resources for taking a new measure of the man. We have none of us known what to make of his thought, and what meaning to extract from it for the dilemmas of today. It has been easy enough to see his glamour and succumb to it. Communists as diverse as Max Eastman and Mike Gold depart from their more drastic attitudes to do homage to him. Socialists and liberals see him on the side of the angels. Technocracy hitched itself to his name, and threatened for a season to become the tail that wagged the dog of his reputation. Yale University has hung his portrait in one of those buildings that were salvaged from the great bull market of the twenties. In Washington itself there are New Dealers high in government councils who use not only his phrases but some of his ways of thought; no doubt if there were any energy left among them for intellectual promotion it would be easier to found a Veblen society than any other.

The situation is a curious one, and not without a dash of irony. Does all this mean that the sallow Norwegian with his enormous intellectual effrontery, his desperate personal shyness, his total absence of our usual suavities, has become all things to all men? A "Norskie," eccentric, who had to eat for the greater part of his life the bitter bread of the alien and the heretic, is now seen as a home-grown product of the American soil. A scholar whose detachment made him a sort of symbol of "idle curiosity" is now talked of as a major influence in economic policy. It is as if history had staged its last theatrical trick to add to the already overgrown Veblen legend.

At the core of the Veblen legend is one of the most tangled and baffling personalities in American history. By the side of it Henry Adams is a study in simplicity. The legend has several phases. One has to do with Veblen's sea-green aloofness from the ordinary concerns of life, as of waters coldly lapping the shores of the world but never mingling with the swift currents. Another has to do with the feckless professor, unintelligible to his classes and his readers, writing on interminably in impossible sentences. Still another depicts the savage ironist who could impale a whole civilization on one of his phrases.

Added to these threads of legend was the mystery of Veblen's personal life—his amazing clothes, his home-made furniture, his noticing on domestic economy (so much more drastically original even than those on political economy), his unmade beds, his dirty dishes packed high in a barrel waiting for the garden hose, his monogrammed cigarettes, his unstable ménages ("But what is one to do if the woman moves in on you?"). The dry talk of the faculty lunch fables was fanned into something like a glow when a new Veblen story was recounted. Here and there on academic campuses young men walked about dizzy with a peculiar and recognizable intoxication, their usually plodding wits reeling because somehow a Norwegian farm boy-turned-scholar had blundered into magical English polysyllables. For many of the generation that came to maturity between the War and the crash Veblen was more than a thinker. He was, like Marx and Nietzsche, a symbol by which men measured their rejection of the values of the established order. And when they found such a symbol their myth-making faculties worked overtime. Mr. Dorfman, by his massive piling-up of the details of Veblen's life has, without diminishing Veblen's stature or complexity' brought the legend down to earth.

But, legend aside, measure Veblen's meaning for today and you will be forced to conclude that his role was not directive but chiefly disillusioning. Read him for direction and you will, as Samuel Johnston said of the plot in *Clarissa Harlowe,* hang yourself first. His starting-point was that of disillusionment with the orthodox systems of economic thought. For almost two decades he was preoccupied either with speaking his mind on the economic theory of Ricardo, Jevons, and their followers or else with making up his mind about the economic and social theory of Karl Marx and his followers. He was infinitely more successful in achieving the first than he was the second. Orthodox economic theory is probably deader today in America than it is anywhere else in the capitalist democracies. Ask for its whereabouts and you will see only the frayed fragments of its graveclothes, peeping out at two or three universities.

But for all his cocksureness about orthodox economics, Veblen had on the subject of Marxism only a painful indecisiveness. He had the hatred that any original mind has for every theoretical system except its own. Even had he accepted Marxism it would have been with a saving skepticism. But he wrote on socialism with a caution and canniness unusual even for him. His first important article, "Some Neglected Points on the Theory of Socialism," was hailed by his associates at Cornell as having nothing to do with the actualities of the class struggle and as being only "a metaphysical disquisition." On the basis of it Veblen got a fellowship the next year. His lectures delivered some years later at Harvard (at the invitation of Professor Taussig) on "The Socialist Economics of Karl Marx and His Followers" were such as to strengthen any doubts about Marxism that may have crept into the minds of his Harvard listeners.

Veblen can never be accused of cowardice. It would have been suicidal for him, desperately dependent as he was for a job upon the good-will of Laughlin and the other academic moguls, to show too much warmth for Marxism. He was writing in the midst of a red scare. No one who reads Mr. Dorfman's book, with its story of the bitterness of Veblen's life until he succeeded in getting some small academic foothold, can wonder that even when his own thought was closest to the Marxian categories he chose to clothe them in other terms.

This is of vast consequence in Veblen's thought. For one thing it means that Veblen's response to the conditions of American life had to be tortuous and indirect. Mr. Dorfman sketches in, as the backdrop against which the amazing enactment of Veblen's life took place, an excellent picture of Veblen's America. But for all the talent and research that he lavishes upon it, much of it is finally indecisive. Veblen lived a remote and abstracted life, never in the thick of things. He took part in no movements, traveled little, shrank from conversation, refused to vote. Even Thoreau was stirred by John Brown's death, but neither the Homestead strike nor the Haymarket trials seem to have left any direct traces in Veblen's writing. Amidst riots and judicial assassinations Veblen was writing "The Economic Theory of Woman's Dress," or framing metaphysical refutations of the marginal-utility school. At least during the first part of his writing career the effect of the American turmoil on Veblen was chiefly negative. The Veblenian irony is a way of saying things and yet not saying them, the Veblenian mystification is a form of protective coloration, the Veblenian vocabulary is triple armor against the charge of agitation, the Veblenian erudition in ethnology and archaeology gives perspectives of the past but never dangerous projections of the future.

But these very qualities have formed the basis of Veblen's acceptance. He was a godsend for the college instructors and other liberals who did not yet wear the stuffed shirts of capitalist apologists but who sought escape from the stridency of populism. He gave our taut generations relief from having to make a choice between brusqueness and passive acceptance. He was a new kind of experience for the American mind. You could discuss the economic problem in his terms without having to take sides. His intellectual method included most of the qualities that have since become the sacred cows of liberalism—disinterestedness, complexity, subtlety, irony, elusiveness, indecisiveness, realism, an awareness of one's own preconceptions, and an emphasis on "institutions" (harmless but magic word). Armed with these qualities you could transvalue all values and lay bare the desolate and jangled wasteland of economic life, but the blessed thing was that you could free yourself thus from bondage to your society without having to do anything about it.

Not the least attractive thing about Veblen is that he has been regarded as native American stuff. He is one of the writers most relied upon by liberals who insist upon an "American solution" to our economic problems, and radicals who would rather point to a nativist revolutionary tradition than a Marxian one. Actually the only one of Veblen's books directly addressed to the "case of America" is *Absentee Ownership,* written at the end of his life. In his other books, as far back as the *Theory of the Leisure Class,* he uses the American scene merely as a convenient ledge on which to perch while surveying the human comedy. His strength lay not in that he concentrated on American life but in that he enlarged the perspective in which American life could be viewed. He was not one of the American mind and American essence hunters. In fact there are few instances in American thought of such complete isolation from other American writers. Veblen seemed to come from nowhere.

If his mind took its temper from any tradition it was, as Mr. Dorfman convincingly points out, the hard-bitten, land-tenacious tradition of Norwegian agrarianism rather than anything uniquely American. Most of his reading and ideas derived from European sources—chiefly the Marxians and the anthropologists. His originality lay for us in his application of these European perspectives to our own life, and his canniness in seeing that the crucial time had come for transforming economic theory by recasting it in terms of the newer anthropology and psychology. His drive was toward economic realism, and he preferred to construct his theory of business enterprise from the United States Steel Corporation rather than from David Ricardo. If ever a government investigating commission justified itself, the Industrial Commission of 1900-02 did because of the use Veblen made of its *Report.*

And yet his greatest theories were brilliant intuitions rather than careful inductions from American material. He was not one of your statistical economists, and he was rather horrified at the prospect that economics "in the calculable future" would consist mainly of detailed factual monographs on business practices. As often as not, in reading Veblen, when you are just at the point where a factual survey would clinch the analysis you find that he has re treated to neolithic times.

With the outbreak of the War a change seemed to come over Veblen's life. It had never been a life sensitive to outward changes. Veblen's first book already reveals his distinctive traits of thought and tricks of style, and for fifteen years after it there are no marked changes in either. But the sweep of events after 1914—war and peace and revolution—added to the final loss of his academic posts, combined to fashion a rather new Veblen. He became less of a recluse, he came to New York, he mingled (although always ill at ease) in intellectual circles, he wrote for the journals. The tempo of his writing quickened and a succession of books flowed from his pen. To the period between 1915 and 1921 belong *Imperial Germany, The Higher Learning, The Nature of Peace, The Vested Interests, The Engineers and the Price System.*

The tone of Veblen's writing grew more bitter and more direct, while retaining much of its elaborate ironical apparatus. The first draft of *The Higher Learning,* finished in 1916, out-Marxed the Marxians in its analysis of direct business pressures upon education and drew from one friend the comment that people would think Veblen had gone mad. *The Vested Interests* repelled many Veblen disciples because of the savageness of its tone: their liberal sensibilities were ruffled. *The Engineers and the Price System* went so far as to suggest the only line of strategy Veblen ever advanced—a general strike of the technicians and the formation of a technical soviet, which with the aid of an economic directorate would carry on the productive processes of the nation after the seizure of power.

With his expulsion from the University of Missouri Veblen had definitely burned his bridges. He no longer needed to hide his meaning behind elaborate anthropological analogies. His irony was still there, but it was soaked in vitriol. His appearance of detachment, which he probably maintained more out of habit than policy, seemed almost gruesome now amidst his talk of war and revolution and collapse. It was like a plague-stricken group out of one of Poe's stories observing the punctilios of a formal evening party.

This was no complete and abrupt change. Veblen's writing had always contained revolutionary implications, and there remained in it now a good part of his liberalism. In the mixture of these two elements lie both his confusion and his richness, his lack of direction and the incalculable possibilities of his thought.

Out of all the welter of his thinking we can extract certain ideas that are still usable. Their value goes beyond the excitement or consolation they may have offered to Veblen's readers over the span of a quarter-century. They still retain some validity for understanding and confronting the dilemmas of our own day. Set down categorically they are:

1. *The rigor and potentialities of the machine process.* Veblen showed the insurmountable barrier that every system of economic organization must face—the fact that the physical necessities of a complicated industrial civilization must be produced by a method dictated by the machine and its rhythms rather than by us and our own rhythms. The implication is that no program can turn its back on the requirements of an industrial technology. But an equally far reaching implication is that we are living in an economy of potential plenty.

2. *The antithesis between industry and business.* This was probably the basic cadre of Veblen's thinking. The machine process and the pecuniary structure that has been erected upon it look toward entirely diverse purposes. One is concerned with the fulfillment of needs, the other with the creation of money values. The tragic irony of such a collapse as we are now suffering is deepened by the fact that the recovery and extension of industrial efficiency must wait upon the rebuilding of the pecuniary structure.

3. *The anti-social tendency of business enterprise.* The essence of business enterprise lies in the restriction of production in order to maximize profits. Veblen found in business rather than in labor the real sabotaging—the "conscientious withdrawal of efficiency." For many of his disciples this has led to a declaration of the need of a program of social control of business, so that this inherent tendency may be restrained, and profits maintained by maximizing production and lowering prices. Veblen's own thought, far from bolstering such a hope, constitutes rather a denial of the possibility of its realization.

4. *Legal and political institutions as the vesting of economic interests.* Veblen defined a vested interest as a "legal right to get something for nothing." He saw law and politics as primarily molded by the drive to create and maintain these rights. The current radical analyses of the trend of Supreme Court decisions owe much to this view. Any program of social control of business, since it operates through the same legal mechanisms, must face the valuation of the extent to which it entrenches existing vested interests or creates new ones.

5. *The compulsive force of idea-patterns.* Veblen's explanations of the origins of institutions tend on the whole to run on the technological plane; his explanations of their persistence tend to run on the ideological. By his stress on the latter he focuses our attention on the basic importance of ideas which, however outworn and archaic, still move men to action or inaction. Here lies much of the explanation of middle-class inertia in the face of widespread economic collapse, and here also the sources of strength on which the industrialists who propel fascist movements may rely. Through his stress on the compulsive force of ideas Veblen can explain a good deal of the power that pecuniary values have upon our lives that cannot be explained by a theory of direct business pressures or even of vested interests.

6. *The bankruptcy of leisure-class (business-class) values and of a culture dominated by them.* Here Veblen has added much ammunition to the attack on bourgeois values along the cultural front.

Granted that all this in Veblen is still usable and even powerful, the pressing question is: Where do we go from Veblen? Here, in his lack of direction, lies Veblen's greatest weakness. Veblen's followers have been uniformly mobile and footloose in their economic allegiances. Many of them entered the Wilson war administration and either helped determine policy behind the lines or sought to implement the peace through research. There is a special irony in the fact that *Imperial Germany* was deemed by one branch of the government good grist for the propaganda mills at the same time that another branch of the government sought to censor it. In fact, this symbolizes Veblen's entire position. He was too well aware of the weaknesses and paradoxes of the existing economic structure to desire its continuance; yet he saw too clearly the tenacity with which the ideas and habits flowing from that structure hold onto our lives to have any hope of realizable radical change. He was finally forced to locate the revolutionary process in that most unlikely place, the minds of engineers and technicians, hoping that in them the force of business values would be more than counterbalanced by the force of the values and habits flowing from the machine process. The tenuous character of this hope is the measure of Veblen's confusion. It was ultimately as great, although on a more subtle plane, as the confusion of the wasteland generation whose plight he so clearly revealed.

Veblen's disciples have given a more straightforward answer to the question of direction. Their answer is embodied in much of the rhetoric of the New Deal. I say rhetoric rather than logic, because the essential logic of the New Deal flows still (1935) from the *modus operandi* of American business enterprise. The NRA embodies a further limitation of production in a business system already founded on the principle of a "conscientious withdrawal of efficiency," while the AAA extends the same principle outside the business system proper into agriculture. Industrial self-government through the code authorities and the control of each code by the largest operators involve a further handing over of business power to those whom Veblen called the "guardians of the vested interests."

But a few of the New Dealers are still sincere Veblenians, and it may be said that in so far as there are forces in Washington working in a liberal direction they owe as much to Veblen's ideas as to those of any other thinker. Their central idea is one not found explicitly in Veblen but implied in his writing—the idea of social and legal control of business enterprise. The final aim is the curtailment of the limits of a profit economy, a tempering of the extravagances of the pecuniary system, a clearing of the way for technological efficiency, and an eventual controlled capitalism. The aims themselves are to be found fitfully stated throughout the history of the New Deal; genuine adherence to them is probably restricted to the liberals. The idea of social control itself, while its economic roots are chiefly to be found in Veblen, is really a composite of his work and that of other American theorists. Its social theory traces back to Cooley and Ward, its philosophy of experimentalism to Dewey, its legal technique to Brandeis.

But a New Deal, even if it were a genuine one, is only one of the several programs that could be founded on Veblen's thinking. He would himself undoubtedly have found most of the features of the administration program obnoxious to his deepest intellectual drives. His skepticism would have eaten through the very rhetoric of the New Deal that to such an extent derives from him.

A final judgment on the force of Veblen's ideas in American history will not be possible until we see what happens to the Roosevelt program. Veblen's thought has gradualist elements that will be confirmed if that program succeeds; it has also revolutionary implications and consequences that are still suspended in the context of history. If the middle road of the New Deal should prove impossible or should finally deviate too far from the middle, in every one of Veblen's basic ideas there is dynamite that may burst asunder the whole fabric of institutions and habits that capitalism and the capitalist state have built up. Veblen himself just before he died admitted that he saw no other way out than communism. The conclusion that he drew from his own thought can be drawn by others, but it will need a new generation of Veblenians to draw it. Veblen's tragedy is not only that his intellectual system lacks a program and a strategy; it lacks also a clear historical analysis that would have indicated the direction of further development in the "calculable future." His fate as a thinker is thus concealed in that very chamber of history-to-come for unlocking which he furnished no key.

1935

Veblen's World

WESLEY MITCHELL'S anthology of Veblen's writings[3] reminds us, if we needed to be reminded, that Veblen has already become a classic. In this "Norskie" farm boy who grew up to be a college professor America has produced its most considerable and most acid intelligence in the realm of social thought. In these lumbering six-syllabled sentences, with their devastating understatement and their poisonous indirections, America has produced a unique literary manner. In this man at once fierce and desperately shy, rooted in the soil like a giant in the earth and yet wandering nomadically from one university to another, turning his "swift wit and slow irony" on you so that you recoiled in fear, mumbling his lectures incoherently yet gathering disciples wherever he went—in this curious personality America has produced one of its complex and legendary figures. The five hundred pages selected from his twelve books and the definitive essay on Veblen by the editor constitute a gateway to Veblen's world.

What sort of world is it? Its outlines have the essential unity of any great theoretical system. It is a fluid unity, however—not, like that of Marx or Kant or Herbert Spencer, one in which all the pieces fit, or can be made to fit, together, but rather a *Gestalt* that comes into being after you have soaked yourself in Veblen's writing and approached with him, by roughly the same paths, one problem after another. For there can be no doubt that Veblen is repetitious to the point of despair. He traverses and retraverses the same ground, from *The Theory of the Leisure Class* in 1899 to *Absentee Ownership* in 1923. In a sense the core of his entire body of thought can be found in his early essays and his first book. The rest was elaboration, sharpening, strengthening.

Partly this is to be accounted for by the fact that Veblen waited until he was forty before he wrote his first book. When he first flashed through the American heavens he was a meteor already fully formed, with all his strength and brilliance gathered and tightly knit. Partly also it is to be accounted for by the fact that Veblen lived so secluded a life that he was able to create an intellectual world with unmistakable features of its own. It has its own landscape, its own heaven and earth, its own seasonal moods, its own mythology and demonology. He buried himself in his reading and his brooding. He read the economists, the anthropologists, the socialists—and the nineteen-volume *Report of the Industrial Commission*. While Veblen knew America and seemed able to breathe a sense of America into his pores, he lived insulated against its passing fashions and follies. His greatest generalizations were brilliant intuitions or uncompromising deductions from daring premises. The unity that his thought has is a unity not so much of structure as of mood and method.

Since Veblen does not have a "system," the body of his thought defies any easy analysis. The key idea is generally held to be the antithesis Veblen finds between industry and business—the one concerned with satisfying human needs, the other with creating artificial pecuniary values. Industry is with Veblen a continuing evolutionary process, starting with the savage state of the industrial arts and coming to its present climax in the modern machine technology. Business is the art of getting something for nothing—also an evolutionary process, starting with the predatory barbarism that followed the peaceful savage state and ending with present-day corporation finance and the techniques of the holding company. Industry and business are the economic forces operating in a psychological medium—in a world of instinct and habit. The deep unrests in our life now arise from the fact that the habituations of the industrial process, based on the instinct of workmanship and the parental bent, are moving ever farther away from the "idiot" institutions of our society maintained by the vested interests. When the gap has become so great that it has strained the limits of tolerance of the engineers and the workers, we may expect a change. Meanwhile there is still a considerable social lag which limits "the prospects of an overturn."

Thus, despite Veblen's delvings into neolithic times and his wanderings in the morass of instinct psychology, there is a Veblen who has meaning for today. And he belongs to the present for the reason that he has so searchingly explored the past and analyzed the economic and psychological roots of our modern being. I have pointed out elsewhere[4] that there are two Veblens rather than one. There is Veblen the liberal, with his fetish of disinterestedness, his awareness of his own preconceptions, his lingering irony, his Olympian detachment from the real struggles of a real America. This is the Veblen who offered, and still offers, consolation to those unwilling to take sides in the planetary turmoil of an era of finance capitalism, yet eager to liberate themselves from the values of a leisure-class society. There is also the second and more revolutionary Veblen, implicit in the first from the very beginning, yet emerging with ever-greater clarity after the outbreak of the War and the coming of peace. This was the Veblen who began to think in terms of the collapse of a decaying world and the seizure of a power. My only quarrel, if I have one, with Mr. Mitchell's anthology is that he overvalues the interest that the earlier Veblen—especially Veblen the destroyer of the idols of classical and hedonist economics—has for us, and undervalues the real interest of our generation in Veblen the revolutionary thinker.

Apply Veblen to the issues that confront us today and you get some notion of his continuing vitality even for a world that is no longer agitated by Darwin and Spencer. In a sense Veblen was part of the movement of populist thought in the first decade of this century and therefore part of the progressive tradition in America. Yet in a curious way he seems completely out of place amid the writings of the Progressive Era, at once strident and indecisive. By the same token his approach to the problems of this generation would be quite different from that of the other progressives and radicals. He would not so much rail at the patrioteers and the Liberty League as calmly destroy them by detached analysis of how closely their mental temper corresponds to that of dementia praecox. He would seek the roots of fascism not only in the immediate struggle for power but more searchingly in the entire history of the predatory barbarian tradition. He would understand why it is that middle-class patterns of ideas still linger sufficiently in the minds even of our workmen to make a united labor party a thing of long-run rather than of immediate concern, and he would stress the peculiar need for an alliance between the workers and the technicians. On the issue of neutrality and the war he would get away from the immediate debates sufficiently to analyze the character of the dynastic state under capitalism and its compelling urge toward war. And when he came to the Supreme Court he would probably analyze it not so much as a judicial agency as in terms of its economic utility or wastefulness, much as he did in his unparalleled economic evaluation of the churches, which may be found in a long footnote in *Absentee Ownership.* I am sorry that Mr. Mitchell did not find a place for this passage, which represents Veblen at his maddest and best.

None the less, most of the famous Veblen passages are in this book, and one comes upon them with a delight that can be explained only by the fact that Veblen is stylist as well as thinker. You will often have someone come up to you in an exasperated sort of way and ask why it is that Veblen is so unintelligible. The answer is that he is not. The manner of his writing is one that was beautifully calculated to achieve the purpose of his thought. He has, to be sure, a vocabulary of his own, but it is not merely an erratic vocabulary. Such phrases as "conspicuous waste," "absentee ownership," "vested interests," "leisure class," "invidious distinction," "calculable future," while not always of his own coining, have been given his peculiar stamp. They have worked themselves into the texture of our own vocabulary in a way that shows the enduring appeal of Veblen's writing. He had to create a new style because he was dealing with a range of ideas which completely cut under the prevailing range of ideas in America. The important thing about his style is that his entire intellectual method, with its satire and its detachment and its indirection, is implicit in it. Any anthology of American prose in the future and any history of American literature will ignore Veblen at its peril.

Notes

1.   This biographical sketch I wrote originally for the *Dictionary of American Biography* and it is printed here with the restoration of a few cuts the editors found necessary. It is based largely upon the material gathered by Joseph Dorfman in his *Thorstein Veblen and His America*. The interpretation is, however, my own responsibility: I should not want Mr. Dorfman to suffer for any quirks of mine.
2.   *Thorstein Veblen and His America.* New York, Viking, 1935.
3.   *What Veblen Taught.* New York, Viking, 1936.
4.   See above the essay "What Is Usable in Veblen?"

5

Thorstein Veblen: Scientism and the Modern Mood

E. Digby Baltzell

All human actions and social relations are concrete. Men, on the other hand, and especially intellectuals, have always been highly adaptable and creative in relation to both their human and natural environments, largely because of their ability to abstract from reality in the form of generalized concepts. This is true of all language and particularly the language of science. For the scientist, consciously and purposely, makes no attempt to describe the world in all its concrete chaos but rather to order and make sense of it by simplifying its complexities in a series of abstract laws, or, best of all, in quantitative equations. Thus Einstein once touchingly confessed that he was really an escapist by nature who had always shunned the muddled and confusing world of affairs by seeking shelter in the ordered world of scientific abstractions. Just as language can be both a vehicle and an obstacle to understanding, so, I think, the language and logic of science, when applied to human affairs rather than the natural world, may have certain undesirable consequences. In other words, I should like to suggest that there is an ever-present danger in the social sciences of moralizing abstractions, of turning concepts into epithets, and, above all, of downgrading the dignity of man.

Though the history of natural science, even since its coming to maturity in the ages of Galileo and Newton, has been full of examples of brilliant men who have become emotionally involved in defending outworn and erroneous concepts, it is in the social sciences that concepts are constantly evolving into ideologies which whole classes of men have loved or hated and have been willing to live and die for. Thus the Darwinian concepts of "natural selection" and "survival of the fittest" certainly involved no invidious comparisons or moral judgments among oysters, dogs, or dinosaurs, yet they easily, and perhaps unavoidably, became epithets and ideologies when races, classes, or national honor were involved. While the concept of the inheritance of acquired characteristics, believed in by Darwin, was eventually replaced by new concepts in biology, it was instructive to see that the Lysenko controversy raged in a culture founded on the ideology of science rather than in the West where men were still living, as moral rentiers to be sure, on the older, Judeo-Christian tradition.

It is indeed no accident, as more than one anthropologist and student of race has noted, that the liberating and enlightening Darwinian concepts in the field of biology have, at the same time, contributed to the intensification of class and racial conflicts and many other forms of social Darwinism which have marked our liberal and scientific age with unprecedented examples of man's inhumanity to man. (Tocqueville immediately saw that his friend Gobineau's classic work on race was fundamentally opposed to Christian teachings and predicted that it would one day be taken up by the Germans.) All of which is to suggest that, while new concepts in the social sciences begin by shedding light on the causes of human behavior and the nature of the historical process, they also, in turn, all too often end up by influencing, and causing, the behavior they once conceptualized. The concept of gravity, for instance, has no effect on the behavior of the tides of the sea, nor natural selection on the behavior of dinosaurs. Yet, as soon as the average man learns that life is no longer a moral journey in preparation for an afterlife but rather a competitive struggle for survival among higher animals (individual in classical, and classes in socialist, social theory), he will begin to behave quite differently towards his neighbors. Nor will he necessarily possess more dignity if he believes that his leaders are merely capitalist exploiters or members of a leisure class rather than God's elect or apostles of Christ. By their faiths in abstractions ye shall know them.

Not only do concepts in the social sciences eventually become causal factors in the historical process; they also, especially those modeled on natural-science concepts, exhibit a tendency to belittle, dismiss, and debunk the higher motives, dignity, and aspirations of men. Thus such psychological terms as rationalization or projection, along with such sociological abstractions as capitalist or bourgeois, begin as neutral, and useful, conceptualizations of reality but soon become ways of dismissing the values, motives, or rational arguments of those one dislikes or disagrees with. The altruism or Christian charity of a great lady like Jane Addams, or the motives of Lady Bountifuls in general, are cleverly dismissed by the initiated as merely projections of their sexual frustrations or rationalizations of their leisure-class guilt; all the virtues of thrift, cleanliness, good manners, punctuality, parental responsibility, deferred gratification, and sexual restraint, whether practiced by pharisees, philistines, bourgeois, or the modern squares, all too easily become, to the bohemians of one age or the beatniks of another, merely ways of avoiding truly authentic and healthily human emotions or spontaneously natural human contacts, rather than the inevitable disciplines practiced by most solid citizens in all civilized communities.

And of course the United Fund, the YMCA, and the Church become merely ways of perpetuating the power of the vested interests or, as Veblen would have it, the kept classes. Thus it follows that one of my Veblenian colleagues (who never contributes to the United Fund drive because it offends his sincere socialist convictions that the government could handle these problems more efficiently) dismisses the building of Mont Saint Michel or Chartres, as well as the atom bomb, as merely examples of how the leisure classes in two historical cultures have engaged in conspicuous consumption. A faithful follower of Feuerbach, Freud, and Durkheim in their scientific studies of religion, he also dismisses the concept of God as merely the projection of man's frustrations or a useful symbol of communal solidarity. But then, as sociological surveys have shown, we social scientists are less likely to believe in God than our less sophisticated natural-science peers. Perhaps my friend is himself merely an example of what Veblen called the "trained incapacity" which characterizes the faithful practitioners of all disciplined ways of thinking.

Though he was hardly of the stature of Marx or Freud, whose concepts have now become common coin in the language of all literate (and not so literate) men, Thorstein Veblen was certainly one of the American masters at coining abstract epithets. After reading a recently published biography of Veblen,[1] I reread his classic work, *The Theory of the Leisure Class*. I was particularly interested in rereading this one book of his because I have had the impression that its theme was causally related to the pervasive decline of authority in America today, as manifested in the rising rates of juvenile delinquency (especially among the upper and middle classes), the lack of leadership and widespread avoidance of leadership roles by many of the most talented members of the younger generation, and, perhaps most interesting of all, the radical revolt from authority on our college campuses and among the beatnik sons and daughters of some of our more concerned and affluent citizens. I should like, then, to briefly outline just enough of Veblen's theory of the leisure class to suggest how its debunking tone—much of which still forms part of the tacit assumptions of many of our leading intellectuals and academicians, as well as their brighter students—may have contributed to this modern mood.

To understand Veblen, I think, one must see him as a brilliant and ironic essayist, using the language of science to hide his own passions and frustrations behind a wealth of anthropological and historical detail which was, in turn, ingeniously ordered in highly abstract concepts. In fact, he conceptualized the history of human evolution in terms of his own hatred for the predatory and crude capitalism of the Gilded Age and, like his contemporary, Mark Twain, ended up in a mood of pure despair. Unlike Twain, he left us a host of abstractions rather than Huck Finn or Tom Sawyer (both innocents in the Garden of Eden before the knowledge of science and industrial technology transformed the face of America).

Veblen had his own highly abstract Eden, which he conceptualized as the stage of "savagery," and saw all the evils of civilization as variations on the theme of "barbarism," the next higher stage in the evolutionary process. Thus private property, conspicuous consumption, leisure classes, idle curiosity, good manners, and especially predatory sports and capitalism were all examples of man's Fall. In many ways, Veblen was a feminist (as was Marx except when he found that his favorite daughter was living in "sin" with one of London's most notorious "bouncers"). He definitely preferred the feminine to the masculine elements in society. The Fall came when the predatory patriarchal principle replaced the peaceful and egalitarian matriarchal one. Thus he wrote that "a leisure class coincides with the beginning of ownership...the earliest form of ownership is the ownership of women by the able-bodied men of the community...the ownership of women begins in the lower barbarian stages of culture, apparently with the seizure of female captives...who seem to have been useful as trophies."

Veblen was also the extreme egalitarian. All distinctions were "invidious" ones. His ideal was the "masterless man," and he saw no need for leaders or differentiation of function within institutions (he saw college and university administrations as examples of "total depravity"). In fact he was actually against all institutions (he was in the habit of rewarding all his graduate students at Chicago with an equal grade of "C," partly because of his egalitarian values and partly to confuse the administration). He idealized the simple stage of savagery largely because both men and women are still engaged in productive labor and living in small, static, and egalitarian communities.

Being somewhat of a technological determinist, Veblen naturally saw the Fall as the result of the invention of the tool, and its counterpart the weapon, which allowed for the rise of the predatory and barbarian stage of culture. Distinctions were now possible and a leisure class, "conspicuously exempted from all useful employment," developed; the normal occupations of this class were "government, war, sports and devout observation," all examples of predatory, not productive, employment; yet all were honorable pursuits and engaged in, incidentally, by men rather than women.

As Civilization "advanced," this leisure class of predatory males (women were mainly "trophies") developed all kinds of hierarchical devices. Veblen, in his own inimitable style, describes the process as follows: "As the population increases in density, and as human relations grow more complex and numerous, all the details of life undergo a process of elaboration and selection; and in this process of elaboration the use of trophies develops into a system of rank, titles, degrees, and insignia, typical examples of which are heraldic devices, medals, and honorary decorations."

Conspicuous leisure, "closely allied with the life of exploit," was of course the ultimate test of high rank. For leisure allowed for all kinds of unproductive accomplishments which, according to Veblen, included "knowledge of the dead languages and the occult sciences; of correct spelling; of syntax and prosody; of the various forms of domestic music and other household art; of the latest proprieties of dress, furniture and equipage; of games, sports, and fancy-bred animals, such as dogs and race-horses." One of the most important consequences of leisure and the predatory culture was the growth of good manners or "breeding, polite usage, and decorum." Thus manners, according to Veblen, "hold a more important place in the esteem of men during the stage of culture at which conspicuous leisure has the greatest vogue"; and "manners have progressively deteriorated as society has receded from the patriarchal stage, as many gentlemen of the old school have been provoked to remark recently." But naturally to Veblen, a clean functionalist long before houses were conceived as "machines for living," the "pervading principle and abiding test of good breeding is the requirement of a substantial and patent waste of time."

At least as of Veblen's publication of *The Theory of the Leisure Class* in 1899, this leisure class of predatory gentlemen of good manners and some grammar was still in the habit of keeping both its ladies and its "lackies," as well as its children, in their proper places. Veblen ingeniously illustrates this in a discussion of the differential use of intoxicating beverages and narcotics, some of which I must quote directly:

> From archaic times down through all the length of the patriarchal regime it has been the office of women to prepare and administer these luxuries, and it has been the prerequisite of the men of gentle birth and breeding to consume them. Drunkenness and the other pathological consequences of the free use of stimulants therefore tend in their turn to become honorific, as being a mark, at the second remove, of the superior status of those who are able to afford the indulgence. Infirmities induced by overindulgence are among some peoples freely recognized as manly attributes.... The same invidious distinction adds force to the current disapproval of any indulgence of this kind on the part of women, minors, and inferiors.... Where the example set by the leisure class retains its imperative force in the regulation of the conventionalities, it is observable that the women still in great measure practice the same traditional continence with regard to stimulants.

How far have we progressed, at least in the democratization of drunkenness, since Veblen's day!

It is of course not my purpose to give a complete outline of Veblen's theory of the leisure class in all its wealth of fascinating detail and debunking epithets. I hope to have given enough, however, to show that, behind all his bitterness and brilliant irony, he was trying to show how all advanced civilizations (in their various stages of barbarism, including the Gilded Age) depend on a class of men who have been able to rise above the purely productive level which traps all men, women, and children in the egalitarian stage of savagery. And the barbarian stages of civilization depend on the differentiation both of function and style of life. Most important of all, I think, was his realization that, at least in his day, the leisure class style of life still possessed authority as far as the rest of the community was concerned. Thus he wrote:

> The leisure class stands at the head of the social structure in point of reputability: and its manner of life and its standards of worth therefore afford the norm of reputability for the community. The observance of these standards, in some degree of approximation, becomes incumbent upon all classes lower in the scale.

Veblen is remembered primarily as the man who debunked gentlemen of the leisure class who bought clothes, lived in correct neighborhoods, cultivated good manners and good grammar, went to church, and built cathedrals purely to impress others, especially those beneath them. But he was interested in far more. He was interested in no less than a comprehensive theory of civilization, in an age when he didn't like very much what it had produced. And due partly to his own temperament and partly to the intellectual climate of opinion in his day, he was led to debunking all civilized institutions, which must inevitably involve hierarchy and leadership, as barbaric departures from the peaceful, stagnant, and egalitarian stage of savagery, a point of view which has of course had a long tradition ever since the days of the eighteenth-century philosophs.

In many ways this tradition of debunking institutions and institutionalized authority in general has been successful. There is hardly a leisure class in Veblen's sense in America today (surely the nervous pleasure-seekers in the jet set do not know what either leisure or manners mean), and what leisure and conspicuous consumption there still is has slowly slid down the socioeconomic scale since the Second World War. And it is not beyond the realms of possibility that the behavior of the beatnik is inspired by folk values of the stage of savagery idealized by Veblen, or that the recent Berkeley and Columbia revolutions against the modern and permissive Captains of Erudition could have used Veblen's *Higher Learning in America* as their bible. All civilization may be sinful, but the longing to return to Eden is pure folly.

But more than this, I think there is a possibility that Veblen and so many others of his school, both before him and since, have somehow missed the point. It is not, in other words, that conspicuous consumption (the behavior might have been conceptualized as "setting an example") is wrong, but rather whether men seek to impress others by building cathedrals or atom bombs, by inspiring us with the Seagram's building or depressing us with the Pan American monstrosity atop Grand Central; whether the young aspire to emulate Liz Taylor or the idealized ladies of Charles Dana Gibson, Frank Merriwell or Elvis Presley, the Beatles or the queen, their peers or their parents.

Similarly, I suppose, sexual frustration will always be with us in spite of the modern permissive and hedonistic temper. Yet is makes all the difference in the world whether these frustrations are projected in one way rather than the other; in creating Hull House or decorating the Sistine Chapel rather than in rabid racism, pornography, or blatant homosexuality; in the idealization of sexual satisfaction as in the art of D.H. Lawrence rather than in its degradation in the theatre of Tennessee Williams or Edward Albee. Thus a leisure-class inheritance and the frequency of guilt which goes with it has produced Jane Addams, Eleanor Roosevelt, and Adlai Stevenson as well as Marx and Engels, Leopold and Loeb, and even Veblen himself, who married well and never held a full-time job until he was thirty-five. On the other hand, the frustrations which go with less fortunate choices of parents produced both Lincoln and Adolf Hitler. It is, then, not necessarily the class of abstract pathologies, whether psychological or sociological, which are the main problem but rather how concrete individuals, influenced by the values of their time, class, and culture, of course, are inspired to handle them. It is, after all, the injured and not the healthy oyster which produces the pearl. The modern passion for perfect social justice or psychological adjustment through the materialistic means of social equality and permissiveness may well prove as undesirable as it surely is utopian. No well-rounded man ever produced anything of lasting value, and surely there are more well-rounded and happy men living in the stages of savagery today than there are along Madison, Park, or Pennsylvania Avenues here in the United States.

But perhaps, after all, Veblen himself had a clue to our problem, which may lie in the "trained incapacity" of the scientific mind to go beyond the analysis of the material causes of our troubles to the theology of hope and the art of inspiration.

Note

1. Douglas F. Dowd, *Thorstein Veblen* (New York: Washington Square Press, 1966).

Part II

6

Essays in Our Changing Order

Scott R. Bowman

Thorstein Bunde Veblen was born on a frontier farm in Wisconsin on July 30, 1857, and died in Palo Alto, California, on August 3, 1929. His lifetime coincided with the rise of modern industrial capitalism and concomitant growth of integrated national markets, the resurgence of monopolies through various forms of corporate combination, and the subsequent transformation of economic, social, and political life under the regime of corporate capitalism. Like many of his contemporaries, Veblen sought to decipher the driving forces behind these developments. In that endeavor, he succeeded brilliantly and entirely on his own terms. What he documented more lucidly and with greater depth than any other scholar of his generation was the manner in which the rise of the large corporation had fomented a reorganization of the structure of power in American society. It is a testimony to the ideological propensities of social scientists, about which Veblen had much to say, that this monumental contribution is not widely appreciated today.

Veblen occupies a unique position in the pantheon of American political and social thinkers. Standing astride two centuries with a foot firmly planted in each, he was both a social theorist in the grand tradition of the nineteenth century and a contemporary critical thinker whose radical vision reshaped the contours of intellectual debate in the twentieth century. His writings invite comparisons with such luminaries as Karl Marx, Auguste Comte, Herbert Spencer, Max Weber, Emile Durkheim, Sigmund Freud, Vilfredo Pareto, John Dewey, and Charles Beard. Evolutionary theorist, economist, philosopher, anthropologist, ethnologist, sociologist, and political theorist of the

99

corporation, Veblen refused to cabin his expansive intellect within the specialized precincts of the academic disciplines. Our intellectual lives are incalculably richer for that decision.

This collection of essays was published posthumously in 1934, at the direction of Leon Ardzrooni, a close friend and former student of Veblen. It spans the entirety of Veblen's intellectual life and offers a panoramic view of the breadth and variety of his scholarship. The book intersects in some fashion with virtually all of the author's seminal ideas. In many cases, essays in this anthology articulated or anticipated the themes of Veblen's major works. It is helpful to know these connections, and I will point them out as I proceed. However, *Essays in Our Changing Order* does stand on its own as an introduction to an extraordinary intellectual legacy. Indeed, it is the most diverse and representative group of writings under one cover by this prolific author.

By all accounts, Veblen was quite eccentric and undisciplined in his personal affairs, remarkably disciplined and focused in his intellectual life, erudite but uninspiring as a teacher, and iconoclastic to the point of infuriating and regularly offending the powers that be in higher education.[1] He is something of a folk hero to anti-establishment intellectuals and academic free spirits. His professional life, however, was more often than not a source of frustration and frequent disappointment. He did not ascend above the lowest rungs of the academic ladder of success, even after having attained considerable fame as an author. His unconventional views did sometimes frighten publishers. On more than one occasion he paid for the costs of publishing a book. But, clearly, his own errors in judgment greatly contributed to his misfortunes, making his academic sojourn more difficult than it might have been. His philandering was well known and widely discussed. Scandals drove him from one institution to another, and still he refused to behave. In this regard, it is accurate to say that his reputation always preceded him.

A moral deviant by Victorian standards, Veblen was also an intellectual misfit in the genteel environment of higher education. His parents were Norwegian immigrant farmers. For the first seventeen years of his life, Veblen lived in culturally insular and often embattled Norwegian-American communities in which the native tongue was the primary language spoken both at home and in school. This formative experience greatly contributed to his defiant ways and especially his intellectual self-image as an outsider. Although a miscreant in some respects, Veblen possessed tremendous integrity as a scholar and craftsman of ideas. Deeply committed to the pursuit of truth in higher education, he believed that academic professionalization and its ethic of "salesmanship" signaled the eclipse of a venerable institution by the businesslike leaders of the modern university system.

Veblen is perhaps best known as a founder of institutional economics, champion of technocracy, bitter foe of finance capitalism, and savvy social critic who exposed the hypocrisies and absurdities of upper-class mores and institutions. No doubt his first book, *The Theory of the Leisure Class* (1899), which has sustained its popularity for a century, is largely responsible for this widely held, yet incomplete, assessment of his work. Veblen's analysis in that early work of the evolutionary origins of modern pecuniary culture shaped the entirety of his thought, but the whole fabric of his social theory was not woven together until his later works completed the tapestry, especially *The Theory of Business Enterprise* (1904), *The Instinct of Workmanship* (1914), and *Absentee Ownership* (1923). His theory did not undergo dramatic shifts or evolutionary leaps so much as it matured with age. One will not find in his voluminous writings an "early Veblen" comparable to an "early Marx," for example. Veblen's analysis of history, culture, politics, economics, and social change remained remarkably consistent from beginning to end, from his cultural critique of the leisure class in the late 1890s, to his analysis of war and peace two decades later.

It is difficult to do justice to Veblen's social theory from the standpoints of current disciplinary perspectives. To appreciate the profundity of his work we must seek a vantage point that allows us to survey all of its intellectual terrain. I propose to reconstruct Veblen's social theory with reference to its central unifying themes: (1) the dynamic interrelationships between instinct, habits of thought, environment, and social change in human evolution; (2) the essential contradiction between business and industry rooted in the evolutionary past and sustained by the instinctual dominance of "pecuniary exploit" over "workmanlike efficiency"; and (3) the self-delusion of the species through ideological and animistic thinking and its implications for the state of our knowledge and social engineering.

I hope to show that these elements embrace the whole of Veblen's social and political thought and related writings. In the course of this reconstruction, I will highlight numerous essays in this anthology to demonstrate their relevance to the texture of his thinking. Moreover, my reconstructive efforts will require frequent departures from the editor's organization of the text. The sequence of discussion, however, follows a certain logic and endeavors to impose its own order on the material consistent with the themes outlined above.

II

Veblen maintained that from its earliest beginnings, the social existence of human beings, like that of other species, was a struggle for survival. In the course of this struggle, a process of natural selection had compelled the gradual adaptation of human nature and behavior to changing social conditions. Human institutions and their corresponding modes or habits of thought, however, were not only a result of a "selective and adaptive process," but they were in themselves "efficient factors of selection."[2] Social change or evolution, according to Veblen, was therefore a product of a complex process in which human thought and behavior, by adapting to a changing social environment, transformed the institutional basis for later selection. The fact that selective adaptation would take different forms in societies, depending upon the character of the people, further complicated this process. In other words, the dominance of certain innate characteristics in a nation or a people would either facilitate or hamper the process of adaptation. To fully grasp Veblen's theory of social change, therefore, we must examine the theory of instincts and conception of human nature that informed it.

Human behavior, Veblen observed, was rooted in and conditioned by a complex of "instinctive proclivities and tropismatic attitudes." Instinctive action was purposeful or teleological; that is, it involved "consciousness and adaptation to an end aimed at." Unlike tropismatic behavior, which was purely psychological and could not be consciously altered or controlled, instinctive behavior was shaped by social norms, customs, and habits. Consequently, even though human instincts were innate, the way in which the instinctive ends of life were worked out would depend upon a host of cultural factors.[3]

Veblen's analysis of instinctive behavior focused primarily on three major instincts—workmanship, the parental bent, and idle curiosity. Essential to the material well-being of a people, workmanship re-

ferred to the human propensity for effective work including the efficient use of resources and technological mastery: "[man] is in an
eminent sense an intelligent agent...possessed of a discriminatory sense
of purpose, by force of which all futility of life or of action is dis-
tasteful to him." The parental bent induced a concern not only for
the welfare of one's off-spring, but for the community as a whole.
Like the instinct of workmanship, the parental bent was also necessary to the survival of the species. Idle curiosity motivated the quest
for knowledge for its own sake. Human curiosity was "idle," Veblen
argued, because it had no utilitarian aim. This did not imply, however, that knowledge produced by this instinctive disposition could
have no practical application. Indeed, the development of science
and technology provided ample evidence to the contrary.[4]

Instinctive action, according to Veblen, was always a product of
an interplay and overlapping of the various instinctive dispositions.
Because of the interdependence of human instincts, the modification or accentuation of one instinct due to environmental factors
would result in a "mutual contamination" of other instincts and
thereby bias the process of selective adaptation.[5] At any given
point in the evolution of a society, human nature therefore consisted of a set of instinctive proclivities which had been selected
for specific economic and social conditions. But once modified,
instinctive dispositions would affect future selection by either
facilitating or hampering adaptation. In the author's view, this fact
clearly revealed the fallacy of the simplistic idea of progress often
associated with human social evolution. In fact, Veblen characterized the notion that "the institutional outcome of men's native dispositions will be sound and salutary" as "an article of uncritical
faith [taken] from the historic belief in a beneficent Order of
Nature." This is not to say that he rejected the idea of survival of
the fittest, only that what was fit and unfit carried no normative con-
notation.[6]

While Veblen believed human beings to be purposeful creatures—
agents "seeking in every act the accomplishment of some concrete,
objective, impersonal end"—his analysis of the evolutionary process suggested that human behavior was largely constrained and
determined by external forces. Societies evolved, he argued, when
individuals were compelled to adapt their habits of thought and hence
their institutions to an "altered environment." Social change therefore occurred "in response to pressure from without," which was

"of the nature of a response to a stimulus." Whereas a variety of factors contributed to the evolution of societies, "the forces which made for readjustment of institutions, especially in the case of a modern industrial community," Veblen related, were "in the last analysis, almost exclusively of an economic nature."[7] Forces generated by existing economic institutions eventually outgrew their institutional mode: "as population increases, and as men's knowledge and skill in directing the forces of nature widen, the habitual methods of relations between the members of the group, and the habitual method of carrying on the life process of the group as a whole, no longer give the same result as before."[8]

Social evolution therefore was largely induced by changing economic forces which, in turn, were driven by advances in the industrial arts, that is, by technological improvements. Veblen's theory of social change clearly embodies a type of technological determinism, albeit qualified by his premise that the development and application of technology will be affected by the institutions and instinctive proclivities of a people. Furthermore, he argued that the impact of technological change on human behavior and thought might vary within a society depending upon the degree to which different groups or classes had been exposed to the forces of change. Prospects for change must also be weighed in light of the fact that power was usually exercised to conserve and not to transform social arrangements. Veblen also contended that, as creatures of habit, human beings generally resisted innovation. Thus when adaptation finally did occur, however haltingly, the adjusted institutions and habits of thought once again were on the verge of being outmoded by newly arisen economic forces.[9]

Because this process of selective adaptation could "never catch up with the progressively changing situation in which the community finds itself at a given time," the dominant beliefs and institutions of a society would be conservative, though some more so than others. This evolutionary process of adaptation resulted in a more or less persistent condition of cultural lag in which the knowledge, beliefs, and customs of a society (with the exception of scientific knowledge) did not accord with the material advances made possible by technological change. This state of affairs, moreover, legitimated prevailing power relationships since the dominant ideas of a society were those of its rulers. Veblen's theory of social evolution therefore would seem to imply that individuals can never completely control their own destinies precisely because human thought and behavior always lag behind economic change.[10]

In four classic essays first published in the 1890s—"The Beginnings of Ownership," "The Barbarian Status of Women," "The Economic Theory of Women's Dress," and "The Instinct of Workmanship and the Irksomeness of Labor"—Veblen outlined the basic themes of his evolutionary theory. Although he had not fully developed his theory of instincts, he already had worked out his critical anthropological analysis of ownership and its relationship to patriarchy, as well as the relevance of these institutions to American economic and cultural life. These seminal essays, which were published shortly before *The Theory of the Leisure Class*, introduce us to the Veblenian concepts or interpretations of pecuniary emulation, animism, the instinct of workmanship, conspicuous consumption, conspicuous waste, the leisure class, and the institution of ownership-marriage. One will also encounter the penetrating intelligence, iconoclastic style, and sharp wit that would become his hallmark for the remainder of his intellectual life.

While rejecting the notion that human social evolution proceeded according to immutable laws of development, Veblen maintained, on the basis of evidence, that certain broad generalizations were possible. Throughout his writings, he identified four major eras or periods of social evolution in human history, each of which corresponded to a different stage in the advance of technology and social organization—the era of primitive or peaceable savagery, the barbaric or predatory era, the era of the handicraft economy, and the modern era of machine technology. It was during the transition from the period of peaceable savagery, which was characterized by a crude technology and a subsistence economy, to the stage of barbarism, that the institution of ownership emerged.[11]

Veblen observed that despite the fact they occupied "the two extremes of economic speculation," classical economists and socialists both agreed that "productive labor" was the foundation of the institution of property ownership. This "conjectural history of the origin of property," which was based on "the preconceptions of Natural Rights and a coercive Order of Nature," assumed that the institution of ownership, and with it production and wealth, derived from a "self-sufficing individual."[12] Besides being illogical (production is necessarily a social, as opposed to individual, activity that requires cooperation and sharing of technical knowledge and tools), this natural rights preconception prevented economists from under-standing the actual origins of ownership. Indeed, to grasp the very beginnings of this institution in the early barbarian culture, the scholar must adopt the point of view of that culture.

As a habit of thought that presupposed a way of viewing people and things, ownership could not exist until individuals distinguished between their organic persons and things that were not a part of their organic persons. The primitive savage, who viewed material and immaterial things as extensions of personality, made no such dis-tinction. Ownership, therefore, did not derive from instinctual ca-pacities; rather, it was a "cultural fact which [had] grown into an institution in the past through a long course of habituation." Owner-ship was established when societies recognized an individual's "cus-tomary right of use and abuse over an object which was obviously not an organic part of his person." Veblen argued that this practice first appeared in cultures in which non-consumable goods and people, especially women, were seized and hence claimed as prop-erty, and that the ownership of property presupposed certain tech-nological advances which made possible the accumulation of wealth which, in turn, often encouraged aggression.[13] Captive humans were obviously not part of the organic person of the captor and could be readily apprehended as possessions or trophies of war. As trophies, women brought distinction to their male owners who eventually cre-ated the institution of marriage as a means of laying exclusive claim to their captive property. Veblen thus concluded that the institution of "ownership-marriage" seemed to be "the original both of private property and of the patriarchal household."[14]

Veblen's analysis of the original marriage ceremony provides in-sight into the pervasiveness in both predatory and modern societies of "animism," the practice of attributing a teleology or purpose to inanimate things or events. The barbarian, he observed, "looks upon external objects and sequences naively, as organic and individual things, and as expressions of a propensity working toward an end." Ritual is accepted as reality by the animistic mind: "if once the mo-tions leading to a desired consummation have been rehearsed in the accredited form and sequence, the same substantial result will be attained as that produced by the process imitated." Understood in this way, religious ceremonies, anthropomorphic beliefs, superstiti-ons, and ritualized social practices all have their basis in animistic thinking. The very concept of ownership is animistic in that it attributes to the individual certain intangible powers (e.g., prowess or force) associated with capture or possession, whereas, in reality, ownership is a social institution. Emulative behavior—for example, competition designed to produce invidious distinctions—is also animistic because it involves the same mental process whereby humans project onto things or events a teleology.[15]

As the institution of ownership-marriage acquired legitimacy and came to represent "the good and beautiful attitude of the man toward the woman," it became necessary to arrange the marriage of free women, especially the daughters of men of high standing. By the same token, status and reputability among males, which was achieved by a more or less constant demonstration of prowess, could not be sustained without marrying (owning) a woman or women. For these reasons, Veblen surmised, the marriage ritual or ceremony of "feigned capture" originated and, in time, came "to be appreciated unreflectingly as a deliverance of common-sense and enlightened reason." The price of social acceptance for women was servitude. Free women—that is, "masterless, unattached" women—were shunned or relegated to a lower social status than "captured" women. Exceptions to this social convention could be found in societies that had enjoyed a long period of "peaceable industrial life" in which the maternal household had thrived. In these (non-predatory) maternal cultures, "the household of the unattached woman" developed in place of ownership-marriage, although the two institutions usually blended to create a hybrid form at a much later date.[16]

Veblen's account of the historical development of ownership significantly influenced his general theory of social evolution. The institution of ownership-marriage in predatory societies, he argued, gave rise to a class division—a leisure class and a working class—based on a discrimination between employments: the "honorific employments which involve a large measure of prowess" and "the humiliating employments, which call for diligence and into which the sturdier virtues do not enter."[17] Veblen explained that the "invidious distinction" between exploit (prowess) and industry flowed from the institution of ownership and its underlying motive of pecuniary emulation. The possession of wealth became a symbol of prowess and thereby conferred honor just as the lack of wealth relegated one to an ordinary or ignoble social position. One will find, the author observed, that the material and psychological foundations of the leisure class—the institution of ownership and pecuniary emulation—had been substantially developed in predatory societies and, from that point on, remained basically unchanged, even though the class itself did not fully mature until a later stage of social evolution.

Both patriarchy and class domination, therefore, had their origin in the institution of ownership-marriage which nourished, and was nourished by, predatory and animistic habits of thought. Besides ownership-marriage, no other convention better illustrated the barbarian status of women in modern society than did the social rules that applied to women's dress. Dress (which must be distinguished from mere clothing) originated with "adornment" in primitive peoples and evolved to represent the wealth of the "social unit" in more advanced predatory societies. As trophies and later (captive) wives, women, "in a peculiar degree," served the purpose of exhibiting "the pecuniary strength" of the male owner-husband "by means of a conspicuously unproductive consumption of goods." Conspicuous consumption demonstrated prowess by virtue of the capacity of the male head of household to display "conspicuous waste." The practice of conspicuous waste, Veblen observed, adhered to three "cardinal principles": expensiveness ("with respect to its effectiveness as clothing, apparel must be uneconomical"), novelty ("apparel must afford *prima facie* evidence of having been worn but for a relatively short time"), and ineptitude (the apparel "must afford *prima facie* evidence of incapacitating the wearer for any gainful occupation"). The "highest manifestation" of this form of dress was "unquestionably seen in the apparel of the women of the most advanced modern communities." Thus, the "most advanced" cultures of the modern world were also the most sophisticated of the predatory societies.[18]

Not only dress, but virtually all of upper-class culture, as well as popular culture (which aped the upper class), especially sporting contests, were outgrowths of a long habituation to predatory life and its corresponding modes of thought. During the evolutionary process, pecuniary exploit had thoroughly "contaminated" the instinct of workmanship and, in modern times, had become the dominant propensity of the two. However, this instinctual blend is a more complex matter in Veblen's theory than this descriptive account suggests. Veblen argued that, in primitive societies, the instinct of workmanship created its own nemesis in the form of a competition or emulation that began when individuals aspired to an "ideal of efficiency." With the growth of technology, especially weapons, predatory culture slowly emerged and supplanted the peaceable industrial community in which the predominance of the instinct of workmanship had become manifest in the values of efficiency, serviceability, and group solidarity. Certain conditions had to be present for predatory culture to develop (e.g., increase in populations, confrontations between groups), but to a large extent, exploit actually grew out of the early industrial culture in which the instinct of workmanship predominated. In short, the psychological propensity necessary for predatory societies to develop was present from the beginning.

Emulation and competitive behavior, therefore, would seem to be part of the human condition. Indeed, Veblen observed that these propensities were also present in the peaceable savage communities in the form of competition for food and sex.[19] He underscored this point in *The Instinct of Workmanship* where he argued that "the most destructive derangement that besets workmanship" was its "self-contamination." This phenomenon was endemic to the activity of work because human beings naturally endowed their actions with significance, thereby imputing a teleology to objects and events. Out of this mental process grew myth and religion which supplanted naive animism with a more sophisticated anthropomorphism.[20] This same innate teleological process, moreover, produced emulative behavior. The putative superiority (or prowess) that invidious distinctions aimed to establish was the ability to control or influence environmental forces. In other words, prowess was not only, or even primarily, a function of demonstrating physical domination. It was a matter of an individual apparently exercising power or, as Veblen would say, "force" over the course of events.

Another way of stating the problem is that Veblen did not believe that human history should be viewed either as a tragic loss of innocence or an idyllic past betrayed. Rather, he argued that both emulation (rooted in animism) and workmanship had co-existed from the beginning and that the development of technology and the advent of predatory culture were inextricable insofar as technical knowledge led to more sophisticated methods of production. Thereafter, workmanship and exploit were blended, with one or the other having greater influence on social institutions, which is to say, habits of thought. The irony of human history, so to speak, was that the prime mover in the evolutionary process was technology (technical knowledge), which initially served the salutary ends of workmanship but, in so doing, also contributed to emulative behavior and the beginnings of predatory society. Technology largely determined the economic structure of a society and hence the conditions under which instinctual proclivities would be expressed. Measured solely by the growth of technology, each era in human history represented an advance over its predecessor. At the same time, the habits of thought that directed the application of technical knowledge continued to be shaped by a mixture of workmanlike efficiency and exploit. The essential contradiction of this developmental process, as Veblen explained it, was that insofar as human beings remained captive to predatory habits of thought, they could not realize the full productive potential of their own creations; but these habits of thought also encouraged the growth of technology and industry.

In Veblen's evolutionary scheme, the handicraft era marked the transition from the predatory to the peaceable commercial phase of pecuniary culture. This stage roughly corresponds to what scholars generally label the transitional period from feudalism to capitalism. For Veblen, the era of handicraft constituted the pre-industrial phase of capitalism, the stage in which the small-scale competitive economy developed around the activities of craftsmen and petty traders.[21] By combining technological mastery with the quest for profit, the craftsman joined the skills of industry and business. Both of these skills "counted equally," for the handicraft system remained "a practicable plan of economic life only so long as the craftsman [could] combine both of these capacities in good force and only so long as the technological exigencies [would] admit the exercise of both in conjunction."[22]

As it became increasingly productive, the handicraft system planted the seeds of its own destruction. Technological advances in various crafts eventually made the cost of equipment prohibitive for most craftsmen. Soon crafts became organized within industrial plants that were owned by individuals with sufficient wealth to purchase the means of production. Improvements in methods of communication, transportation, and trade facilitated, directly and indirectly, the process of industrial advance. Eventually, the handicraft system broke down, or perhaps outgrew itself, and the rudiments of an industrial system began to take shape. In the process, however, a division of labor separated the two skills once embodied in the craftsman. Under the new system, pecuniary control was vested in a class of owners while the tasks of production were consigned to a propertyless class of workers.[23]

Although the Industrial Revolution in England definitively ushered in the era of machine technology, its formative principle—the dominance of business over industry—grew out of the handicraft economy. The progressive separation of these two realms of economic activity constituted the dominant trend of modern technological development. With the ascendancy of the business class, moreover, new relationships of power were established:

> The transition from the original predatory phase of the pecuniary culture to the succeeding commercial phase signifies the emergence of a middle class in such forces as presently to recast the working arrangements of the cultural scheme and make peaceable business (gainful traffic) the ruling interest of the community…. It is the conscious interest of this class to further the gainfulness of industry, and as this end is correlated with the productiveness of industry it is also, though less directly, correlated with improvements in technology.[24]

Society thus became organized in the interests of business or profit making; and pecuniary principles or habits of thought soon acquired "supreme dominance…both as standards of efficiency and as canons of conduct." This "pecuniary system of social organization" further instituted "class divergence of material interests, class prerogative and differential hardship, and an accentuated class disparity in the consumption of goods."[25] The rise of the bourgeoisie in the era of modern industry had initiated the final stage of the conquest of exploit over industry.

III

Veblen reminds us throughout his writings that the split between business and industry did not occur suddenly but developed very gradually with the growth of modern industry. This division initially became apparent with the phasing out of the independent craftsman and the ascendancy of the first great class of business leaders, the so-called "captains of industry." The captains of industry were in actuality entrepreneurs who possessed, in varying degrees, considerable industrial expertise.[26] It was during the "era of free competition"—roughly the period which "lies between the Industrial Revolution of the eighteenth century and the rise of corporation finance in the nineteenth"—that the captain of industry emerged as a major economic, political, and social force. For nearly a century, the captain of industry was "the dominant figure in civilized life, about whose deeds and interests law and custom have turned, the central and paramount personal agency in Occidental civilization." Yet, as technology became more complex and scientific in character, as the efficiency and output of industrial production increased, and as business transactions expanded, "the function of the entrepreneur, the captain of industry, gradually fell apart in a two-fold division of labor, between the business manager and the office work on the one side and the technician and the industrial work on the other side."[27] With this most recent split between business and industry, which amounted to a division between financial and industrial management with the former retaining ultimate control, the era of corporate dominance began.

The rise of the corporation in the late nineteenth century, Veblen argued, coincided with the failure of the competitive system to prevent excessive (i.e., unprofitable) production. In order to limit production and thereby prevent retrenchment of assets or earnings, the pecuniary captains increasingly resorted to the corporate form of business enterprise. The corporation, he explained, "is a business concern, not an industrial unit;" moreover, it is a "business concern which has been created by a capitalization of funds, and which accordingly rests on credit." While corporations may have indirectly facilitated industrial expansion, their purpose has always been investment for profit. "Business enterprise may be said to have reached its majority," he asserted, "when the corporation came to take first place and became the master institution of civilized life."[28]

The proliferation of corporate enterprise in the last quarter of the nineteenth century marked the beginning of a new order of industry and business.[29] Scientific advances in chemistry and physics revolutionized industrial technology; and the operations of industry increasingly came under the supervision of scientifically trained experts or technicians. The "modern machine process," as Veblen called it, gave rise to greater specialization and division of labor within industry. It created industrial interdependence through standardization of processes, machinery, and labor requirements, and ultimately standardized and routinized all of social existence—work, consumption, leisure—as though it were merely an extension of the mechanical workings of industry. Built upon the precepts of science and "matter-of-fact thinking," the modern machine process held forth the promise of industrial efficiency on a scale hitherto unimagined. This promise, however, was continually thwarted by the overlords of business. Unlike the scientifically oriented technicians and engineers who were concerned with the efficient operation of industry, the business magnates, the czars of finance and the rulers of the great industrial corporations, were driven solely by the quest for profits. Modern business enterprise and the credit economy upon which it rested were designed to stabilize prices, and therefore profits, by regulating competition and limiting production. Because they provided for centralization of control, allowed for routinization of business transactions, and created a greater interdependence within the financial community, corporations constituted the institutional foundation of the new order of business. The rise of the corporation therefore represented the demise of the captain of industry and the triumph of the modern business leader, the "captain of finance."

Veblen's ground-breaking theory of business enterprise focused primarily on three interrelated aspects of the economy—the use of credit, the nature of corporate capital, and the dynamics of business crises and depressions.[30] In "The Overproduction Fallacy," published in 1892, twelve years before the publication of *The Theory of Business Enterprise*, Veblen criticized the inability of conventional economic theorists to explain the phenomenon of overproduction and its relationship to depressions. His enduring contribution to this debate was to shift its footing from the terrain of classical economic theory, which could not account for the economic facts including the decisions of capitalists, to a theory of modern business enterprise that could explain the interrelationships between credit extensions in various forms, their impact on prices and markets, and the cyclical nature of depressions in the era of corporation finance. This same theme runs throughout "Credit and Prices," which was written in response to an issue raised at the American Economic Association annual meeting in 1904: "Does the use of credit raise general prices?" While emphasizing that a rise or fall in prices was correlated with the extension or contraction of credit, Veblen also examined theoretical implications of the causal relationship between credit and prices in this essay.

Veblen maintained that during the era of competitive capitalism and prior to the ascendancy of corporate finance, the extensive use of loan credit gave rise to periods of speculative expansion, rising prices, and business prosperity. Eventually, such periods of prosperity waned and prices dropped, with the result that many businesses had difficulty meeting their financial obligations to creditors. Because loans had been secured on the basis of an inflated earning capacity, a steady drop in prices revealed the extent to which businesses had overextended themselves.[31] The discrepancy between the putative and actual collateral basis of capitalization became apparent to the creditors and a period of liquidation and business depression ensued:

> Such a divergence between the accepted valuation and the actual value of capital may seem an inadequate basis for an economic fact of such magnitude as a period of industrial depression. And yet an industrial depression means, mainly, a readjustment of values. It is primarily, to very great extent, a psychological fact. Secondarily, it is largely a matter of shifting of ownership rather than destruction of wealth or a serious reduction of the aggregate productiveness of industry as measured in goods.[32]

Liquidation resulted in a redistribution of ownership of collateral property among creditors, a period of adjustment and re-capitalization, and eventually another speculative movement. Veblen maintained that prior to the 1870s, the discrepancy between capitalization and actual earning capacity was never too great to prevent a renewed speculative advance. As a consequence, depressions during this period tended to be short-lived and rarely disabled the economy as a whole.[33]

Under modern conditions, however, technological advances reduced costs at such a great rate that there existed a chronic discrepancy between capitalization and earning capacity. As technological improvements persistently out-stripped the readjustment of capitalization, a steady decline in profits resulted, thereby preventing a renewed speculative expansion of the type that had occurred in the earlier decades of the nineteenth century. Furthermore, depressions in the era of modern machine technology took on a systematic character due to the interdependent nature of the industrial system. The technological factor not only complicated the problem of credit inflation, but basically altered the nature of depressions as well. So long as business was conducted on a competitive footing, chronic depression, Veblen observed, was "normal to the industrial situation."[34]

Veblen concluded that competitive business practices were incompatible with the increased efficiency and productivity of modern industry. Accordingly, the dominant business interests in the latter decades of the nineteenth century had sought to eliminate competition by controlling prices and limiting production, mainly through combination and monopoly. In this fashion, the first lords of high finance proceeded to reorganize the economy through mergers and trust building. Thus, high finance—the buying and selling of enterprises, the financing of mergers, and the control of credit—came to dominate business enterprise. The investment banker reigned supreme as the master of high finance, and what the trust builders had initiated in their quest for profits, within a few decades, acquired an institutional basis in the major banks and the Federal Reserve System.[35]

The structure of corporate power, which is to say, the organization of power within the ruling business class, therefore, could be conceived as a hierarchy in which the large financial interests dominated, followed by the business managers of the key industrial corporations, and below them, the managers of the remaining industrial and manufacturing concerns whose livelihood largely depended upon the strategic decisions of the ruling business interests. According to Veblen's theory of modern industrial society, the pecuniary interests of the business class as a whole (which included the leisure class) stood opposed to the community's interest in efficiency and serviceability. Increasingly, this conflict took the form of a confrontation between the interests of the "One Big Union of Financial Interests" and their agents in government, on the one hand, and the vanguard of modern technology, the new class of technicians and engineers, on the other. The contradiction between business and industry, therefore, boiled down to a conflict between an exploitative class interest in profit making and a general social interest in full production and efficient use of technology and resources.[36]

IV

Just as the ascendancy of the captain of finance established the supremacy of pecuniary exploit over workmanlike efficiency, so did the era of corporate dominance represent the highest development of pecuniary culture. In shaping the styles and tastes of the ruling class, and ultimately the underlying population, business principles and ideology also served to justify class rule. Because class governance in advanced capitalist societies depended upon widespread ideological consensus, control over the production and dissemination of ideas was of vital importance to the perpetuation of existing power relationships. Indeed, the institutions of higher learning, according to Veblen, were dominated by individuals thoroughly imbued with pecuniary and non-scientific habits of thought, a fact that was clearly evidenced in the biased curriculum of these schools.

While scientific thinking had made some inroads, the system of higher education continued to be administered on the basis of businesslike principles, to propagate the ideas of pecuniary culture, and to serve the needs of the business class.[37] Schools of business and law, and to a lesser extent other vocational schools, "serve the advantage of one class as against another" because they "increase the advantage of such men as already have some advantage over the common run."[38] Thus, even though Veblen did not employ the actual phrase, it is clear that he adhered to a conception of the ideological hegemony of liberalism in the era of corporate rule.

Interpreted within the logic of Veblen's social theory, ideological hegemony was as much a product of cultural lag as of overt control. Ideological justification of the new order of business and industry, he argued, consisted of principles of ownership derived from the era of the handicraft economy.[39] Both the legal and moral foundation of the corporate order rested on the Lockean theory of property rights which posited a unity of ownership and workmanship, that is, of business and industry. This theory, however, like all habits of thought or ideological beliefs, had long since ceased to depict the reality which it justified. In fact, once the split between business and industry had become established in the competitive era, the unity of ownership and workmanship gave way to the institution of absentee ownership. Despite the fact that absentee ownership separated the productive use of property from its ownership, its legal and moral justification stood squarely on Locke's defense of property rights.

Veblen's critique of natural rights preconceptions also included an analysis of animistic habits of thought which, he argued, derived from the earliest primitive societies and remained a factor throughout the evolutionary process. Although its influence was progressively decreasing with the growth of matter-of-fact scientific thinking, Veblen identified animistic preconceptions as a significant influence on the precepts of liberal political thought and classical economic theory. The confluence of animism and liberal ideology was well illustrated by the hedonistic or utilitarian doctrine that informed classical economics and its progeny, such as marginal-utility theory. This latter theory ignored the social reality of production in the era of business enterprise and assumed that a mechanical hedonism was the natural psychological state of humanity from time immemorial. Marginal-utility theory substituted "sufficient reason" (rationalization) for "efficient cause" (cause and effect). It was teleological, Veblen argued, because it assumed an end or purpose rather than demonstrating a causal sequence or process: "this preconception imputes to things a tendency to work out what the instructed common sense of the time accepts as the adequate or worthy end of human effort."[40]

Veblen used the occasion of reviewing two books by economist Irving Fisher—*The Nature of Capital and Income* (1906) and *The Rate of Interest* (1908)—to illustrate how the preconceptions of economic science (marginal-utility theory) limited its ability to explain the reality of economic life. In "Fisher's Capital and Income" and "Fisher's Rate of Interest," published respectively in 1908 and 1909, Veblen took issue with the failure of the author to define the concepts of capital, income, and interest with reference to the actual social context in which they were applied. Veblen deemed Fisher's books to be "taxonomic" works based on a "primordial metaphysical postulate," the "hedonic principle." Although "capital" did not hold the same meaning for businessmen that it did fifty years earlier, practitioners of "modern" economic theory were unable to explain this fact. "Intangible assets," a phenomenon very familiar to real people involved in corporate finance, was not only excluded from Fisher's concept of capital, but was absent altogether from his analysis. This omission, which was to be expected in marginal-utility theory, was a chief cause of its failure "to give an intelligent account of credit and crises." The failure was not Fisher's as such, but that of the theory: the "shortsightedness of the taxonomic economist is a logical consequence of the hedonistic postulates of the school, not a personal peculiarity of the present or any other author."[41]

Fisher's concept of income, "a perfect flower of economic taxonomy," erroneously reduced income to "psychic income" and, for the sake of taxonomic precision, unnecessarily distinguished income from "increase of capital." Income must be assessed in terms of "pecuniary, not of hedonistic magnitudes."[42] Modern business was a pecuniary institution—a credit economy that developed out of a money economy—that had left behind in important ways the simpler economic life that Bentham's utilitarian calculus idealized. The same criticism applied to Fisher's analysis of the rate of interest: the "primordial metaphysical postulates," those hedonistic preconceptions of a bygone era, did not (and could not) explain the present

significance of interest, which was "a phenomenon of credit transactions only." Interest was a quintessential business (pecuniary) concept of the credit economy: "The whole matter lies within the range
of a definite institutional situation which is to be found only during
a relatively brief phase of civilisation that has been preceded by
thousands of years of cultural growth during which the existence of
such a thing as interest was never suspected."[43] Marginal-utility
theory failed because it assumed exactly what needed to be explained—namely, the economic behavior of individuals in society
under historically specific conditions.

Veblen argued that both animism and emulation had contaminated
the instinct of workmanship. Animistic thinking, which was an archaic form of anthropomorphism, was especially important in the
development of religion:

> So an animistic conception of things comes presently to supplement, and in part sup-
> plant, the more naive and immediate imputation of workmanship, leading up to farther
> and more elaborate myth-making; until in the course of elaboration and refinement there
> may emerge a monotheistic and providential Creator seated in an infinitely remote but
> ubiquitous space of four dimensions.[44]

Monotheistic religions, therefore, developed in conjunction with
predatory culture and patriarchy. Like pecuniary emulation, contemporary religious belief was a throwback to the era of barbarism.
Both had animistic origins and both limited or interfered with the
instinct of workmanship. This was Veblen's position throughout his
writings with one important and curious exception—"Christian Morals and the Competitive System," which he published in 1910. It is
not entirely clear why Veblen changed his position in this paper only
to abandon it thereafter. Whatever the reason(s) for these decisions,
the essay offers an unusual glimpse of another side of the author.
There is a hopefulness that pervades the argument, an aberrantly
cheerful tone, that is reminiscent of a few other occasions when
Veblen perhaps sensed that social change was possible or imminent.
Even a theorist of his erudition, it seems, was occasionally prone to
wishful thinking.

As he did in all of his research, Veblen sought in "Christian Morals and the Competitive System," to explain habits of thought—in
this case, Christian morality and pecuniary emulation—with reference to the material environment and changing social conditions.
Noting that both Christian morals and the morality of pecuniary com-

petition were "institutional factors of first-rate importance in this culture" both seemingly occupying a "dominant position," Veblen posed the central issues of the paper in the form of questions: "Taken at their best, do the two further fortify one another? do they work together without mutual help or hindrance? or do they mutually inhibit and defeat each other?"[45]

To answer these queries it was first necessary to identify the basic principles underlying the moral doctrines of Christianity and pecuniary competition, principles that had been present in them from the outset and that still broadly shaped their significance in all of their cultural permutations. The principles of Christianity were "non-resistance (humility) and brotherly love," the latter of which was "in some sort an atavistic trait" inherited from the peaceable communities of savages. Non-resistance, on the other hand, which could not be "traced back as a culturally atavistic trait," belonged "almost wholly to the more highly developed, more coercively organized civilisations, that are possessed of a consistent monotheistic religion and a somewhat arbitrary secular authority." Christianity first took hold under Roman rule "among the lower orders of the populace especially, who had been beaten to a pulp by the hard-handed, systematic, inexorable power of the imperial city." In short, Christianity started out as the religion of the oppressed before it became the official doctrine of the ruling classes during the Middle Ages. Its enduring appeal, however, had more to do with its compatibility with traits selected during the peaceable savage era of human history ("by far the most protracted and probably the most exacting of any phase of culture in all the life-history of the race") than with any of the institutional forms it had taken on during subsequent centuries.[46] By contrast, the principles of pecuniary competition were derived from the natural rights philosophy of the eighteenth century which had been devised in large part to justify economic changes associated with the growth of handicraft and petty trade. With the transition from feudalism to capitalism, pecuniary exploit had supplanted chivalric exploit. These habits of thought, however, were being outmoded by habits of life instilled in "the current era of machine industry, credit, delegated corporation management, and distant markets."[47]

Veblen concluded that the "two codes of conduct, Christian morals and business principles," were "the institutional by-products of two different cultural situations." Yet, they also shared common ground: Christian brotherly love had its analogue in the ethic of fair play observed under the regime of pecuniary competition. Indeed, the connection was even stronger in view of the fact that the "very deeprooted and ancient cultural trait" of brotherly love was "forever reasserting itself in economic matters, in the impulsive approval of whatever conduct is serviceable to the common good and in the disapproval of disserviceable conduct even within the limits of legality and natural rights." This principle of Christian morals, Veblen reasoned, seemed to be "nothing else than a specialized manifestation of the instinct of workmanship, and as such it has an indefeasible vitality that belongs to the hereditary traits of human nature." The author's surprising conclusion was that as habits of thought that developed from pecuniary competition during the handicraft era lost their sway in the era of machine industry, the "ancient impulse" of brotherly love (and hence workmanship) would gain ground and eventually eclipse the moral doctrine of pecuniary exploit.[48]

A similarly hopeful view did not characterize Veblen's analysis of the famous protest march on Washington, D.C., by several thousand unemployed men in 1894. Coxey's Army, also known as The Army of the Commonweal, was in reality several separate "armies," only one of which was actually organized and led by Jacob Coxey, a businessman and reformer from Ohio. Members of the Army of the Commonweal demanded that the federal government take action to solve the chronic problem of unemployment. This sentiment was especially widespread in 1894 due to the millions left without jobs as a result of the depression of 1893. In "The Army of the Commonweal," Veblen explained that the conviction among American workers that local economic problems required national solutions was the product of a fundamental and thoroughgoing change in industrial methods and organization: "[T]his attitude is but an expression of the fact latterly emerging into popular consciousness, that the entire community is a single industrial organism, whose integration is advancing day by day, regardless of any traditional or conventional boundary lines or demarcations, whether between classes or between localities." The protest itself was an indication of incipient change in popular perceptions; however, the actual agenda of the protesters reflected an inchoate blend of state-centered and paternalistic ideas of recent years—bimetallism, greenbackism, protectionism, religious (and patriarchal) paternalism, and state socialism. The support for the protest indicated to Veblen that a significant social movement might eventually develop out of this changing sentiment, but to have any effect on the actual course of events, it would have to catch up with the reality of the industrial process.[49]

Veblen came to a similar conclusion in his assessment of the "arts and crafts movement," which sought to restore or rediscover the ethic of an earlier period of handicraft capitalism wherein the artist and craftsman were joined in the same individual. His critique of this romantic quest in his essay, "Arts and Crafts," was incisive and unforgiving. Pointing out that modern industry showed no signs of returning to an earlier stage of technological development, he explained that the machine process "ubiquitously and unremittingly" shaped the workmen's habits of thought rooting out whatever elements were "alien to its own technological requirements and discipline." The implications were fairly obvious to everyone except the aristocratic "Dreamer of dreams, born out of his due time": "'Industrial art,' therefore, which does not work through and in the spirit of the machine technology is, at the best, an exotic. It will not grow into a dandelion-like 'weed of cultivation,' for it has no chance of life beyond the hothouse shelter of decadent aestheticism."[50]

Given his impatience with backward-looking reformers and his commitment, in principle, to progressive movements capable of altering the structure of power in American society, one might have expected Veblen to champion the cause of socialist revolution. Despite the many similarities of his social theory with classical Marxism, however, Veblen rejected the Marxist conception of class war between the proletariat and bourgeoisie. Although the business class dominated the whole of society, the potentially decisive class confrontation, in his view, was between the leaders of business and the new class of technicians and trained engineers, the vanguard of modern industrial methods and thinking. Veblen outlined his theory of revolution in a series of optimistic essays written in 1919, subsequently compiled in *The Engineers and the Price System*. While discounting a (Marxist) proletarian revolution as such, he emphasized that the prospect of revolution did indeed depend upon an alliance between the vanguard class and industrial workers. After 1919, Veblen continued to believe that the engineers and technicians could shape the direction of social change, but he never again expressed this view with the same enthusiasm.

V

Veblen maintained that while the rule of the business class in the United States derived its ideological sustenance, in the main, from the traditional theory of property rights, it also found justification in the sentiment of nationalism. Originally a means for ensuring loyalty to feudal overlords, nationalism or patriotism in its modern form served as a guise to mask the imperialist ambitions of the business class.[51] Through an evolutionary process of adaptation and rationalization in response to changing social circumstances, the institutions of ownership and nationalism continued to justify the predatory aims of society's rulers.

Veblen viewed the state or nation as an institutional outgrowth of the dynastic period of early modern Europe in which "the rival princely or dynastic establishments...each sought its own advantage at the cost of any whom it may concern." In modern times, "the divine right of the prince has passed over into the divine right of the Nation," but the predatory animus of the era of state-making remained in the imperialistic ambitions of the business interests. With the advent of this latest stage of predatory culture, he argued, the ruling class ensured its dominance through control of the state.[52]

In one of his more prescient essays, "Japan's Opportunity," published in 1915, Veblen applied his evolutionary theory of social change and his theory of the state to analyze the unusual blend of monarchical rule and industrial development then at work in Japan. Arguing that an opportunity had presented itself to Japan's rulers to realize their imperialist ambitions, Veblen shrewdly assessed the probable consequences that Japan's rapid industrial development would have on its social and political order. In essence, he argued that Japan had reached a point in its history where it could take advantage of the strengths afforded by a combination of feudalism and capitalism. Japan's rulers would experience for a short time the best of two worlds, so to speak—a feudal social structure and a modern industrial economy. This transitional phase would last a generation or so after which the deteriorating impact of industrialization on feudal institutions would begin to weaken this powerful combination of dynastic rule and modern technology. The Japanese case resembled in some respects that of the German people who "allowed their new-found technological efficiency to be turned to the service of dynastic politics." Yet Japan had outdistanced all of Europe in the degree to which it had exploited the modern state of industrial arts "by recourse to the servile patriotism of the common man."[53]

In detailing the likely course of change that Japanese social and political institutions would undergo in the coming years, Veblen argued that the business corporation would play an essential role in this transformation both as a means of instilling commercial values and of exploiting the modern state of industrial arts for dynastic ends. However, this bearer of pecuniary culture inculcated the logic of business principles which did not mesh well with the ceremonial trappings of dynastic politics. In the long term, business enterprise would thoroughly transform the face of Japanese society: "Wherever it reaches it carries a 'commercialization' of human relations and social standards, and effects a displacement of such aims and values as cannot be stated in terms of pecuniary gain; and so it throws pecuniary solvency into that position of first consideration that has been occupied by pedigree and putative excellencies of character."[54]

Veblen's writings during World War I covered a wide range of topics that reflected his considerable expertise in international relations, comparative government, economics, philosophy, and what has since been labeled "modernization theory." Many of the essays he wrote during this period reveal the sometimes awkward merger of the realistic social scientist and the social critic still hopeful that progressive change might come out of the most tragic of circumstances. One also suspects that the bitterness Veblen harbored following the many disappointments associated with the War—the failure in his view of the peace agreement to really make the world a safer or better place, the continued oppression of the "common man" at the expense of the vested interests, the mindless backlash against the American left in the wake of the Bolshevik revolution—might have encouraged or fueled the revolutionary zeal he expressed on behalf of the new class of engineers in 1919, while serving as an editor of *The Dial*.

Veblen wrote several papers and one book addressing the philosophical basis and practical implementation of a peace settlement.[55] He contributed two of his papers, "Suggestions Touching the Working Program of an Inquiry into the Prospective Terms of Peace" and "Outline of a Policy for the Control of the 'Economic Penetration' of Backward Countries and of Foreign Investments," to the committee or "Inquiry" formed by Colonel House at the request of President Wilson, in 1917, to explore possible terms of a peace agreement.

Four other essays, "The Passing of National Frontiers" (1918), "A Policy of Reconstruction" (1918), "Peace" (1919), and "The Economic Consequences of Peace" (1920), were published in various political and academic journals. A common theme runs throughout all of these papers. When conceived as a permanent condition and not as a temporary or partial solution put in place between wars, peace could be achieved only when the root cause of war—the rivalries between dynastic states fueled by imperialist policies—no longer held sway over the peaceful industrial interests of the great majority of the world's people. In the essays submitted to Colonel House's "Inquiry," Veblen outlined a peace settlement based on a "Pacific League," an idea that might have influenced President Wilson's ill-fated "League of Nations." The vision of the "New Order" that Veblen laid out in these and later papers, however, was not one that Wilson would have fully embraced. Veblen urged that the Pacific League adopt and implement the following policies or objectives: abolition of national frontiers to encourage free trade and the spread of industrial technology, submergence of national distinctions whenever possible through federations or disincentives, protection of natural resources of less developed countries from exploitation by the dominant (imperialist) business interests, and punishment of belligerent nations.[56]

Veblen also argued that the World War had made possible, if not necessitated, a "reconstruction" of the American commonwealth, which entailed "a revision of vested rights, for the common good."[57] Considerations of efficiency in preventing destructive competition among business owners as well as conflict between employers and workers that produced industrial strife and waste justified two "remedial measures":

(1) Disallowance of anything like free discretionary control or management on grounds of ownership alone...whenever the responsible owner of the concern does not at the same time also personally oversee and physically direct the work in which his property is engaged...

(2) To take over and administer as a public utility any going concern that is in control of industrial or commercial work which...[can be] habitually managed from an office by methods of accountancy.[58]

This argument, which seems to anticipate his essays in *The Engineers and the Price System*, illustrated well the blend of realism and hopefulness that characterized so many of his writings during this period. Veblen insisted that his recommendations were "a simple matter of material expediency," and contained neither "socialist iconoclasm" nor the "slightest animus of moral esteem or disesteem."[59]

Veblen supported the war effort but also defended the right of dissenters to oppose it and openly assailed the Red Scare policies that came in its aftermath. In 1918, he had worked five months for the Food Administration in Washington, D.C., writing policy papers. In this capacity, he penned several memoranda, including "Farm Labor for the Period of the War," "Farm Labor and the I.W.W.," "A Memorandum on a Schedule of Prices for the Staple Foodstuffs," "The War and Higher Learning," and he wrote an article for *The Public*, "Menial Servants During the Period of the War," which was also based on research he had done while working for the Food Administration. Two of these essays are especially noteworthy as examples of Veblen's efforts to influence government policy in conformance with his political ideals. "Farm Labor and the I.W.W.," which ostensibly began as a report on the "conditions surrounding the prospective grain crops of the prairie states," evolved into a very enlightening analysis of the ongoing class warfare between farmers and farm workers, on one side, and the "vested interests" (big business and the commercial clubs) in league with local, state, and federal governments, on the other. In addition to arguing that a labor shortage could be avoided by allowing the 50,000 members of the I.W.W. affiliate, the Agricultural Workers Industrial Union, to work free of harassment and to be paid the minimum wages they demanded, Veblen went out of his way to plead for intervention by the federal government on behalf of many Wobblie members who had been illegally jailed, unfairly punished, or beaten.[60]

Veblen's tack in "The War and Higher Learning" was also ingenious. With many European academic institutions in turmoil and a state of disrepair, which included a lack of financial resources and threats to academic freedom, Veblen sensed an opportunity to propose a two-part plan that might loosen the hold of the vested interests over higher education. First, he proposed that an open-door policy for foreign educators would have to be instituted at all American universities. The continued diffusion of knowledge, after all, was in the interest of all nations even if it did run counter in some respects to the American method of businesslike competition among universities. Second, an international forum or center for higher education that involved "an inclusive co-ordination of these Ameri-

can schools" would be established. In addition to preventing dupli-
cation and hence wasted funds, a "central office" would "serve as a
common point of support and co-ordination, which would at the
same time serve as a focus, exchange, and center of diffusion for
scholarly pursuits and mutual understanding, as well as an unattached academic house of refuge and entertainment for any guests,
strays, and wayfaring men of the republic of learning."[61]

For Veblen, these policies no doubt did not seem idealistic or utopian. They were, in his view, consistent with the direction of social
change and with the best interests of the nation as a whole. One
might question, however, whether his highly critical assessment of
the peace settlement (see "Peace," "Between Bolshevism and War,"
and "The Economic Consequences of Peace") combined with his
strong reaction to the childlike paranoia fomented by the Red Scare
(see "Dementia Praecox"), might not also have affected his ability
during this period to assess realistically the actual content and direction of Bolshevik policies. In "Bolshevism is a Menace—to Whom?"
published in February of 1919, Veblen observed that "the Bolshevik
is the common man who has faced the question: What do I stand to
lose? and has come away with the answer: Nothing."[62] Bolshevism
was indeed a menace, he surmised, but only to the vested interests.
One would expect Veblen to hold this view when the Russian Revolution was fresh and its course had not yet been firmly set. Two
years later in 1921, however, he compared the Soviet form of administration to a New England town meeting that had assumed juris-
diction over "all items of absentee ownership" and, in nearly the
same breath, he reported matter-of-factly that the Soviet had displaced democracy and representative government because they had
"proved to be incompetent and irrelevant for any other purpose than
the security and profitable regulation of absentee ownership."[63] This
seemingly cavalier attitude toward the squelching of democracy in
Russia was more indicative of the hopefulness mixed with despera-
tion and anger Veblen experienced during this period than of a doctrinaire support for communism. Like many other critical thinkers of
his generation who had nurtured the hope that the future would bring
a more just and humane society, the failure of fundamental social
change to occur in the aftermath of the war, combined with the chill-
ing effect of the anti-Red mob-mentality on progressive thinking,
eventually left him disillusioned and bitter. Indeed, in his last and
perhaps most comprehensive and mature work, *Absentee Owner-*

ship, Veblen did not even mention the prospect of revolutionary change. Rather, he seemed resigned to the continued dominance of the business class.

VI

Essays in Our Changing Order touches upon every aspect of Veblen's social theory and political writings. It is also a volume of firsts and lasts. Veblen's inaugural academic publication, "Kant's Critique of Judgment," marked the first and last time he published a strictly philosophical essay that was not about his own social theory. This essay appeared in the prestigious *Journal of Speculative Philosophy* in 1884, shortly after Veblen received his Ph.D. in philosophy from Yale. Unable to secure a university position in philosophy (most philosophers at that time were divinity students), he left the academic world for several years, returning to take graduate courses at Cornell in 1891, and subsequently embarking on a career as an economist. Despite the considerable gap in time (ten years) that separated this first publication from his later writings on evolutionary theory, the paper is nevertheless useful for understanding Veblen's intellectual development. It sheds significant light on his methodological assumptions and his insistence on using inductive, as opposed to deductive, reasoning in empirical research.[64]

Veblen's last published essay (which is first in order of appearance in this volume), "Economic Theory in the Calculable Future," might serve equally well as a conclusion to this book. In his inimitable style, Veblen dryly observed that economists of the coming generation would be predictably behind the times in their thinking but also more securely wedded to the creed of businesslike principles. Most economists, he explained, would study only what is useful to business, just as academic institutions increasingly would become business schools. "Mr. Cumming's Strictures on 'The Theory of the Leisure Class'" originally published in 1899, was the first and last time Veblen defended any of his books in print. This is unfortunate. Veblen's spirited defense is well worth the read, especially his closing remarks explaining his choice not to adopt the style of writing that had "long afflicted economics" and had "given that science its reputed character of sterility."[65] To continue my theme, the last essay Veblen wrote in his life, "An Experiment in Eugenics," which was rejected for publication when he was alive, was first published in this posthumous collection. A somewhat confusing ethnological analysis that tests eugenics theory with respect to Scandinavians, this piece is not up to Veblen's normally high standards. Like many of his contemporaries influenced by Darwinian theory, Veblen considered ethnology to be a science. To the contemporary reader, his ethnological or racial generalizations might give offense or seem comedic depending on the context. However, many of his writings in this area were connected with his broader social critique of the predacious habits of thought that sustained modern pecuniary culture. It should be noted that Veblen rejected as unscientific the notion sometimes associated with eugenics theory that certain races were superior to others based on genetic endowment.

In closing, there is one gem left to admire—"The Pre-eminence of Jews in Modern Europe." This too would have made a fitting conclusion for this book because it describes so effectively the intellectual perspective of an outsider. There is no doubt that Veblen identified with those intellectuals and scientists (e.g., Marx, Freud, Einstein) whom he dubbed "renegade Jews," gifted thinkers who became citizens in the "gentile republic of learning."[66] These outsiders were an odd hybrid of cultural influence. Denizens of two worlds, they belonged completely to neither. But their alienated existence was also the wellspring of their intellectual strength and vision. They saw more clearly than those whose eyes were shrouded by convention. They had pierced the veil of accepted wisdom and beheld the naked truth. This paralleled Veblen's own experience. The son of immigrant Norwegian farmers, he had always been a stranger in the land of his birth. Not only did this allow him to study American society with a certain detachment, but he also infused his written observations with an unfamiliar bias, not unlike a social anthropologist whose "objective" assessments of another culture are sifted through the prism of his own life experience. Perhaps this is why Veblen's deadly serious accounts of the ludicrousness of American pecuniary culture often have been mistakenly interpreted as satire. There can be no doubt that Veblen took great pride in his formidable wit and that his playfulness with words often revealed a sardonic sense of humor. He even loved practical jokes. To be sure, some of his writings *were* brilliantly satirical, but one wonders how often he actually intended them to have that effect. The satirist indulges in a form of cultural self-parody, a critique from the inside as it were. It is a literary technique that combines ridicule and irony to delve beneath the layers of conventionality to excavate the truth. Mark Twain, the social conscience of his generation, was a master of satire. Thorstein Veblen, the outsider, was a renegade intellectual. He documented the truth as he saw it which, we all know, is sometimes much funnier than fiction.

In describing the plight of the Jew in the land of the gentile, Veblen seems to have unwittingly crafted his own eulogy. On second thought, perhaps that is exactly what he wanted us to believe:

> For him as for other men in the like case, the skepticism that goes to make him an effectual factor in the increase and diffusion of knowledge among men involves a loss of that peace of mind that is the birthright of the safe and sane quietist. He becomes a disturber of the intellectual peace, but only at the cost of becoming an intellectual wayfaring man, a wanderer in the intellectual no-man's-land, seeking another place to rest, farther along the road, somewhere over the horizon. They are neither a complaisant nor a contented lot, these aliens of the uneasy feet...[67]

Notes

1. The most comprehensive biography of Veblen is Joseph Dorfman's, *Thorstein Veblen and His America* (New York: The Viking Press, 1934).
2. Thorstein Veblen, *The Theory of the Leisure Class: An Economic Study of Institutions* (New Brunswick, New Jersey: Transaction Publishers, 1991), p. 131; Veblen, *Essays in Our Changing Order*, edited by Leon Ardzrooni (New York: The Viking Press, 1934), p. 80; Veblen, *The Place of Science in Modern Civilization* (New Brunswick, New Jersey: Transaction Publishers, 1990), pp. 241-242.
3. *Essays*, pp. 80-81, 85; Veblen, *The Instinct of Workmanship and the State of the Industrial Arts* (New Brunswick, New Jersey: Transaction Publishers, 1990), pp. 1, 4, 6-8, 30-31; *Leisure Class*, pp. 29, 146.
4. *Essays,* p. 80; *Leisure Class*, p. 29; *Instinct of Workmanship*, pp. 25-27, 31-37, 84-89; *The Place of Science*, pp. 6-19.
5. *Instinct of Workmanship*, pp. 11, 40-41.
6. Ibid., p. 50, note 1; see also *The Place of Science*, p. 76.
7. *Essays,* pp. 80-81; *Leisure Class*, pp. 29, 133-134; see also *Absentee Ownership and Business Enterprise in Recent Times* (New York: B.W. Huebsch, Inc., 1923), pp. 16-17, 206.
8. *Leisure Class*, p. 134.
9. Ibid.; see also *Instinct of Workmanship*, p. 40; Veblen, *The Theory of Business Enterprise* (New Brunswick, New Jersey: Transaction Publishers, 1978, pp. 146-148; *Absentee Ownership*, p. 17.
10. *Leisure Class*, p. 133, 138-142; see also *Absentee Ownership*, pp. 18, 43; Veblen, *The Vested Interests and the Common Man* (New York: The Viking Press, 1933), pp. 4-11.
11. *Essays*, pp. 42-49; *Instinct of Workmanship*, pp. 146-160.
12. *Essays*, p. 33.
13. Ibid., pp. 42-49, 92; *Leisure Class*, pp. 33-34; *Instinct of Workmanship*, pp. 149-161. Veblen's main concern was to locate the beginnings of ownership, not to posit a necessary causal relationship between that institution and a particular social prac-

tice. "Whether property provokes to predation or predation initiates ownership," he concluded, "the situation that results in the early phases of the pecuniary culture was much the same" (ibid., p. 160).

14. *Essays*, p. 48.
15. Ibid., p. 58.
16. Ibid., pp. 56-58, 60-61.
17. Ibid., pp. 50, 93; *Leisure Class*, pp. 25, 26, 35, 43.
18. *Essays*, pp. 68, 74-75.
19. Ibid., pp. 88-94; *Leisure Class*, pp. 30-32.
20. *Instinct of Workmanship*, pp. 52-61.
21. For Veblen's analysis of the handicraft era, see ibid., pp. 209-298; *Absentee Ownership*, pp. 40-49.
22. *Instinct of Workmanship*, p. 211.
23. Ibid., pp. 210-214, 228-229, 233-234, 277-282.
24. Ibid., pp. 184-185.
25. Ibid., pp. 216, 187. It should be noted that Veblen did not consider pecuniary exploit to be an instinct. Rather, it is a "self-regarding sentiment" or "motive" rooted in pecuniary emulation. Veblen argued that pecuniary exploit, which, of course, is essential to the institution of ownership, had come to thoroughly dominate the behavior and thought of the business (and leisure) class as well as large segments of the rest of society. In short, pecuniary exploit had imposed its own bias on the instinctive proclivities of individuals living in pecuniary culture. Thus, pecuniary exploit and the institution of ownership affected the way in which the instinct of workmanship was expressed. Veblen argued that with the emergence of pecuniary culture, the system of "free workmanship" (i.e., cooperation, common use of resources and technology, social equality) gave way to pecuniary control of industry (i.e., self-interest, ownership, class distinctions). See ibid., pp. 142-151.

    The fact that Veblen did not classify pecuniary exploit (or pecuniary emulation) as an instinct does not seem to be important to his analysis inasmuch as he often referred to pecuniary exploit and/or pecuniary emulation as though it were an instinct. His decision in this matter, however, would appear to serve an ideological purpose since instincts, according to Veblen's theory, were essential to the survival of the species.

26. Veblen's most systematic analyses of the captains of industry will be found in: *Absentee Ownership*, pp.101-118; *The Engineers and the Price System* (New Brunswick, New Jersey: Transaction Publishers, 1983), pp. 27-51.
27. *Absentee Ownership*, pp. 101, 102, 106; see also ibid., pp. 70-71. To avoid terminological confusion, it should be noted that the era of machine technology in Veblen's analysis actually comprises two periods or eras—free competition and corporate finance.
28. Ibid., pp. 78-79, 110-111, 331-353; *Business Enterprise*, pp. 115-116, 123-127; *The Engineers*, pp. 36-38; *Absentee Ownership*, pp. 82, 86.
29. Veblen discussed the financial and industrial characteristics of this new order at length in several works. See, generally, ibid., pp. 205-397; *Business Enterprise*, pp. 7-127; *Instinct of Workmanship*, pp. 299-355; *The Engineers*, pp. 38-82; *Vested Interests*, pp. 35-113.
30. For Veblen's theory of business enterprise, see *Business Enterprise*, pp. 49-127; *Absentee Ownership*, pp. 82-100, 326-397.
31. *Essays*, pp. 110-112, 114-120, 126-131. Veblen argued that the extensive use of loan credit, especially in the form of "notes, stock shares, interest-bearing securities, deposits, call loans, etc." had become a normal practice in modern business. In effect, credit of this sort allowed for a greater rate of turnover of capital and served

"much the same purpose, as regards the rate of earnings," as did "time-saving improvement in the processes of industry" (*Business Enterprise*, pp. 49-50). Because resort to loan credit provided a competitive advantage, however slight at first, loan credit soon became necessary in order to achieve a "reasonable" return on investment (ibid., pp. 51-52; *Absentee Ownership*, pp. 356-358). The use of credit, however, also had the effect of enlarging business capital. Recapitalization on the basis of credit extension inflated the money value of an enterprise which at this point diverged from the actual value of the industrial capital upon which the credit was based. This inflated value, plus the intangible asset of "good-will," provided the basis for a further extension of loans, and so on, with the result that the capitalized value of an enterprise came to rest in large part on credit which had no collateral basis (*Business Enterprise*, pp. 52-58; *Absentee Ownership*, pp. 345-348, 218-220). These inflated values therefore created a discrepancy between capitalization or putative earning capacity and actual earning capacity.

32. *Essays*, pp. 112-113.
33. *Business Enterprise*, pp. 94-100, 117-120.
34. Ibid., pp. 109, 120-121.
35. Ibid., pp. 115-116, 123-127. *Absentee Ownership*, pp. 331-353; *The Engineers*, pp. 47-49. On the role of the Federal Reserve system in consolidating the rule of corporate finance, see ibid., pp. 50-51, and *Absentee Ownership*, pp. 223-224 and 352, note 13.
36. Ibid., pp. 229-250. Although Veblen believed that the new class of engineers and technicians constituted the vanguard of social change, he conceived the basic division within society to be between the business (and leisure) class and the "underlying population," i.e., workers, farmers, small business people (ibid., p. 399; *Vested Interests*, p. 175).
37. Veblen, *The Higher Learning in America* (New Brunswick, New Jersey: Transaction Publishers, 1993); see also *Leisure Class*, pp. 235-258.
38. *Higher Learning*, p. 212.
39. My reconstruction of Veblen's ideological critique is based upon the following works: *Absentee Ownership*, pp. 12-68, 205-210, 398-445; *Business Enterprise*, pp. 37-48, 128-176; *Leisure Class*, pp. 131-164; *Vested Interests*, pp. 1-34, 114-137, 174-176; *Instinct of Workmanship*, pp. 340-355; *The Place of Science*, pp. 82-251.
40. Ibid., pp. 65, 236-237. Veblen examined this problem in detail in several essays published in *The Place of Science*. Economists regularly indulged in teleological explanations, he argued, precisely because their discipline employed *a priori* or deductive reasoning based on a set of normative principles. Modern economics was, therefore, largely a "taxonomic" or classificatory enterprise.
41. *Essays*, pp. 148-50, 154-157.
42. Ibid., pp. 157-60. "According to the hedonistic postulates the end and incentive is necessarily the pleasurable sensations to be derived from the consumption of goods, what Mr. Fisher calls 'enjoyable income' or psychic income…" Hence, "men prefer present to future consumption. This is the beginning of economic (marginal-utility) wisdom; but it is also the end of the wisdom of marginal utility" (ibid., p. 141).
43. Ibid., p. 142.
44. *Instinct of Workmanship*, p. 59.
45. *Essays*, pp. 200-201. John P. Diggins has argued that this essay constituted Veblen's response to Max Weber's *The Protestant Ethic and the Spirit of Capitalism.* See Diggins, *The Bard of Savagery: Thorstein Veblen and Modern Social Theory* (New York: The Seabury Press, 1978), p. 92.
46. *Essays*, pp. 203, 205-207, 209.

47. Ibid., pp. 210-214.
48. Ibid., pp. 214-216.
49. Ibid., pp. 101-103.
50. Ibid., p. 197.
51. *Absentee Ownership*, pp. 35-36, 47.
52. Ibid., pp. 22, 25, 31-39; see also *Vested Interests*, pp. 123-131; and *Business Enterprise*, pp. 135, 139-140.
53. *Essays*, pp. 250-251; see also Veblen, *Imperial Germany and the Industrial Revolution* (New Brunswick, New Jersey: Transaction Publishers, 1990).
54. Ibid., p. 262.
55. Veblen, *An Inquiry Into the Nature of Peace and the Terms of its Perpetuation* (New York: B.W. Huebsch, 1917).
56. *Essays*, pp. 355-390.
57. Ibid., p. 391.
58. Ibid., p. 396
59. Ibid., p. 387.
60. Ibid., pp. 319-336.
61. Ibid., p. 345.
62. Ibid., p. 414.
63. Ibid., p. 441.
64. On the relationship between this essay and Veblen's methodological assumptions, see the Murray G. Murphey, "Introduction," *The Instinct of Workmanship and the State of the Industrial Arts* (New Brunswick, New Jersey: Transaction Publishers, 1990), pp. ix-xiv.
65. Ibid., p. 31.
66. Ibid., p. 226.
67. Ibid., p. 227.

7

The Theory of the Leisure Class

C. Wright Mills

THORSTEIN VEBLEN is the best critic of America that America has produced. His language is part of the vocabulary of every literate American; his works are the most conspicuous contribution of any American to American studies; his style, which makes him the only comic writer among modern social scientists, is an established style of the society he dissected. Even the leisure class, which has now been reading Veblen for more than a generation, talks a little like him.

Veblen would have appreciated the fate his work has suffered. An unfashionable mind, he nevertheless established a fashion of thinking; a heretic, his points of view have been received into the canon of American social thought. Indeed, his perspectives are so fully accepted that one is tempted to say there is no other standard of criticism than the canon which Veblen himself established. All of which seems to prove that it is difficult to remain the critic of a society that is entertained by blame as well as praise.

Veblen is still read, not only because his criticism is still plausible, but because his style makes it so, even when the criticism is not taken seriously. Style is not exactly a strong point of American social science; in fact, most sociologists avoid style, even as some historians cultivate it. And, in this respect, Veblen is more historian than "social scientist." At any rate, it is his style that has kept this rather obscure and unsuccessful sociologist of the "Progressive Era"—he died in 1929—alive, after the immediate scene he anatomized has become history.

George Bernard Shaw, in his Preface to *Man and Superman,* remarks that "...he who has something to assert will go as far in power of style as its momentousness and his conviction will carry him. Disprove his assertion after it is made, yet his style remains. Darwin no more destroyed the style of Job or Handel than Martin Luther destroyed the style of Giotto. All the assertions get disproved sooner or later; and so we find the world full of a magnificent debris of artistic fossils, with the matter-of-fact credibility gone clean out of them, but the form still splendid."

That is true of Veblen—although in his case we cannot say that all "the matter-of-fact credibility" in his works has "gone clean out of them."

2

In a grim world, Veblen's style is so hilarious that one would wish to see it left intact as a going force for sanity. One may not always be sure of his meaning today, but his animus remains unmistakable and salutary. Whether or not his style in this, his first book, is his best, Veblen's books as a whole do constitute a work of art, as well as a full-scale commentary on American life.

As works of art, Veblen's books do what all art properly should do: they smash through the stereotyped world of our routine perception and feeling and impulse; they alert us to see and to feel and to move toward new images, many of them playful and bright and shrewd.

Veblen creates a coherent world in which each part is soon understandable and which is peopled by fascinating types of men and women who are soon though newly recognizable. We might learn from him that the object of all social study is to understand the types of men and women that are selected and shaped by a given society—and to judge them by explicit standards. Much of Veblen's comedy comes simply from his making his fresh standards explicit.

The form of Veblen's books and their content are one. It is as much the exact way he says things as what he says that one appreciates in his work. His phrases stick in the mind, and his insights, if acquired early, often make a difference in the quality of one's life. No, his thought could not properly be expressed in any other form than the form which he gave it. And that is why, like all works of art, you must "read" his work for yourself.

3

Thorstein Veblen realized that the world he lived in was dominated by what one might call "crackpot realism." This was, and one must use the word, Veblen's metaphysic—his bone deep view of the nature of everyday American reality. He believed that the very Men of Affairs whom everyone supposed to embody sober, hard-headed practicality were in fact utopian capitalists and monomaniacs; that the Men of Decision who led soldiers in war and who organized civilians' daily livelihoods in peace were in fact crackpots of the highest pecuniary order. They had "sold" a believing world on themselves; and they had—hence the irony—to play the chief fanatics in their delusional world.

No mere joke, however, but a basic element of his perspective caused Veblen to write in 1922 what might with equal truth be written today: "The current situation in America is by way of being something of a psychiatrical clinic. In order to come to an understanding of this situation there is doubtless much else to be taken into account, but the case of America is after all not fairly to be understood without making due allowance for a certain prevalent unbalance and derangement of mentality, presumably transient but sufficiently grave for the time being. Perhaps the commonest and plainest evidence of this unbalanced mentality is to be seen in a certain fearsome and feverish credulity with which a large proportion of the Americans are affected."

The realization of this false consciousness all around him, along with the sturdiness of mind and character to stand up against it, is the clue to Veblen's world outlook. How different his was from the prevailing view is suggested by his utter inability to be "the salesman."

4

We are told that even as a youth Veblen mumbled and so seemed incomprehensible. His students thought him dull, and he did not pretend to be fond of them. Veblen never got a decent academic job. He was not what the nineteenth century called a decent man. He was a sure-footed old man who hated sham, realistically and romantically protesting against it by his manner of living as well as by his life work. Veblen was one of those lean, masterless men, who are hated by plump flunkies. He was an idle, curious man, watching bustling citizens and pompous spokesmen beat him at games he refused to play.

It has been fashionable to sentimentalize Veblen as the most alienated of American intellectuals, as the Prince outside even the ghetto. But Veblen's virtue is not alienation; it is failure. Modern intellectuals have made a success of "alienation" but Veblen was a natural-born failure. To be conspicuously "alienated" was a kind of success he would have scorned most. In character and in career, in mind and in everyday life, he was the outsider, and his work the intellectual elaboration of a felt condition.

He was almost a foreigner, except if someone had told him, "If you don't like it here, go back where you came from," it would have had to be Wisconsin or Minnesota. He was born, in 1857, to Norwegian immigrants in Wisconsin and he was moved to Minnesota by his father, an artisan-farmer, when he was eight years old.

After nine more years on the farm he was packed off to Carleton, a small Congregational school in Northfield, Minnesota, where he was regarded as impressive but likely to be unsound. After graduating with the class of 1880, he tried to teach in a middle-western academy. The next year he went to Johns Hopkins for graduate work and in 1884 he took his Ph.D. at Yale. No job was available for Thorstein Veblen. He went back to the farm. He married a girl from a family of university administrators. Still no job. For six or seven years he lived in idle curiosity. The farm had no place for a scholar, although on the Veblen farm scholarship was not out of place. Veblen talked much with his father and learned much from him.

In 1891, Veblen went to Cornell for further graduate work, and shortly thereafter finally got his first academic job at the University of Chicago. He lived eccentrically, and his wife kept going away and coming back again. Girls, we are told, liked Veblen, and he did not really object. He was requested to resign. With his wife again, he got a job at Stanford, where the Chicago story was more or less repeated. His wife now gone for good, Veblen began to teach at the University of Missouri, where he wrote four or five of his best books while living in the cellar of a colleague's house.

During World War I, Veblen went to Washington, filling a minor post in the Food Administration. He was not successful. After the Armistice, Veblen went to New York to write for an unsuccessful

little magazine and to lecture at that future haven for refugee scholars, The New School for Social Research. He was not a successful
lecturer. Then he went to Stanford and lived in a shack in the nearby
woods, where he died on August 3, 1929.[1]

There is no failure in American academic history quite so great as
Veblen's. He was a masterless, recalcitrant man, and if we must group
him somewhere in the American scene, it is with those most recalcitrant Americans, the Wobblies.[2] On the edges of the higher learning,
Veblen tried to live like a Wobbly. It was a strange place for such an
attempt. The Wobblies were not learned, but they were, like Veblen,
masterless men, and the only non-middle class movement of revolt
in twentieth-century America. With his acute discontent and shyness
of program, Veblen was a sort of intellectual Wobbly.

5

Two schools of sociological study have flourished in America since
Veblen's time. One of them makes a fetish of "Method," the other of
"Theory." Both, accordingly, lose sight of their proper study.

The Higher Statisticians break down truth and falsity into such
fine particles that we cannot tell the difference between them; by the
costly rigor of their methods, they succeed in trivializing man and
society, and in the process their own minds as well.

The Grand Theorists, on the other hand, represent a partially organized attempt to withdraw from the effort plainly to describe, explain, understand human conduct and society: they verbalize in tur-
gid prose the disordered contents of their reading of eminent nineteenth-century sociologists, and in the process mistake their own
beginnings for a finished result.

In the practice of both these leading schools, contemporary Social Science becomes simply an elaborate method of insuring that
no one learns too much about man and society, the first by formal
but empty ingenuity; the second, by formal but cloudy obscurantism.

The work of Thorstein Veblen stands out as a live protest against
these dominant tendencies of the higher ignorance. He always knew
the difference between the trivial and the important, and he was wary
of the academic traps of busywork and pretension. While he was a
man at thought, he kept the bright eye of his mind upon the object
he was examining. Veblen was quite unable to be a specialist. He
tried philosophy and he was trained as an economist, but he was

also a sociologist and a psychologist. While specialists constructed a world to suit only themselves, Veblen was a professional anti-specialist. He was, in short, a social thinker in the grand tradition, for he tried to do what Hegel and Comte and Marx and Spencer and Weber—each in his own way—had tried to do:

To grasp the essentials of an entire society and epoch,

To delineate the characters of the typical men within it,

To determine its main drift.

The results of Veblen's attempt to do these things exist in some ten books. His first attempt, published in 1899, is the book you hold in your hand. Five years later he published *The Theory of Business Enterprise,* and then, in 1914, *The Instinct of Workmanship.* When World War I occurred, naturally Veblen turned to it, publishing *Imperial Germany* in 1915, and *The Nature of Peace* in 1917. After that, published a few years apart, he produced *The Higher Learning* and *The Vested Interests;* his more technical essays were collected in *The Place of Science in Modern Civilization.* He wrote *The Engineers and The Price System,* published as a book in 1921, and *Absentee Ownership*—which many consider his best single volume— in 1923. After his death, *Essays in Our Changing Order* was published. These constitute the heritage Veblen left for the use of the human community. There is no better set of books written by a single individual about American society. There is no better inheritance available to those who can still choose their own ancestors.

6

Since the intelligentsia, just now, are in a conservative mood, no doubt during the nineteen-fifties Veblen, when he is not ignored, will be re-interpreted as a conservative. And, from one rather formal viewpoint, Veblen was a profoundly conservative critic of America: he wholeheartedly accepted one of the few unambiguous, all-American values: the value of efficiency, of utility, of pragmatic simplicity. His criticism of institutions and the personnel of American society was based without exception upon his belief that they did not adequately fulfill this American value. If he was, as I believe, a

Socratic figure, he was in his own way as American as Socrates in his was Athenian.

As a critic, Veblen was effective precisely because he used the American value of efficiency to criticize American reality. He merely took this value seriously and used it with devastatingly systematic rigor. It was a strange perspective for an American critic in the nineteenth century as it would be in our own. One looked down from Mont St. Michel, like Henry Adams, or across from England, like Henry James. With Veblen perhaps the whole character of American social criticism shifted. The figure of the last-generation American faded and the figure of the first-generation American—the Norwegian immigrant's son, the New York Jew teaching English literature in a Midwestern university, the southerner come north to crash New York—was installed as the genuine, if no longer 100 percent American, critic.

If Veblen accepted utility as a master value, he rejected another all-American value: the heraldry of the greenback, the world of the fast buck. And since, in that strange institution, the modern corporation, the efficiency of the plain engineer and the pecuniary fanaticism of the business chieftain—are intricately confused, Veblen devoted his life's work to clarifying the difference between these two types and between their social consequences.

7

The America Veblen saw seemed split in two. Running through everything Veblen wrote was the distinction between those activities and moods that are productive and useful and those that are ostentatious and honorific, workmanlike as against businesslike, industrial and amiable in contrast to pecuniary and predatory.

In the course of history, his account ran, material labor had become unworthy; predatory exploit had become the very essence of high dignity. Labor, Veblen believed, became irksome because of the indignity imputed to it; it had not become undignified because it was irksome. By "leisure" Veblen really meant everything that is not of the world of everyday, productive work and of the workmanlike habit of mind.

The key event in the modern history of the leisure class was its involvement with private ownership. Originally, Veblen tells us, predatory warlords seized property—especially the women—of an enemy, and hence their ownership of the booty revealed their prowess. This was of course honorific, because it was an assertion of superior force. In due course, the struggle for existence became a competition for pecuniary emulation: to own property was to possess honor; it was to set up an invidious distinction, a better-than-thou feeling on the part of absentee owners: those who own more than they could personally use, against those who did not own enough for their livelihood.

Popular esteem thus came to be based upon property, and accordingly became the basis for "that complacency which we call self-respect." For men judged themselves favorably or unfavorably in comparison to others of their general class in point of pecuniary strength, and this led to an insatiable, restless straining for invidious distinction.

But would not such a pecuniary struggle lead men to industrious and frugal lives? Perhaps for the lower classes, but not for the higher. Being useless in the struggle for status that had succeeded the struggle for existence, productive work was held to be unworthy. The better classes abstained from it while at the same time they emulated one another. It was not enough to possess wealth in order to win esteem; one had to put it into evidence; one had to impress one's importance upon others. Conspicuous leisure, according to Veblen, did just that— it put one's wealth and power on social display. That was the value of leisure for this pecuniary society. When one's group was compact and all its members intimately known, either leisure or consumption served to demonstrate one's wealth. But when one moved among wider circles of urban strangers, it became necessary to advertise one's wealth. Conspicuous consumption was then needed as a means of ordinary decency. With what was obviously expensive and wasteful one could impress all transient and anonymous observers.

So mere idleness was not enough: it had to be the idleness of expensive discomfort, of noble vice, and costly entertainment. It had, in short, to be conspicuous consumption: the obvious waste of valuable goods as a means of gaining reputability.

Opposed to all this, there stand in Veblen's world the industrial interests of the modern community, and the honest, prosaic man who would serve these industrial interests. But such peaceable men, having a "non-emulative, non-invidious interest in men and things" lack what passes for initiative and ingenuity, and end up as amiable good-for-nothing fellows. For what is good for the community is, of course, in a regime of crackpot realism, "disserviceable to the individual."

By his master split, with businessmen on the pecuniary side, Veblen linked the theory of the leisure class with the theory of business enterprise. For ownership and acquisition belonged to the pecuniary range of employments, to the moneyed life. And the "captain of industry" was misnamed, for his was a pecuniary rather than an industrial captaincy.

This, all too briefly, is the kind of real, never-never world you who are to read this book for the first time are about to enter. "All this is incredible," Veblen suddenly remarks in the middle of one of his books, "but it is everyday fact." Veblen has made Alices of us all, and dropped us through the looking glass into the fantastic world of social reality.

8

What Veblen said remains strong with the truth, even though his facts do not cover the scenes and the characters that have emerged in our own time. He remains strong with the truth because we could not see the newer features of our own time had he not written what and as he did. Which is one meaning of the fact that his biases are the most fruitful that have appeared in the literature of American social protest. But all critics are mortal, and some parts of Veblen can no longer live for us. In the criticisms of Veblen which follow, I shall examine only his theory of the leisure class.

9

Veblen's theory is not "The Theory of the Leisure Class." It is *a* theory of a particular element of the upper classes in one period of the history of one nation. It is a criticism of the *nouveau riche*, so much in evidence in Veblen's formative time, the America of the latter half of the nineteenth century, of the Vanderbilts, Goulds, and Harrunans, of Saratoga Springs and Newport, of the glitter and the gold.

Moreover, what he wrote about was mainly Local Society and its Last Resorts, and especially the women of these worlds. He could not of course have been expected in the eighteen-nineties to see the meaning for the *national* status system of the professional celebrities, who have risen as part of the national media of mass communication and entertainment, nor the major change in national glamour, in which the debutante is replaced by the movie star, and the local society lady by the military and political and economic managers— the power elite—whom crackpot realists now celebrate as their proper chieftains.

10

The spleen of Veblen is due to the assumption, in his own words, that "the accumulation of wealth at the upper end of the pecuniary scale implies privation at the lower end of the scale." He tended always to assume that the pie was of a certain size, and that the wealthy class withdraws from the lower classes "as much as it may of the means of sustenance, and so reducing their consumption, and consequently their available energy, to such a point as to make them incapable of the effort required for the learning and adoption of new habits of thought." Again, the moral edge of the phrase, "conspicuous consumption" lies in the fact that it tends "to leave but a scanty subsistence minimum…to absorb any surplus energy which may be available after the pure physical necessities of life…." All this, strangely enough, was a sort of survival in Veblen's thought of classic economic conceptions of scarcity, and betrays a lack of confidence in technological abundance which we cannot now accept in the simple terms in which Veblen left it.

Veblen, thinking of the immigrant masses of his time and of the enormously unequal distribution of income and wealth, did not leave enough scope for the economic pie to expand—and what has happened, especially since the second World War, has meant that the majority of the U.S. population can consume conspicuously. In fact, in the absence of "lower classes on a scanty subsistence," the term "conspicuous consumption" becomes a somewhat flat description of higher standards of living because the invidious element is lacking. Of course the aesthetics of Veblen's case remain applicable.

11

In depicting the higher style of life, Veblen seemed to confuse aristocratic and bourgeois traits. Perhaps this is a limitation of his American viewpoint. He did this explicitly at one or two points: "The aristocratic and the bourgeois virtues—that is to say the destructive and pecuniary traits—should be found chiefly among the upper classes...." One has only to examine the taste of the small shop-keeper to know that this is certainly not true.

Conspicuous consumption, as Veblen knew, is not confined to the upper classes. But today I should say that it prevails *especially* among one element of the new upper classes—the *nouveau riche* of the new corporate privileges—the men and women on the expense accounts, and those enjoying other corporate prerogatives—and with even more grievous effects on the standard and style of life of the higher middle and middle classes generally. And of course among recent crops of "Texas millionaires."

12

The supposed shamefulness of labor, on which many of Veblen's conceptions rest, does not square very well with the Puritan work ethic so characteristic of much of American life, including many upper class elements. I suppose, in the book at hand, Veblen is speaking only of upper, not middle classes—certainly he is not writing of wealthy Puritan middle classes. He did not want to call what the businessman does "work," much less productive work. The very term, leisure class, became for him synonymous with upper class; but, of course, there is and there has been a *working* upper class—in fact, a class of prodigiously active people. That Veblen did not approve of their work, and in fact refused to give it that term—work being one of his positive words—is irrelevant. Moreover, in this case it obscures and distorts our understanding of the upper classes as a social formation. Yet for Veblen fully to have admitted this simple fact would have destroyed (or forced the much greater sophistication of) his whole perspective and indeed one of the chief moral bases of his criticism.

13

Veblen was interested in psychological gratification; he tended to ignore the social function of much of what he described. He would not, in fact, have liked the term "function" to be used in this way, because, given his values, the solid word "function" is precisely the sort he would have reserved for workmanlike men and forces. Consider merely as illustrations three close to hand:

Many of the social scenes with which Veblen had so much fun were, in fact, meeting places for various elite of decision, for prestige behavior mediates between various hierarchies and regions. Hence prestige is not merely social nonsense that gratifies the individual ego: it serves a unifying function; leisure activities are one way of securing a coordination of decision between various sections and elements of the upper class.

Such status activities also coordinate high families; they provide a marriage market, the functions of which go well beyond the gratifications of displayed elegance, of brown orchids and white satin: they serve to keep a propertied class intact and unscattered; by monopoly of sons and daughters, anchoring the class in the legalities of blood lines.

And "snobbish" exclusiveness, of course, secures privacy to those who can afford it. To exclude others enables the high-and-mighty to set up and to maintain a series of private worlds in which they can and do discuss issues and decisions and in which they train their young informally for the decision-making temper. In this way they blend impersonal decision-making with informal sensitivities, and so shape the character structure of an elite.

14

There is another function—today the most important—of prestige and of status conduct. Prestige buttresses power, turning it into authority, and protecting it from social challenge.

"Power for power's sake" is psychologically based on prestige gratification. But Veblen laughed so hard and so consistently at the servants and the dogs and the women and the sports of the elite that he failed to see that their military, economic, and political activity is not at all funny. In short he did not succeed in relating their power over armies and factories to what he believed, quite rightly, to be their funny business. He was, I think, not quite serious enough about prestige because he did not see its full and intricate importance to power. He saw "the kept classes" and "the underlying population," but he did not really see the power elite.

15

Perhaps Veblen did not pay appropriate attention to the relevance of status to power because of his theory of history. The members of his "leisure class" are no history-makers; in fact, they have no real function in history. For in modern societies, Veblen held, industrial forces are the motors of history, and the leisure class is a survival and a lag, an anachronism or a parasitical growth. In fact, Veblen explicitly believed that "they are not in the full sense an organic part of the industrial community." For in that matter-of-fact community, it is the innovator who counts, and in the leisure class the innovator is vulgar, and innovation, to say the least, bad form.

Technological innovators are the history makers, and next to them, according to Veblen, those who are forced to change their ways in order to meet new technical conditions. Today, we cannot go along with what seems to us this over-simple view of the relations of technology to the institutions and the men who adapt and guide its developments and uses. This is one of the several Marxist overtones in Veblen, the assumption that those who are functionally indispensable to the community are the men who count and that those who are parasites are doomed. In our time, of course, we have seen too many technically parasitic men gain power and hold it with authority to believe in this rational, optimistic theory of history.

16

Veblen had an inadequate view of the effect of industrial efficiency upon the rationality of the men close to the machine process. He failed to recognize the terrible ambiguity of rationality in modern man and his society. He assumed that the skilled workmen and the engineers and the technicians would increasingly come to embody matter-of-fact rationality—as individuals and as strata. It was, in fact, upon these strata that he rested as he lectured about the "leisure class." And this, again, is a result of his over-simple split between the honorific and the workmanlike.

Veblen failed to appreciate that the increasing rationality of the efficiency-machines does not at all mean that the individuals who are linked together to run these machines are personally more rational or intelligent—even inside the fabulous engine room itself, and certainly not inside the mass society of which it is a part. In fact, the judgment of "the technicians" and their capacity for general intelligence, especially in social and political affairs, often seems quite paralyzed and is no better than that of the pecuniary fanatics. The rational apparatus itself has expropriated the rationality of the individual to the point where we must often assume that those in charge of the big institutions are normally quite stupid. Moreover, the few key individuals who are able rationally to understand the structure of the whole are no more likely to be engineers than workingmen.

What Veblen called industrial efficiency, "the opaque run of cause and effect," does not necessarily increase the substantive rationality of independent judgment. Nor does close contact with the big machine increase in men any of those amiable, sane traits that Veblen stuffed into his "instinct of workmanship." For in truth, Veblen's "workmanship" is an ideal set forth by a man afraid to set forth ideals, and it is more socially at home in some simple artisan society than in the modern social disorder we are trying to live in and understand.

17

Just what does all the pretentious monkey business about status, which Veblen analyzed so well, have to do with the operations of the political economy? I have intimated that the local society of the very rich—about which Veblen wrote—turned out to be too economically unstable and too politically weak to become an enduring center for a national system of prestige. The professional celebrities of the mass media are without power of any stable sort and are in fact ephemeral figures among those we celebrate.

And yet there is an upper-class demand for some sort of organization of enduring and stable prestige, which Veblen's analysis somehow misses. It is a "need" quite consciously and quite deeply felt by the elite of wealth and especially the elite of power in the United States today.

During the nineteenth century neither the political nor the military elite were able to establish themselves firmly at the head or even near the head of a national system of prestige. John Adams's suggestion—in his *Discourses on Davila*—which leaned in that direction, was not taken up. Other forces and not any official system of distinctions and honors have given such order as it has had to the polity. The American economic elite and for this very reason it is uniquely significant—rose to economic power in such a way as to upset repeated attempts to found national status on enduring family lines.

But in the last thirty years, with the managerial reorganization of the propertied class, and the political roles assumed by the managerial elite, there have been signs of a merger of economic, political, and military elite in a new corporate-like class. Together, an as elite of power, will they not seek, as all-powerful men everywhere have always sought, to buttress their power with the mantle of authoritative status? Will they not consolidate the new status privileges, popularized in terms of the expense account but rooted deeply in their corporate class? And in view of their position in the cultural world of nations—as they come more fully to realize it, will they be content with the clowns and the queens—the professional celebrities— as the world representatives of their American nation?

In due course, will not those we celebrate come to coincide more closely with those who are the most powerful among us? In due course, will not snobbery become official, and all of us startled into our appropriate grade and rank? To believe otherwise, it seems to me, is to reject all that is available and relevant in our understanding of world history.

18

We must remember that we could not entertain, at least not so easily, such criticisms and speculations had Veblen not written. And that is his real and lasting value: he opens up our minds, he gets us "outside the whale," he makes us see through the official sham. Above all, he teaches us to be aware of the crackpot basis of the realism of those practical Men of Affairs who would lead us to honorific destruction.

Notes

1. Joseph Dorfmann, in his *Thorstein Veblen and His America* (Viking, 1934), has written a detailed account of Veblen's life and work.
2. The Industrial Workers of the World (I.W.W.): an industrial labor union, having a syndicalist ideology, founded in 1905.

8

The Engineers and the Price System

Daniel Bell

Periodically, there is a renewed wave of interest in Thorstein Veblen's *The Engineers and the Price System.* The sudden vogue of technocracy in 1932 led to the reissue of the book, and for a while it became a best seller, with an average sale of 150 copies a week. In recent years, the rapid expansion of the technical class of employees (in 1900, there was one engineer for every 225 factory workers; in 1950, one for every 62; and in 1960, one for every 20), the rise of computer technology and automation, the engineering exploration of space, and the new prestige of the scientist have all focused attention on the strategic importance of the technologists, and these speculations recall the excitement that greeted Veblen's book when it was first published as a series of essays in 1919 in *The Dial* and then published in 1921 as a book.

The reasons for this excitement are not hard to find. *The Engineers and the Price System is* one of Veblen's few prophetic books. The tantalizing "Memorandum on a Practicable Soviet of Technicians," the concluding essay, is *not,* as the blurb writer proclaimed on the jacket of the 1932 reissued volume, "to the engineers what the Communist Manifesto purported to be for the proletariat," for Veblen opens and closes that chapter with the ironic statement that "under existing circumstances there need be no fear, and no hope of an effectual revolutionary overturn in America" that could "flutter the sensibilities" of the Guardians of the Vested Interests. But the context of the book does seek to establish a drift of history and an agenda for the future.

Revolutions in the eighteenth century [Veblen wrote] were military and political; and the Elder Statesmen who now believe themselves to be making history still believe that revolutions can be made and unmade by the same ways and means in the twentieth century. But any substantial or effectual overturn in the twentieth century will necessarily be an industrial overturn; and by the same token, any twentieth century revolution can be combated or neutralized only by industrial ways and means.

In this respect, *The Engineers and the Price System is* squarely in the center of the preoccupation that has attended the rise of sociology since its beginnings in the nineteenth century: namely, the scanning of the historical skies for portents of "the new class" which will overturn the existing social order. Henri de Saint-Simon, the master of Auguste Comte and one of the fathers of modern sociology, initiated this quest in 1816, when he began publishing an irregular periodical, *L'Industrie* (though he did not actually coin it, he popularized the term *industrialism),* which sought to describe the society of the future. Past society, Saint-Simon said, had been military society, in which the chief figures were priests, warriors, and feudal lords—"the parasites" and consumers of wealth. The new industrial society, he said, would be ruled by the producers—the engineers and the entrepreneurs, the "coming men" of the times.[1] Karl Marx, of course, made the confrontation of capitalist and worker the central figure of his drama of modern history, but already in his time, some of Marx's opponents, such as Mikhail Bakunin and Alexander Herzen, were warning the workers that the victory of socialism would lead not to a classless society but to the emergence of a new class, the intellectuals ruling in the name of the workers.[2] The identity of this new class has been central to the elitist sociology of Mosca, Michels, and Pareto. James Burnham achieved a flash of notoriety in the early 1940s with his theme (a vulgarization of the work of two European syndicalists, Waclaw Machajski and Bruno Rizzi) of "the managerial revolution" as the coming stage of collectivist society. In American sociology, Harold Lasswell has written (most notably in his *World Politics and Personal Insecurity)* of the "skill groups" that must inevitably dominate any future society.

And in this regard Veblen, too, must be ranked on the side of the elitists. *If* a revolution were to come about in the United States—as a practiced skeptic, he was highly dubious of that prospect—it would not be led by a minority political party, as in Soviet Russia, which was a loose-knit and backward industrial region, nor would it come from the trade-union "votaries of the dinner pail," who, as a vested interest themselves, simply sought to keep prices up and labor supply down. It would occur, he said, along the lines "already laid down by the material conditions of its productive industry." And, turning this Marxist prism to his own perceptions, Veblen continued: "These main lines of revolutionary strategy are lines of technical organization and industrial management; essentially lines of industrial engineering; such as will fit the organization to take care of the highly technical industrial system that constitutes the indispensable material foundation of any modern civilized community."

The heart of Veblen's assessment of the revolutionary class is thus summed up in his identification of the "production engineers" as the indispensable "General Staff of the industrial system."

> Without their immediate and unremitting guidance and correction the industrial system will not work. It is a mechanically organized structure of the technical processes designed, installed and conducted by the production engineers. Without them and their constant attention the industrial equipment, the mechanical appliances of industry, will foot up to just so much junk.

Thus the intellectual commitment was made: "The chances of anything like a Soviet in America, therefore, are the chances of a Soviet of technicians" although, as was his wont, Veblen immediately backs off by remarking that "anything like a Soviet of Technicians is at the most a remote contingency in America." Given his style of exaggerated circumlocution and deliberate indirection, this is, at best, what we can pin Veblen down to saying: *If* a revolution ever could come about in the United States, a revolution that would break the power of the vested interests, it would come from the engineers, who have a true motive for revolution—since the requirements of profit-making must traduce their calling—and who have the strategic position and the means to carry through a revolution.

In a curious way, all of this represented a radical departure for Veblen. Before 1919 he had paid little attention to the engineers, though one of the persistent themes of his major work, *The Theory of Business Enterprise, is* the inherent conflict between "business," the financial interests who are concerned primarily with profit, and "industry," those forces which are geared to production. His fundamental concept, the idea of the "machine process," implied that because of the rationality of the machine a new race of men was being bred who replaced rule-of-thumb methods or intuitive skills with reasoned procedures based on the discipline of science. Yet he had never before tied these themes to the engineer. Typically, Veblen always left his concepts magnificently abstract, or he skillfully played the game of personification (e.g., "the captains of industry"), in which the social role rather than the person was manifest. Now, in 1919, Veblen seemingly made a basic sociological commitment—the identification of a concrete social group as the force that could, and possibly would, reshape society.

The postwar period was a critical one in Veblen's life, and the books he wrote at this time, *The Vested Interests and the State of the Industrial Arts* and *The Engineers and the Price System,* bear a somewhat different relation to his purposes than does the rest of his work. It would be too much to say that Veblen in this period had hopes of becoming a revolutionary leader; this was out of keeping with his dour personality and the heavy personal armor with which he kept most of the world, and even his friends, at a distance. But it does seem to be the case that at this time Veblen suddenly felt that he might become a prophet (he had always been an oracle, and his writings were suitably Delphic) who would rouse the latent forces of change in America. And among these forces—or so he was led to believe by some of his disciples—were the engineers.

The Academic Floater

In 1919, at the age of sixty-two, Veblen had begun a new life, although two years earlier it had seemed that his career was at an end.[3] Less than twenty years before, he had written his first book, *The Theory of the Leisure Class* (having had to guarantee almost all the costs of publication himself), and this book, largely through the efforts of William Dean Howells, had gained him widespread attention. His second book, *The Theory of Business Enterprise,* published in 1904, won him the even more intense admiration of an eager group of young economists. But "professionally" this farm-boy son of Norwegian immigrants was a "failure."

Throughout his life, Veblen was unable to find a permanent niche in the academic hierarchy. Although he had completed his Ph.D. at Yale at the age of twenty-seven (itself a remarkable achievement, considering the fact that he spoke almost no English until he entered the preparatory division of Carleton College, when he was seventeen), Veblen did not get his first academic job until he was thirty-five, when J. Lawrence Laughlin, with whom he had studied economics at Cornell, took him along to the nascent University of Chicago as a Fellow. Veblen stayed at the University of Chicago for fourteen years, but the administration regarded him with a cold eye (as much for his amatory difficulties as for his economic heresies), and he never rose higher than an assistant professorship, despite his publishing the aforementioned books, editing the *Journal of Political Economy,* and writing half a dozen major essays, including those on Karl Marx and socialist economics, reprinted in *The Place of Science in Modern Civilization.*

In 1906, Veblen was offered a post as associate professor of economics at Stanford University by David Starr Jordan, who was trying to strengthen the school's academic reputation. For the first time, Veblen had an opportunity to move up the academic ladder, but his stay at Stanford University was dismal. Veblen was indifferent about his courses and uninterested in his students, and, to cap it all, he got involved in an adulterous episode that became a campus scandal. In December of 1909 he was forced to resign his post.[4] For a year Veblen was unable to find another job, and then, through the intervention of a former student, H.J. Davenport, he was invited to the University of Missouri as a lecturer.

For seven years Veblen suffered the small-town oppressiveness of Columbia, Missouri. He tried desperately to leave, going so far as to apply to the Library of Congress for a routine bibliographical position—he was turned down as being too bright for the job. During the dispirited years at Missouri, Veblen's output slackened. He wrote *The Instinct of Workmanship,* an uneven book that reflects more sharply than any of his others the evolutionary anthropology that guided his viewpoint, and (after a summer in Europe in 1914) *Imperial Germany and the Industrial Revolution,* a brilliant account of the way German feudal culture had grafted a highly advanced technology on the society in order to promote dynastic ends.

In 1917, by "mutual consent," Veblen took a leave of absence from the University of Missouri to go to Washington; he never returned to formal academic life. A year later he celebrated his departure by publishing *The Higher Learning in America,* whose subtitle, "A Memorandum on the Conduct of the Universities by Businessmen," only hints at its savage indictment of higher education. (The manuscript, written a few years before he left Missouri, had been withheld from publication at the suggestion of the university's president; its original subtitle had been "A Study in Total Depravity.")

The war itself engaged all of Veblen's attention and energy. His stay in Germany and his tolerance of Woodrow Wilson (not his faith in Wilson, since Veblen was incapable of any such commitment) led him to support the Allied cause. He believed, moreover, that the war not only would demonstrate the requirements of rational planning, because of the need to mobilize total capacity, but would allow the victorious Allied nations to make an attempt at social reconstruction. In 1916, working at feverish speed, Veblen had written *An Inquiry into the Nature of Peace and the Terms of Its Perpetuation* (published largely at his own expense), which expounded these ideas. Making a distinction between democratic and dynastic governments, Veblen noted that in the latter the survival of "barbarian" impulses made them consistently more aggressive and warlike; "perpetual peace," he concluded, could be maintained not only by finally disposing of all monarchic regimes, but by eliminating everywhere "the price-system and its attendant business enterprise"—Veblen's euphemism for capitalism.

The book came out at a propitious psychological moment. By the spring of 1917, when *The Nature of the Peace* was published, virtually the entire intelligentsia of the progressive movement (Herbert Croly, Walter Lippmann, John Dewey) as well as the intellectual leaders of the Socialist party (William English Walling, John Spargo, A. M. Simons, Jack London, Upton Sinclair) were supporting America's entry into the war and repudiating their earlier anti-war stands.[5] *The Nature of the Peace* allowed the intelligentsia both to justify their attitude against German militarism and to hope for the emergence of a new rational society after the war. The book was an immediate success, and was praised in all the liberal magazines. Francis Hackett, an editor of the *New Republic,* which was the organ of the progressive intelligentsia, called it "the most momentous work in English on the encompassment of lasting peace," and the Carnegie Endowment for International Peace purchased five hundred copies for distribution in colleges and universities. Veblen quickly became an international figure, and letters were written to him from all parts of the world. "Now," he said, "they are beginning to pay some attention to me."

It was in this mood that, in October 1917, Veblen went to Washington. As his biographer, Joseph Dorfman, remarks, "He wanted to be at the centre of things, and he hoped that he could be made use of on the paramount questions of the plans for peace." He saw Newton

D. Baker, the secretary of war, and Supreme Court Justice Louis D. Brandeis, but no one in a high position was interested in Veblen's ideas. He was invited to submit some memoranda to a group (whose secretary was Walter Lippmann, then of the *New Republic*) that had been set up by Wilson's confidant, Colonel Edward M. House, to prepare material on the terms of a possible peace settlement. One of Veblen's two memoranda discussed the problem of creating a "League of Pacific Peoples"; the other, on the "Economic Penetration of Backward Countries and of Foreign Investments," proposed the regulation of investment by the "Pacific League." Both were duly filed, but Veblen, discouraged, took a job with the statistical division of the Food Administration, where, with the aid of Isadore Lubin, he prepared a study of price control on foodstuffs.

Meanwhile Veblen's books, with their cool, sardonic tone, were getting its author into trouble. Although the Committee on Information, an official propaganda agency, praised his *Imperial Germany,* the Post Office Department, which was in charge of censorship, declared the book nonmailable under the Espionage Act. The American Defense Society and other jingoist groups complained to the Department of Justice about Veblen's attitude in *The Nature of the Peace* and *Imperial Germany* (complained, that is, about its mocking treatment of the democracies).

> The book was read by an agent of the department who, although he could not understand Veblen's vocabulary, found the programme for the punishing of Germany so far ahead of anything that had been proposed by the entente, that he concluded that Veblen was a superpatriot, and refused to pay any attention to the complaints.[6]

The University of Missouri was behind him, his fruitless work with the Food Administration had ended, and Veblen was again without a job. Negotiations with Cornell University came to nothing. Two of his former students, Walton Hamilton and Walter Stewart, arranged for Veblen to give a series of lectures at Amherst in May 1918, and shortly afterward Jett Lauck, another former student, who was executive secretary of the War Labor Board, offered Veblen a job with the board as an examiner, at $4,800 a year—ironically, higher than any academic salary he had ever received. Veblen at first agreed to take the job, but when through the intervention of Horace Kallen he was invited to join the editorial board of *The Dial,* he gladly accepted. *The Dial* was to be the occasion of a short but significant new phase in his life.

Postwar Disillusionment

In June 1918, Veblen moved to New York and joined *The Dial.* The magazine had an old and honorable name in American letters. The first *Dial* had been founded by Ralph Waldo Emerson and Margaret Fuller, in 1840, and was the parent of all the hundreds of little magazines that followed. Like many of its progeny, the original *Dial* had a short but brilliant life. Failing to gain more than three hundred subscribers, it suspended publication in 1844. In 1880, a Chicago publisher revived the name and continued to publish it as a sedate fortnightly review; in 1916 it was reorganized by Martyn Johnson as a literary journal with a staff consisting of Conrad Aiken, Randolphe Bourne, Padraic Colum and Van Wyck Brooks.[7] Two years later, under the influence of one of its owners, Helen Marot, a liberal woman who had written *American Labor Unions, by a Member, Helen Marot,* the magazine announced its removal to New York and a broadening of its scope to include "internationalism and a program of reconstruction in industry and education." The editors were to be John Dewey, Thorstein Veblen, Helen Marot, and George Donlin,[8] and the magazine set out to compete directly with *The Nation* and *The New Republic.* Veblen, clearly, was its star.

His experiences in Washington had left him bitter and resentful. The extraordinary thing was that he had lived his entire life, if not in an ivory tower, at least in its academic banlieus; and his protective tone of irony, his superior gamesmanship in the mimetic combat of pedantry, had not really prepared him to operate in the bureaucratic labyrinths of power. As David Riesman remarks:

> In all this, Veblen appears to have been somewhat naive to assume that an elderly professor, inexperienced in practical affairs, would be eagerly welcomed, even by sympathizers in office. He expected miracles from the War itself—and possibly also as a result of his own willingness to come out, at long last, from behind his shell.[9]

A woman spurned in love turns to reform as a second choice; a man scorned by power often turns to revolution. Veblen had always been subversive in his verbal irony; now, in the next two years, from 1919 to 1921, he began to entertain hopes, always somewhat masked, of becoming an active political force. A sense of revolutionary excitement was in the air and Veblen responded to it strongly. Writing as a journalist for the general public, he slashed out, more overtly than he ever had before, at the "vested interests" and their control of industry. He became intensely interested in the Russian Revolution (though he was never active in the "worker's soviet" formed at *The Dial* in the summer of 1919!); and in an article in *The Dial,* "Bolshevism Is a Menace—to Whom?" Veblen interpreted Bolshevism simply as the carrying of the principle of democracy into industry, or as just another name for the industrial republic.

More than that, Veblen was becoming popular, even something of a fad. *The Theory of the Leisure Class* had been reissued; it was approved by *Vanity Fair,* the magazine of the sophisticates, and had become required reading in intellectual circles.[10] The essays in *The Dial* were widely read, although an old friend of Veblen's, Walton Hamilton, felt that as a journalist Veblen the agitator and phrasemaker was taking precedence over the thinker. Reviewing in the *New Republic* the first group of essays, published in book form as *The Vested Interests,* Hamilton remarked that even though readers would take over the phrases—in many cases they were quite imponderable when analyzed—sympathizers would get more "psychic income than intellectual ammunition from the volume."

But Veblen's savage mood reflected accurately the combination of postwar disillusionment, revolutionary anger, nihilism, and dadaism that was dominating the intellectual circles, and he, in turn, responded to these currents.[11]

It was during this period, too, that Veblen wrote one of his most incisive essays, "The Intellectual Pre-Eminence of Jews in Modern Europe" (in the *Political Science Quarterly* of March 1919),[12] which is at the same time a revealing self-portrait of the Norwegian farm boy who had left his own hermetic culture. The intellectually gifted Jew, he wrote, like other men in a similar position, secures immunity from intellectual quietism

at the cost of losing his secure place in the scheme of conventions into which he has been born, and…of finding no similarly secure place in the scheme of gentile conventions into which he is thrown.… He becomes a disturber of the intellectual peace, but only at the cost of becoming an intellectual wayfaring man, a wanderer in the intellectual No Man's Land, seeking another place to rest, farther along the road, somewhere over the horizon. They are neither a complaisant nor a contented lot, these aliens of the uneasy feet.

In April 1919, Veblen began a new series in *The Dial,* on "Contemporary Problems in Reconstruction," which, according to an announcement in the magazine, was intended to be "a concrete application of [Veblen's] theory, outlined in *The Modern Point of View and the New Order.*"[13] These essays, later brought out in book form, became *The Engineers and the Price System.*

The heart of the book is in the last three essays. The first three sketch themes Veblen had already discussed in previous writings, although at this point he singled out the investment banker rather than the corporation head as the dominant figure in economic life ("regulating the rate and volume of output" in industrial enterprises under his control); and the old corporation financier is no longer a captain of industry but a lieutenant of finance. Specifically the last three essays, beginning with the chapter "On the Danger of a Revolutionary Overturn," represent a political departure from his earlier work.

These essays were written at the height of the "red scare," the drum-fire campaign initiated by Attorney General A. Mitchell Palmer, which included wholesale roundups of suspected radicals, raids on various radical meetings (including the breakup of the underground convention of the nascent Communist party in Bridgman, Michigan), and the deportation of anarchists. Against the same threat of revolution, about twenty states began passing criminal syndicalist laws, which made advocacy, rather than acts, of violence a crime.

Veblen's essays, as Dorfman has noted, were "conspicuous for their recklessness and their savage use of inverted meaning." Bolshevism, Veblen says, is the danger that

> the Vested Interests are facing," and "the Elder Statesmen are…in a position to know, without much inquiry, that there is no single spot or corner in civilized Europe, or America, where the underlying population would have anything to lose by such an overturn of the established order as would cancel the vested rights of privilege and property, whose guardian they are.

Some observers, continued Veblen, foresee a revolutionary overturn in two years; others, less intimately acquainted with the facts, predict a later date. Veblen, tongue in cheek, constantly reiterates that the Guardians of the Vested Interests have nothing to fear, but in each case the statement carries the sly addition "just yet." It is in this context that Veblen began to write of the engineers in words which seemed to say, "And now, I hear the tocsin of revolution, and it cannot be far away."

Hitherto these men, who so make up the general staff of the industrial system, have not drawn together into anything like a self-directing working force [he writes. *But*] Right lately these technologists have begun to become uneasily "class-conscious" and to reflect that they together constitute the indispensable General Staff of the industrial system. Their class consciousness has taken the immediate form of a growing sense of waste and confusion in the management of industry by the financial agents of the absentee owners.... So the engineers are beginning to draw together and ask themselves, "What about it?"

In all this, Veblen's mode of calculated ambiguity and abstracted specification heightens the tension, building up hints of an extraordinary ground swell among the engineers. But no persons are ever identified, no groups are ever named. In pointing to the sources of unrest, Veblen refers generally to "the consulting engineer" and "the management expert" who, in appraising the efficiency of business enterprises for the investment banker, have come to understand the "pervading lag, lack and friction" in the industrial system; and to the "younger generation," trained in the "stubborn logic of technology," who are "beginning to draw together on a common ground of understanding."

And yet it was Veblen, and not the Guardians of the Vested Interests, who was deceived. The movement that he thought was a "class-conscious effort" by engineers to end the "all-pervading mismanagement of industry" was, in its most immediate organizational thrust, an attempt to give engineers a distinct "professional" status in society. In its extremely vague import, it was a chimerical "technocratic eudaemonism" which resembled, if it resembled anything at all, Plato's *Republic,* but ruled by the engineer rather than the philosopher.

The "movement," if it can even be characterized by that term, was largely the work of two men, Morris L. Cooke and Henry Gantt. And, such is the comedy of the thing, it represented not a revolutionary dissenting group, but an effort by messianic disciples of Frederick W. Taylor, the "father" of scientific management, to extend Taylor's ideas, as they understood them, to American society at large.

The Gospel of Efficiency

Frederick W. Taylor, a fascinating, if nowadays neglected, figure was indisputably the shaper of "modern" capitalism. If any social upheaval can ever be attributed to a single person, the logic of efficiency as the rule of contemporary life is due to him. For what he did was to establish the principle and methods for the rationalization of work. But Taylor was more than an engineer. In his own mind's eye, he was a prophet who felt that he had discovered the "scientific principles" that would settle all social conflicts.[14]

This *éclaircissement* began when Taylor in 1882, then working as a mechanical engineer at the Midvale Steel Company in Philadelphia, became discouraged by the fact that the workmen he directed refused to work as fast as he thought they should. The solution, he felt, lay in the fact that no one knew what constituted a "fair day's work," and one reason was that not even management had any notion of a man's capacity, the fatigue a specific job engendered, the pace at which a man should work, the number of pieces that could be turned out in a specified period of time, or the speed at which any particular set of operations should take place. Out of Taylor's reflections (and his own compulsive character) came the idea of scientific time study and, more broadly, the measurement of work—for it is with the measurement of work and the idea of unit costs, rather than with the introduction of the factory as such, that modern industry gains distinctive meaning as a new way of life—and, following this, the practice of scientific management.

Taylor's principles were based upon the following: the time it takes to do a specific job; incentives and bonus systems for exceeding norms; differential rates of pay based on job evaluation; the standardization of tools and equipment; the fitting of men to jobs on the basis of physical and mental tests; and the removal of all planning and scheduling from the work floor itself into a new planning and scheduling department, a new superstructure, the responsibility for which was in the hands of the engineer. By setting "scientific" standards, Taylor felt that he could specify the "one best way" or the "natural laws" of work, and so remove the basic source of antagonism between worker and employer—what is "fair" or "unfair."[15]

Morris L. Cooke, one of the two men Veblen had in mind when he spoke of the "uneasy...sense of waste and confusion" felt by the "General Staff of the industrial system," was a Philadelphia-born mechanical engineer who, while working in a number of shipyards before the turn of the century, was "sickened by the heartlessness on the part of the employers" and the "inefficiency on the part of the workers."[16] Discovering the work of Frederick W. Taylor while he was in this mood, Cooke responded like a religious convert.

To Cooke, and to many other young engineers, Taylor's ideas were excitingly "progressive," and the standpat resistance of turn-of-the-century industry to these innovations only reinforced their fervor. Moreover, Cooke and the others felt that such a conception of the engineer gave him a new professional status and that crucial recognition which hitherto he had been denied. Even further, Cooke was lured, as were other engineers, by Taylor's gospel declaration that "the same principles [of scientific management] can be applied with equal force to all social activities: to the management of our homes; the management of our farms; the management of the business of our tradesmen large and small; of our churches, our philanthropic institutions, our universities, and our governmental departments."[17] In effect, the engineer was to be the hierophant of the new society.

About 1910, when Taylor's ideas were beginning to catch on rapidly, hundreds of persons proclaimed themselves "efficiency engineers," promising to install his "system" in half the two to four years' time Taylor had felt necessary for the conversion of a plant. The prophet of scientific management openly announced that only four engineers were authorized to teach his theories. "They were men who had worked with him intimately and knew his every thought and wish." These four were C. G. Barth, H. K. Hathaway, Morris L. Cooke, and Henry L. Gantt. "Taylor let it be known that these four only had his blessing and that all others were operating on their own."[18]

Henry L. Gantt had been Taylor's chief assistant in the early experiments at the Midvale Steel Plant and later at the Bethlehem Steel Company. Later, he became an independent consulting engineer, installing the Taylor system into many different factories and earning the enmity of the American Federation of Labor, which, in 1914, had opened a campaign against "scientific management." In 1916, a year after Taylor's death, Gantt became the spokesman of a new technocratic orientation. Under the influence of Veblen, whose works he had begun to read, and of Charles Ferguson, an engineer and "an eccentric social gospeller, who wanted to reform business in order to develop its spiritual potentialities,"[19] Gantt founded an organization called the New Machine. Gantt attacked the incompetence of the "financiers" and argued that the community should not have to bear the costs of such inefficiency. He assumed that the business system was going to collapse, and that the ground had to be prepared for his successor. In one of his essays, Gantt declared, "We can no longer follow the lead of those who have axes to grind, disregarding economic laws; but must accord leadership to him who knows what to do and how to do it for the benefit of the community. This man is the engineer."[20]

The New Machine, however, was never a formal organization. It held a few discussion meetings which brought together about thirty-five interested engineers, but its only official act was to send a letter, in February 1917, to President Wilson, arguing that the industrial system would grow "only through a progressive elimination of plutocracy and all other forms of arbitrary power." Most of the group was quickly involved in war work, including Gantt, who, working with the Ordnance Department, produced the famous Gantt Charts, a graphical analysis designed to permit quick and easy understanding of the state of production at any given time, and the New Machine lay dormant. Gantt, who never met Veblen, though he was friendly with Veblen's disciple, Leon Ardzrooni, was thus one of the chief sources of Veblen's idea of the impending revolutionary consciousness of the engineers.

Morris L. Cooke, whom Veblen did meet, was the other chief source, and it was Cooke's effort to reform the American Society for Mechanical Engineers that Veblen mistook for a new "class conscious" activity.[21] In 1905, when Frederick W. Taylor became president of the Society, he asked Cooke to conduct an analysis of its affairs and reorganize its procedures in accordance with the principles of scientific management. At this same time, Cooke began to realize that the Society was dominated by engineers employed by big business firms and the public utilities. In 1911, he became director of public works for the city of Philadelphia, as part of a reform administration. Seeking to examine the electric rates charged the city by the private utilities, Cooke was outraged to discover that while these utilities were able to enlist the services of the most eminent members of the engineering profession, almost no prominent engineer was willing to act as a consultant for the city.

In 1915, Cooke was elected a vice-president of the A.S.M.E. and became the leader of a faction seeking to reform the organization. He attacked the Society's ties with the corporations, charging that the professional status of the engineers was being compromised by their subordination to big business. By 1919, Cooke had succeeded. The A.S.M.E. was reorganized to sever its ties with business and trade associations, and a new code of ethics was adopted, which stated that the first professional obligation of the engineer was to the standards of his profession, not to his employer. Thus, the ferment within the American Society of Mechanical Engineers, and some of Cooke's papers that led to the reorganization of the Society, provided another source for Veblen's memorandum about the "Soviet of Technicians."

Veblen had been introduced to the writings of Cooke and Gantt by a friend at Stanford University, Guido Marx, who was a professor of machine design. Cooke supplied Marx with copies of his papers, and probably of Gantt's as well; Marx, who had kept up a correspondence with Veblen, in turn sent them on to him. It seems clear that, in the heightened political excitement of the day, Veblen not only had some literary plans about the engineers, but that he—or his disciples— also nursed some vague expectations of actually inspiring a new movement that would look to him for prophetic leadership.

In the fall of 1919, Veblen left *The Dial,* which, in the course of reorganization, had become a literary magazine, and he joined the faculty of the newly founded New School for Social Research. The New School was an experiment in higher education. It set out to maintain postgraduate standards in the character of its courses, but to dispense with degrees, ceremonials, professional hierarchies, and other trappings of academe. It assembled a distinguished faculty, which, besides Veblen, included Charles A. Beard, James Harvey Robinson, Wesley Clair Mitchell (all of whom resigned from Columbia University), and some other distinguished American figures in the social sciences.

When the New School began to function, Veblen was writing his series of articles on the "Soviet of Technicians." As Dorfman puts it, "He had become obsessed with the important role of the technician, and felt that the New School provided the opportunity and headquarters for the group he planned." In October of that year, Veblen wrote to Guido Marx, stating that

> it is an intimate part of the ambitions of the New School to come into touch with the technical men who have to do with the country's industry, and know something about the state of things and the needs of industry. At the same time, he continued, " the younger generation among the technicians appear to be getting uneasy on their own account…and are loosely drawing together, and entering on an inquiry into the industrial conditions and speculating on a way out of the current muddle."

In sum, Veblen asked Marx to come to New York to give a course at the New School, and to help in the direction of an industrial inquiry. Actually, Veblen saw Marx as a potential leader of these "young engineers." The suggestion was made directly to Marx by Leon Ardzrooni, Veblen's amanuensis, who was on the faculty of the New School. In December, Ardzrooni wrote to Marx:

The situation is this: I have been hobnobbing with some of the members of the A.S.M.E. and find that they are very much upset about the present industrial muddle throughout the country. Some of them, with the connivance of certain prominent newspaper men, had nearly perfected plans to get together and discuss matters, under the guidance of H.L. Gantt. They are all convinced that there is something wrong somewhere, but they are still groping and need proper leadership. As you have probably heard, Gantt died quite recently, and, in speaking about the plans of these engineers, I told them we had in you the proper leader and, in case it was possible for you to come to New York, you could meet with them once a week, or oftener, and talk things over.[22]

Marx assumed that some large movement was under way, and modestly suggested that Morris Cooke would be the more logical person to replace Gantt as the leader of engineers, but Ardzrooni "preferred Marx, doubtlessly because he was already something of a convert to Veblenism."[23] Marx came to New York, and found, as he put it, that "no mature members of the A.S.M.E. appeared in the picture." A man named Howard Scott appeared proclaiming himself to be an engineer, but as Marx observed, "I could not believe he was a trained technician, his use of technical terms being highly inaccurate and his thought processes, to my mind, lacking in logical structure and being basically unrealistic." A conference was organized by Marx ("in line with what I thought would best fulfill Veblen's plans") bringing together some of the new leaders of the A.S M.E. (including Colonel Fred J. Miller, the president, and Cooke) and some of the New School faculty, but after a desultory session nothing further came of any proposed collaboration. Apparently Veblen continued to see Cooke, in particular to discuss a Giant Power Survey being undertaken by the engineers, but as Cooke remarked, "I must say that all my contacts with him were rather tenuous because he struck me as a man who was almost too frail for any kind of contacts. He was a bully good counsellor, but only as to theory. There was too little physique there to help on action."[24]

This seems to have been the sum total of all those dark hints about the emerging class-consciousness of the "indispensable General Staff of the industrial system." Marx returned to California; Howard Scott organized a pretentious Technical Alliance, with himself listed as chief engineer, and a temporary organizing committee which included such personages as the architect Frederick Ackerman, the electrical engineers Bassett Jones and Charles Steinmetz, and some younger economists (Leland Olds and Stuart Chase), as well as Veblen (though, as Ardzrooni noted in a letter to Marx, enclosing the prospectus, "I have learned that most men whose names...appear here [including

Veblen] were never consulted or informed of any meeting.").

In February 1921, *The Engineers and the Price System* appeared in book form. The country was on its way back to normalcy. The American Society of Mechanical Engineers had settled down into its conservative groove. A similar reorganization had taken place in the American Institute of Mining Engineers, and its leader, Herbert Hoover, had become the national spokesman for all the insurgent engineers. (Cooke, who felt that Hoover was the "engineering method personified," had in 1919 endorsed Hoover for the Republican presidential nomination.)[25] There was little to indicate that a Soviet of technicians was in the offing. Curiously, though, Veblen let his words stand as written, with no editorial revision or foreword. And so it stands, a record of misunderstanding.

Veblen's remaining life was a sorry epilogue to these disappointed hopes of establishing his intellectual leadership in the country. In 1922, the New School was drastically overhauled and, of the "Big Four," Beard, Mitchell, and Robinson resigned. Veblen wanted to leave, but had nowhere to go. Efforts to find him a job in the city universities proved unsuccessful. His last major book, *Absentee Ownership,* was proving to be a grueling effort, and, as Dorfman writes, "he resorted more often than before to Roget's *Thesaurus."* The book, which picks up and elaborates more directly the arguments of *The Theory of Business Enterprise* of two decades before, was only indifferently received—the conservatives felt that the prevailing prosperity seemed to refute Veblen's argument, and the radicals were annoyed because Veblen had asserted that "the standard formalities of 'Socialism' and 'Anti-Socialism' are obsolete in the face of the new alignment of economic forces."

His appointment at the New School having come to an end, for the next few years Veblen lived on small stipends contributed by a former student and, for a while, on some "winnings" from a quixotic foray in the stock market. He neglected economic writing, and as "one of the things men do, when they grow old," he remarked, he turned back to the Norse tales and completed the translation of *The Laxdaela Saga,* which he had begun thirty-seven years before. After the death of his first wife, Ellen Rolfe, in 1926, Veblen returned to California to live at his absentee properties in Stanford. New investments proved a failure, and Veblen, anxious about money, was supported by the generosity of his friends. On August 3, 1929, he died of heart failure.

Veblen, the Utopian

The Engineers and the Price System is a "short course" in the Veblenian system, and it can serve as a simplified introduction to his ideas. Veblen always felt the need in all his writings to start from "first principles" (since these were so much at variance with classical economics), and so almost all his books after *The Theory of the Leisure Class* seem inordinately repetitious. But if they are read in sequence, one can discern a spiral in which themes set forth in earlier books are picked up and elaborated as the basis for further argument. Thus the opening chapter of *The Engineers and the Price System* begins with a tongue-in-cheek account of "sabotage," a word hitherto used to describe the tactics of the radical syndicalists, but which Veblen defines as the restriction of output practiced by business in order to maintain levels of profit. This thesis, already set forth in *The Theory of the Business Enterprise,* Veblen now ties in with the role of the investment banker, whom he regards, in his postwar analysis, as the key figure in the organization pooling system of the Federal Reserve; the investment banker becomes not only the stabilizer of the business system but also the figure who, in his effort to inflate values and restrict production, is responsible for business cycles and depressions. Thus the tension between nonutilized capacity and restriction becomes the central motif of the book and the basis for Veblen's conviction that if the engineer were to take over the direction of American society, there would be "the due allocation of resources and a consequent full and reasonably proportioned employment of the available equipment and manpower" of society.

There is much in *The Engineers and the Price System* that is surprisingly accurate and relevant to the present-day American economy. The 1958 Kefauver Committee reports on "administered prices" in the steel and auto industries read like a gloss of the opening chapter in Veblen's book.[26] His wry comments on "salesmanship," the argument that salesmanship is a substitute for price reduction ("It is the chief factor in the ever-increasing cost of living, which is in its turn the chief ground of prosperity among the business community...") still has a telling bite. And the discussion, in Chapter 2, of the cumulative "state of the industrial arts" as one of the chief contributions to progress (as against the older emphasis, in classical economics, on land, labor, and money capital as the co-ordinates of production) points up the increasing concern today with education, or "human capital," as the basic resource for technological and productive advance in society. The neglected point Veblen makes is that technology (the "state of the industrial arts") is a joint stock of knowledge derived from past experience—a social asset, which is no man's or no firm's individual property, though it is often claimed as such.

But his reiterated emphasis on technology also reveals the one-sidedness, or inadequacy, of the Veblenian system. He was indifferent to the social relations within the factory—both the elements that created bureaucracy and those that, as in the case of the engineers, made for insistence on professional status as one means of overcoming the impersonality that the rationalization of work imposes on modern life.[27] In his concentration on the machinations of credit, Veblen slighted the imaginative social invention that is the "fiction" of credit. If one looks at the nature of capital accumulation in a historical perspective, credit, a nineteenth-century device, is a "due bill" on the future, an expression of faith (necessarily based on political stability) in the growth of an economy; through such a lien on the future, one is able to employ resources that normally would have lain fallow. Credit thus becomes, as Schumpeter has pointed out, the basis for entrepreneurial activity.

Veblen's proposal to do away with the price system reveals a naive notion of planning—akin to Marx's idea that the interest rate is merely an exploitative device, rather than an instrument to test the efficiency of capital, and has no place in a socialist economy. It is evident that direct physical planning of production (as in the experience of the American War Production Board during the Second World War, or the Soviet system of a "mobilized economy") can rapidly increase the output of a *few* final products—regardless of cost—to an astonishing extent. But it is also equally evident that any complex planning mechanism seeking to distribute resources efficiently (i.e., to assess relative costs) in the production of tens of thousands of *different* products can do so best, as even the socialist economies have discovered, only through a price system.

And, finally, the idea that revolution in the twentieth century can only be an "industrial overturn"—itself a syndicalist idea—underscores the "rationalist fallacy" that lies behind so much of Veblen's thought. No matter how increasingly technical the underlying social processes become—and in the advanced industrial countries, with the rise of computer technology and its consequent effect on the labor force, this process is rapid indeed—social change, at bottom, is a *political* decision; or rather, the crucial turning points in a society are ultimately determined not by crescive social changes, but only as these changes come to a head in some political form. Thus, in the case of the United States, the Veblenian analysis, because it is essentially *apolitical,* neglects the role of government, or of the federal budget, as the crucial determinant of economic growth and social power.

To generalize the concerns of a political sociology: in the advanced industrial, as well as in the newly industrializing, societies it is the military and political forces that remain the "movers and shakers" of change.

In all this—in his evolutionary schemes, his emphasis on the economics of production, his savage critiques of commerce and money (as well as in his neglect of other forces)—Veblen betrays his true intellectual lineage, one that his involuted style was successfully able to obscure.[28] This ancestry is not Marxist (in an effort to assert his own originality, one of the few forebears that Veblen attacks by name is Marx), but the utopian socialism of Fourier and Saint-Simon. The parallels with Fourier in Veblen's writing are astonishing. To show his contempt for the academic learning of his time, Fourier phrased the system he recapitulated endlessly in his various works in a set of neologisms that were deliberately meant to be incomprehensible to the laity. ("Fourier was conscious of the fact that he was pouring forth a torrent of newfangled words, and in his manuscripts he occasionally indulged in facetious self-mockery on this account. 'Hola, another neologism! Haro on the guilty one! but is this any worse than *doctrinaire?*'")[29] Fourier's description of the earlier stages of society as *savagery* and *barbarism* were taken up by Veblen in *The Theory of the Leisure Class.* And Fourier's indictment of capitalism—the *locus classicus* of such criticism, as Professor Manuel points out—concentrates on the thievery in the stock market, the "corruption of commerce," the miseries of economic crises, hoarding and speculation and the squandering of natural resources as all being endemic to the system.

Perhaps the most binding link between Veblen and the French Utopians is their two-fold view of society based on the pre-eminent virtue of production as the basic "good." For Fourier, as it was to be for Saint-Simon and, in his own way, for Veblen, those persons not directly connected with production—soldiers, bureaucrats, merchants, and lawyers—were parasites who lived at the expense of the producers.[30] (Veblen insisted that the elimination of salesmanship and all its voluminous apparatus and traffic would cut down the capitalized income of the business community by half.) And Saint-Simon, who constantly harped on the social waste, maladjustment, and friction produced in a nonrational society, felt that a "natural elite"—in his view, the men of science—would come to the fore in the inevitable development of the industrial order.[31]

The distinction between productive and unproductive labor, between industrial and pecuniary employments, runs as a peculiar thread through the writings of the Utopians, as it does through Veblen's[32] and reflects at bottom the hatred—and fear—felt by the artisan mentality toward metropolitan life. What Veblen disliked about capitalism, as T. W. Adorno has shrewdly pointed out, was not its exploitation of the people but its waste of goods; and, like Frederick W. Taylor, he disliked every "superfluous" action. In the end, falling back on the "instinct of workmanship" as the basic virtue, Veblen the technocrat longed for the restoration of "the most ancient." It is the final irony, as Adorno indicates, "that in Veblen faith in Utopia necessarily takes the form which he so vigorously condemns in middle class society, the form of retrogression or 'reversion.' Hope, for him, lies solely with the primitive history of mankind. Every happiness barred to him because of the pressures of dreamless adjustment and adaptation to reality, to the conditions of the industrial world, shows him its image In some early golden age of mankind."[33]

Central to all this—to return to our earlier theme of the new class— is the elitist image, which was given its most mechanical shape in the doctrines of technocracy. Most of Veblen's admirers have sought to discredit the similarities[34] but the resemblance is clear, and while Veblen's doctrines cannot be held accountable for the later phase of technocracy—which flared again briefly in 1940 as a quasi-fascist movement, replete with gray uniforms and a monad symbol—the "elective affinity" between Veblenianism and technocracy is evident not only in the formal content of the ideas but in the temperamental derivatives: the qualities of inhuman scientism and formal rationalism, which in the end become an attack upon culture itself.

The central feature of contemporary life is bureaucracy—that vast cobweb of rules and procedures which lays down "rational" grades or levels of accomplishments and orderly prescriptions of conduct as the defined steps for rising or finding a place in the world. It is an age of the specialist, the expert, and the technician. Karl

Marx, in his metaphysical simplicity ("Man will be a hunter in the morning, a fisherman in the afternoon"), never envisaged that this would be the fate of the socialist dream. Veblen, with his ironic military metaphors, had a more profound insight; for him the technicians constituted the indispensable general staff of the economic army, and one day, when the dawning consciousness of their power became clear to them, they would presumably take over as the rulers of the new society. That the actual historical story—the literal contact with the engineers—is a myth is less important than Veblen's need to envision and proclaim such a myth as true.

In the coming decades, as any reading of changes in our occupational structure indicates, we will be moving toward a "post-industrial society," in which the scientist, the engineer, and the technician constitute the key functional class in society. The question remains whether Veblen, in envisaging such a change, which is the striking portent of *The Engineers and the Price System,* finally abandoned the cautions that had made him the "outsider" all his life, and placed himself at the head of this wave of the future—saying, in effect, that the technological rule of society was good—or whether, in some final, mordant irony, in seeing such a society as the mechanized end-product of the "instinct of workmanship," he was playing a joke—and if so on whom?

Notes

1. For a more intensive discussion, see Frank E. Manuel, *The New World of Henri Saint-Simon* (Cambridge: Harvard University Press, 1956), especially Chapter 16, and *Selected Writings of Henri Comte de Saint-Simon,* edited by F. M. H. Markham (Oxford: Basil Blackwell, 1952).

2. For a summary of these concerns, see Max Nomad, *Aspects of Revolt* (New York: Bookman Associates, 1959).

3. In this section, and the next few, I have drawn largely on Joseph Dorfman's fine biography of Veblen, *Thorstein Veblen and His America* (New York: Viking Press, 1934), and, in particular, on two unpublished doctoral theses, Samuel Haber's "Scientific Management and the Progressive Movement" (Berkeley: University of California, 1961) and Edwin T. Layton's "The American Engineering Profession and the Idea of Social Responsibility" (Los Angeles: University of California, 1956). In addition, I have profited considerably from Mr. Layton's article "Veblen and the Engineers," in the *American Quarterly*, XIV (Spring 1962), although I think he overstates Veblen's confusions of the distinctions between different types of engineers. Additional sources were the article "Veblen and Technocracy," by Leon Ardzrooni, in *Living Age* (March 1933); *Scientific Management and the Unions,* by Milton Nadworny (Cambridge: Harvard University Press, 1955); the biography of Morris L. Cooke, *The Life and Times of a Happy Liberal,* by Kenneth Trombley (New York: Harper & Brothers, 1954); and David Riesman's provocative psychoanalytic interpretation, *Thorstein Veblen* (New York: Charles Scribner's Sons, 1953).

4.   For a sad but charming account of Veblen at this time, see a memoir by R.L. Duffus, *The Innocents at Cedro: A Memoir of Thorstein Veblen and Some Others* (New York: Macmillan Company, 1944).

5.   For a discussion of this episode, see my monograph, "The Background and Development of Marxian Socialism in the United States," in *Socialism and American Life* (Princeton, NJ: Princeton University Press, 1952), pp. 312 passim.

6.   Dorfman, *Thorstein Veblen and His America*, p. 382.

7.   For a history of the successive changes in the makeup of *The Dial,* see Frederick J. Hoffman, Charles Allen, and Carolyn Ulrich, *The Little Magazine: A History and Bibliography* (Princeton, NJ: Princeton University Press, 1946), p. 7, and pp. 196-208.

8.   The associate editors were Clarence Britten, Harold Stearns, Randolph Bourne, and Scofield Thayer.

9.   Riesman, *Thorstein Veblen*, p. 31.

10.   "In 1919, Mencken wrote an essay on Veblen, in the magazine, *Smart Set,* which was later republished in his first *Prejudices.* Until 1917, said Mencken, Professor Dewey was the great thinker in the eyes of the respectable literary weeklies, a role he had fallen into after the death of William James. 'Then, overnight, the upspringing of the intellectual soviets, the headlong assault upon the old axioms of pedagogical speculation, the nihilistic dethronement of Professor Dewey—and rain, rain, rah for Prof. Dr. Thorstein Veblen!'

    "'In a few months—almost it seemed a few days—he was all over *The Nation, The Dial, The New Republic* and the rest of them, and his bookstand pamphlets began to pour from the presses, and newspapers reported his every wink and whisper,' and 'everyone of intellectual pretensions read his works. Veblenianism was shining in full brilliance. There were Veblenists, Veblen clubs, Veblen remedies, for all the sorrows of the world. There were even in Chicago, Veblen Girls—perhaps Gibson Girls grown middle-aged and despairing.'" Dorfman, *Thorstein Veblen and His America*, p. 423.

11.   "The hero of Ben Hecht's novels is a disgusted young man; everywhere he sees people and institutions designed to trap him, to cut him down to their size. He is a 'philosopher' fond of commenting upon the dreary stupidity of his inferiors and of quoting the 'best authorities' he has read. The authorities he knows best are Nietzsche and Veblen, though he also remembers the titles of many books." Frederick J. Hoffman, *The Twenties: American Writing in the Postwar Decade* (New York: Viking Press, 1955), p. 93.

12.   Reprinted in *Essays on Our Changing Order,* edited by Leon Ardzrooni (New York: Viking Press, 1934).

13.   That is, the essays published from October 19, 1918, to January 25, 1919, and published in book form under the title of *The Vested Interests and the State of the Industrial Arts.*

14.   For a discussion of Taylor and his influence, see my essay, "Work and Its Discontents," in *The End of Ideology* (Illinois: Free Press of Glencoe, 1960).

15.   See Frederick W. Taylor, *The Principles of Scientific Management*, p. 10, reprinted in the compendium *Scientific Management* (New York: Harper & Brothers, 1947).

16.   Trombley, *The Life and Times of a Happy Liberal*, p. 8.

17.   See Taylor, *Principles of Scientific Management*, p. 8.

18.   Trombley, *Life and Times of a Happy Liberal*, p. 9. The proselytizing efforts of the Taylorites and the formation of the Taylor Society, the forerunner of the present Society for the Advancement of Management, is a fascinating study of the engineering and progressive mentalities, but far beyond the scope of this essay. For the best accounts of these efforts, see Milton J. Nadworny, *Scientific Management and the*

      Unions, and the unpublished doctoral thesis of Samuel Haber.

19.   I have relied upon Edwin Layton's doctoral thesis for this characterization of Gantt.

20.   Nadworny, *Scientific Management and the Unions*, p. 107.

21.   I follow here largely the article by Edwin Layton in the *American Quarterly,* his unpublished doctoral thesis, and Trombley's biography of Cooke.

22.   Dorfman, *Thorstein Veblen and His America*, pp. 452-53.

23.   Layton, "Veblen and the Engineers," p. 69.

24.   Cited by Dorfman, *Veblen and His America*, p. 455. Curiously enough, the only biography of Cooke extant (written twenty years after Dorfman's biography of Veblen), by Kenneth E. Trombley, the editor of *The American Engineer,* though it is replete with references to Cooke's relations with Brandeis, Franklin D. Roosevelt, Frankfurter, David Lilienthal, Philip Murray, and dozens of others, contains no mention of Cooke's short tryst with Veblen. Since the "book was developed in the glow of the subject's irrepressible personality and soul-stirring inspiration," according to the author, Cooke's failure to talk about Veblen may be taken as evidence of the thinness of such a contact—from Cooke's point of view.

      Layton, who worked through the Cooke papers (which included some exchanges between Cooke and Guido Marx), writes "Marx contacted Cooke and arranged for him to give one of the lectures for the course at the New School. He also obtained from Cooke, a list of engineers who might be interested in the course and arranged a meeting between Veblen and Cooke. A meeting between the insurgent mechanical engineers and Veblen's group was held. But the engineers were unwilling to accept the leadership of Veblen and Marx. Cooke, though friendly, regarded them as spokesmen for the 'extreme left.'" "Veblen and the Engineers," pp. 69-70.

25.   "Veblen and the Engineers," p. 72. In assessing Hoover, as is the case with many other figures, there is always the danger of reading present-day images back into the past. Hoover, in 1919, because of his war-relief work, was widely regarded as a "progressive Republican" and was looked at askance by the conservative Republicans of the day. It is still relevant, though, that the highly touted "insurgency" of the engineers was actually an effort to "professionalize" their status, rather than to change the social order. For a contemporary evaluation of Hoover, which does remarkably well in reconstructing the mood of the wartime years and after, see Lewis L. Strauss, *Man and Decisions* (New York: Doubleday & Company, 1962), pp. 7-56.

26.   We can best understand how such market control is exercised by examining the price-setting system, the so-called standard-volume concept employed by the auto industry. This system, which was developed by Donaldson Brown for General Motors in 1924, is based on an equation of three variables—price, net return on investment, and estimated average rate of plant operation. The price set for a single car is a function of the other two variables. But how are these determined? Net return on investment is simple: General Motors decides that it must get roughly a 20 percent return after taxes each year. "Estimated average rate of plant operation" is more complicated. Because of seasonal and other fluctuations in demand, General Motors estimates that in its *best* year it will utilize about 80 percent of its maximum operating capacity. In an *average* year it figures on reaching 80 percent of the production in its best year. Thus it figures, theoretically, on using 64 percent of its capacity in any normal year. In actual practice, the "standard volume" has been calculated on a 55 percent capacity. In effect, therefore, General Motors so sets its prices as to plan for a return of 20 percent a year on its investment on the assumption that its plants will operate through the year for a total of only 180 days, or 36 weeks. From 1950 to 1957, General Motors' actual sales were, on the average, about 30 percent higher than the "standard volume" on which the company set its prices.

Thus in 1950, General Motors estimated its "standard volume" at 2,250,000 units in order to give it a 20-per-cent return on investment, and sold 3,812,000 units, or a 69 percent "margin of safety."

The concept of "standard volume" is related to the idea of the "break-even point" (a measure that is based on the relationship between costs, both fixed and variable, and sales), or the figure at which a company begins to turn a profit. General Motors, in the 1950 decade, had a "break-even" point at about 48 percent of sales; and if one took full capacity into account, the "break-even point" would come to between 40 and 45 percent of capacity. In other words, General Motors could significantly reduce its prices, and still make enormous profits. As things stand, the "marginal firm" in the industry, Chrysler, holds up a neat "price umbrella" for General Motors.

For an elaboration of this data, and its consequences for the economy, see my article, "The Subversion of Collective Bargaining," in *Commentary,* March 1960.

27. These are themes, of course, which are central to the writings of Weber and Durkheim, and which have been deeply evident in sociological writing in recent years.

28. "[Veblen's] usual failure to cite his sources in his writings would seem to have been due, to some extent, to a desire to seem original—a 'natural'—and to a slightly greater extent to a desire to evade another academic ritual, another debt, but, in addition, to some inner fear that a citation would act as a constraining force, limiting what he could say. Thus, for instance, if he should rest a particular statement about the handicraft era on Sombart's treatment of it, he would either have to put himself under obligation to Sombart's interpretation or to show why he departed from it, whereas by a rare vague, and general reference he maintains his superiority to his sources. This practice, and many other elements in his make-up, led him to seek the doubtful security of abstraction—including an endlessly abstract and earnest call to other economists to be concrete. For abstraction allows one to glide over difficulties presented by individual instances...." David Riesman, *Thorstein Veblen,* pp. 15-16.

29. Frank E. Manuel, *The Prophets of Paris* (Cambridge, MA: Harvard University Press, 1962), p. 201.

30. *The Prophets of Paris*, p. 217.

31. Manuel, *The New World of Henri Saint-Simon,* pp. 303-04.

32. The distinction between productive and unproductive labor exists in Adam Smith as in Marx, but in Smith, and to a great extent in Marx, the distinction is used analytically as a means of establishing a labor theory of value, whereas in the Utopians and in Veblen, the distinction becomes "ideological"—a stick for beating the enemy.

33. T. W. Adorno, "Veblen's Attack on Culture," *Studies in Philosophy and Social Science*, IX (1941), 389-413.

34. Though Leon Ardzrooni, Veblen's most faithful disciple, was quick to claim such credit in the winter of 1932, when the spreading vogue of technocracy led some of its followers to state that Howard Scott, the leader of the Technocratic movement, had inspired Veblen's thinking in *The Engineers and the Price System.* Ardzrooni wrote: "From this brief narrative it should be clear that Veblen had laid the foundations and worked out the details of what passes current as Technocracy and before his contact with Howard Scott." Ardzrooni then sketches the story of Veblen's (and his) efforts to provide leadership for the young engineers, though in his account ("Later on, at the earnest solicitation of Veblen and at some expense to the New School, a prominent and experienced engineer joined the group, chiefly for the purpose of consulting with Scott") the emphasis is put, surprisingly, and apparently for the purposes of establishing Veblen's originality, on consultation with Scott, rather than with the followers of Gantt or with the Cooke groups in the American Society of Mechanical Engineers. See Leon Ardzrooni, "Veblen and Technocracy," *Living Age*, March 1933.

9

The Higher Learning in America

Ivar Berg

It would be to deny readers a great many pleasures of discovery and revelation if these introductory pages identified all of the several analytical premises on which this and others of Veblen's books were based, but it will be helpful to consider a few of them in preparation for a reader's satisfying recognitions of others.[1] I will begin with some general comments, then offer an outline of the book and, finally, I will discuss a few of Veblen's chapters. Until we come to the end of this esquisse, the treatment I accord Veblen will be essentially sympathetic; in the final paragraphs the treatment will be a tad less appreciative of the applicabilities of some of Veblen's ideas to the quiddities on today's quads and the reasons for some shortfalls that detract only slightly from this gifted analyst's basic statement.

Overview

First off, Veblen was a full-fledged founding member of a school, in the discipline of modern economics in its earlier days, that has essentially been given over to sociologists, economic historians, and cultural anthropologists, in favor of *far* more narrowly drawn analyses whose banks of equations are constructed from the postulates of price theory, and the "marginalist" principles with which it is applied.

The basic premises of price theory and marginalism have been whimsically but not entirely misleadingly summarized in a revision of a popular aphorism: "A thing worth doing at all is worth doing—until marginal costs exceed marginal revenues." While Veblen, with others, attacked price *theory* the version it took in the 1890s on technical grounds, his larger target was the price *system* on grounds very clearly implied by the paraphrased epigram; he would take the same aim today.

The work of economists, in accord with price theory, distinguishes between what Victor R. Fuchs terms allocative efficiency and distributive justice. Economics nowadays, he tells us with just enough confident prose to lead most moderns to read right along, "has a great deal to say about the former, but the justice of any particular distribution of income cannot be established by economics...the economic perspective can help clarify the effects [of public policies, for example] but it cannot provide the final answers. These must come from our values." [2] One possible implication is that the economist's own work, like the physicist's, is entirely value free, even when it offers us "tradeoffs" between unemployment and inflation with clear ideas about the economist's preferences between these woes depending, of course, on whether they are "Keynesians" or "supply-siders." An alternative implication: economists, themselves, can separate their pure, technical findings about policy options from their personal predilections when they testify before congressional committees, write letters to op-ed pages, or write columns for *Business Week* and *Newsweek* magazines; the many faces of Eve.

Professor Fuchs then admiringly quotes an oft-cited dictum of Sir Edwin Chadwick's that "when the sentimentalist and the moralist fails, he will have as a last resource to call in the aid of the economist." [3] The economist, in the event, would presumably not be a Marxist even though he would be at least as much an "economic determinist." In summing it all up, Professor Fuchs borrows a bottom line to end all bottom lines for his discipline from Professor Gary Becker whose version of "human capital theory" in 1962 and reissued, without modifications in 1991, stands in very marked contrast with the main themes about education in the volume by Veblen that we here introduce. Thus Becker tells us that "the combined assumptions of maximizing behavior, market equilibrium, and stable preferences, used relentlessly and unflinchingly, form the heart of the economic approach." [4]

Were Veblen alive, as Sam Goldwyn, the master of malapropisms once said about Abraham Lincoln, he would turn over in his grave, upon reading Becker's definition. A comparison of Becker with Veblen is an important one because Becker's position, as an evangelist for neo-orthodox economists' faith, more than half a century after Veblen, represents well the essential and unfortunate rejection by most modern economists of Veblen's school of thought in favor of what has come to be known as the marginalist school. Veblen's institutionalist perspective helped to give the name to an alternative school of thought about economic processes, a set of perspectives that lent itself admirably to parallel analyses by Veblen's contemporary and admirer, John R. Commons, and by Commons' colleagues who elaborated, significantly, on the institutionalist tradition of what came to be known as the "Wisconsin School."

For Veblen the exchanges of quids and quos contemplated by economists are embedded in sociohistorical cultures, from which economists detach them, that have evolved—literally in Veblen's case—from those dominated by barbarians, then by military conquerors, then by religionists, and finally, at the turn of the century in America, by businessmen and their "pecuniary values"—price theory, in effect was made into what John Kenneth Galbraith characterized in the 1950s as the conventional wisdom.

Veblen would have relished Galbraith's truly oxymoronic phrase but he was more attentive to "Captains of Industry" and the intellectual merit popularly *assigned* to the preachments of Captains of Industry (because, he argued, of their business successes) than he was to the numerous citizens who admired the achievements of the leading men of commerce; these leaders' own preachments Veblen might well, with the same touch of irony, have called the sapient orthodoxy. For Veblen, prices embodied the sums of genuine value added to a good by all those who crafted and produced it and an additional "unearned increment" accruing to the essentially wasteful "efforts" of peddlers, procurers, predators, promoters and parasitic brokers.

One of Veblen's chapters, as we shall see, elaborates upon business leaders' "conduct" of the American academy in ways that are totally subversive of one of the most reputable bodies of modern economics—Becker's aforementioned "human capital" theory. While this theory allows, in writers' prefaces, that "cultural benefits" attach to higher education, the main focus of the theory is perforce upon its (more measurable) social and private economic returns. For Veblen, however, the costs to the higher learning of the displacing effects on the higher learning's missions generated by the academy's roles in preparing college and professional school grads for careers in the service of "pecuniary interests," are enormous.

These costs receive no attention whatever in "human capitalist's" reckonings regarding human capital, specifically *because* their economizing value systems and their conceptualizations do not join "R and D" in the modern model they construct around differentially educated earners. It is also difficult to convert displacements of the higher learning's missions into costs except to note, by implication, that the displaced missions simply suffer from changes in demand, as will happen when markets operate as economists conceive of things. The modern economist's measurement of the *value* of the higher learning is found in aggregated data either on the "effective demand" for the higher learning, among those able to pay the asking price, or on the economic value of some research efforts; these educational products are measured separately. Price *says* it all, but it most assuredly does not *tell* it all.

In Veblen's view one could truly and fully understand the ways of actors in economies only by going well beyond supply, demand, and prices, by examining the prevailing norms, the governing sentiments, and the "the habituations of thought" in a society, the formulation he borrowed from the philosopher-logician, C.S. Peirce; Veblen called them a culture's "human institutions." These human institutions shape widespread practices alongside cash and credit transactions—Veblen repeatedly refers to the "cash nexus"—we can detach from their social contexts, to which we can attach numerical "pecuniary" values, and which we may reduce to detailed equations to be solved with the aid of subtle if not always sensitive mensurational techniques.

Veblen, the quintessential skeptic, would have enjoyed the application of Oscar Wilde's characterization of the cynic as "one who knows the price of everything and the value of nothing" to much of economics and, as we will later see, to modern economics sister social sciences, as well. In their dogged pursuit of these variable forces to which numbers can be attached and, as Fuchs more or less implies, in their detachment from matters that do not lend themselves to quantification, economists are playing, consciously or otherwise, in Veblen's perspective, at the cynic's game.

The market is not a dismembered, unseen hand for Veblen but the doings of several hands, sometimes all thumbs, of a number of key members of what Veblen conceived to be the business class. The shifting intersections of demand with supply curves encapsulate a great many phenomena in helpful and somewhat revealing ways but they also approach the logician's fallacy of "misplaced concreteness."

Veblen would, in fine, deny that social scientists might achieve the objectivity claimed by Fuchs, Chadwick, or Gary Becker, simply because social scientists' efforts—especially in their choice of problems, in the definitions and characterizations of phenomena under examination, and in the methods used in pursuit thereof—borrow heavily from a culture's offerings; these cultural offerings both shape and color the social scientist's findings in significantly though generally unexamined ways. As a case in point, economists have debated over whether slavery up to the Civil War was a profitable arrangement and, later, that discrimination against black Americans was and is, "in economic terms," inefficient. Slavery and discrimination may thus be treated as special cases of economic exchange for economists' purposes, rather than as component parts of institutional arrangements that enjoy popular sanction. The facts that a pair of economists found slavery to be efficient, and another one that discrimination is inefficient, would be counted hardly at all in the reckonings of plantation owners, and bigots, respectively. The salaries and fees of an almost inestimable number of public and private civil rights lawyers, meantime, turn up in economists' measures of gross national product, but not in their cost-benefit analyses of discrimination. Just think of the jobs we would lose, for example, were we to eliminate most crimes, the fastest growing economic sector we have.

The results of noninstitutional analyses, as Veblen saw them, are simply to gainsay the fact that values do play a part in the constructions of policy options of the types Fuchs and his colleagues will generate in their works. I will elaborate upon Veblen's point a little later in these pages, principally in connection with modern economists' conceptions and analysis of higher education, since an important—to him the most important—part of higher education, Basic research" today, is the subject of Veblen's *The Higher Learning in America;* for modern economists, once again, the role of basic research, which they study in connection with "R and D," is separated from the role of the academy in mobilizing human capital except insofar as account is taken of the education of scientists and engineers. For Veblen, the latter mobilization hinders the former because universities have come to letting the pedagogic tail wag the scholarly and scientific dog.

My plan is to consider a major point or two in each of several chapters in Veblen's guided tour through higher education in the period from the end of the Civil War until he finally went to press in 1918, with a manuscript he had completed some dozen years earlier. I will leave to his readers to learn, from his two prefaces, of Veblen's thoughts about waiting a dozen years, after a certain university president's death, to publish this trenchant volume. Speaking autobiographically, I must note that growing up Norwegian, as Veblen and I did, can leave one with very considerable capacities for controlling one's emotions, especially if one might be accused by others of mean motives and thus suffer feelings of guilt. It was his intent, Veblen suggests, to use the university leader he depicts, with acerbity, as an archetype, not as an archenemy, an intention that, he felt, obliged him to allow a decent interval to pass after his bête noir died.

The point in this introduction will be to juxtapose some of Veblen's main points with a number of circumstances in today's academy by recalling them to many readers' minds and, additionally, by attempting, now and again, to divine how Veblen might have viewed them. One test of a classic work of social criticism in the social sciences—and Veblen belongs with the best of such critics, as well as he belongs in the pantheon of the social sciences—is to see if the critique's central logics generally remain applicable beyond the critic's own times.

As we will see, Veblen's judgements apply in general ways to present day American higher education very well indeed. It turns out, *well over three quarters of a century later,* that the more many things have changed since Veblen took out after "The Strongman," his archetype, the worse, in many respects, they have become. Successive generations of university presidents and their satraps and entourages—provosts, deans, and other factotums on the academic factotum pole, and the faculties of colleges (Veblen called then Captains of Erudition and Schoolmasters, respectively)—have not behaved in too many ways that lie more than "one half of a standard deviation beyond the mean," as rigorous colleagues might like to put it, that materialized in Veblen's calculus.

As most readers well know, a large crop of books on higher education have appeared—one, from the University of Chicago, has even bloomed, briefly—since the 1960s: technical analyses of higher education and economic growth and income distribution; on curriculum; and on academic politics. Foundations, organized interest groups, the leaders of sundry modern causes and reform movements, federal agencies, and even a few American presidents have joined innumerable individual private observers in blessing and damning university administrators, researchers, and teachers.

The topics they address range from tuition rates; the "political correctness," or lack thereof, of faculties; the legitimacy of the roles of "Western civilization" core courses, and fraternities; college graduates' earnings; the "appropriate" balance between instructional and scholarly pursuits; admissions policies; the use of SAT tests; fiscal problems; the "Ph.D. glut" of the 1970s; the legitimacy of classified research, draft deferment policies, and the "overhead" costs of research; university accounting practices; "publishing or (and!) perishing"; student "stresses"; student "uprisings"; intercollegiate athletics; and financial aid. With the exceptions of Jacques Barzun's magisterial book, *The American University,* a major success d'estime, the works of the late Lawrence Cremmins, one of American education's major historians; and Lawrence Veysey's comprehensive history, *The Emergence of the American University;* and David Reisman's writings; and Robert Paul Wolff's *The Ideal of the University;* most of these efforts will be soon forgotten, though the issues modern authors have sought to join will not likely go away any time soon. To put it another way, most recent critical efforts are targeted on single issues and on discrete, analytically distinguishable developments, rather than on the higher learning's present day *estate.*

Nicholas Murray Butler, a contemporary of Veblen's, who led Columbia University after Veblen wrote his book, and Chicago's Robert Maynard Hutchins buckled enough swashes, as presidents of their schools, to leave enduring traces of their ways and means on *many* aspects of higher education, but these deeper going types of traces are overlooked, in the current literature, in favor of analyses of specific issues. These newer works by recent scribes and chroniclers will likely interest only authors of Ed.D. theses who only rarely aspire to lima the essences, the quiddities, of modern higher education.

When they do so aspire, they do not do it at all well because they generally isolate developments they examine from those in the nation's widergoing culture; they tend to treat causes and effects, both, to be immanent in the educational system itself, not in the larger cultural and social scheme.

If these writers do reach beyond the academy's parietal walls, they grasp only an element in the larger culture, and shake it vigorously. Allan Bloom's attack on America's intellectual crisis, the "vulgarized continental idea of nihilism and despair, of relativism disguised as tolerance," comes to mind.[5] Clusters of ideas are interesting, of course, but they do not make up into persuasive "independent variables" in discussions of causes and effects. Veblen's pioneering study will survive, however, because it offers a "generic" explanation for what amounts to be a significant—that is, very large number of special cases of the types suggested by the foregoing enumeration of recent and current topics.

Veblen urges that we trace the imperatives of the *business* system, a structure populated by actors with needs for growing numbers of polished graduates[6] with pecuniary values; for universities increasingly managed in accord with pecuniary values; and for universities that make more and more room for usable, practical, that is, marketable, programs and ideas, than for the play of "idle curiosity" (curiosity that is essentially unfettered by significant concern by scholars with the marketability of results except in the market place of ideas), and for scholarship for its intrinsic value. In so doing Veblen offers us a way of explaining the ways and means of the academy as an embodiment of a "[business] culture's" "habituations of thought" that are manifested in almost all aspects of social life. These habituations do not enter Bloom's analysis, an analysis that focuses on the eddies and flows of Western thought, not on changes in social structures and in the hierarchies of power whose members have vastly differentiated capacities to shape a society and thus its educational system.

Veblen's analysis is thus institutional; it is ultimately a lamentation over the distracting pressures on detached, curious scientists and scholars, not a condemnation, not a criticism per se, of one or another of the failings and fragile decencies of university presidents and students, or of professors' neglect of' "true learning," of alumni conceits, donors' edifice complexes, fraternity boors' miscreant ways, or of readily intimidated faculty, of zealous "multiculturists," or of academicians who spread themselves widely and thereby risk becoming interdisciplinary dilettantes who pool their ignorance.

Though Veblen stalked, found, and accorded tongue lashings to those who commit these sins, it is their distracting effect on the learning enterprise that provokes Veblen, not their errant ways per se.

Veblen writes of the avarice of financiers and the hypocrisies of university heads, but he is far more concerned about limiting the influences of their ways on the academy than about damning or reforming them. Veblen would likely have agreed, in the end, with Owen D. Young, a major business leader, author of the Young Plan for German reparations after World War I, and early leader of General Electric, who said that "it is not the crook in modern business we need fear, but the honest man who doesn't know what he's doing," especially, for Veblen, in higher education.

Veblen, as I have noted, distinguished "business" from "industry." An almost fervent admirer of those who make (and effectively lead those who make) goods and services, Veblen was a contemptuous urticant, in all of his works, of those businessmen involved essentially only in making money in exchanges that were singularly pecuniary, in that their offerings to society were socially useless. He might call several of their reincarnations, in recent history, "Captains of Acquisitions and Leveraged Buyouts."

Indeed, in his views of what, in the lexicon of capitalism's critics was called *Finanzkapital,* Veblen's generally biting wit was, well, biting, as readers will shortly see. Veblen virtually foresaw an economy that, by the beginning of this century's last decade, had been Boeskeyed, Milkenized, mergered, "divestitured," acquisitioned, "offshored," "downsized," and regularly recessed, even after the passage of a salmagundi of regulatory measures, since the trust busting era, designed to temper if not exactly to tame the bulls and bears who take seasonal turns in their runs through Wall Street's canyons— and who were thus so aptly though admiringly pictured a few years ago, in their television ads, by Merrill-Lynch. Exposés of R.J. Nabisco, Salomon Brothers, Drexel-Lambert, and of several other financial "holdings" corporations, over the past five years, are entirely in line with Veblen's more institutional analysis of pecuniary high rollers.

Veblen would be intrigued by the very language generally used in characterizations of financiers' present-day professional(!) activities: "raiders," "shark repellents," "poison pills," "greenmail," "white knights," "pac man defense" and the rest. Indeed Veblen pointed to the military metaphors in financespeak as clear evidence of the atavism of potent Wall Streeters, their recapitulations of barbarians' ways.

The fact is that Veblen was writing during what some historians in the 1950s called the Age of Big Business; he was there, as in the cliche, at the conception of what he presciently saw was the founding of the institutionalization of a new version of civilization. Well instructed in the Lutheran catechism he could amend the obligatory preface to the required answer to questions about meaning in every catachistical canon, "Thou shalt fear and love God..."; the Captains of Industry's version would be "Thou shalt tolerate priests of learning but befriend the schoolmasters and vocationalists who prepare a table before me in the presence of my competitors."

We may also note in this introduction that there have occurred only a few major developments in present day higher education for which the underlying theory in his book did not make significant room:

- the pressures to make colleges atone for some of the sins of primary and secondary education, by admissions policies and remedial programs in universities, to serve victims of adults who have wasted their victims' early lives in the holding tanks that have succeeded yesterday's primary and secondary schools in major urban centers; the business community can neither be credited nor blamed, depending upon how readers feel, for this singularly significant addition, in modern times, to higher education's roles. In 1990 corporations donated $1.4 billion to education, 264 million of which was given to precollegiate education; the latter figure was double the amount in 1986.

- Senator Joseph McCarthy's frontal attacks on "effete" professors— later Vice President Agnew's "nattering nabobs of negativism"—who, in, a study by Columbia University investigators Paul Lazarsfeld and Wagner Thielens, turned out frighteningly often to be feckless self-censorers who feared the senator, the senator's admirers on their universities' boards, the senator's terrorized targets in innumerable universities' presidential mansions, and the academic deaneries whose heads' personal anxieties could so easily compromise them as leaders of free speaking writers and lecturers. The business community knew a few of the senator's sympathizers well but only a few; one of his main targets, a secretary of the army, was on leave from his own corporation, J.P. Stevens.

- The move by liberal democrats, many of them on university faculties, to lay the ground work in the sixties and seventies, for expanding the opportunities of what U.S. Presidential Executive Order #11246 called protected groups. Some of these groups have, since that time, used their new empowerment, as it is called, to organize what, here and there, have become bloodless lynchings of colleagues and, at other times, have led what have become fairly vicious "multiculturist" movements, in battles over curriculum contents. In still other moments, some of these persons have led patronizing efforts to treat minorities as modern beneficiaries of updated notions about the white man's burden; again, the business culture has observed most of these battles from a distance as its members seek, whatever their personal predilictions, to comply pretty much with regulations pertaining to employment practices in their own precincts.

*   The very large financial investments of funds in higher education by Uncle Sam and, paraphrasing Veblen in a different context, by Uncle Sam's fifty retail outlets; the business community has supported these expenditures, for the most past, out of interests in basic research, defense and human resource development, that is for productive purposes rather than for strictly "pecuniary" gains.

Veblen also saw clearly the interests of businessmen in science but he did not anticipate the portion of President Dwight Eisenhower's military-industrial complex that would be allocated to academic physicists, chemists, biologists, engineers, medical scientists, and psychologists, for all manners of projects. At the moment, with the completed thaw in the Cold War and the reduction of the defense establishment's budgets, discussions among scientists, their university leaders, and opportunistic business leaders are leading to contracts between some corporations and universities that critics fear, as Veblen would, will have very subversive effects on the free dissemination of scientific knowledge. It remains to be seen whether new social technology can be invented that will help to serve both industry's interests in protecting proprietary information and academic interests in the publication of research results.

Veblen's Eight Categories

Veblen organized his thoughts—not a few of which are slings and arrows—under eight rubrics; each body of his remarks will assuredly make a key group of modern academic citizens wax defensive as, in turn, they are smarted. I suspect, though, that modern arts and sciences types, humanists especially, will take more kindly to Veblen's characterizations. Though colleagues in arts and sciences almost always take themselves more seriously than their ways and means entirely justify, they tend by and large, to be somewhat abler at self-mockery than are the more self-righteously practical majorities that surround them in the academies' professional and vocational school faculties.

Those, for example, who train graduate and undergraduate students of business and management at my own university, potential inside traders among them, include some of the most acerbic critics arts and science's faculties will ever meet. Many of them resist degree requirements applicable to undergraduates that can only be fulfilled by arts and sciences course offerings; such collegiate courses are labeled "nebulous," "ornamental," "insubstantial," "frothy." Like other business schools they have sought to teach their own version of economics ("managerial economics") because "academic" economics is "too theoretical," (and costly to their dean's budget) and to offer the social sciences, otherwise, under such titles as "human behavior in organization." These residual social sciences are cast in terms of their usefulness in shaping the values, norms and motives of employees in the service of productivity and, with a few notable exceptions, are taught by social scientists manqués.

As Veblen pointed out, some vocationalists draw their self portraits with utilitarian pride in their valuable contributions to technological progress, to practical discoveries, and to "progressive" management; today, others sense their importance from the consulting fees they earn from corporate clients who manage enterprises beyond universities' parietal walls and pay handsome tribute for their advisors' counsel. Older vocationalists, in my experience, often reduce whatever idealism their younger colleagues, with moist-eyed visions of learning may have, by passing on the lower-paying offers they receive from their patrons to probationers, whose financial needs are not trivial, and whose academic career aspirations are not well served by ungracious responses to senior colleagues' offers of dollars and implied sponsorship; many of the novitiates abandon the faith and, themselves, become dry-eyed and sometimes vulgar pragmatists.

Veblen's Rubrics

The Place of the University in Modern Life

This constitutes an overview of the author's distinction between the higher learning, on one side, and the preparation for careers of professionals, sundry kinds of para-professionals and practitioners, and undergraduates, on the other.

The Governing Boards

The (to Veblen, irrelevant) business successes of the Captains of Industry lead to their appointments as trustees who control and "conduct" what they (most evidently, to Veblen) can't understand.

Academic Administration

The archetypes of these administrators in modern times for Veblen could well be Nicholas Murray Butler, had he known this younger contemporary as Columbia's president, and Michigan State's John Hanna, in the 1950s and beyond.

The latter, who would have out-pointed the Chicago and Stanford presidents on Veblen's scorecard for entrepreneurial and distracting derring do, could have been an "ideal type" model for this, his third chapter. Dr. Hanna was one of the architects of the undemocratic deferment of college students—"the cream of America's youth," they were called—during the Korean "police action," a war that was pointedly waged against communists who threatened democracy and free enterprise. Those of us who were recalled to active duty, in the event, felt that both the policy means and the political objectives, in the immediate service of South Korea's dictator and his autocratic successors, were essentially fraudulent. Through Dr. Hanna's good connections, his university later trained leaders of notoriously brutal tiger cage tenders, at U.S. taxpayers' expense, to fill the South Vietnamese government's police forces' needs for effective control over political and other prisoners. Such barbaric ways would have further persuaded Veblen of the atavistic streaks in a business culture. Otherwise, Dr. Hanna nurtured his university's football team's fortunes—large ones during his tenure—and rooted it on into membership in the Big Ten Conference, while he persuaded his state's regents to "upgrade" his school from that of a huge college to formal status as an even larger university. Veblen, in disgust, and Hanna, in envy, would both have gnashed their teeth had they watched the Rose Bowl game on 1 January 1992 and heard from a reporter that the University of Washington earned a $10 million profit from its football team in 1991, and that it thus had a budget surplus of $5.3 million. Hanna would have been surprised to learn that the University of Washington has used these funds to support women's soccer and softball teams. Veblen, very substantially a feminist, would however enjoy women's growing campus opportunities for cultivation of their "instincts for sportsmanship," atavistic instincts, once again, that Veblen deemed to be very serviceable to combative male bulls and bears in a "business culture."

Butler, "Nicholas Miraculous," meantime made possible the "leisure of the theory class" by urging the Carnegie Foundation to buy off classicists at New York's City College though attractive pensions in order to make faculty places for young "radical" intellectuals among Lower East Side New York Jews (the distinguished philosopher of science, Morris Raphael Cohen, among them). America's academicians by now know these sources of postcareer benefits as their generous pension program, TIAA-CREF, but few know that they derive from the prejudices of a stereotyper.

Academic Prestige and Material Equipment

This chapter's title speaks well for itself, a chapter in which we learn that the so-called edifice complexes of universities' leaders and large donors who sought to have their names graven over ivied gymnasiums, neo-gothic dormitories, and richly columned applied chemistry labs, were as much a part of academic life before World War I as they were in the muddy, bulldozing era on campuses during the first several decades following the Second World War. Much of this construction came, then as now, at the expense of regular maintenance and of sensibly designed classrooms. Then as now, wealthy donors were only rarely ecstatic over acknowledgments that their beneficences made it possible to putty and paint windows, repair leaking roofs and, otherwise, to replace rickety furniture, mend cracking foundations, and repaint the bricks and stones under the nonsymbiotic vines that are celebrated in songs and promotional video cassettes.

Academic Personnel

The biggest discontinuities between Veblen's academies and ours will be discerned in this chapter: we now make professors of many more persons than those from among the business classes' sons, as in Veblen's day. And, today, faculty wives—especially the younger women among them—would no doubt cry over the pitiful lots accruing, according to Veblen, to his colleagues' spouses.

The democratizing process (too slow to please all, to be sure) meanwhile, has reduced, more than a little bit, the docility and deference academicians visited upon business leaders in Veblen's time.

There is hardly a campus in the republic, nowadays, without a large caucus of pedantocrats, liberal and conservative, that vie with each other for opportunities to lead faculties against universities' policies. What power top level administrators have retained derives, less and less, from their unilateral authority than from the fragmentation of universities in which separate and fairly autonomous schools fight each other to garner resources at each others' expense.

But most others of this chapter's observations describe life in the four universities in which I have served over the past thirty-three years fairly adequately, indeed: give or take one-fifth of university faculties truly do the higher learning; another three-fifths sit on committees, senates, and councils to absolutely no evidently significant academic purposes, with time out for class lectures; and one-fifth grouses about the other two groups. Presidents and their decanal point persons seek, sometimes successfully, to understand and capitalize on the first fifth, exploit the second group as instrumental proof of their putatively democratic administrations, and either buy off or otherwise placate or co-opt the last third during "office hours" and in ad hoc advisory agencies, for service on which most of these irritating fleas can readily be co-opted. The most engaging members of the last group write droll letters about bloated administrations and intellectual freedom to which presidents and provosts respond with what they, sometimes quite gratuitously, expect readers to regard as urbane wit.

The Portion of the Scientist

In this chapter Veblen assays the "business value" to the president, of well-ranked scholars and scientists who become charms on the watch fobs of their universities' Directorates" and who generally play their roles well at banquet tables and in road shows in cities with large alumni clubs. A dean I have known coached a member of the National Academy of Sciences on how to help distract the dean's school's visiting "overseers" from their urges to help manage the school, by waxing on some scientific findings: "They will be as happy as pigs in [swill]," he assured his colleague.

Vocational Training

The turn towards practical education, the preprofessionalization of students in the undergraduate departments of the Arts and Sciences, twists the question "what profiteth it a man…?" from its poetic biblical concerns about faithless materialism, to its profane, secular meaning.

Veblen here even anticipates the modern pleas, by defensive arts and sciences spokespersons, to those who would listen, that four years of liberal arts and sciences is a sound business proposition and, in unspecified ways, a useful preparation for the success-hungry masses of those who move, in graduate exercises each spring, from campuses to corporate settings.

I must confess, as a college dean in a university for four and one half years, that I have somewhat shamelessly lectured prospective applicants and their nervous parents, in auditoriums and hotel ballrooms all over the country, on the rewards the college grads will earn as what we may call Corporals of Business Bureaucracies, in the service of Captains of Industry, following exposures to the Schoolmasters in one of the Captains of Erudition's rank and file. Such reassurances were, of course, always tacked on, with studied casualness, to longer and serious disquisitions about the joys of learning, intellectual growth and inquisitiveness, in well-informed anticipations of the question and answer period that always follows presentations on these "admissions trips"; one is obliged to render unto Mammon what, after all, truly is Mammon's, by treating Mammon's pecuniary pursuits as worthy, even lofty ends. Consider that a visiting dean can scarcely neglect the aspirations parents nurse regarding their children's prospects for leaving their nests and feathering their own, especially so as the price of tuition, alone, for 104 weeks of classes over four years can approach $100,000, even if significant numbers of their offspring, urged by freshman orientation program speakers to become well-rounded men and women, turn out to be cultural doughnuts.

Summary and Trial Balance

And now to a discussion of the materials under these rubrics.

The Place of the University in Modern Life

In his opening essay Veblen stakes out his views about the precious and, at the margins, the precarious roles of the higher learning in Western cultures. Veblen conceived the higher learning in each developmental stage to be the product of the idly curious who seek to build and elaborate upon bodies of knowledge, including theoretical apparatuses, that hold the segments of civilizations—barbarian, military, religiously oriented, and "industrial," by turns, on their courses, and that show how (and how far) institutional factors, "habituations of thought," help and hinder realizations of a civilization's ideals. Priests in "seminaries of learning" do so by identifying evolutions of answers to deep-going questions, in each epoch, about "what it all means."

For Veblen, learned men reassert their idle curiosity (Veblen's term of approbation for detached and dedicated learning) over the "habitual [pecuniary] preoccupations" of other classes, thereby to claim the resources they require. The successes of the truly learned minorities in "seminaries of learning," in their periodic reassertions of their significance in modern industrial society, he reasoned, is aided by the fact that the subversive interests of the majority—the classes preoccupied with expedient solutions to practical problems—are unable to reach a consensus strong enough to *compromise* the true learning enterprise, however much these classes' preoccupations *hinder* the "learned priesthood" in its detached pursuit of knowledge for its own sake.

For Veblen, those who hinder the higher learning in a business culture are specifically those men of business (among others he thinks more legitimate) whose exclusively pecuniary values become ends, not means to loftier ends; these values cause them additionally to pressure universities to expend their resources in support of colleges that essentially polish and thus fit youths for careers in commerce, and to support of professional schools that prepare their students for vocations in law, medicine, engineering, and in schools of commerce that unapologetically prepare graduates to go for what Veblen acidly calls the main chance.

The pursuit of the higher learning, for Veblen, was the exclusive raison d'être and province of graduate schools in the arts and sciences. Veblen does not deny the marginal social value of collegiate and professional education (the word education first appears seventeen pages into the book). Rather, he views them as inevitable distractions from and thus as challenges to the higher learning's true seminarians.

Readers will find it difficult to deny that the values informing college faculties' programs and their colleges' curricula are regularly wedded to all the other operations of the academy, to the disadvantage of true science and scholarship and to the advantages of

Captains of Erudition, on one side, at the urgings of Captains of Industry, on the other. Veblen, in short, would undoubtedly identify many patterns in today's universities to be in linear continuity with those he limned seventy-five years ago.

Though he saw fairly quiet attacks on "socialists" in the 1890s, he could not, of course, have predicted the *details* of later incisions into the higher learning made by the sharpened edges of pecuniary values, especially since the end of the Second World War. Consider many Americans' concerns about capitalism's safekeeping against the threat of USSR-brand communism, during the 1950s that Senator McCarthy exploited so mercilessly in his formal attacks on university folk.

According to findings by the Columbia University social scientists mentioned earlier, significant numbers of tenured university faculty members, by their own admissions, censored their work, in and out of classrooms, to reduce risks of quickening the attentions of campus leaders sensitive to the possible indignation of large donors and constituency-conscious legislators, in Washington and in state capitols, over effete intellectuals, pinkos, and fellow-travellers who might warp or even poison young minds.

Veblen mentions, in his review of the academy's uneasy fellowship with the business culture, the termination of Scott Nearing by the University of Pennsylvania's Wharton School for left-leaning utterances that disturbed the alums of what continues to be a pre-eminent school of commerce and finance. The mention of the Nearing case provokes discussions, on that and other campuses, of encroachments on academic freedom in universities to this day, as does a similar case involving W. E. B. DuBois, the productive and celebrated African-American who was also obliged to leave the Wharton School. It is of particular importance that these cases occurred in the Wharton School, where American social sciences had many of their beginnings, where the title Professor of Social Sciences first appeared in 1890, and where, compared with other schools, Veblen's "pecuniary values" are most conspicuously operative.

That college students with "B" grade point averages could be deferred from service during the war with China and North Korea during the McCarthy period would not have surprised Veblen, who noted (but did not name) "grade inflation" in his own observations about the ways in which professors treated the "gentleman C's" sent to them from the families of the well-to-do. He would also easily assimilate these developments into his assessment of colleges' roles as finishing schools for more fortunate youths. Neither the democratic nor the academic values Veblen espoused were served by these gifts of deferments to collegians and to the treasurers in private universities who collected their tuition payments.

Nor would Veblen have been surprised by the transformation of many campuses, during the Second World War, into military academies with corps of officer candidates hopping over obstacle courses in mathematics and physics. The bulk of private college alumni in the nation's most prestigious four-year and university-based colleges in the classes of 1946-48 were in fact cadets left stranded on campuses from "NavyV-5" and "V-12" programs, Army Al2 programs, and from ROTC programs, when the war ended in 1945.

Veblen would probably have been as impressed by the conscientious dedication of the veterans' attentions to genuine intellectual development *and* to career goals, however, as their professors were pleased by them; the democratization of admissions to para-military colleges thus ushered in a brief period in which "gentleman C's" were in classroom company with many more serious students than populated colleges in prewar days.

Speaking of wars, in 1918 Veblen appended a section, to his first chapter, in which he ruminates about the prospects for post-World War I exchanges of scientists and scholars between the U.S. and what came later to be known as Western Europe, Germany, especially; he would have endorsed the Fulbright Grant Program's financial support from European governments, after World War II, for American academicians to study and lecture abroad in payment by these countries for the valuable military equipage left behind by homebound U.S. troops; this program squared well with Veblen's views of learning as an end unto itself. Not a few departments in European universities were enabled to catch up on much in the nonarmament related sciences and scholarship, generally, the pursuits of which had been interrupted by the war. Veblen's hopes in these regards were far less fully realized in the period immediately after his book went to press in 1918 than they were after World War II.

The G.I. Bill of Rights' offerings of assistance to school- and college-bound veterans after World War II would probably have bothered Veblen at least a little bit, however, because the benefits were endowed by a Congress that was fully aware, already in 1945, of the colossal expansion in the domestic demand for a labor force segment known by census takers as "professionals, managers and technicians." While the bill's beneficiaries took to their humanities courses, for example, with something very much akin to alacrity and generated from among themselves a considerable number of future scientists and scholars, now beyond their sixtieth year, the *plan* was mainly conceived to thank former military servants for their sacrifices and to help to turn most of them into economically valuable citizens. For many of us who exchanged helmets for freshman beanies in the mid-forties, but attended classes in leftover government issue jackets and trousers, it did not take long to recognize that we would need new dress suits, by the senior year to qualify us additionally for interviews with recruiters from Proctor and Gamble, Anaconda, Continental Can, Chase Manhattan Bank, IBM, and other corporations of which the editors of *Fortune* magazine and investors in stocks thought well. The classmates who won multiple offers earned the grudging envy of classmates who called them Darlings of Industry; Veblen could have easily coined the appellation!

By the 1970s the staffs of "career and placement offices" were housed in prime (and precious), well-appointed university spaces. These staffs have been increasingly well briefed on data about corporate hiring plans from surveys of employers, late each fall, by professional job watchers at Michigan State and Northwestern Universities. Where high school seniors can read endless details about the "supply side" in ubiquitous guides to colleges, college seniors read about job survey results on campus bulletin boards where they can also sign up for interviews with corporate "head hunters" during their annual roundups.

Few professors do more than frown over the vacant seats of career-bound absentees from their classes who are jetting hither and yon in quest of post-senior livelihoods. With white collar workers' annual rates of unemployment increasing more rapidly nowadays than the annual rates of increases in service sector jobs, these job seekers do not leave their mentors with any sense that they are awed by their prospective employers, by the way; many of them, in fact are alternately frustrated, angry, and distressed about the problematic course of the Republic's economic future.

In marked contrast with Veblen's graduate and undergraduate degree candidates, in the early years of the century, moreover, about half of today's would-be scions of commerce are laden with debts incurred for their post-secondary educations. These debts reflect the investment-colored character of many students' (and their parents') motives, a fact that confirms Veblen's earlier apprehensions about college and even post-college enrollments.

The mounting indebtedness of students includes significant portions of universities' own funds that are siphoned away from the fiscal resources from which these institutions pay for their operating expenses. It was one of Veblen's main points that undergraduate studies and other attachments to the higher learning's missions involve disturbing reallocations of resources. These reallocations are even more distracting when nearly half their undergraduates are aid recipients whose merits as young intellectuals are not uncommonly modest.

According to my own estimates in 1970, meantime, about one quarter of all college graduates accepted jobs performed splendidly by high school graduates only fifteen years earlier.[7] But by 1980 American primary and secondary schools' educational efforts had quite apparently continued to deteriorate so significantly that employers who had needlessly upgraded job qualifications for their jobs in the fifties and sixties were increasingly driven to do so later by the declining "human capital" value embodied in America's precollegians.

In the earlier period, better-"educated" persons were paid better, according to Professor Becker and adherents to his "human capital" theories, because the better educated were ostensibly more productive; absent direct evidence that *might* (or might *not)* prove that better-educated people are more productive than their less educated peers, most economists have indulged and comforted themselves with a tautology: better educated souls earn more because they are more productive, and we know that they are more productive precisely because they earn more! Veblen stated very crisply, in *Theory of the Leisure Class,* that the parameters of the distribution of income in the U.S. were not "natural" in the sense that they reflected differences in income recipients' *merits.* Many economists still believe that the "rationality" of distributive processes in our society approximates the rationality of the production process. Justice is not, in the event, as justice does, but as normatively informed income distribution patterns dictate.

Productivity, notoriously, is not easily measured directly and, as noted earlier, we tend to avoid institutional questions, about "habits of thought" for example, that lead us to practices that are not exactly on the cutting edge of pure reason. In place of explanations of employers' job requirements that are less than rational, that is, hinted at but undemonstrated in terms of efficiency, we *assume* the behavior to be reasonable and formulate questions posed in terms that permit quantitative measures, measures of "pecuniary value."

We can, of course, measure educational achievements crudely, but instructively, in years of attendance, and we can measure incomes in dollar units. We link the two equal interval scales—a requirement for a number of statistical machinations—by assuming that competition, especially over the long term and in accord with postulates undergirding marginalist price theory, forces the businessman to buy only the educational achievements he truly needs. Thus went the faith.

The deterioration of primary and secondary educational apparatuses has recently come to redeem the faithful in the earlier period in their religious devotion to formal education as a necessary means to occupational salvation. Veblen, the student of institutions, would enjoy the fact that silk purses could be converted into sows' ears, and back, in the period 1950-1980. It may be in the economic interest of academics to seek to salvage a few eighteen-year-olds from among those admitted to colleges with deficient pre-college exposures. But it would very likely be more sensible, in economic terms, to invest in primary and secondary schools and in their pupils, thereby to salvage far larger percentages of disadvantaged youths!

The pecuniary lessons urged about "human capital" formation in the early 1960s were learned especially quickly, in the sixties and seventies, by minorities whose college enrollments shot upward. And universities in the event, always attentive to what Veblen repeatedly refers to as the main chance, subsequently joined labor market demand schedules to demands for "multicultural" diversity and have since converted universities into the single most focused of organized American efforts to make what some critics, black and white, call patronizing amends for slavery and for the historical denigration of women. The race to recruit minority faculty, to invent novel curriculum programs about oppressed persons, and to design anti-harassment programs followed in due course. Veblen, whose Norwegian immigrant father and his fathers' countrymen were compared very pejoratively to "Negroes," by their Wisconsin neighbors transplanted from New England, would be at least a little surprised by this turn.

Given the proximity of colleges to graduate programs, as Veblen notes, these dramatic elaborations on higher education's growing involvements as instruments for providing multiple services to society, impact on graduate studies in correlative ways. And universities, bent on serving so many social purposes, become supermarkets that offer the equivalent of the varieties in offerings, in such stores, that range from "hamburger helper" to gourmet items, like snail shell's for serving escargot, and imported goose liver pâté.

The hordes of para-students, legions of upwardly mobile and unemployed adults, phalanxes of minorities, and herds of careerists, otherwise, are not uncommonly directed to the hamburger helper on the academic shelf; I have frequently heard undergraduate advisors refer these intellectually indifferent souls to "accessible" courses. These courses, "guts" commonly among them, are widely available, and offer a useful consummation: they bring together witless students and witty teachers, in unwitting support of enrollment drives among competing departments. Even Veblen could not have foreseen that how-to-do-it evening courses would be taught in universities by stockbrokers, arts and crafts specialists, professional bridge tournament players, real estate brokers, and cabinet makers, in drives to use space more fully, to augment universities' incomes, and to prove their responsiveness to the citizenry; town and gown, and all that. He would have approved of a few of these; the New School's mini-courses, in New York City, afford highly stimulating intellectual fare to stimulus hungry citizens, and evening schools of general education are well-deserved blessings for those not able to enter universities directly from high school. Judging from the post-college awards these "extension" students win, several of them salvage very valuable talents, including talents for scholarship and science.

Veblen's higher learning generally has thus become the focus not only of otherwise skeptical Captains of Industry in search of employees but "targets of opportunity" for those who seek to make universities key instruments of social reform and political correctness as well as of economic productivity.

Much of the higher learning is described by those given to the newer learning as sexist and racist, however, as are the academy's own political and social structures. Veblen's concerns with Germany's attacks on "Christendom" in the period of World War I, might reasonably suggest that he would be sympathetic, today, to grievances about the longtime second class citizenship suffered by many Americans, but he was out of sympathy with roughly equivalent versions of political correctness imposed by the university leaders of the 1 890s and might likely be equally unsympathetic with a few of those on America's historically iconoclastic, liberal left who, in recent years, seek an orthodoxy of their own that, in some extreme articulations, distills into intellectual terrorism of Thermidorian dimensions.

Both the milder, timid and the grosser, nosier, versions of the sanitizers' rhetoric would appall Veblen, but he would be surprised by the fact that the indulgences with which the purifiers are increasingly endowed are granted not by the *business* culture's princes but by some of the priests of higher learning, including a few academic prize winners, and not a few of their presidents. Even after being properly instructed by today's students of youth about the importance now commonly attached to Urole models" for the young, he would probably be surprised that some lists of role models held in highest esteem include persons on campuses in charge of newfangled "advocacy centers" whose performance on behalf of constituents, in their pursuit of defendants, sometimes resemble Madame Defarge's style of support for Robespierre.

Veblen's idealized version of the higher learning—idle curiosity turned, by liberation from exclusively material aims, to science and scholarship—has, of course, not died on many campuses, but the academy's role as an agency, in Clark Kerr's fine phrase, that makes people safe for ideas, rather than the reverse, is increasingly harder to realize, as costs rise and as more and more new campus claimants to shrinking resources proliferate well beyond the "side shows" in the academy identified by Veblen in a later chapter. Some of these new claimants and their causes' champions augment their fiscal demands with angry, even blistering criticisms of those into whose company they have been enthusiastically recruited, but among whom they seek to enjoy privileged rights.

Governing Boards

Veblen grudgingly admired business leaders for their pecuniary wizardry, the artfully dodging Chicane" of some, and the productive genius of others. But he was harsh, indeed, in his judgments about whether the *popular adulation,* in the Age of Big Business, of their pecuniary wizardry (their capacities to make money, rather then goods, as an end) thereby qualified businessmen to conduct the higher learning through their governance of the academic enterprises that house "seats of learning." Readers will enjoy this essay and some may conclude that his pointed attacks on academic administrators have gained more force in the past seventy-five years than have his attacks on the motives and actions of trustees. I know of no universities in which the majority of faculty members do not angrily begrudge the expansion of academic administrators.

One may even suggest in passing, and while looking at businessmen in the 1980s, as well, that Veblen did give his trustee devils (and a few of our modern boardsmen) their due. The successors of the would-be rational masters of pecuniary chicane he grudgingly admired had, by mid 1989, truly mastered the arcane arts of mergering, acquisitioning, leveraging managerial "buyouts," conglomerating, and insider trading, while, too often, neglecting goods production and consumers' interests in quality and in competitive prices.

It is evident even in 1992 that quite a few business tycoons are still tardy in fully recognizing consumers' reason's for years—long interests in imported goods of high quality, and in nursing doubts about the salaries, bonuses, stock options, and "perks" that top executives secure themselves. These mostly regressive economic developments arguably led us to observe the fiftieth anniversary of Japan's submergence of naval vessels at Pearl Harbor, 1941 on the eighteen-month anniversary of our economy's submergence in recession in just plain peril. And the Captains of today's industry show as little promise of helping to stem the falling tides that have lowered all ships in recent years as do the rest of what has come to be called the establishment, including government leaders, neo-orthodox economists, pundits and consultants, and labor leaders.

A good part of Veblen's critique of businessmen's involvement in the conduct of higher education, meanwhile, was *rooted precisely* in the fact that businessmen *were* successful in business, though such success was "irrelevant" to higher education except (in *very* limited ways!) in the conduct of universities' fiscal affairs. Trustees from business circles are still prominently numerous on university boards today, however, *despite* the sad circumstances of so many of their own enterprises. But Veblen might well be pleased by the adequacy of his earlier tracings of cause and effect for understanding today's scene: trustees have considerably less control over the modern university than they did in Veblen's era; their declining influence in the academy may reflect the malperformance of America's present-day business culture, as exemplified by America, Inc.'s problematic performance in competition with Japan, Inc., Germany, Inc. and the smaller but booming economies in S. Korea, Malaysia, and Taiwan. When businessmen *are* successful, popular sentiments support their roles in higher education, and when their fortunes decline, their influence on campuses declines with them. Veblen would be grateful for the "downside" of this cycle.

Among additional sources of the reduction in trustees' potency are those stemming from the changes, over three generations, in businessmen's sensibilities about learning and about science and scholarship, incident to the business community's members' own rising educational achievements, their growing self-consciousness that they, themselves, have troubles "Meeting a payroll," and the growing numbers of them with spouses, sons, and daughters (Veblen would be very happily surprised to note the spouses and daughters) with Ph.D. degrees from many of the largest, best-established, and most prestigious of academic departments.

It is also the case that many industries employ large numbers of Ph.D.s—geologists, physicists, mathematicians, chemists, anthropologists, demographers, economists, and psychologists, to name a few. The business culture has clearly helped, in significant ways, to shape the academy, as Veblen argues, but academics' cultures have their own imperialists occupying what Max Weber, on viewing lower Manhattan from a ship, called the fortresses of capitalism. Much creative work in the fields of computing, economic forecasting in brokerage houses, mineral exploration, acoustics, pharmaceuticals, aerodynamics, nuclear energy, environmental science, cosmetics, and the for-profit, health related field, is contributed to industry by corporations' own platoons of susquepedalians with Ph.D. degrees, who dress with studied negligence in jeans and docksiders, and consume inconspicuously, otherwise, as matters of pride and life-style.

Most thoughtful academicians, in company with many other Americans, would thus acknowledge disappointments over the performance of business leaders since they were first faced with the full force of postwar foreign competition. But they would likely take issue with Veblen's implied argument that knaves and poltroons among our Captains of Industry who serve on university boards have, as such, exercised undue controls over the best of the higher learning's best and brightest since the late 1960s.

It is true that an Ivy League trustee caused problems, a few years ago when, with considerable gains resulting in his own fortunes, he brought his university's funds into "Pennsy" stocks just a little short of this railroad's failure. But, overall, the pecuniary advice trustees have accorded to universities has been both welcome and beneficial. There are few faculty among the top universities who do not cheer when the size of their universities' endowments are annually ranked well in *The Wall Street Journal*(!); a few are pleased when they are appointed to an endowed chair with a corporate name.

And, since the McCarthy witch hunts in the 1950s inspired proportionately more sickeningly sympathetic behavior from many government officials than from most business leaders, there have been few instances of flagrant violations of academic freedom by business tycoons on university boards beyond the walls of sectarian colleges.

One of the most significant exceptions was a trustee of the University of Texas, in Austin, who appointed himself a vigilante in hot pursuit of undergraduate newspaper editors and their faculty sponsors in the 1970s. But if the American Association of University Professors censures a university for infringements on faculty freedoms it is virtually always a president, a provost or a dean, not a trustee, who has been specifically indicted for heavy-handed treatment of one or more academic citizens. At this writing, meantime, Dartmouth College's beleaguered president has been ably defended by his college's board against attacks by a hyperconservative alumni group, led by William Simon, a financier who served for a time as secretary of the treasury under President Nixon, whose collective sensibilities were offended by black student protesters.

And most trustees have been responsive to Veblen's values: several board members acted like fully responsible intellectuals and heroic financiers in 1969-72 when Columbia faced extraordinarily high operating deficits and attacks from (mostly) middle-class "barbarians at their gates," graduate as well as undergraduate, who shut the university down for several weeks during April 1968.

Indeed, trustees were a good deal less ideologically impulsive than some of the institution's own faculty and administrators; the board members emerged as strong proponents of the academic freedoms of all parties during the mind-numbing "politicalization" of the totality of campus life, a six building-wide police Bust," and the paralysis of the university's central administration.

The board's chairman was as agonized over these developments as the sanest faculty at a time when, as a colleague likes to put it, the sanity coefficient at Columbia was not very high. One of these trustees, the late Benjamin Buttenwieser, an investment banker, and Democratic party fund raiser, was rejected seventy-seven years ago by Columbia's doctoral program in nineteenth-century English poetry because, at seventeen, he was too young. Buttenwieser was perhaps more prominent than most other colleagues on the board, but he was not alone as a champion of Veblen's higher learning. The equivalent board at Berkeley was also, for the most part, stalwart in its self-control even with critical governors, Ronald Reagan and Edmund Brown, looking over the board's shoulders at the University of California.

Interestingly, the present-day trustees of the Rockefeller University, in New York, preside over the *only* "seat of learning" that precisely meets Veblen's standards for this designation: its faculty is chock-a-block with members of the National Academy of Sciences, it has no undergraduates, no schools of business, journalism, pharmacy, Communications," or home economics; it has no football team, no fraternities, and no career counselling service, and offers *very* few formal classes. The university's founding father and benefactor, meantime, was a general, compared to most of Veblen's Captains of Industry, however much Veblen resented the earlier Rockefeller who founded the University of Chicago, where Veblen was resident soon after the university came into being. And Nelson Rockefeller managed, as governor of New York, to finance his university, the State University of New York, owning retail outlets all over the state, with other's funds.

The Academic Administration

Presidents and their high-level associates, meantime, are more the victims, at this writing, of multiple crosspressures and less the polishers of apples for their trustees, than they were when Veblen delivered himself of this book to his publisher. Most presidents now come, as they did in his time, from the para-scholarly ranks of their own or others' faculties; not a few have been deans and provosts (and have often been candidates who have been running for presidencies) with some sense of university administrative matters. However well equipped to mobilize and lead universities they may be, though, presidents today face problems Veblen could not easily have imagined and his arch comments at the turn of the century might be softened (somewhat) were he able to visit campuses today.

Consider that the majority of standing faculty in universities today can now claim long-term tenure—beyond age seventy, in many cases. Their tenure claims (granted by acts of trustees!) assure those among them with integrity (and even a few without) the right to make themselves heard on matters over which they have strong disagreements with their universities' heads; faculties could not meaningfully vote "no confidence" in their administrators in Veblen's day as they can—and do with increasing frequency—on campuses these days.

Even as I write, the present-day heir of one of the presidents under whom Veblen served is living the last days of his tour of duty as Stanford's leader, as he prepares to depart from office in 1992, after resigning in 1991, following widespread sentiments of trustees and faculty that his administrative underlings' mismanagement of overhead cost reimbursements from Uncle Sam made him an embarrassment; press treatments in distinguished academic publications reported frequently, in 1991, on his faculty's criticisms. At this science center, Stanford's researchers, in common with others elsewhere, have generally begrudged their universities' overhead reimbursements from Uncle Sam on the grounds that their grant proposals become uncompetitively expensive and that the proceeds help to sustain "bloated"—a common epithet—administrative staffs, and to equip and decorate administrators' homes.

And Columbia's president and its provost left office in 1968, without ceremony, when the trustees acted responsively to thoughts about the university's situation from members of an ad hoc faculty committee that even included some erstwhile admirers of these two leaders.

Other cases, less celebrated, would make it clear as Veblen would recognize, that strongmen, like his bêtes noires in this book, no longer terrorize faculties; presidents simply "lose their faculties," as wags often put it, when they engage professors on one or another issue considered vital on a given campus at a given time. The turnover rates of university presidents have been notoriously high since the 1960s, as they buckle under the pressures of fund raising, critical faculty committees, skyrocketing operating costs, federal grant monitors, and disaffected alumni. As for deans, "they are to faculties," as a senior colleague helpfully declared to me on my becoming associate dean of Columbia's faculty, on the heels of the revolution in '69, "as fire hydrants are to dogs." Veblen, to mix metaphors, would have cheered the turning of the worms.

This is not to argue that presidents, provosts, and deans since Veblen's day have become simply "ceremonially adequate" figures; a few of them have managed long periods in office during which they have served their own visions well—for both good and ill. But while local responses will vary in the points at which hostile faculty tempers reach high fever pitch, presidents and their subalterns may be completely confident, nowadays, that when the fever point is reached on a given campus, their days in office will be numbered. Many of the Rockefeller University's faculty, for example, opposed the appointment of Dr. David Baltimore, a Nobelist in biological science, to the institution's presidency and worked very diligently at forcing his resignation, not too many months later, in the late fall of 1991, following his allegedly misplaced support of an associate accused of fudging scientific data in a research report.

Veblen would also find it interesting that senior academic officers are sought after by committees in which faculty members generally constitute a majority. And he would find it very amusing that the priests of learning tend to be as unsympathetic towards officers they actually helped to select, after a very few years, as was the case, years earlier, towards those picked unilaterally by trustees!

Nor are deans—"mice aspiring to be rats," in the now-friendly academic joke—typically very powerful at this juncture. Strong, that is, strong-armed, deans tend to sense that their prospects dim after three or four years, and so they often make themselves available as candidates for higher offices in other academic venues. The fact is that many, many heads of academic departments—bureaux, in Veblen's "academic bureaucracies"—more often became formidable since the 1960s as a result of the academic stars and academic prize winners in their departments' tenured ranks, than because of their own typically modest talents.

It is also the case that highly visible, accomplished faculty members can and do walk off campuses when they feel that they or their colleagues have been trifled with by petty bullies or unappreciative dilettantes, and these leaders pay a price for the losses. New decanal appointees, at the same time, are far more likely to preside over budget cuts, struggle with operating deficits, suffer undergraduate newspaper reporters, and bargain with teaching assistants' unions, than lead faculties in pursuit of academic visions. Deans and provosts, like Columbia's Jacques Barzun, with visions are only a little less rare than chaste persons in houses of ill repute. Self made academic leaders, for the most part, they are generally the products of their own semi-skilled intellectual labor and of groping search committees consisting of politically sensitive souls representing all relevant campus interests.

Many readers will be somewhat surprised, meantime, to learn from Veblen that the very considerable blurring of the lines between graduate and undergraduate instruction, now so common, was well advanced by the 1890s, as collegiate studies came to be more and more dominant in shaping the ways and means of all of university life. Prescribed curricula and "the elective system," permitting early specialization, were to be found just about universally on university campuses in Veblen's time, and the custom of graduate students fulfilling residence requirements in Supper division" undergraduate courses was well institutionalized. And, as in many modern universities, undergrads could "submatriculate" in graduate degree programs. The fact should also be noted, however, that the Ph.D. "glut" of the 1970s discouraged many able candidates from applying to graduate programs; many professors accordingly took pleasure in working with the best undergraduates at the expense of significant numbers of less talented post-collegians who, borrowing from Veblen, were so often men and women of "indifferent composition."

As Veblen saw it, the generalization of undergraduate arrangements permitted the same "economies of scale," the same routinization of the learning enterprise, and the same system of grading, marking, and credit-granting that control collegians, to be employed in graduate studies. Thus came graduate program contents, curriculum, and instruction to be "driven," as they are today, in considerable measure by undergraduate college programs.

These arrangements, for Veblen, added up to the same standardization and academic "accountancy" of intellectual effort for graduate students as for undergraduates: grade point averages, course credits, scheduled class meetings, and term intervals, have to be reconciled across academic ::ac departments in order that all students' progress could be marketed by a single "multivariate" calculus; however different the contents of one or another discipline might be from most others, however intellectually uncongenial conventional calendar divisions were, uniformity became an administrative necessity in Veblen's time; it remains so. We have simply refined these systems, in or our times, by adding religious holidays during which even totally secularized students will absent themselves, by adding "stress breaks," and by instituting, "reading periods" in advance of incredible numbers of examinations. On some campuses I have visited I have wondered whether they might not consider more intermittent brief vacations so that many undergraduate and a few graduate students, after a few heavy reading assignments, could, as Veblen might well have said, rest their tired lips.

It was remarkable then, and it is remarkable now, that more than two dozen different bodies of knowledge in a typical school of arts and sciences represented by departments (as the meat and produce units in supermarkets, are called) could be reduced to the same formulas of hours, weeks, terms, and years, without more than a remonstrating doubt, now and again, being expressed by the majorities of graduate and undergraduate faculties who are obliged to be complaisant about the routines. If one could teach a course in six weeks, stretch it out to twelve. If one needs eighteen weeks, stretch it to twenty-four or compress it into twelve weeks. Except in medical schools, learning thus follows the agricultural calendar (with a midyear totemic,: celebration of the winter solstice), the clock, and a department's needs for courses that trade off meeting times between faculty and students' preferences, from art history to zoology. A great portion of learning can putatively take place in classrooms 'twixt nine amend two, preferably not above the second floor, and in courses in which 70 percent of the students earn A's or B's. I draw these inferences from reams of "printout" afforded me, as a dean, by an "associate dean for administration," in a world in which the students likewise the professionals, become rank empiricists.

The benefits of these businesslike arrangements are, of course, very agreeable to hosts of department chairs, deans, registrars, and their technical staffs who are obliged, variously, to staff courses, monitor student performance, and assign classroom and laboratory spaces; administrators thus are dispatchers in the academic equivalents of motor pools, with faculties to operate the vehicles in accord with established procedures and schedules, and licensed to do so by those who award them their Ph.D. degrees. Their roadmaps are contained in bulletins, catalogues, handbooks and streams of memoranda. Schedules, like timetables, are produced up to three years in advance. Academic "Five-Year Plans" are ubiquitous.

In further emulation of industrial practices, even in the most elite universities, the most pretentious and often prideful presidents and provosts acknowledge neither shame nor embarrassment in discussions of their faculty colleagues' total pedagogic efforts as "teaching loads"; their graduates as "products." Faculty members are routinely referred to, in countless university handbooks, as "officers of instruction"; intellectual centers of advanced studies are "think tanks"; admissions personnel are "recruiters," (new faculty members are also "recruited"); generous benefactors, like attractive investors on Wall Street, are "fat cats" while colleagues of independent bent are "oddballs."

On my own and on innumerable other campuses the inducements offered to attract celebrated candidates for appointments have recently come to include "sign up bonuses," just as they are added to the inducements tendered to highly talented "intercollegiate" athletes who go on to perform as professionals, especially on basketball courts and in football stadia, after four years of tutoring by professors of English, history, business, and by these learned persons' academic peers in sprawling departments of athletics who Veblen noted, generally hold ranks of "professors of physical education." "Gym requirements" have pretty much disappeared, though; the "healthy minds" now have "healthy bodies" without their attendance being noted by "athletic scholarship" winners.

Veblen's treatment of intercollegiate sports, by the way, occurs in his third chapter in the context of a discouraged discussion of student activities in passages that will elicit nervous chuckles from even the most cynical of academic pragmatists. His contempt for the hordes of people on a given campus who provide long lists of "student services," sometime headed by a vice provost, would turn to outrage were he to look at my university's telephone directory's departmental lists of names of personnel who afford such services. *Hundreds* of persons are listed in any university directory who, among other chores, advise, treat, tutor, succor, counsel, coach, provoke, feed, house, try and punish, hire and support, an place undergraduates some professional school grad students) in jobs. In recent years universities have added Advocacy" centers, for students who feel themselves oppressed, or need help m becoming mindful of their circumstances, that are staffed by directors, consciousness raisers, harassment detectors, and the usual cadres of supporting staff.

Given the reach of crimes by their neighbors, and sometimes by what Veblen called universities' own inmates, furthermore, the nation's larger universities also have constabularies as large as those that keep the peace in middle-size cities. These forces for law and order are generally about as effective in reforming the rowdy and misanthropic ways of social fraternities, meantime, as are presidents who are caught, paralyzingly, between fraternity alums, on one side, and those who are outraged by stripteasers, at fraternity initiations, and who regard fraternity brothers, sometimes quite accurately according to the *Chronicle of Higher Education*'s reports, as sexists in training to become rapists, on the other. Veblen took a dim view of these "side shows to the main tent" but reports that they were, in his times, only scenes of "innocent dissipation."

There can be little wonder that top campus leaders must have pecuniary skills if they are to manage and equip huge phalanxes of people in need of uniforms and weapons, football pads, automobiles and trucks, corporate liaisons, sports stadia, landscaping implements, cafeterias, magnetic resonance imagers, post offices, travel offices for those who seem to hold endowed chairs on airplanes, computing centers, employee training centers, buckets and mops, clean animal cages, and the physical spaces in which these legions of "infrastructural" experts, servants, and experimental beasts of scientific burden, do their extra-academic chores. Universities' purchasing officers, like their "planners," accountants, admissions officers, travel department directors, and administrative computing centers' leaders, have their own national professional associations, where they may attend technical seminars to learn of the newest tricks of their trade.

And the end, stretching back from Veblen's time, is nowhere in sight, as university leaders and their faculties become gatekeepers who operate the sluices through which the middle and upper echelons of most of the American labor force's members, with or without intellectual merit, scholarly and scientific imagination creative impulses, decent tastes, or civilized manners, must eventually flow on their way to their work, whether in hospitals, sports arenas, television studios, supermarkets, cigarette manufactories, churches, schools, dog kennels, cabinet secretaries, cruise ships real estate agencies, army regiments, universities, automobile dealerships, banks, prisons, tax offices, gambling casino's headquarters,[8] and in innumerable other mills, shops, labs, mines, forges and, of course, in "offices."

Veblen, as the reader will see, was ever the optimist however he felt that the true believers in the higher learning would, at least embody the loftier wishes of society for a richer understanding of their social, aesthetic, political, and scientific worlds, and that the citizens of society would ultimately resolve to leave the best of the higher learning's citizens free to pursue knowledge as an end in itself, given that their efforts would underpin inventions and conventions that would ultimately make the living of their lives easier healthier, and in the best sense, fuller.

Whether college enrollment booms on university campuses can be continuingly prevented from shattering the fragile barrier between the higher learning and the distractions there from, and whether universities can continue, with a modicum of support, as "seats of knowledge," are vexing questions—and then some. We can thank Veblen (and a precious few others) for worrying about it and for sketching our upward trend lines towards materialistic goals that, while they may slow, are not likely to head down either steeply or any time soon. The expansion, in recent decades, of the so-called service sector assures that we will have more schools and departments of hotel administration, health management, retailing, dental hygiene, and advertising.

Veblen also deplored the competition among academic departments for undergraduate enrollments, the results of which skew the allocation of academic resources and lead to proliferations of courses, such that professors would be dispatched to drive vehicles for which their academic licenses do not, in fact, qualify them. Such competition would force the priests of learning to prostitute their standards in favor of course admissions, and further drain off scholars from their higher earnings into pedagogic "schoolmaster" roles with collegians; college teachers, for Veblen, are too often academic middlemen who distribute to their students what others have learned and discovered. When the truly learned scholars at a university are driven to teaching undergraduates, they thus become for Veblen, more and more, their own and others' salesmen. Biologists, for example, often complain that they are in service departments for "pre-meds."

Competition, he correctly predicted would lead many teachers to accord higher and higher grades to serve their chairmen's drives for more enrollments—which, for Veblen was good business but not higher learning, especially when so many students are more interested in "politely blameless dissipation"—athletics, clubs, fraternities, "'student activities'...'side shows'"—than in scholarship. Veblen's view of this competition could only grow dimmer seventy-

five years later, as he would quickly observe the cutthroat competition among universities, the "privates" especially, for the shrinking
supply of teenagers in the marketplace owing to the greater conti-
nence of baby busters' parents than that of the fertile parents of the
baby boomers, in the period 1945-1962.

Veblen's comments on the role of scholarships designed to attract
students to graduate programs will strike familiar notes m many
readers' minds, but he could not have anticipated the sensible substitution of the term "financial aid" for "scholarships" accorded to
about half of private schools' undergraduates, a *great* many of
whom receive support in spite of their measurably deficient academic aptitudes, as universities seek to increase the diversity of
their student bodies and to accommodate the least prepared among
them with costly remedial programs, late summer "pre-matricula-
tion" crash courses in mathematics and English, and by reducing
course requirements, designing special course sections in watered-
down sciences, and by sponsoring advocacy programs designed
to help raise the consciousness of "newcomers" to the academy of
the parochially "majoritarian" flavor of college courses and campus norms that do not adequately address these newcomers' "social histories." There is something historically Historical about an
increasingly prevailing view that the wretched victims of poverty
and political oppression on this earth were never with us before It
has been several seasons, meantime, since the post-collegian Minnesota Vikings have enjoyed the legitimate right to bask in memo-
ries of the violence of Veblen's and my forebears; we can almost
understand the resentments of Native Americans over the logos of
college teams like the "Dartmouth Indians" and the Redmen from
St. John's. Animal rights advocates will not presumably trouble over
California's Bears, Minnesota's Gophers, Penn State's Nittany Li-
ons, or Texas's Longhorns. But who can tell about interest groups
on given campuses?

Finally, Veblen's observations about the essentially careerist interests of the majority of the undergraduates of his day were widely
expressed by youths, themselves, in national probability surveys of
1980s undergraduates. He might have found surprising however,
the hostility towards pecuniary interests and toward corporate
America that were expressed during the brief interlude of campus
disorders and student protests, 1968-1975, that were often led by
graduate students.

Indeed, Veblen's own published work enjoyed considerable favor during that period in which students' watchwords were to do "one's own thing," "to trust no one over thirty," and to pursue studies that were "relevant"; this book had particularly wide currency, and Veblen's subtitle, "A Memorandum on the Conduct of Universities by Businessmen," was appealing, indeed, among those who quickened the demiurge that universities be centers for those who sought to "restructure" work, welfare, politics, race and "gender" relations, income distribution, and policies regarding drugs foreign affairs, sexual "preferences," and abortion. Among the gurus to some of these free spirits were Timothy Leary and Edward Alpert, Harvard faculty members at the time, both sons of business leaders, and both authoritative lecturers on the joys of "tuning out," "dropping acid," and "dropping out." Interestingly, many others of the rebels were also business leaders' and other professionals' sons and daughters, and card-carrying subscribers to the American Express Company's credit division; they were at least as angry toward industrialists as they were toward university leaders; Alpert's father, for example, was president of the Pennsy.

Academic Prestige and Material Equipment

Veblen begins this essay with a wonderfully cynical treatment of businessmen's efforts to stimulate customers' sensibilities about the "prestige value" of the goods and services produced by craftsmanlike employees that they market thorough less useful traffickers—advertisers and marketers. The publicity-generating process for Veblen, created an "immaterial increment of illusions" about their corporations' offerings and an "intangible and expensive utility [that attached to] advertisers' or salesmen's work—work spent not so much on the goods as on the customer's sensibilities" about the value in a business culture of what Veblen elsewhere mocked as "conspicuous consumption." Such "a body of accumulated and marketable illusions" he writes, "constitutes is known as 'good will.'"

Veblen would not be shocked to learn that, in December 1991, the House of Representatives agreed, with White House encouragement, to allow payments for a takeover in the excess of the value of a target corporation's real assets to be treated as valuable goodwill that thus can be added to the acquiring company's tax deductible costs, a decision that was specifically reached to help give a new lease on life to the currently (1991) flagging market for corporate takeovers. Veblen's view of our society's affections for intangibles make abundant room for what, with his fondness for puns, he would unquestionably forgive me for calling legerdemain. While *this* particular new boon will be welcomed in corporate financial circles it will not directly help today's "university directorates"; it will however help faculty pensions to the extent that these funds' directors "capitalize" on the stock market effects of mergers and acquisitions.

But Veblen recognized that university directorates fully appreciated the role of publicity and the possible heaps of good will it promised to generate, even though he seriously doubted whether "this notoriety and prestige, or the efforts that go to their cultivation, will conduce in any appreciable degree to any ostensible purpose served or awarded by any university. These things, that is to say, rather hinder than help the cause of learning, in that they divert attention and effort from scholarly workmanship to statistics and salesmanship." Once again, Veblen's distinction between industry and pecuniary business.

Veblen goes on to say, emphatically, that "The gain...from such an accession of popular illusions is a differential gain in competition with rival seats of learning, not a gain to the republic of learning." He then points out that prestige actually does not do much to help serve a university's pecuniary interests—he likens efforts to impress potential donors to the drawings of a lottery—but that prestige attaches itself to buildings and equipment which, for the "unlettered," are visible evidence of credibility whereas the work of the academy's "learned men" is generally unseen and even more rarely understood by those whom university presidents are determined to please.

Veblen's characterization of the ways in which professors would avoid controversial pronouncements, thereby to avoid offending widely held beliefs, especially those treasured by business leaders, apply to a number of academicians in the arts and sciences especially into the early 1960s. I can recall that the CEO of one of the "Big Steel" companies threatened, in 1962, to withhold payment of a pledge made to a dean to endow a huge classroom in a proposed building because I had taken him to task, in a Columbia University journal, for testimony before the U.S. Senate Anti-Monopoly Committee. Senators may think that differences in steel prices are desirable, the CEO told the late Senator Kefauver, but that his own "concept is that a price that matches another price is a competitive price.

I say the buyer has more choice when the other fellow's price matches our price ... if all steel prices are the same then the customer is free to buy from any producer he chooses," but "if prices are different, then the buyer has no real freedom of choice because he must buy from the company that sells the cheapest." The dean felt generously disposed toward academic freedom and defended his (then untenured) junior colleague before the chastened CEO. Veblen would have been proud of the dean, an ex-officer of Esso, now Exxon!

Since that time the social scientists Veblen chided for the very conventional—uncritical—treatments they accord their subjects have become far more critically free-spirited in their demystifying studies of most of the very "habituations in thought" to which Veblen showed the way. And he most assuredly did show the way, however much his means, his trenchant English prose, has given way to polysyllabic jargon and opaque argot.

Coda

Veblen's title for his concluding chapter is "Summary" to which, given his larger mission, he not surprisingly adds, "and Trial Balance." It would be a formidable task to confront this essay with distillation in mind (with one important exception); first off, it would be unfair to Veblen's triumphant success at outdoing himself in concentrated applications of Veblenesque prose; an admiring contemporary called Veblen's "a cactus style"; bowing to more modern newspeak, it is not an exaggeration to state that, in this chapter, he writes in a scorched earth, carpet-bombing style.

A second reason for leaving this chapter essentially for readers' delectation is that, if it describes the heads of universities in his time with considerable accuracy, it at least caricatures the heads of today's academies. Good caricatures simply offer little exaggerations in the interests of a larger truth, as so often is the case when distinguished scholars are introduced to audiences; the marginal overstatements do not mislead, they capture essences of their subject with a large number of small excesses. Veblen's descriptions of president "Strongman's" powers, as I have already suggested, do not fit today's presidents at all well, but he stresses other aspects of presidential proclivities in his concluding chapter that too often do apply, and therein lies an exception to my feelings that readers should "have at" Veblen's final words without my intercession.

The exception: Veblen himself boils his book-long critique down to two basic points, or as he call them "two foci [notoriety; and the academic executive] about which swings the orbit of the university world...having virtually but a single centre, which may perhaps indifferently be spoken of as the university's president or as its renown."

I will begin to take leave of these introductory pleasures by noting that Veblen's preoccupation with the matter of renown should also guide any modern academic insider who seeks, in serious ways, to afford us a timely new study of the higher learning. We live in an age in which prestige, and the publicity aimed at achieving it, after all, remain matters of very high priority. Indeed, it is my sense that universities' determined efforts to enhance their images, generate favorable publicity, and elevate their competitive statuses, have been significantly increased as their funding problems have multiplied, and as birth rates stabilized at lower post-baby-boomer rates.

Virtually every university's so-called development office has grown, and new capital fund drives pop up across the Republic with the first crocuses each February, and with them, so have publicity departments. These publicity departments are also important in helping a university to deal with news headlines about the use of federal contract funds, laboratory animals' rights, athletic recruiting irregularities, and the high (and low) jinks of fraternities.

The pace for most academic departments is set by "the top ten," so ranked, literally, by national organizations of immense prestige. And universities and their schools are ranked by their budgets, book collections, prize winners, and endowments, in surveys of deans, presidents, alumni, and by popular newsmagazine editors. Well-ranked departments are celebrated, sometimes even with a touch of arrogance, by their members, their chairs, and by their deans, provosts, and their presidents, in reports, news releases, "job" offers to attractive faculty candidates, and to parents of prospective admissions candidates. In turn, the latter candidates can add, in both cases, to additional increments of prestige if they raise a faculty's "visibility" and its undergraduates' avenge College Board scores, respectively. In my and many others' universities the most demanding departments—physics, chemistry, mathematics, and biology, economics and (sometimes) psychology—contrive, with provosts and deans, to compare their majors' SAT scores, intramurally, with those of other majors. And "P.R." departments need no 3 a.m. calls from university presidents with orders to deliver champagne to a large lecture hall for 9 a.m. toasts to newly minted Nobel medal winners in which journalists are seated in the front rows. Flash pictures appear in the *New York Times* complete with "bios" conveniently provided by campus "news offices."

And, during half time "breaks" in televised intercollegiate football games both contenders' universities are described, in all their telegenic splendor, as founts of truth, artistic accomplishment, disciplined science, and literary excellence, on videotapes provided by appropriate campus offices. One reputable school of business sends videocassettes to high school seniors with professionally made tapes about its charms.

On New Years Day 1992, a massive and energetic cornerback for Texas A & M was lauded, in a "graphic" afforded the television broadcasters by his university, for his masterful scholarship in his field, "Recreation, Parks, and Tourism." Sports columnists at the *New York Times* wondered, on January 2nd, whether this gladiator's professor is Smokey T. Bear. Few presidents, in meetings with large city alumni groups, can resist a disarming quip, at the end of a speech about alma mater's academic distinctions: "So you see, we are continuing to make ours a university that the football team can be proud of," a way, one reckons, of fighting forest fires with back fires.

One mentions these mixtures of types of urges to notoriety less to serve the spirit of Veblen, deserving though it is, than to point out that the urges can be perverse insofar as these urges know absolutely no bounds as between Veblen's higher learning and Veblen's "side shows." These urges encourage hired publicity specialists to treat universities as three-ring conglomerates of science wizards, intellectual havens, and pre-occupational boot camps for lawyers, athletes, investment bankers, and many other economic actors.

Veblen's "renown" is present on almost every campus; it visits some faculty members regularly as magazine "cover story" journalists and public radio and television staffers call "experts" about one or another matter on their news desks. Through the good offices of Saddam Hussein, Boris Yeltsin, and Mikhail Gorbachev, a dozen political scientists became almost as famous as America's retired generals and admirals during the early months of 1991.

Veblen's university presidents, however, the other of his two "foci," have failed to measure down, nowadays, to the levels of arrogant behavior that earned their predecessors his contempt. He likes the word "notoriety" to describe what presidents thirst after but the most notorious presidents, in the calendar year preceding my scribbling these lines, included only one fairly strong Strongman, in Veblen's usage (Derek Bok), who retired from Harvard after many years in office and who has offered his alums and sundry committees and commissions insightful observations on many matters pertaining to higher education.

The others were a man who allegedly played games with the University of South Carolina's fortunes; a man who allegedly preyed upon male students in Georgia; a man whose subalterns' accounting practices obliged Stanford to reimburse Uncle Sam for irregular expense charges to federal grants and contracts, and one, at the Rockefeller University, whose name was allegedly mixed up in a science scandal, as noted earlier.

Presidents, continue to bask in public glory with star faculty—"world-class scholars" they are called—a few more of whom they may even personally respect then did presidents in Veblen's time. But these modern proxies had best be prepared to be vilified, over the course of a given academic year, for their insufficient (even if frequent) efforts to support, unconditionally, the needs—demands, more often—for resources, succor, the approbation of their causes, and the condemnation of their appointed antagonists, of a staggering number of well-organized interest groups among students, alumni and, occasionally community neighbors.

The president of Dartmouth has been attacked by alumni, as I have noted, who support a nonuniversity sponsored conservative student newspaper whose columns have often offended Jews and African Americans. And the former president of a university in Pennsylvania was driven out of office in 1989, following charges that he touched one of his female aide's knees, under the table, at an out-of-town dinner. Veblen would indeed be shocked to observe how far presidents have fallen from the self-constructed pedestals on which they sat in the 1 890s. And where presidents hypocritically and insincerely accorded esteem to Veblen's most distinguished colleagues, it is nowadays faculty colleagues who merely tolerate or barely suffer, their universities' officers.

Only Veblen's wider going—and ultimate—concerns about the larger subversions of the higher learning by a business culture's values, remain in need of comment. Put crisply, Veblen's judgments, on this count, must be revised today. While universities are even more "bureaucratic" now than in Veblen's era, with more conformities to schedules required, more standardizations, and all that, the business culture is no longer the key contributor to values on campuses beyond those this culture gives to the values of a few "professional schools" faculties.

Indeed, the cultures on most (nonsectarian) campuses today lend themselves hardly at all to easy characterizations in large part because universities have literally become, all things to all persons—and innumerable causes. In the event, it is possible for many scholars and scientists to do exemplary and highly regarded work, while presidents, provosts, and deans distractedly deal with legislators, university donors, reformers, faculty colleagues with spectacularly attractive job offers, students with acne of the spirit, scrupulous government contractors' auditors, animal rightists, and student newspapers—among others with appointments on overfilled daily schedules.

If professors are still distracted significantly from their basic research, they are protected from "strongmen" administrators because administrators, now, are also distracted today—from fulfilling their erstwhile "adminocratic" preferences. It is not an easily challenged proposition that these campus figures allow about thirty minutes to most issues (the budgets they construct among the exceptions) that come daily to their desks. One senior leader I've had occasion to observe alerts those comparatively few who bother to meet with him at all, to the imperatives of his necessarily well-ordered life by a little pinging sound, on the half hour, from a high-tech digital wrist watch. A neat index card in his shirt pocket, to which he refers, almost autonomically, at the pinging, tells of his next half-hour *pflicht*; his weariness does not let itself be masked, as his academic visions are sacrificed in favor of those who seek his endorsements of multiple intent group supplicants. What a change from the impresarios cum autocrats to whose librettos so many of Veblen's colleagues at Chicago and Stanford sang and danced.

At the same time that universities are put upon by growing numbers of not-so-friendly users, the business community has, itself, become far more differentiated; the House of Adam Smith, who was a professor of moral philosophy at Glasgow, now has many mansions. Such fragmentation does not a homogenous culture make, their neo-Marxist critics' protestation's generally, we might say, withstanding.

And faculties themselves, in the most reputable universities, have managed better than in Veblen's time, to combine teaching with research, with the help of leaves, research funds (though not as ample as in the 1960s and 1970s), teaching assistants (who are often very competent), fewer course obligations, and more choices regarding how and what will be taught.

If my readers include gamblers on matters of future trends in academic schedules, courses, and grades, I would suggest that they bet that there will be more seminars, fewer courses that meet often; fewer courses required for graduation; and more "A's"—the latter will reduce office hour wranglings with students—and thus contribute to more higher learning by the twenty percent of faculty who live for their subjects and, for the others, more time for senate meetings, committee sessions, and for grousing. Such readjustments will also assure that "downsized" faculties will not be obliged to do the work of departing colleagues and teaching assistants whose obligations will simply disappear.

Much in *The Higher Learning in America is* sufficiently applicable to make this volume very much "well worth a read," as they say in bookstores. It will be disquieting to those younger ones, who, with Veblen, care deeply about learning as an end unto itself, and cannot be optimistic that arrangements familiar in his time will soon yield to reformers.

Older newcomers to Veblen's words will be reminded of the axiom, in high school biology, that "ontogeny recapitulates phylogeny"; in the event, in the gestation period of each new generation of university arrangements, the "parents'" arrangements are recapitulated. Veblen was an evolutionist in his thinking and would feel very much vindicated, in this particular, could he visit with us.

I join the publisher in welcoming those who care, those who know that to care is to worry, those who enjoy wordplay by a whimsically angry wordsmith, and those who enjoy having their unexamined assumptions contested even if the contesting author, as an antagonist, is given to exaggerations in the service of truth.

The fact of the matter is that we continue do most of things to the higher learning in a modified business civilization that were done to it when this civilization was in its adolescence. As Veblen put it metaphorically in *The Theory of the Leisure Class,* "The adoption of the cap and gown is one of the striking atavistic features of modern college life," and atavists, in some degree, we remain. Veblen—with the heart of a socialist and brains enough to be skeptical of socialism's prospects—would most assuredly not be altogether surprised to learn that faculties' participation in the control of the university that lay so close to his heart would add up to yet another distraction for the modern, boggled, academic mind. But he would be pleased that presidents and administrators may be even more distracted by the quotidian realities of late twentieth-century academic life than are their faculty colleagues.

Notes

1. For a recent and very successful effort to examine the philosophical underpinnings of Veblen's work, see Murray G. Murphey, "Thorstein Veblen: Instinctive Values and Evolutionary Science," in Murray G. Murphey and Ivar Berg, editors, *Values and Value Theory in Twentieth-Century America: Essays in Honor of Elizabeth Flower,* (Philadelphia: Temple University Press, 1988), 122-145.
2. *How We Live* (Cambridge, MA: Harvard University Press, 1983) p. 5.
3. Ibid., p. 12.
4. Ibid., p. 1.
5. From the dust jacket of Bloom's best-seller. Bloom does not mention Veblen but comes out about the same place after a review not of American institutions but of its academicians' waywardness. *The Closing of the American Mind* (New York: Simon and Schuster, 1987).
6. I should alert readers, that Veblen correctly uses "sophisticated" in the sense long, long assigned it, *not* as a term of approbation!
7. *Education and Jobs: The Great Training Robbery* (New York: Praeger, 1970).
8. The references to occupations here are not rhetoric; I have one or more former students at work in these among other settings.

10

The Theory of Business Enterprise

Douglas F. Dowd

Thorstein Veblen was born in Wisconsin in 1857, and he grew up in Minnesota. There, in the heartland of the United States, Veblen was one of twelve children of a Norwegian immigrant farm family. On the surface, then, a quintessential member of nineteenth-century U.S. society; only on the surface, though, for Veblen turned out to be most peculiar. His personal history and social setting gave him the opportunity to undertake his numerous, far-reaching, and penetrating studies; his personal quirks and drives added impulse and genius to opportunity. The results include the present book, the first and still one of the most pertinent analyses of the evolution, the nature, and the meaning of U.S. capitalism.

The Theory of Business Enterprise (1904) is the most powerful and impressive of Veblen's studies of the United States—powerful because of its underlying theoretical framework, impressive because it foretold so well what we now live with and under: the system of monopoly capitalism. In his own time, and until his death in 1929, Veblen was alone in perceiving the comprehensive socio-political-economic-global system that could emerge, and that after World War II did emerge, as it had to if capitalism was to be resuscitated and reinvigorated after its decades of self-inflicted wounds—World War I, the Great Depression, and World War II. Nothing approximating an equally systematic treatment of the capitalist need for and possibilities of such a system has come from any but Marxists, and that not until 1966 with the publication of *Monopoly Capital* by Paul Baran and Paul Sweezy. Mainstream professionals remain innocent of such knowledge, still, though their nervousness increases as their theoretical constructs fall one after another from the weight of social realities. In the two decades after *The Theory,* Veblen went on to broaden and deepen his analysis (most notably in *The Nature of Peace,* 1917, and in *Absentee Ownership,* 1923); it is remarkable how self-contained and how germane *The Theory* is when read today.

Even a meager recounting of Veblen's own history and of his time sheds some light on what made him peculiar; even the fullest biography leaves his genius unexplained.[1] First, the farm family of which Veblen was a member was anything but typical. The father and mother would be classified as intellectuals by today's standards, and both were much more self-reliant and multiskilled than is customary, whether among farmers or intellectuals. Veblen was like them in all these ways; if anything, more so. He remained deeply respectful of them for his entire life. From what we know, the table talk in the Veblen home was superior to what one finds at a faculty gathering today—which, upon reflection, may be damning the Veblens with faint praise. Be that as it may, Veblen was encouraged to go to college (Carleton, in Minnesota) and on to the Ph.D. (at Yale, in philosophy). Most of his education before Carleton was picked up at home, and most of that was in Norwegian, German, Latin, and Greek. When he enrolled at Carleton he was already a scholar, but he had to take what now would be called "English as a second language."

Veblen had a hard time financing his education at Yale; after getting his degree in 1884 he entered harder times still: he could not get a job. He got jobs beginning in 1891, in economics, but he could never hold one. That in itself is a fitting commentary on the employment criteria of universities; Veblen repaid them all—and most especially Chicago and Stanford—in his still applicable *The Higher Learning: A Memorandum on the Conduct of Universities by Businessmen* (New York: B.W. Huebsch, 1918), whose original subtitle was "A Study in Total Depravity."

Toward the end of his life some appreciative economists sought to have his achievements recognized honorifically through the American Economics Association. Veblen scorned the effort—whether out of bitterness, contempt, or both is a matter of dispute. He died just as the stupefying depression of the 1930s began—a condition and process, in the absence of what he called "inspired waste," Veblen saw as chronic for "the New Order." Monopoly capitalism has found those essential and inspired ways to waste labor and resources—and not least among them the massive military expenditures *after* World War II (well over two *trillion* dollars in the United States since 1946). The man who wrote the following words (in the last chapter of *The Theory*) would not have been surprised:

> The modern warlike policies are entered upon for the sake of peace, with a view to the orderly pursuit of business.... At the same stroke they direct the popular interest to other, nobler, institutionally less hazardous matters than the unequal distribution of wealth or of creature comforts.... In this direction, evidently, lies the hope of a corrective for "social unrest" and similar disorders of civilized life.... Such is the promise held out by a strenuous national policy.

Veblen has been claimed and rejected both by sociologists and economists as being one of theirs. He enriched and attacked both disciplines, as he did so many others: philosophy, history, social psychology, politics, and linguistics. Veblen took all knowledge as necessary and relevant to adequate understanding of anything. Though he eschewed it or any other classification for himself, he was a practicing "dialectician," a holistic analyst of the social process. He was both an astute student and severe critic of Marx and Marxism; his criticism there was friendly, but savage for the conventional pundits. Marxism needs Veblen's broad social focus and needs to learn how to practice what it has so long preached, and in which all of Veblen's writings are soaked: the treatment of *all* matters within their real historical process. Veblen's own approach, suffering from the defects of its virtues (to use a favorite phrase of his) lacks sufficient theoretical clarity and consistency. But no possible combination of Marx and Veblen would by itself be sufficient for raising, let alone answering, all the questions that pertain to the range of objective and subjective processes characterizing the contemporary world. Such a combination *might* constitute the best starting point for achieving the framework of adequate social theory.[2]

The effort to appreciate and assess Veblen's analytical contributions can be enhanced by further comparing him with other important strands of social thought—important because dominant or (which is usually to say something different) important because useful for understanding. Comparisons may be made in terms both of method and content.

Veblen is often accused of being non-theoretical (or even antitheoretical) by social analysts of conventional and radical persuasions. The charge would be valid, if by "theory" were meant some particular kind and some particularly high level of abstraction, for

Veblen could not move very far from the social realities without becoming analytically uneasy. But he was anything but a mere empiricist or observer of the passing scene; indeed his critiques of such work as "taxonomic"—that is, mere exercises in definition and classification—were for him the same as saying pre-scientific, not at all concerned with "questions of the class which occupy the modern sciences—that is to say, questions of *genesis, growth, variation, process* (in short, questions of a dynamic import)...."[3]

In that brief statement Veblen identifies the notion of science as being the same for the natural and the social sciences, and reveals his dependence upon Darwin—and Marx, if not what became Marxism. Except that Veblen found Marx to be "teleological," "metaphysical," and overly rational: teleological because he saw Marx's analysis as being guided by its desired consequences, instead of the consequences emerging from analysis; metaphysical because the theoretical core of Marx's *Capital,* value, had no empirical counterpart; and overly rational in emphasizing the calculating inclinations and abilities of people in general (not least the working class) while neglecting almost entirely the ways and degrees in which peoples have moved far and fast in response to irrational—i.e., self-destructive—tendencies and exhortations. All this was said of Marx, and more, while Veblen also saw Marx as by far the most scientific of Western social thinkers.[4]

The level of abstraction of a theory may be determined with rough accuracy by noting the areas of reality left unexamined in the analysis: the "other things" that are "equal" or "do not change." Conventional economics still today sets aside all qualitative and historical matters (i.e., social relations and processes) in its "theory" and examines only a few quantitative relationships between typically imaginary variables—in order, as Joan Robinson once put it, to explain the imagined difference in price "between an egg and a cup of tea." But the Marx of *Capital* sets aside as much in his theory as did his classical predecessors and the neoclassicals who followed: e.g., all labor is uniform in skill and function, as is technology and capital; the functions of the state and the real world in almost all other respects are (temporarily) set aside: "other things are equal." What Veblen has to say of such procedures applies with almost as much force to the Marx of the labor theory of value as to the mainstream economists he was targeting:

There are certain saving clauses in common use…:"Given the state of the industrial arts"; "Other things remaining the same"; "In the long run"; "In the absence of disturbing causes." Now…, the state of the industrial arts has at no time continued unchanged during the modern era; consequently other things have never remained the same; and in the long run the outcome has always been shaped by the disturbing causes.…The arguments have been as good as the premises on which they proceed.…[5]

Of the many and important differences between Marx and conventional economists, of course, one was that he knew all these things too, and showed that he did in his trenchant and voluminous writings; but the theory of *Capital* depends upon its assumptions, as do all theories. It was that theory Veblen found critically detached from relevant segments of social reality.

C. Wright Mills (1916-1962) was an intellectual descendant of Marx, of Veblen, and of Max Weber. Like Veblen, he was a product of "middle America"—in his case, Texas. Of the many similarities between the two men, one most relevant to the preceding discussion was Mills's insistence on finding an area for analysis that lies between "grand theory" and mindless empiricism. His own work was in that area, as was Veblen's. Both men spent their thinking lives as sustained critics of their professional colleagues and of their own society—whether that is defined as U.S., capitalist, or "western." They were both gloomily prescient; unfortunately, neither has yet been shown to have been too gloomy. The frequent accuracy of their storm warnings may be assumed to connect in some systematic way with the "middle level" of their analyses.[6]

That Veblen *was* prescient is all the more interesting considering his general position that all social prediction is hopeless, that the process of social change is one of "blind drift." His ability to pay attention to and anticipate developments outside the U.S.—most notably in Germany and Japan—have if anything attracted more attention than what he saw coming for the U.S. That ability, due to a variety of intellectual strengths of Veblen, depended heavily on his inclination to gaze steadily and carefully at the importance of the irrational in the social process.

As he saw it, most systematically in *The Theory of the Leisure Class* (a work as fundamental in Veblen's development as *Capital* was for Marx), rule had been maintained since prehistoric times through the ancient techniques of "force and fraud." Force had to be used surprisingly little, considering the oppressiveness of rule of "the leisure class" (or "vested interests"); although, of course, it has been used often enough. Force is used sparingly because of the greater weight of its ally "fraud"—a term used by Veblen to cover the blandishments of the church, of ideology in general, of patriotism, of "bland acceptance of what is, lest a worse fate befall." "Fraud," as Veblen means the term, matches what Marxists influenced by Antonio Gramsci have come to call the "ideological hegemony of the bourgeoisie," which helps to explain the consenting acceptance by the general population of its own undoing.

That "hegemony" has always had nationalism and patriotism among its strongest supporting pillars; nor have their twin brothers, religion and tradition, been far behind. In one measure or combination or another, all these Veblen saw as working both in Germany and Japan (as of 1915) to produce the strengthening of a literally reactionary (feudal/dynastic) political process and power structure which, in combination with rapid industrial development, would strengthen the hand of militaristic aggression abroad and (what came to be called) fascism at home.[7]

In 1915 such thoughts concerning either Japan or Germany were unique, but by the 1930s the processes Veblen had anticipated were firmly and tragically in place in both countries. It is worth noting here that although he had hopes for the U.S. in 1904 that it would avert such a fate—because of the greater looseness of our history— he had given up on that by 1923, when he finished his last book (*Absentee Ownership*). The militarism that came out of German and Japanese traditions he saw arising in the U.S. out of economic need and the rule of business troglodytes.

Now it is time to turn to the book in hand; being in hand, of course, it can speak for itself. Still, it may help to preview what will be found here in contemporary terminology—although neither the order nor the same words will be found.

In the realm of what is now called "macro" or "aggregative" economics, there is a theory of business fluctuations (or, the business or the trade cycle), a theory of economic growth that posits both chronic tendencies toward depression (or "stagnation") and inflation, and there is joined to that the positing of numerous socioeconomic changes and policy steps that can and will be taken to keep all that in control to the advantage of the "vested interests"—steps enhancing militarism, imperialism, consumerism, and a lubricating media establishment to transform the necessary into the actual.

In the realm of what is now called "micro" or "partial equilibrium" economics and its correlative assertions about industrial organization and behavior, Veblen provides a full anticipation of the Berle and Means and Burnham theses regarding the concentration and bureaucratization of corporate power and of the emergence of the modern, intrusive, representative (of the "vested interests") state, the obverse side of the corporate bureaucracy. In addition, Veblen, like Marx, sees a justified and bitter struggle between capital and labor; unlike Marx, Veblen sees that struggle as eventuating more in the taming of labor (through patriotic appeals and material enticements) than in a socialist revolution. There is much more in *The Theory*: the elements of a sociology of knowledge, a rationale for economic planning, and neither least nor last, Veblen's ironic expectation that this society, ruled and managed by a business elite and its eager allies, is on a path of social and economic development which, if business is to keep its class enemies from triumphing, will most likely mean a defeat for business principles too; will mean that if business is to avoid socialism of one sort or another it will be able and inclined to do so only by supporting and, for a while, embracing fascism, of one sort or another: "It seems possible to say this much, that the full dominion of business enterprise is necessarily a transitory dominion. It stands to lose in the end whether the one or the other of the two divergent cultural tendencies wins, because it is incompatible with the ascendancy of either."

Those were the very last words of *The Theory of Business Enterprise,* written over seven decades ago. Three decades later, the business classes of Germany and Japan had accepted the support of social maniacs in order to avoid what they saw as a greater evil. Subsequently, these same business classes came under the control of those whom they thought they were using, and saw themselves and their nations go down to defeat—to arise once more only under the sheltering wing of U.S. monopoly capitalism.

Today, as chronic depression once more looms, joined startlingly by a chronic inflation that is an organic outgrowth of what made monopoly capitalism "healthy" for two decades or so, customary state and social policies have lost their brief ability to create or even to maintain simultaneous social and economic stability and expansion. As capitalist rulers once more search about for ways—*any* ways—of holding on to their power and profits, it behooves us all to study the works of those, Veblen surely included, who could see before the fact what the facts might become, and why.

Notes

1. Joseph Dorfman has provided the "fullest" possible treatment of Veblen and his social context, in *Thorstein Veblen and His America* (New York: Viking, 1934), an indispensable if also dry-as-dust study of the man, his works, and his era. Considerably more succinct and often more insightful are the introductions by Wesley Clair Mitchell and Max Lerner to the collections of Veblen's essays edited by them in, respectively, *What Veblen Taught* (New York: Viking, 1936) *and The Portable Veblen* (New York: Viking, 1948). See also the perceptive introduction to Veblen's *The Theory of the Leisure Class* (New York: Mentor, 1953) by C. Wright Mills— of whom, and some comparisons with Veblen, more later.
2. For some of the sociological, psychological, and philosophical issues that are relevant the following books are among many worth consulting: Carl Boggs, *Gramsci's Marxism* (London: Pluto Press, 1976); Harry Braverman, *Labor and Monopoly Capital* (New York: Monthly Review Press, 1974); Erich Fromm, *The Sane Society* (Greenwich, Conn.: Fawcett, 1955); Jules Henry, *Culture Against Man* (New York: Vantage, 1963); Henri Lefebvre, *Everyday Life in the Modern World* (New York: Harper & Row, 1971); Robert J. Lifton, *The Life of the Self* (New York: Touchstone, 1976); Herbert Marcuse, *One Dimensional Man* (Boston: Beacon, 1964); Bertell Ollman, *Alienation* (Cambridge: Cambridge University Press, 1976); Herbert I. Schiller, *The Mind Managers* (Boston: Beacon, 1973); Richard Sennett and Jonathan Cobb, *The Hidden Injuries of Class* (New York: Vintage, 1973).
3. My emphasis. This is found in his essay, "Professor Clark's Economics," in Thorstein Veblen, *The Place of Science in Modern Civilization* (New York: B.W. Huebsch, 1919; Russell & Russell, 1961), p. 192. J.B. Clark was Veblen's teacher at Carleton and something like the Samuelson of his day.
4. The gist of Veblen's position is put forth in his two-part essay, "The Socialist Economics of Karl Marx," in *The Place of Science in Modern Civilization.* For sheer critical savagery, and considerable wit, see his critiques of the conventional economists, well-exemplified in "The Limitations of Marginal Utility," in the same volume.
5. Thorstein Veblen, *The Vested Interests and the Common Man* (New York: B.W. Huebsch, 1919; Viking, 1946), pp. 85-86.
6. Mills was the first of U.S. social thinkers to notice how very far along the road to a garrison state—the euphemism for which has become "military-industrial complex"—the U.S. had gone already by the mid-1950s, and how very much that was in the service of a corporate elite, in his *The Power Elite* (New York: Oxford, 1956). His *The New Men of Power: America's Labor Leaders* (New York: Harcourt, Brace, 1948) all too accurately foresaw the bureaucratization of organized labor, and the draining away of at least some social hope thereby implied. And, among others of his extraordinarily prolific and valuable writings, his *The Sociological Imagination* (New York: Oxford, 1959) does once more what Veblen sought to do in his *Place of Science...*essays: to enable serious people to screw their thinking caps on straight.
7. Germany was dealt with in Veblen's *Imperial Germany and the Industrial Revolution* (New York: Macmillan, 1915), and Japan in his essay "The Opportunity of Japan," in his *Essays in Our Changing Order* (New York: Viking, 1943).

11

Absentee Ownership

Marion J. Levy, Jr.

THE title of *Absentee Ownership* is itself typical of Veblen's use of language. True, on the title page of the original book the full title is given: Absentee Ownership (in large caps) and Business Enterprise in Recent Times (in smaller caps) and The Case of America (in smaller caps yet), but the title on the cover of the original book is *Absentee Ownership,* and I confess that not until I turned to this introduction did I realize that the title technically included the words cited here. For me, and I would wager that for 99 percent of its readers, the book was *Absentee Ownership.* Even in this Veblen is peculiar. For ordinary folk *Absentee Ownership* is two words but for Veblen the two really constituted one word, "Absenteeownership." Veblen was extraordinarily concerned with the precise use of words. J. Dorfman states (*Thorstein Veblen and His America,* Viking Press, p. 324), "He was so meticulous in this respect that he declared that there are no synonyms in the English language." Veblen did not actually create words de nouveau, but he did create neologisms out of words lying about. These neologisms were a major base for his claim to be the number one prose stylist of American social analysts—or for that matter of the English-speaking world after the eighteenth century. These new words were almost all composed of two perfectly well-known words lying about. It is easy to list some: leisure class, conspicuous consumption, ostentatious display, business enterprise, putative profits, parental bent, idle curiosity (defined by four words, the propensity to pry), higher learning, and, of course, absentee ownership. His works built around these "words" made so powerful an impression that people who never read or even heard of Veblen use them as single words.

Absentee Ownership was not the least of these, and Veblen used it with telling effect. Even in Veblen's day, the vast majority of people were farmers of one sort or another. They lived out their lives on a localized basis with an ideal of as much self-sufficiency as possible. The absentee landlord or his equivalent, the feudal landlord, was and is a figure of dark connotations. He not only represents an intrusion on desired levels of self-sufficiency, but he is usually a person who neither knows nor cares about the local community *if* the members of that community do not thwart his desire to get as much as possible out of the land and out of the people whom he may or may not own as well. He is not only a frustration of desired levels of self-sufficiency; he is an outsider to boot. It is, alas, not true that people have always placed a high value on personal freedom. Throughout history high levels of hierarchy have generally been taken for granted as normal and natural. People have not generally felt that he or she governs best, who governs least—but almost to a person they have felt that he or she governs best who governs most locally. Even though the absentee landlord is technically defined by economic ownership, such allocations of goods (in this case property rights) and services can never be irrelevant to governance—and vice versa. The absentee landlord is thus not only an absentee owner of land; he is simultaneously an absentee source of governance. General governance at great distance may have been a rarity until modern history—high levels of local self-sufficiency were both ideally and actually taken for granted, but high levels of absentee landlordism were not. It is not the role of *landlord* or *ownership* that casts a pall on these relationships, it is the qualifier, *absentee*.

It is safe to say that *absentee* as a term before Veblen was applied most often to landlordism and the holding of political roles, and it always cast the pall of outsiderism and hence an overwhelming probability of lack of empathy with the locals. Hoi polloi never had the luxury of absentee roles. And what does Veblen do with the term, "absentee?" He applies it to virtually the whole of the economic system of any modernized state, although he is presumably only referring to "America." The 1933 edition of and the 1982 supplement to the *Oxford English Dictionary* contain no reference to "absentee ownership." The second edition of *Webster's New International Dictionary* (1954) does not have it, but the third edition (1966) does. It may do an injustice, but I attribute the term's current currency to its use by Veblen.

And how does Veblen use it? He uses it to cast a pall over the whole current system of economic ownership. Years later the *Modern Corporation and Private Property,* by Berle and Means (1934) picked up Veblen's themes of the concentration of power and control and above all of the separation of ownership and control which Veblen certainly attributed to the larger use of loan credit. In the earlier days, the giants of business enterprise had faces—Rockefeller, Vanderbilt, Ford, Edison—but they all turned into faceless bureaucracies. The giants may not have been nice, and they weren't noted for their empathy, but they had faces and human traits. Absentee ownership wiped that out for the common man. He or she had to deal with bureaucratic representatives of huge and distant entities. If your business with them covered more then one visit, you couldn't even count on dealing with the same person. In effect, when absentee ownership became generalized, it become the fate of the common man always to have to deal with a "bastard from out of town." You couldn't know what he was doing or often what ends he sought, but they weren't likely to be your own.

And so *Absentee Ownership* introduces alienation as a characteristic of the system. Veblen sees that, furthered by his distinction between technology and material output on the one hand and the use of credit and the pursuit of profit, however obtained, on the other. The whole of *Absentee Ownership* depicts the common man as a helpless pawn. Sometimes Veblen thinks of the common man as mentally deficient; he is clearly impatient that the common person doesn't do something about the state of affairs. He predicts instability if the present system continues. Veblen died on August 3, 1929. The 1929 crash and the Great Depression were just down the road Veblen delineated. He was another Cassandra; nobody was listening.

I was first given Veblen to read by Professor Clarence E. Ayres at the University of Texas when I was a sixteen-year-old sophomore. I was given *The Theory of Business Enterprise,* and I decided within the first ten pages that Veblen was the best thing since Voltaire. I didn't realize until much later that this was a peculiar introduction to economics in general. It seems even more odd today. I am, as far as I know, the only academic left who got interested in economics through Thorstein Veblen. I didn't realize the virtues of such an introduction at the time. But it gave me perspective and a place to stand that I still appreciate. It was an alternative to what we then referred to as classical economics, and more importantly for a young person like myself, it was an alternative to Marxism. Veblen had an unusual perspective on practically everything, mostly because he was reared in a Norse farmer setting in a rapidly changing American society. He had the same kind of comparative critical advantage that he discussed in his essay "The Intellectual Preeminence of the Jews in Europe." We never met, but reading Veblen gave this comparative advantage to me, in a sense. The economics of my days as a young student was classical economics. Paul Samuelson had yet to work his wonders on the study of economics in the United States. And although American economists could have gotten much from Walras and Pareto, they clearly didn't. On the other side was Marx, who despite his enormous importance, wasn't a very good economist.

I lived at the time in a peculiar intellectual world based on three premises: (1) intellectual matters were more important than anything else; (2) if two people disagreed on an intellectual matter, one of them was right and the other was wrong; and (3) the one who was right was brighter than the one who was wrong. It seemed to me that Veblen had the better of lots of arguments, so I felt he was brighter than any of the other economists around. Although the basis of my position was ridiculous, my conclusion probably wasn't very far off the mark.

Veblen didn't write like anybody else. I was intrigued by his style. When he thought officials were corrupt, dishonest, and so forth, he didn't waste any words. He simply referred to them as *kept* officials. In those days "kept" was a derogatory participle used to stigmatize women. It somehow lent a salacious tone to Veblen's description of those officials. At the same time he could bring to bear the vocabulary of several different fields to make his points about economics. The most famous of these began, "If we are getting restless under the taxonomy of a monocotyledonous wage doctrine and a crypto-gamic theory of interest...." And yet he wasn't fooling around. He wrote, "The physical properties of the materials accessible to man are constant; it is the human agent that changes,—his insight and his appreciation of what these things can be used for is what develops" (Veblen, *The Place of Science in Modern Civilization,* p. 71).

Someone, I can't now remember who, referred to Veblen's tech-nique of writing as "inverse normalization." This first caught people's attention in his first book, *The Theory of the Leisure Class,* where he has a famous passage on how college football is viewed and how he sees it to be. He simply refused to write about economic analysis in the language of the economists of his day. But then he was trying to jog them out of writing that way too. Therefore, many of the things that he wrote, which anticipated the classical or the neoclassical literature in economics, got into the fields of economics through entirely different avenues. Perhaps the most conspicuous of these was the theory of monopolistic competition, the essence of which was published in "The Use of Loan Credit in Modern Business" (1903), later incorporated in *The Theory of Business Enterprise* (1904). In this essay Veblen maintained that the use of credit that would have given a comparative advantage to a single entrepreneur became a competitive necessity for all, adding to the cost of doing business without conferring comparative advantage. Costs were higher and output lower than would have been the case under pure and perfect competition. This didn't get into the general economic literature until the 1930s with the publication of Professor E. A. Chamberlain's book *The Theory of Monopolistic Competition.*

The Theory of Business Enterprise contained a theory of business cycles very close to what came into the general literature with the work of Keynes three decades later. Veblen's concept of putative profits, which he regards as the basis for the decisions of businessmen, is remarkably close to what came to be very much better known as the unknown elements in the schedule of the marginal efficiency of capital.

The heart of the distinction between Veblen's work and the economics he disdained was the distinction between production for output and production for profit on the one hand, and developmental process versus equilibrium situations on the other. There is, as far as I know, no reason to believe that Veblen knew of the work of Walras and Pareto; he died long before their work was known to economists in general in the United States.

Perhaps one of Veblen's most startling insights was that at a time when people saw either capitalism as continuing indefinitely into the future, substantially without change, or socialism as the only alternative outcome, in *The Theory of Business Enterprise* Veblen scouted another alternative. We would call it fascism today, but we didn't have the term then. Remember, this was 1904. But he saw the predatory search for national profits leading to a militaristic state with an emphasis on pomp and ceremony and an accent on national glory.

He carefully distinguished between "modern Socialism," a scheme of society under democratic organization, and what he referred to as "state, church, or monarchical Socialism" (see J. Dorfman, *Thorstein Veblen and His America,* 1934, p. 241). He apparently didn't consider the Russian experiment to be "modern socialism." He assumed that modern socialism would arise under the direction of engineers. He may not have been "right." He wasn't, but his argument sidestepped the available ideologies. Technocracy may have developed out of Veblen, but certainly not vice versa.

For Veblen markets washed out the intrinsic qualities of commodities and services and reduced them all to financial reckoning. Because the analysis of rational action was so little studied or developed in his time, he seems not to have been aware of a function of markets, even less than pure and perfect ones, as one, perhaps the only one, of the few devices mankind ever invented that offset the effects of differing degrees and kinds of ignorance. Markets aren't nice, but they grind exceedingly fine. Veblen was also perhaps the last major American social analyst who really felt that humankind would be benefited if all major decisions regarding allocation were in the hands of engineers who in a modern democratic socialist state would manage everything for output rather than for profits or war. For him, nationalism was not one whit different from chauvinism in general, and he saw surcease from war as only possible with an international organization, not oriented to or determined by local sovereignties.

Veblen really was unusual. He was the quintessential outsider about whom he wrote in one sense in every book he ever turned out. His initial learning was that of a Norse farmhand transported to the wilds of the United States. He was our indigenous Norse pragmatist. It is interesting that there were two great outsiders who viewed America (it is not quite correct to talk about the United States in either case) as a very special setting. The first, of course, was Tocqueville whose primary point of view was that of an elite representative of the enlightenment of France. He was overwhelmingly preoccupied with what he viewed as our political inventions. We wanted to read what Tocqueville wrote. We remember him not least because what he said about us very much appealed to us. Veblen, on the other hand, viewed us from an economic point of view, but always taking the economic results as a function for the setting and types of social action in which we engage. Tocqueville viewed us as a miraculously open class elite system, whereas Veblen viewed us as an anthropologist from another planet or better as a biologist observing termites. But we were a set of termites who all wanted to be queens. We always felt that his values had more to do with his analysis than he let on, but it was very difficult to catch him at it because his most biting revelations were always presented as careful statements of fact "with no intention to disparage"—and they were statements of fact inversely normalized. What he said of religious organizations was in one sense factual, but Veblen alone saw them as sales organizations carried to perfection.

Veblen made another contribution that got lost. More than any other social analyst of his time economic analysis was for him a part of general social analysis. This is clear in all his books, especially so in *Absentee Ownership.* He railed against the general economic concern with materials and things other than with people and their plans and motivations and actions. One searches far in his first volume, *The Theory of the Leisure Class,* for anything that smacks of an ordinary economist's analysis of the allocation of goods and services. And yet he gives us an explanation of why wealthy people cultivate green lawns and elaborate weddings. He uses terms like "conspicuous consumption" and "invidious displays," but those concepts are used to elucidate the allocation of goods and services. It is just that even now, when interdisciplinary approaches are so taken for granted as to duck intellectual responsibility, we regard *The Theory of the Leisure Class* as satire rather than economics. As Veblen said, "people were inclined to giggle." (Dorfman, p. 197)

In Veblen's day the first comers to modernization were just getting their acts and facades in place. The whole panoply of the problems of latecomers to modernization was not on his plate. He saw the structures of modernization being put in place as importantly pathological. He did not see modernization as a kind of universal social solvent. And yet again, there is that strong hint of one of the major still overlooked aspects of all that, the long-term exponentially increasing level of interdependency—the relentless increase of what he referred to as the "delicacy of interstitial adjustments amongst the closely concatenated processes." Had the concept of modernization been available to him, *Absentee Ownership* might have been subtitled, "The Pathological Development of Modernization." Veblen grew up and lived in a period of our increasing confidence and self-assurance. He was awed by the material welfare that could be achieved by the industrial revolution and infuriated by human institutions that thwarted and frustrated the possibilities of material productivity. People who should have paid closer attention to what he had to say let him live out his life on very short rations as a kind of ornament and verification of their own tolerance. If another Veblen appears in our world, liberals and conservatives alike will stone him.

All sorts of people saw the system; Veblen saw through the system. Remember, it was a day when investment bankers were like God Almighty as far as the economic system was concerned. But now there are a whole group of operators in the economic system who have investment bankers jumping through hoops. This is the day of the raider and merger, and we've fallen back to thinking of investment bankers as useful handmaidens to real economic operators. Never mind how unrealistic that is. *Absentee Ownership* is a dividing line book. It can be rightly claimed, I believe, that Veblen did more than foresee the crash of 1929. He was bathed in wonderment that it hadn't happened already. He died, of course, before it happened, albeit by only a few months. But that was the crash par excellence that wiped out what a Norse farm boy economist thought of as the unrealities of the system. And that crash was a dividing line in history. There had and has been no other like it. There is not only the magnitude of that crash and its implications, but also the way it changed the system. Before that crash we thought of government as the ordinary negligible, non-acting part of the system. It wasn't supposed to do much. It was to provide a few public goods, but not too many. Political bosses and their political machines, not the official government, provided what welfare system there was. Only during wars did government become the biggest player in the game. But something happened with the 1929 crash. For awhile people simply dithered, sold apples, and wrung their hands as unemployment took off. And then in 1932, with the election of Franklin Delano Roosevelt, a man who really made a difference in history, the government became the biggest player in the game. It wasn't exactly like Veblen's view of the engineers and the technologists, but business and banking never again became the factor they were before the 1929 crash. There is increasing talk today of taking the government out of the picture, but even the people who are most in favor of that don't really think it is possible. This makes a big difference for people who read *Absentee Ownership* and other books by Veblen now. It is very hard to put ourselves back into the position of looking at the players as Veblen saw them.

Absentee Ownership seems old-fashioned as I reread it now. Of course, Veblen didn't see things the way most people saw them in his day, and that's why he was so hard to take in *Absentee Ownership* and in every other book he wrote. But ever since Franklin Delano Roosevelt and the New Deal came in, the government has been the *big player,* and the accessibility of credit for the government was never in question. Indeed, by our accounting (fictions?), the government doesn't hold any assets of any sort. So there the absentee ownership stands. The crash that Veblen could have claimed to have predicted because what counted as credit and what counted as material objects were quite different, flushed out the system and created a revolution that nobody seemed to be aware of except perhaps for some 12 million unemployed (of a total labor force of 50 million), who weren't very articulate.

The new world of America that came into existence after the Great Crash followed by the Great Depression (Not a "recession," a *depression*!) was a wholly different world, and that fact alone makes it difficult to give credence to the world of America as described by Veblen in *Absentee Ownership*. It's a very worrisome book to read because Veblen obviously takes as real things that just don't seem real to us anymore. Mind you, again, he saw those realities as very different from what other people of his age and generation saw. And much of the value that he contributed to knowledge lay in the fact that he saw them peculiarly. In his time he was regarded as quixotic because he viewed the world differently. Yet, even when you disagreed with what he said, there was a disturbing reality about what he wrote. Even his outrageously funny note about the Propaganda of the Faith (*Absentee Ownership,* pp. 319–25) has a realism about it that shines through all the shock. There is certainly, for example, no other book describing America in the two decades after the twentieth century began that bears any resemblance to the way in which Veblen described it. We can still read that sort of quixotic view, but for us he's doubly quixotic because it's hard to believe that that world he described was ever the world of America. Nevertheless, while it was the world of America that was looked at differently than other people looked at it, it certainly was in some sense the world of America.

There is another aspect of the America described in *Absentee Ownership*. The current faithful, who call themselves Libertarians, along with those who oppose them, don't seem to realize they had their wished for lack of governance from at least 1900 to 1932. Except for the Federal Reserve Board and times of war, there was little governance to give the business community let or hindrance. What government there was more often plundered then prohibiting. Few "public goods" were offered, and the concept of "public bads" (pollution, unemployment, etc.) as a governmental responsibility was unheard of. The absentee owners against whom Veblen railed, though he claimed merely to describe them, had things pretty much their own way. And their ways led directly to 1929 and by 1932 to 12 million unemployed (24.1 percent of the civilian labor force; 36.3 percent of the non-farm labor force) out of a 50 million labor force and a total population of a 125 million people! Veblen would surely be the first to say that the Libertarians have had their shot at U.S. history. They have had their shot at acting as though interdependency had no relevance, as though Veblen's increasing delicacy of the interstitial adjustments of the closely concatenated processes were irrelevancies that would take care of themselves or at least could be ignored by the movers and shakers of absentee ownership, that is, the bankers and business lords.

Had Veblen survived until now, he could have written an *Absentee Ownership, Done and Redone.* How would he see us now? One thing is sure, he would have had a field day with *junk bonds.* He could place Michael Milken alongside the Propaganda of the Faith as an unabashed triumph of salesmanship—of *suppressio veri, suggestio falsi.* Milken and those who took up the junk bond with a whoop and a holler carried the larger use of loan credit to an extreme even a Norse farm boy economist simply couldn't imagine. He thought the absentee owners would protect themselves whilst they plundered the laymen. Even Veblen couldn't predict a feeding frenzy of junk bonds. But in *Absentee Ownership* he descries better than anyone else the road to 1929—no matter how much he relishes flaying the system. Our interdependencies are mounting exponentially. We may be sorely in need of another Veblen to cry havoc.

As each day brings us further along toward the next millennium, our increasing libertarianism tugs the shrill warnings of *Absentee Ownership* back into focus—back into style. There is a new dark cloud to be coped with, exponentially increasing interdependency. Veblen correctly caught its beginnings, but it has gone on nearly seventy years and a Second World War since then. The public bads of libertarianism are far more potent now than they were in Veblen's day, though they brought about the Great Depression even then. While most people saw only onward and upward, Veblen predicted a slippery slope whose angle of inclination steepened. Veblen thought, the more the new lords of business enterprise paid attention to maximizing profits rather than to maximizing material output and its increasingly unimodal distribution to the general public on whom in some sense economic welfare had, in the long run, to be based—the greater would be the reaping of woe.

If we could have Veblen back now, he need not point out the slippery slope. The government is now a major player even though the thought of governmental dismantlement is so popular among articulate political power players. But anyone as perspicacious as Veblen might now be able to devise a system of holding responsible the creators of public bads whether they be government officials or "private players." In the long run the slippery slope does not threaten life as much as a level plane of operation threatens it. The slippery slope invites everyone to seek again the increasing slope of material productivity. The level plane can destroy hope, and our great material productivity is based on reasonable hope. Continually increasing horizons of the possibility of material development have created our dangerous new world of interdependency. Veblen was so preoccupied with calling our attention to the pitfalls we were digging that he didn't show us how to fill them in. His one naivete was his faith in engineers. We could all do with a rereading of *Absentee Ownership;* we are not out of the reach of the horrors of libertarianism. That rereading with the new roles we take too much for granted of the government as a major player in the game might lead us to a solution of the problem of how to keep the "absentee owners" of both the economic and political spheres responsible. We need the energy and the imagination of business and governmental leaders, but we seem at a loss to inculcate responsibility on absentee owners. Disillusionment with the government as a major player undermines a governmental balance wheel for business enterprise. The popularity of politics as a zero sum game makes statesmanship vulnerable to politics. The market can destroy reckless players, but Veblen showed how that could go awry. Competition in the flesh is neither pure nor perfect though its record in the last century has been preferable to overall state planning. Tocqueville told us how good our system could be. Veblen described how bollixed up we could get it. We must now add to our marvelous political system of checks and balances, which has preserved our liberties, a set of checks and balances for economic allocation. We must set absentee ownership a new task in addition to individual enrichment. Politics as a set of checks and balances is one thing. Politics as a zero sum game is quite another. We need an *Absentee Governance* to alert us to the lack of participation and statesmanship that becomes ever more critical as we become ever more interdependent.

12

Imperial Germany and the Industrial Revolution

Otto G. Mayer

Thorstein B. Veblen's book, *Imperial Germany and the Industrial Revolution,* published in the second year of the First World War, is certainly not his best-known work. His *Theory of the Leisure Class* and *Theory of Business Enterprise* take places of pride in that respect. Whether the reader is familiar with his other works, this book is simply a treasure-chest of greatly varied knowledge.

First of all, it is fascinating to see how Veblen outlines and formulates, precisely and to the point, basic concepts that are still being heftily debated in various branches of economics today. This is true, for example, for the transfer of technologies from other cultures (cf. p. 37). The development economics literature on this question today fills entire library shelves under the heading of "appropriate technology." The idea that mature societies run the danger of becoming encrusted and losing their economic and social vitality (cf. p. 30 and p. 233 f.) has recently been further developed and expanded by Mancur Olson in his book *The Rise and Decline of Nations.*

Secondly, it is refreshing for the economist of today, who is confronted daily with PME (problem-model-empirical results) "literature, " to be forced to think again about things which are often brushed under the carpet of assumptions-of-the-model by the advocates of PME. One cannot help but suspect that the authors are hardly conscious of the fact that this apparently neutral approach in fact normatively takes the existing system or—to use the German expression—the existing "order" as given. It thus simply ignores the dynamics that determine human behavior, namely the changing of ideas and institutional dependencies, which are constantly changing along with ideas and technological development. From this it can, however, also be deduced that this network of relationships can be changed by people.

The basic terminology used by Veblen—terms such as "the received scheme of use and wont" and "the new state of the industrial arts"—gives expression to a dialectic which, especially if one takes into consideration (unfortunately Veblen does not expressly do so) the fact that both of these factors permeate and influence each other, means anything but a "necessary" and thus *a priori* foreseeable development of events. This may be comforting for a modern German in the sense that the disastrous, racist Nazi regime was not as "necessary" as some historians and others claim. Here, as in other spheres, it appears that the facts of reality are abstracted from far back enough until a trend, a straight line, forms from Bismarck to Hitler, or even from Martin Luther through Bismarck to Hitler.

Veblen does not do this, and it can be doubted whether Veblen today would agree with Joseph Dorfman's interpretation, that his "story in 1915 of how aristocratic and imperial Germany exploited the development of the machine technology turned out to be so prophetic of the rise and fall of Nazi Germany."[1] In my opinion he would have been more likely to agree with the words of the British historian Alan Bullock, "Nothing in history happens necessarily. On the basis of decades of historical research I am absolutely certain that national socialism and Hitler's dictatorship were not 'inevitable.'"[2]

I fully agree, however, with Dorfman's subsequent statement, "that a new edition of *Imperial Germany and the Industrial Revolution* was called for,"[3] and Transaction Publishers must be congratulated for deciding to publish it.

The reader of Veblen has demonstrated to him in a brilliant way how more general ideas can be used to explain political and economic developments. It is these ideas, or concepts, that make the book definitely worth reading. Some of them are formulated so generally that they can still be used today as "instruments of analysis." The reader automatically draws parallels between his analysis of British society at the end of the nineteenth century and today's Germany (West), which is preparing to realize the shortest working hours in the world. Elsewhere it is not difficult to find analogies to recent developments in Eastern Europe, when one reads, "Its (the mechanistic conception) practical working-out is the machine technology, of which the intellectual precipitate and counterpart is the exact sciences. Associated with these in such a way as to argue a correlation, of the nature of cause and effect, is the modern drift toward free or popular institutions" (c.f. p. 268).

These few examples may suffice to indicate that the reading of Veblen's work confirms the old but often forgotten wisdom that a knowledge of literature protects one from making new discoveries, and secondly, that Veblen in his way belongs to "the giants on whose shoulders we all are standing."[4] Even a dwarf is then in the fortunate position of being able to see somewhat further or somewhat more.

More than seventy years have passed since the publication of *Imperial Germany and the Industrial Revolution.* Veblen wrote his book at the beginning of the First World War and in the light of his personal experience of the rapid economic expansion of the German Empire. He actually wanted to find an explanation for this expansion and for the developments leading towards war. Perhaps this is the reason why Veblen's arguments are tailored in a quite streamlined way to the role of the dynastic state, particularly of the German Empire—a role that is even more pronounced by the comparison with Britain. More recent research on the outbreak of the First World War, into which several countries apparently more or less "slipped," will not be discussed here. Even in view of today's historical knowledge, Veblen's remarks on this (cf. p. 259) are amazing. What will be discussed here—despite the danger of appearing very "dwarf-like"—are two factors to which, in my opinion, Veblen did not pay enough attention.

Although Veblen points out that neither the political nor the economic history of Germany begins with the founding of the Empire in 1871 (p. 61), if one takes institutionalism—which goes back to Veblen, among others—seriously, then consideration must be given to the institutional changes, at least since the beginning of the nineteenth century, which were decisive the economic expansion. The fact that Great Britain was an island, or that the geographical position of the German Empire was in the center of Europe, is treated by Veblen rather as if it were marginal (p. 111). Britain, as an island, had been able to develop relatively unmolested by the outside world, for the foregoing 900 years, whereas the center of Europe, virtually without any natural borders, had always been an arena for very differing ideas, interests and disputes, through to the calamitous devastations of war. It is a fact that the strengths of Veblen's analysis of imperial Germany can only really be appreciated if the reader is familiar with some of the basic facts of Central European history. Veblen simply takes this knowledge for granted, which was perhaps possible at the time, but cannot necessarily be presumed today, neither in the country in the center of Europe nor among English-speaking people.

Although pointless, it would be fascinating to speculate about what the German economic and political scenery, or that of Europe in general, would look like today if energy had not been wasted so often in war and if Germany had not had to start back at square one several times. In some ways Germany's economic history seems to be a "chase to catch up" with the other nations following indescribably destructive wars. And certainly not only the wars but also the "chases" have left their mark on both the Germans themselves and their image in the eyes of their neighbors. The Thirty Years' War (1618-1648) in particular had political and economic repercussions into the nineteenth century. What began as a religious war soon degenerated into a pure struggle for power over the preservation of the German Empire and between Germany's European neighbors to extend their own spheres of interest on German soil.

The effects of the war on the economic and social situation of the population can hardly be assessed. In the areas where fighting took place, 60 to 70 percent of the population was killed. The total population of the German Empire fell from about sixteen million to ten or eleven million. Hunger and epidemics, murder and manslaughter were ubiquitous. In the final year the war was nourished by the war; the result was the economic ruin of the stricken regions. Economic relationships and trade had broken down. Production had reached zero and agriculture had collapsed. Enormous public debts, flocks of beggars and demobbed soldiers lamed the economy's new start. Just as the collapse of the peasant uprisings a hundred years before had lamed the country population for decades, so now the daily shortages deprived the urban bourgeoisie of the time, the strength, and the will to take part in the shaping of public and economic life.

Looking back, it was perhaps more decisive that with the end of the Thirty Years' War German particularism was intensified and perpetuated by the Westphalian Peace Treaty of Münster in 1648, which recognized the territorial rights of each and every minor territorial ruler and thus made them independent of the emperor and the empire. The empire became an association of smallest, small, and middle-sized states and semi-states. Every prince and "semi-prince" received full sovereignty over his land with the right to enter into alliances with each other and with foreign countries. Thus the reigning princes and the aristocracy largely determined political and economic developments in Germany for considerably more than a century. Veblen's statement (p. 66) that the territorial state "has come to its best maturity only among the German peoples, and which has held its place with remarkable tenacity within the limits of a fatherland" is correct, but this is not based on any particular pattern of behavior on behalf of the Germans compared to the British. It is, rather, as stated above, the result of a terrible war and of a structure forced upon them, partly from abroad.

The countryside lay waste, the population drained of its life's blood, the bourgeoisie exhausted, and the economy in total agony—ideal starting-points for an active economic policy on the part of the state or the sovereign representing the state. The economics of the state found its strongest expression in the Prussian variety of mercantilism. While the Great Elector of Brandenburg, Frederick William (1640-1688), created the basis for the establishment of the State of Prussia, Frederick William I (1713-1740) gave shape to the strictly authoritarian military and functionaries' state. It was above all due to these two figures that in Prussia the tradition of a public enterprise economy was formed from the spirit of absolutism and characterized by a lack of capital and the timidity of private entrepreneurs. Not only the economist J. A. Schumpeter sees this as the cause of the fact that, in contrast to Britain or even France, the development of the economy by free entrepreneurs was prevented, or at least hindered, and that this contributed to Germany's falling behind in the later process of industrialization.

For the beginnings of manufacturing—pre-industrial enterprises, organized on the basis of division of labor but in contrast to the later factories as yet unmechanized and largely based on handwork—the first hesitant steps toward "industrialisation" and the formation of a class of energetic, imaginative, and daring entrepreneurs were to be found before the Thirty Years' War in Germany just as in other European countries. This was after an economic philosophy oriented towards gain and profit had finally come to be accepted in the sixteenth century and the Church's prohibitions and commandments regarding usury, monetary transactions, and credit had been overcome.

The best-known examples of large entrepreneurs in that period are the houses of Fugger, Welser, and Hochstätter. Originally weavers, the Fuggers went over to trade in textiles and participated in the Tyrolean silver mines and in Hungarian copper mines. Between 1500 and 1525, they already owned shares in seventy-six mines in Tyrol and Silesia. In the fifteenth century and into the sixteenth century, they were the largest bankers in Europe. Individual popes and the Habsburger, above all Charles V, in whose empire the sun never set, were their greatest debtors. Apart from their main seat in Augsburg, they had major branches in Venice, Rome, Nuremberg, Breslau, and Antwerp, to name only a few. Their competitors, the Welsers, whose seat was also in Augsburg, conducted extensive foreign trade, founded a society for slave trade, and even temporarily won control of trade in Venezuela.

These enterprises had with certainty passed their prime by the end of the sixteenth century. Like the Hanseatic League, a union of free imperial cities that had joined together with other cities throughout Europe several decades previously, they suffered not only from the lack of political and military support of a united and energetic empire—Great Britain's flag, for example, almost always followed her trade—but also from the geographical changes in foreign trade activities due to the discovery and colonialization of the new worlds abroad. Even if the Thirty Years' War perhaps only put the stamp of finality on this decline, it certainly prevented a consolidation and reorientation. The ground was pulled from under the feet of every kind of trade and the small German states, politically and economically disunited and weak, withdrew into themselves.

Whereas at the time of the Thirty Years' War in France Jean Baptiste Colbert (1619-1688) laid the foundations for French mercantilism in a consolidated national state and removed domestic customs barriers almost entirely, these continued to hamper trade within and between the individual territories in Germany far into the nineteenth century. Imagine: alone on the eight-kilometer-long shipping route from Bingen to Koblenz in 1781 there were five customs stations, and en route from the Palatinate to Rotterdam duties had to be paid twenty-eight times. Britain has had a uniform economic territory since at least 1707, when the turnpikes between Scotland and England were dismantled. In addition, the restrictions put on handicrafts by the limiting guild regulations had largely been removed there by the end of the seventeenth century. In France such privileges and monopolies were first removed by the great revolution—a full century later than in Britain. In Germany they began to disappear slowly in the first half of the nineteenth century.

The century and a half to the great reforms of the post-Napoleonic era was characterized by the state economic policy of mercantilism—which, by the way, was prevalent throughout continental Europe—and its German variant, cameralism, which regarded its most important task as being the improvement of the receipts of the sovereign's treasury. Although there had also previously been state activity in the field of economic policy, mercantilism and cameralism were the first to develop extensive economic policy concepts which came fairly close to that which is described today by the words "economic system." Their model was the French unitarian state. Taken over by hundreds of small territorial princes, this system had difficulty in allowing economic development to take place. From this point of view, too, a comparison of Germany's political and economic development with that of France might be more revealing than with that of Britain.

The leading idea of mercantilism was the expansion and consolidation of one's own power. To this purpose one's own economy had to be developed rapidly and extensively. Autarchy, complete self-sufficiency, was regarded as ideal. A rich land was a land with a lot of money, which meant precious metals. Precious metals, however—if they could not be mined domestically—could only be obtained by having a surplus of goods or, as was practiced in Hessen, by selling one's own able-bodied population overseas. The measures to be taken by economic policy followed necessarily from this. In order to be independent of imports, manufacturing and industrial production had to be extended and protected from foreign competition by import restrictions and high customs duties. Agriculture was supported and new areas cultivated to increase the supply of foodstuffs. Foreign trade, again, was favored in order to secure the desired surpluses in the balance of trade. If one believes that this could be a description of parts of today's world, then this belief is certainly correct.

There was another important aspect in Prussia, due to the losses in population during the Thirty Years' War: deliberate population policy in the form of the admission of immigrants. The Catholic states, particularly the Archbishop of Salzburg, the Habsburgers, and France, took care for denominational reasons that the states willing to admit immigrants experienced an abundant flow of religious fugitives. Under Frederick I (1701-1713) and Frederick William I (1713-1740) alone, roughly 25,000 French immigrants were admitted, mainly Huguenots. This extensive immigration policy not only compensated for the population losses, it also improved the structure of the economy, for an overproportionately large number of the fugitives from France especially were at home in branches of manufacturing, the products of which previously had to be imported. The existence of such a refuge and the tolerance connected with it surely also contributed to the population's loyalty to this dynastic state. These are certainly other reasons than those listed by Veblen.

Not only in contrast to the Netherlands and Britain with their relatively open economies based on private entrepreneurs, but also more strongly than in absolutist France, Prussia in fact became a uniform state economy. Whereas beside Louis XIV and the mercantilist Colbert there were also in France strong physiocratic (i.e., supporters of the concept of a natural circulation in the economy, which functioned best without state interference) and liberal individuals, and opposition groups, in Prussia the role of the state as entrepreneur was not even questioned in discussions. If the Prussian economy under Frederick William I was characterized by military armament, under Frederick the Great after 1740 it increasingly became a war economy which only began slowly to return to normal again after the Seven Years' War. But even after that—and Veblen sees this correctly—military considerations were dominant. Thus, for example, Frederick the Great stopped the peasant liberation measures that had been introduced at the beginning of the century because they would have been disadvantageous to the aristocracy, which had defended the country and formed the backbone of the army. A landed economy without serfdom was at that time as difficult to imagine as plantations without Negro slaves.

Manufacturing and industrial policy, on the other hand, represented in a way the peak of Frederick's mercantilism. With the creation of the department for "manufacturing and commercial questions" in 1740, production in the existing manufactories was improved, the setting up of new ones supported, and manufactories were brought in from other countries. However, this form of production should not be overestimated, neither qualitatively nor quantitatively. Qualitatively, because traditional hand techniques still continued to be dominant and advantages resulted essentially only from the greater division of labor between craftsmen or workers, and quantitatively because seldom more than 10 percent of all those employed in production worked in manufactories.

The manufactories were still far from being what we would today consider to be an industrial enterprise. But they were an important transitional step toward the later factories because the various craft activities which until then had been split up were now collected together under one roof and a uniform management. Their numbers were forced to remain modest as they could only take up activities in branches that were not hampered by guild regulations. It was not until the beginning of the nineteenth century that reforms essential for the more extensive development of the economy and the break-through of the technical revolution could be made. These reforms had already been passed in England in 1689 and in France in 1789: removal of guild privileges, freedom to choose a trade, freedom of movement, the freeing of the peasants from hereditary serfdom, and the gradual creation of a uniform economic area.

Veblen equates the rise of Germany with the rise of Prussia, and this has certainly subsequently proved to be correct. But this, too, was not *a priori* "necessarily" the case. It was above all Prussia that suffered immensely under Napoleon and his wars. On top of that, however, in 1806 the German Empire ceased to exist with the abdi-cation of the German imperial throne by the House of Habsburg under pressure from Napoleon. It is against this background that the ideas of romanticism in German philosophy and literature, in almost every sphere, can be understood. Romanticism is less the expres-sion—as Veblen believes (p. 227)—of a "retirement in the direction of the medieval and feudalistic scheme of life." It should, rather, be interpreted as an exaggerated, idealistic concept of the Holy Roman Empire of the German nation as an expression of, and the desire for, nation-building, which other European countries, especially Britain and France, had long since realized—an idea that was revived pre-cisely by the War of Liberation 1812-1813. But the Vienna Con-gress of 1815 did not lead to the re-creation of the German Empire, even if the number of territorial states was reduced from three hun-dred to about thirty.

It was the very structure of the State of Prussia which, with the above background, contributed to its ascending like a "Phoenix from the ashes" after it had shaken off the Napoleonic yoke. As far as the economy was concerned, the manifold reforms conducted at the beginning of the nineteenth century, which were mentioned above, made an essential contribution to the rise. The reforms—connected especially with the names vom Stein and Hardenberg—had quite contradictory effects. The liberation of the peasants gave personal freedom and freedom of movement to individuals who had until then been tied to the soil, but since they had to buy their freedom with payments of money they often lost their property and thus the premise for an independent existence. In the four eastern provinces of Prussia alone, thousands of farms ceased to exist as a result of debts, and tens of thousands were driven from house and home. On the other hand, the dissolution of the old agrarian society set labor free, which provided the necessary reservoir for industrialization. At the same time the liberation of the peasants led to the extension and intensification of agricultural production, which was indispensable to meet the needs of the rapidly growing population. And without the "meal of the poor," the Latin American potato (which had been planted in the Prussian domains as of 1746 on the order of Frederick the Great), perhaps neither the increases in the population nor industrialization would have been possible.

Again, the freedom to choose a trade meant at last that theoretically anyone, whether aristocrat or peasant, could practice to whatever extent, in whatever branch of production and with whatever production technique he chose. The opportunities here—and Veblen analyzes this brilliantly—of applying already existing techniques, especially from Britain, were of great advantage. Partly to the application of new techniques, partly to the reduction in the number of craftsmen's workshops, however, here too labor was set free. It may be doubted whether this was the breeding ground for the unconditional loyalty to the dynastic state which Veblen describes.

Like the measures described above, the creation of a uniform economic area also required more than half a century for its final realization. After Prussia, under the influence of vom Stein, had removed its own domestic customs duties, it attempted to achieve economic union with other German states via the removal of customs duties between them. But it took long negotiations, in which the German economist Friedrich List, father of the idea of a railway network to overcome provincialism, played an outstanding role before the German Customs Union was founded. On New Year's Day 1834, the turnpikes between eighteen German states were removed. But it was not until 1867, when at Königsgrätz the decision as to whether Prussia or Austria would be the leading power in Germany had been taken in favor of Prussia, and Bavaria and Wurttemberg had joined the Customs Union that there were no more restrictions to trade within Germany (excluding Austria).

The effects such a development can have have been described by Veblen (p. 242) in a brilliant portrayal of the argument for free trade. However, it appears somewhat exaggerated to regard the external customs duties, which were kept or even raised, as the most important instrument for the consolidation of the dynastic or imperial state. After all, the backlog demand with regard to industrialization requires—as practiced today by many developing countries—a certain level of protection for infant industries, an argument which in fact goes back to Friedrich List.

Following these reforms, trade and industrialization experienced a stormy boom. The railway was of decisive importance here. Ten years after the opening of the first railway line between Nuremberg and Fürth in 1835, the network already had 2,131 kilometers. Shortly before the outbreak of the First World War, it had more than 79,000 kilometers. The extension of the railway network was not only necessary for trade, but also a permanent impetus to the iron and steel industry, to mechanical engineering, and the building trade, which on their part provided employment and incentives to invest in other branches of the economy.

Just how tempestuously industrialization took place in Germany from the middle of the nineteenth century is shown by a few statistics: the number of steam-engines— symbol of the new form of mechanical energy—in Prussia grew from 419 in 1837 to about 74,000 at the end of the century; the production of textiles and clothing increased, thanks to the mechanization of spinning and weaving machines, by 250 percent from 1835 to 1873 (however, this led to such a great fall in prices that it came to the Weavers' Uprising of 1844—the impulse for Gerhart Hauptmann's drama about the living conditions of the Silesian linen weavers); there were 180 engineering factories in Prussia in 1852, but in 1875 there were already 1196. Coal production rose from only 2 metric tons in 1835 to 30 metric tons in 1873, and 190 metric tons in 1913. Iron production increased in the same period from 0.2 metric tons, through 1.3 to 8.5 metric tons.

Coal and iron, the two most important raw materials of the period, also reflect the rise of Germany in the Club of the Great Powers. Whereas Britain—the leader and prototype of industrialization—

covered half of the entire world's requirements of coal and iron in the 1860s and in 1890 exported twice as many machines as the next-powerful countries, the U.S.A., Germany, and France together, its position was rapidly lost to the U.S.A. and Germany after 1890. On the eve of the First World War, Germany had clearly overtaken Britain in the production of pig-iron and in exports of iron, ironmongery and machines, and there is a certain connection between the fact that the year in which the First World War broke out was also the year in which German coal production was about to overtake that of the British.

This industrial revolution was made possible by a whole new layer of (mainly Protestant) entrepreneurs, which was formed within only a few decades and was recruited largely from craftsmen, peasants, and workers, but also from the landed gentry—a development that led to Max Weber's famous essay, but which was scarcely initiated by the state. It is therefore difficult to follow Veblen when he states (p. 241): "But throughout the imperial area the material fortunes of the nation have consistently been furthered and conserved for the ulterior end of warlike power."

As is the case with every revolution, the industrial revolution, too, had its socially shady side. Urbanization increased, the number of factory workers rose proportionately faster than total population. Whereas in 1870 about so percent of the economically active population were still working in agriculture and forestry, by 1913 the figure was only one-third. At the same time the share of those working in industry and in crafts rose from 30 to 40 percent, and that in a period when the number of workers itself doubled. In spite of increases in income the situation of the workers did not basically improve, as wage increases were largely eaten up by higher prices for dwellings and foodstuffs. The situation worsened further following the economic crisis of 1873, which put an abrupt end to the boom that had begun with the founding of the Empire in 1871. Falling prices, cuts in wages, and dismissals were on the order of the day. Social tensions were thus inevitable. These were, not least important, the reason for Bismarck's Social Laws, which are also the starting point for the social security system in the Federal Republic of Germany. In 1883 health insurance was created, in 1884 accident insurance, and in 1889 old age and invalidity insurance. Altogether, this social policy brought certain material improvements for a section of the working class. Social policy on the one hand and the deviation of the Social Democrats from their "revolutionary" line on the other hand led, after all, to the fact that at the outbreak of the First World War the great majority of the Social Democrats and the working class saw not "the state as exploiter" as endangered, but "the fatherland. "

The prognosis, or rather diagnosis, of Veblen's (p. 239), that "this variant of Western civilisation is evidently an exceptionally unstable, transitory, and in a sense unripe phase" was fulfilled by the end of the war and the abolition of the dynasty. At the outbreak of the war Germany was undoubtedly one of the strongest economic powers in the world. It paid for the war with 2 million killed in action, 750,000 dead of starvation, and 6.5 million inhabitants in the ceded territories: altogether about 14 percent of its total population before the war. The loss of such important economic areas as Alsace-Lorraine and Upper Silesia, the temporary severance of the Saarland, the occupation for a time of the Ruhr valley, exceptionally high reparations, the extradition of almost the entire merchant fleet, the internationalization of its waterways, and the loss of all patents and foreign property set Germany back to the level of an economic province. Added to this was the hyperinflation at the beginning of the 1920s, whose psychological effects are still to be found today in the especially strongly marked German emphasis on monetary stability. Whereas a dollar could be had for 46.30 Reichsmark on November 21, 1919, on the same day four years later it cost 4.2 billion Reichsmark. Only after it proved possible to stabilize the exchange rate in 1924 did a boom of several years' duration begin with surprising speed and strength. This was bought, however, with rapidly growing American, usually short-term, loans with high interest rates, and avenged itself bitterly with the outbreak of the world economic crisis. The collapse of the New York stock exchange led to the sudden withdrawal of such loans and to the collapse of all domestic credit relationships. The lack of credit caused production disruptions and unemployment in every branch of the economy: the unemployment figure rose by leaps and bounds from 1930 onwards and reached six million two years later. Over six million unemployed and three million on short-time (in every second family someone was either unemployed or working short-time) were an ideal breeding ground for demagogues. Certainly— I quote again the British historian Alan Bullock:

Without the person Hitler there would have been no seizure of power.... Historians and publicists like to lie about the personal importance of Adolf Hitler. For ideological reasons they are incapable of recognising and admitting the importance of persons in the shaping of politics. They stare at the social circumstances and the dynamic of the masses.... Of course an important role was also played in the rise of national socialism and Hitler's seizure of power by social circumstances.... But it is simply not true that at the same time as the circumstances the man also appears who understands how to exploit them politically. We know periods in history in which the circumstances cry out for a revolution or another dramatic solution and nevertheless no Lenin or Hitler appears. Several factors have to come together.[5]

Of course Veblen is not responsible for others' interpretations of his work. Important and lasting are the impetus he gives to thought. From this point of view it is Interesting to see that some time ago the circle slowly began to close. The American institutionists in the tradition of the author of *Imperial Germany* have lately been showing greater interest in the neoliberal German school around Eucken, Böhm and others, who made an essential mark on the political shape of the economic system of the new Federal Republic of Germany following the Second World War. The German economic miracle in the 1950s and 1960s is proof of Veblen's basic thesis, that institutional developments have an essential influence on the ruling "scheme of use and wont."

Notes

1.   Joseph Dorfman. "Veblen Centenary Round Table, Source and Impact of Veblen," *American Economic Review,* Supplement, May 1958, Vol. 48, p. 8.
2.   Allan Bullock, interview in: *Die Welt,* September 2, 1989, No. 204, p. 17 (translated by Otto G. Mayer)
3.   Joseph Dorfman, op. cit.
4.   On the origin and history of this word see the wonderful essay of Robert K. Merton: *"On the Shoulders of Giants.* A Shandean Postscript, The Free Press, 1965.
5.   Allan Bullock, op. cit. (translated by Otto G. Mayer).

13

The Instinct of Workmanship and the State of the Industrial Arts

Murray G. Murphey

Thorstein Veblen occupies a curious place in American intellectual history. He was a member of an extraordinary generation that blossomed between the Civil War and World War I, and whose work permanently altered the American scene. His writings are well known; nevertheless his contributions have proven very difficult to assess. Although he is often classed with William James and John Dewey among the prophets of democratic liberalism,[1] his kinship with this group is at least dubious and is usually asserted more on the basis of what he was against rather than what he was for. His *Theory of the Leisure Class* has become a classic of American satire and his terms "conspicuous consumption," "conspicuous leisure," and "conspicuous waste" have become part of the liberal vocabulary. Yet it is not at all clear that Veblen saw himself as a satirist, and there has been such uncertainty concerning his positive doctrine that some observers have thought of him as purely a critical thinker.

Veblen's first book, *The Theory of the Leisure Class,* published in 1899, was by far his most popular. Nevertheless, as I shall seek to show, Veblen had not fully formulated his positive theory when he wrote that book, and some of the theses he advanced there, such as the commanding role of emulation, were later substantially modified. In his second book, *The Theory of Business Enterprise,* published in 1904, Veblen worked out his basic economic ideas and their application to the America of his time, in a manner which is still worthwhile and used today.[2] It was in his third book, the little-read volume, *The Instinct of Workmanship,* published in 1914, that he succeeded in formulating a consistent system of fundamental tenets. In this sense, *The Instinct of Workmanship is* Veblen's most important work, for it is here that one finds the basis of the theory which he elaborated in his other works. Therefore, in introducing a new edition of this work, I should like to describe the premises underlying Veblen's thought and then show how a grasp of these principles leads to an understanding of certain of his major claims in economics. Thus it is hoped that we may come a little closer to understanding this "man from Mars."[3]

Veblen received a Ph.D. in philosophy from Yale in 1884. Not being a minister or even orthodox, he failed to get a job teaching philosophy, and in 1891 he went to Cornell to study economics. Economists were not required to be men of God and Veblen did manage to get work at the University of Chicago in 1892.[4] Given his background it is not surprising that Veblen should have approached economics from a different point of view than most, and his philosophic views are crucial to an understanding of his economics. The only explicitly philosophical piece he wrote which has survived was an article on Immanuel Kant's *Critique of Judgment,*[5] which was published in the *Journal of Speculative Philosophy* in 1887. This article gives some important insights into Veblen's position.

Veblen began the article by setting the *Critique of Judgment* in the context of Kant's other critiques. The first critique, he said established "the notion of strict determinism, according to natural law, in the world"; the second, established "the notion of freedom in the person."[6] Given the division between the phenomenal and noumenal realms, freedom and determinism may not conflict, but for freedom to play any role in the world the free person must be able to act as an efficient cause in nature. If such action is to be rational, it must be based upon a knowledge of the effects that will follow upon the actions taken, and the individual must, therefore, be capable of establishing empirical generalizations which hold for the future. This is possible only through induction, and according to Veblen, the purpose of Kant's third critique was to explain and justify inductive reasoning.

Veblen noted Kant's distinction between the determinative judgment, by which universal rules are applied to particular cases, and the reflective judgment, by which the universal rule is found once the particular cases are given. The problem of reflective judgment is then the problem of induction—of inferring empirical generalizations on the basis of particulars. What justifies such an inference? Only if the reflective judgment is guided by an a priori principle will such an activity be legitimate, because since "the result aimed at lies beyond experience, the principle according to which it is to proceed cannot be given by experience."[7] It also cannot come from outside the reflective judgment, since that would make the judgment determinative, and it must therefore come from the reflective judgment itself. The a priori principle of the reflective judgment is, Veblen said. the principle of the "adaptation on the part of the object to the laws of the activity of our faculties of knowledge."[8] Thus induction will be legitimate only if nature forms an orderly, logical system of the type the human mind seeks to create out of its experience and knowledge. Kant regarded this as equivalent to saying that we must view nature as if it was the product of an intelligent creator who had purposely structured it to fit the needs of the human mind. The stress should fall on the *as if,* for Kant held this principle to be subjective only. We must accept such a principle as a regulative principle for the operation of the reflective judgment, but Kant held that it could not be proven to be true of the world. It is therefore a maxim which guides inquiry—a presupposition of inductive investigations—but subjective rather than objective since the reality of such an intelligent creator lies beyond the possibility of proof. Nevertheless, the principle is crucial for it is the foundation for induction. Only if the world is taken to be systematically ordered and free from chance will induction yield true results.[9]

The test of induction, Veblen held, was a feeling of gratification. This was so because "whenever the intellect finds the objects of its knowledge to be such as to admit of the unhampered activity of the faculties employed about them, there results a gratification such as is always felt on the attainment of an end striven for."[10] To the degree that the object known is adapted to our faculties, their activity will be unhampered and so will produce gratification. With respect to the single datum of experience, where the datum is considered simply in relation to the apprehending subject, the reflective judgment is the aesthetic judgment and the gratification is aesthetic pleasure. But with respect to cognition, it is the relations among concepts and their objects, taken as part of our knowledge of the world, with which the reflective judgment is concerned, and to the degree that these are adapted to our faculties the result will again be a feel ing of gratification. "This feeling of gratification may therefore be regarded as a sanction to the principle of the reflective judgment, and, in the last resort, it is this feeling of gratification alone which can decide whether the principle has been applied successfully in any given case."[11]

Veblen's interpretation of Kant leads to the result that we inevitably impute teleology to the world in our attempts to give coherence to our experience. This imputation is based on a subjective requirement, not objective fact.

> The finality which is attributed to external reality, on the grounds of the adaptation found by the reflective judgment, is simply and only an imputed finality, and the imputation of it to reality is based on the same ground of feeling as every other act of the reflective judgment. Our imputation of finality to things of the world, and our teleological arguments for an intelligent cause of the world, proceed on subjective grounds entirely, and give no knowledge of objective fact, and furnish no proof that is available for establishing even a probability in favor of what is claimed.[12]

This article is a discussion of Kant's third critique, not of Veblen's own position, and to draw conclusions from it about Veblen's views involves some risk. Nevertheless, the ideas discussed here play so important a part in Veblen's later thought that it is impossible not to draw certain connections. Whether he derived it from Kant or not, Veblen certainly believed that experience was a joint product of an active mind and sense data, the first supplying the conceptual order, the latter the material or data. But like many of his contemporaries in the post-Darwinian world, Veblen did not accept the idea of one fixed set of categories which were true for all men at all times. He did follow Kant (and most of the nineteenth century) in holding that Newtonian mechanics was not only true, but the model which all other physical sciences must emulate. He also seems to have followed Kant on the question of teleology. He accepted teleology as a description of the behavior of individual organisms, but rejected it as applying to nature as a whole. However, Veblen's comments about the reflective judgment and induction make it clear he believed we do imput teleology to nature, both to nature as a whole and to particular objects of nature, organic and inorganic. This imputation is subjective, but it is also universal since it is required by the mind. Veblen seemed to have rejected entirely Kant's arguments of the Transcendental Dialectic and the second critique; he did not believe in God, or in a noumenal world, and there is no evidence that he believed in freedom or immortality. But he did derive from the third critique his position on induction, which has the consequence for him that the truth of induction rests on a feeling of gratification signifying a compatibility between the object known and "our faculties." Deleting the reference to the faculty psychology, this becomes a compatibility between what is known and the "apperception mass" brought to bear on it—in other words, it becomes a coherence theory of truth.

Kantian psychology was a faculty psychology, and like most of his contemporaries in America, Veblen rejected this model of the mind. In his early writings (before 1914), Veblen drew heavily upon the "new" psychology of James, Dewey, and their followers. Thus he held that man is an active and unified being; the whole man is involved in every act, and although various aspects can be analytically distinguished in the mental processes, there are no separate faculties. Veblen accepted James's theory of the selective operation of attention upon the stream of thought. He also accepted the use of the term habit to encompass both learned patterns of behavior and beliefs, and the general outline of the doubt-belief theory of inquiry. The role of intelligence is to solve problems created by the failure of existing habits to lead to satisfaction in specific settings, and to create new habits which will provide a more adequate basis for action. The emphasis in this psychology is upon man's ability to overcome obstacles and to solve problems—in short, his ability to adapt to the world. Little emphasis is laid upon the invariable features of human nature which might limit the scope of adaptability. Veblen does introduce at least one instinct in this early period—the instinct of workmanship—but he does not discuss instinct as a psychological phenomenon and there is no evidence in these early writings that he used the term in any sense different from William James.[13]

In 1908, William McDougall published *An Introduction to Social Psychology*.[14] McDougall's psychology was an instinct psychology, and the function of the instincts was described as providing the "essential springs or motive powers of all thought and action."[15] If these instincts could be defined and shown to be common to all men, McDougall believed, they would "afford a much needed basis for speculation on the history of the development of human societies and human institutions."[16] McDougall divided these innate tendencies into two classes—the instincts proper, and general non-specific tendencies arising from the constitution and processes of the mind. Of these two groups, the first is the more important. His most precise definition of instinct was:

We may, then, define an instinct as an inherited or innate psycho-physical disposition which determines its possessor to perceive, and to pay attention to, objects of a certain class, to experience an emotional excitement of a particular quality upon perceiving such an object, and to act in regard to it in a particular manner, or, at least, to experience an impulse to such an action.[17]

These three aspects of instinctive action were designated "the cognitive, the affective, and the conative aspects, that is to say, every instance of instinctive behavior involves a knowing of some thing or object, a feeling in regard to it, and a striving towards or away from that object."[18] From this it is clear that instinctive action is teleological, usually having for its end the welfare of the group or the individual. Furthermore, instinct involves the action of consciousness and intelligence, and so is fundamentally distinct from a mere reflex or tropism. Of particular importance for Veblen was the cognitive aspect of the instinct, which McDougall described as follows:

Now, the psycho-physical process that issues in an instinctive action is initiated by a sense-impression which, usually, is but one of many sense impressions received at the same time; and the fact that this one impression plays an altogether dominant part in determining the animal's behavior shows that its effects are peculiarly favored, that the nervous system is peculiarly fitted to receive and to respond to just that kind of impression. The impression must be supposed to excite, not merely detailed changes in the animal's field of sensation, but a sensation or complex of sensation that has significance or meaning for the animal; hence we must regard the instinctive process in its cognitive aspect as distinctly of the nature of perception, however rudimentary.[19]

There is a functional similarity evident here between the Kantian categories and McDougall's instincts. Both are conceived to be generic to the human species and to be the fundamental grounds of thought and action. Both involve an active mind acting upon sense data through a preset mental process—i.e., an innate tendency of the mind to order its data according to these principles. In both cases mental action is teleological and its innate principles are assumed to be basically unchangeable.

We do not know when Veblen first read McDougall, but he had certainly read him by the time he introduced his own instinct theory in *The Instinct of Workmanship*[20] in 1914. Although he cited McDougall as the source of his instinct theory, [21] Veblen's instincts are not McDougall's. He defined them as general tendencies which arise from a combination of more specific psychological elements, but which for the purposes of the social sciences may be treated as irreducible. Like McDougall's instincts, Veblen's are teleological; they are "teleological categories" which are best defined by reference to the end that each serves. But the underlying psychological processes out of which the instincts arise are not teleological. They are "of a quasi-tropismatic or physiological nature"[22] which, while functional for the organism, involve no conscious purpose. Thus, the teleological character of behavior, which Kant imputed to man (among other organisms) as a subjective requirement of the reflective judgment, is here grounded on the nature of instinct, but it arises as an effect of "mechanical" processes in the organism. Instincts are not only purposive, they involve consciousness and intelligence, but the role of intelligence is limited to the finding of means to the attainment of instinctively given ends. Intelligence therefore functions within the framework provided by the instincts and cannot transcend it. Veblen's instincts, like McDougall's, serve as a priori syntheses of thought and action.[23]

The most basic of these instincts Veblen called the "parental bent." Such specific instincts as the instinct of reproduction and the so-called maternal instinct he regarded as components of the parental bent, but the latter is more general and is taken to include all feelings of solicitude for the welfare of others, and particularly for the welfare of the community at large. By welfare Veblen meant material welfare—the satisfaction of the community's needs for food, shelter, heat, clothing, etc. The term "community at large" refers not just to the specific group (family, village, town) to which the person belongs, but to the wider set of people who are linked to the person by economic interdependencies. In the modern world, this means the earth's population.[24]

The second instinct is idle curiosity. That curiosity was an instinct was generally agreed; Veblen's labelling of it as "idle" was specifically intended to assert its non-teleological character. This means of course that idle curiosity does not really fit his definition of an instinct as a teleological category, nevertheless, he named it as one of the three basic instincts. Veblen actually introduced idle curiosity as an instinct in 1906—before McDougall published—but his description of it is so similar to McDougall's that he could have cited the latter's authority for almost everything he said about it. Veblen accounted for idle curiosity psychologically by arguing that the selective processes of the mind in thinking leave some data which are rejected, and that some account must be given of their effects. Such data, Veblen thought, set up their own subsidiary chain of reactions which results in a wholly aimless curiosity. It is just because idle curiosity is idle—i.e., not teleological—that it can lead to the apprehension of facts in terms of efficient cause rather than final cause, and it is from idle curiosity, Veblen believed, our matter-of-fact and scientific knowledge was derived.[25]

In many respects the most important instinct is the instinct of workmanship. Like idle curiosity, it does not precisely fit the definition of instinct, for it belongs to the category of means rather than to that of ends, yet like the parental bent it is teleological and does have its distinctive end—a desire for a job well done, for the efficient use of means, and hence for effective workmanship. The end of the instinct of workmanship is thus the efficient use of the means which are employed in attaining the ends specified by the other instincts—e.g., the parental bent.[26] But this is not an adequate description of this somewhat ubiquitous instinct, for its influence seems to pervade the mind to a greater degree than that of the other instincts. The reason for this is its peculiar relationship to intelligence. Both are in the category of means, both are teleological, and both are closely connected with the knowing process. It was primarily to the instinct of workmanship that Veblen attributed the rise of man from the brute to his present position. Moreover, it is from the instinct of workmanship that the phenomenon of contamination results—a factor which is of the greatest importance in Veblen's system. It is therefore necessary to consider somewhat more closely the nature and role of intelligence.

On Veblen's analysis of human nature, man was essentially an active and purposive creature who strove to satisfy certain instinctive desires. The ends of action were determined by instinct; therefore intelligence had nothing to do with the choice of ends. But instinct is differentiated from tropism because it involves intelligence and consciousness. The role assigned to intelligence is that of finding the means whereby instinctive ends may be attained. It follows, therefore, that the pattern of intelligence—its mode of operation—is teleological; it operates within the framework of the instincts or teleological categories. Knowledge produced by intelligence conforms to this pattern. Instincts act selectively in the field of cognition and order the data of sensation in a fashion analogous to the way Kantian categories operate. Human knowledge is thus systematized according to its general compatibility with these categories.

Because action and thought are teleological, the mind seeks to find the means to attain its ends. But even here it is under the control of instinct, for it is the peculiar function of the instinct of workmanship to regulate the choice of those means. The end of this instinct is efficiency, and intelligence will therefore seek to find such means as will attain the ends with the maximum of efficiency. Once action patterns which serve as means have been found, they will be repeated, and the constant repetition of one mode of action or thought results in the production of a habit, or a resistance to changing the established mode of action. When the process of habituation is extended over a protracted period, resistance to change may acquire sufficient strength so that habits are perpetuated even when they have become grossly inefficient. Like instincts, habits, in proportion to their strength, become principles which affect the ordering of sense data in a selective fashion. The mental framework may thus be conceived as composed of two basic factors; instincts and habits, the former providing the ends, the latter the means.[27]

Veblen held that "habits of thought are an outcome of habits of life."[28] This claim does not imply a strict determinism, nor a simple copy theory. Action is related to thought in several ways. First, ideas are plans of action[29] and the outcome of executing those plans can force a revision of the ideas. There is thus an interaction between thought and action, each modifying and modified by the other. Second, and more broadly, thinking occurs within a problem context defined by the failure of some habit of doing to work successfully, and so is conditioned by the action context in which the problem occurs. Man satisfies his instinctive values by doing, and thinking is called for only where action fails. Habits of life thus give rise to habits of thought because thought is essentially a tool for developing habits of action which will produce satisfactions of the instinctive ends.

It is from this composition of the mind—a combination of instincts and habits in interaction—that one form of the phenomenon of contamination arises, for it follows from the vague and general character of the instincts that there will be a certain degree of overlapping among them, and hence to some extent the same mental processes will be involved in each. From this it further follows that habits contracted in the service of one instinct will to an appreciable extent carry over into the service of another, thus producing "contamination" of one instinct by another.[30] Superficially, the general nature of this contamination is that of obstruction—the blocking of the free operation of the instinct by habit—but the true seriousness of this situation can be seen only through Veblen's use of the "apperception mass":

> All facts of observation are necessarily seen in the light of the observer's habits of thought, and the most intimate and inveterate of his habits of thought is the experience of his own initiative and endeavors. It is to this "apperception mass" that the objects of apperception are finally referred, and it is in terms of this experience that their measure is finally taken.[31]

The "apperception mass" comprises the whole of the instincts and habits, desired ends and formulated knowledge, that the mind contains and that it brings to bear upon sense data in the process of knowing. On Veblen's theory of knowledge, data are systematized in terms of this "apperception mass" with the result that sense experience is interpreted through principles some of which are already outmoded and false. It follows then that human knowledge is never abreast of the actual situation, and there is always a time-lag between environmental and institutional change. To the dictum whatever is, is right Veblen answered whatever is, is wrong, at least to some extent.[32]

There are two further types of contamination that are important for Veblen's theory. One of these is emulation, which arises from a contamination of the instinct of workmanship. Emulation is a crucial factor in Veblen's theory, but its analysis must be postponed to a later point. The second, and most important type of contamination is animism or anthropomorphism. Veblen spelled out the significance of this phenomenon as follows:

> But the most obstructive derangement that besets workmanship is what may be called the self-contamination of the sense of workmanship itself.... The difficulty has been spoken of as anthropomorphism, or animism—which is only a more archaic anthropomorphism. The essential trait of anthropomorphic conceptions, so far as bears on the present argument, is that conduct, more or less fully after the human fashion of conduct, is imputed to external objects.[33]

Animism means the imputation of teleology to what are actually matters of fact, and hence a failure to understand the true relations among these factors. To this end the first type of contamination contributes. For in any act of knowing, the "apperception mass," or complete body of knowledge, habits and instinct in the mind comes into play, and the new data are brought into harmony with it. Data thus become assimilated to our knowledge of reality just in so far as we are able to bring them into a relation of logical consistency with our other knowledge. Since the action of the mind under its instinctive proclivities (idle curiosity excepted) is teleological, data are systematized under the cannons of teleological order with reference to the teleological ends in view. The instinct of workmanship, by focusing attention on the means used in the attempt to attain ends, leads to a consideration of the means apart from the ends—regarding what they are in themselves, as opposed to what can be done with them—and so comes to explain their character on teleological grounds on the assumption that things have ends of their own.[34] This leads to an animistic habit of mind whereby general efficacy is referred to some further ground of "intention" or "purpose" on the part of natural objects.

Veblen's catalog of instincts seems at first glance entirely arbitrary. Other instinct psychologists posited the existence of instincts similar to Veblen's, but they also posited the existence of a number of further instincts—pugnacity,[35] self-assertion,[36] emulation,[37] acquisitiveness,[38] etc. What justification had Veblen for making the selection he did? Veblen had two answers to this question. The first was that rather than posit a long list of instincts it is more parsimonious to posit a minimum set of instincts and then to show that other phenomena which might occur on such a list can be derived from the minimum set. It is obvious that Veblen chose his minimum set so as to emphasize man's altruistic motives and minimize the selfish ones. The problem then becomes one of explaining why human beings, who are basically altruistic, are so patently selfish, and this requires a method of deriving the egotistic motives from the altruistic. One function of contamination is precisely to permit the derivation of such motives as emulation and self-assertion from the three basic instincts. The second answer lies in his theory of cultural evolution—a theory which seems bizarre by today's standards, but was based on impressive authorities at the time he formulated it.

The basic scheme of social evolution Veblen took from Lewis Henry Morgan. In *Ancient Society* Morgan advanced a linear progressionist evolutionary scheme which he asserted to hold universally.

As it is undeniable that portions of the human family have existed in a state of savagery, other portions in a state of barbarism, and still other portions in a state of civilization, it seems equally so that these three distinct conditions are connected with each other in a natural as well as a necessary sequence of progress. Moreover, that this sequence has been historically true of the entire human family, up to the status attained by each branch respectively, is rendered probable by the conditions under which all progress occurs, and the known advancement of several branches of the family through two or more of these conditions.[39]

Morgan posited three major stages of evolution, two of which were trichotomized. Beginning with the most primitive, these were: Lower Savagery, Middle Savagery, Upper Savagery, Lower Barbarism, Middle Barbarism, Upper Barbarism, and Civilization. Each was correlated with a particular cultural configuration and the transition from one to another was marked by an invention or cultural innovation, such as the introduction of pottery or the domestication of animals. Moreover, Morgan believed the stages formed a geometrical progression, with savagery having by far the longest period.[40]

Veblen borrowed this general scheme from Morgan, but modified certain elements of it for his own purposes. He believed that habits of thought are an outcome of habits of action. Habits of action in turn are determined by the modes of production and distribution which prevail in the community, for the requirements of survival are the most imperative demands faced by people and determine most of their activity. But the modes of production and distribution themselves are determined by the state of the industrial arts—i.e., by the knowledge underlying and embodied in technology. Hence Veblen saw the state of the industrial arts as the chief dynamic factor in social evolution. The industrial arts are of course knowledge—i.e., habits of thought—so we have a closed process in which the industrial arts, having determined a given mode of production and distribution, and thus certain habits of action, will in turn be modified by those habits of action. The process so defined is dynamic and will generate an endless sequence of changes; it is also cumulative in that at each moment the course of the process depends upon the outcome of the process up to that time, and it is continuous in that change is always underway. For analysis and description, Veblen used the stages drawn from Morgan, but these were not steady states with leaps from one to another; they are rather segments of a process of continuous change.[41]

The earliest stage Veblen called savagery in accordance with Morgan's scheme. It was characterized by group struggle for subsistence in the form of agriculture and herding, with minimal technology, and with peace, poverty, group cooperation, considerable animism, and a matriarchal family structure.[42] When technological knowledge reached the point where indirect production became important—where the means of production became important apart from the product—and where a surplus could be produced, the transition to barbarism occurred.[43] This stage was marked by the appearance of war, since there was now a surplus worth seizing, patriarchy, ownership of booty leading to the development of private property, increasing inequality of wealth, emphasis upon status, slavery, tyranny, emulation, animism, monotheism, and pecuniary control.[44] Barbarism developed in two forms which often overlapped, the predatory phase, in which ownership rested upon seizure by prowess, with war as the principal means, and the commercial phase, in which war gave way to commerce based on ownership by prescriptive right.[45] Barbarism in turn gave way to civilization. Veblen distinguished two phases, the earlier handicraft phase and the later machine era. The handicraft phase began in the late feudal age and extended to the eighteenth century, a period of five or six hundred years, and was initiated by the growth of handicraft production, itinerant merchandising, and industrial towns. Central to this era was the "masterless man" or independent craftsman, who was at once the maker and marketer of his own goods, and so was involved in both industrial and pecuniary concerns. Technological progress was rapid in this era, but it was for the sake of pecuniary gain as goods were rated in terms of price, and pecuniary acquisition was the objective. The emergence of the price system led to new methods of accounting, which in turn led to the development of statistics, and so furthered the development of science. Indeed, science made rapid strides in the handicraft era with the concept of efficient cause—itself based on the model of the craftsman producing his product—as its fundamental postulate.[46]

With the industrial revolution of the late eighteenth century civilization moved into the machine era, and that is its present state. The machine era began with the development of mechanical means of production too extensive to be owned and operated by independent craftsman. As mechanization grew ownership of the means of production became divorced from operation; owners specialized increasingly in the pecuniary manipulation of production and distribution while the actual operation of the machines became the domain of wage labor. The result was a separation into classes of owners and workers, the former becoming increasingly removed from actual contact with productive processes while the latter came to be almost entirely occupied with them. The institutional effects of the machine process are as yet unclear, owing to its recent appearance, but Veblen particularly emphasized its impact upon scientific thought and upon thinking about causality in general. Instead of the handicraft notion of an efficient cause producing its effect as a craftsman produces his product, Veblen believed the machine had introduced a new concept of efficient causality as a cumulative sequence of change free from any anthropomorphic residue. It is this essentially mechanistic view of causality that Veblen believed the discipline of the machine was instilling into those who tended it. and thus will become the premise of the industrial arts of the machine age.[47]

Veblen's process of social evolution was an evolution of "institutions," whereby habits of thought have become established in the community. But with respect to human nature itself, Veblen believed the process of evolution to be quite different. Here he confronted conflicting theories: on one hand was Darwin's theory of fortuitous variation, on the other, Mendel's theory of stable types. Veblen opted for the latter, as amended by DeVries's theory of mutations. Extreme environmental pressure, Veblen believed, caused similar mutations simultaneously in a number of members of the group. Stable types thus originated as mutations from pre-existing types and remained constant until some further occurrence of extraordinary environmental conditions produced a further mutation or until hybridization, that is, interbreeding with other types, altered genetic endowment. In the former case, the result was an alternation of the basic physical and psychological structure, the psychological structure for Veblen being the instinctive endowment, while in the latter case greater variability was added to the population and thus greater adaptability.[48]

Veblen applied this theory to the origins of the "races" of men, using the term "race" with the latitude customary in the early years of the twentieth century. His most detailed treatment of this subject concerned the origin of the "dolichocephalic blond race" of northern Europe.[49] The earliest traces of this race, he believed, went back to the late glacial period and post dated the early traces of the Alpine and Mediterranean races in Europe. Veblen argued that the Mediterranean race had entered Europe from Africa, and that shortly thereafter the Mediterranean bridge had sunk, cutting off their retreat. The advance of the last glacier would have sufficiently altered the climate in the Mediterranean basin to cause mutations among the members of the Mediterranean race. The result was a wide variety of mutants, including the dolichocephalic blond. Under the environmental conditions caused by the glacial invasion, the vast majority of these mutants would have been eliminated, but the blond was one of the survivors, apparently the only major one. As the glacier retreated, the blond followed it north in order to remain in climatic conditions favorable to its survival, and finally settled in the Baltic area where such conditions were relatively stable. The blond thus appears as a mutant of the Mediterranean stock. Furthermore, he was a hybrid because he was produced in the midst of another stock, where there had been constant crossing and recrossing of parent and mutant lines. Veblen thought this conclusion was confirmed by contemporary evidence which indicated there was no pure blond community in existence, and none where the proportion of blonds exceeded fifty percent. The result of this hybrid character was greater adaptability than a pure bred race would have.[50]

The point to be noted here is that the survival of the dolichocephalic blond was not a matter of adaptation. The range of adaptability, even of a hybrid stock, was relatively narrow. The blond survived because by native endowment he happened to be fitted to survive under the conditions then and since prevailing, not because he could change his genetic make-up to meet the situation. The environment selects by eliminating those whose native endowment does not permit an adequate adjustment; ability to adapt has a relatively limited role for Veblen, unlike some of his contemporaries.

What is true of action in the natural environment is also true, Veblen held, of action in the social environment. The genetic endowment of a race must permit its members to meet the requirements of the culture under which it lives or the selective process will operate to eliminate that race. The selective action of the social environment, however, requires a long time to operate decisively. Veblen followed Morgan in believing that the period of savagery was much longer than the subsequent periods, and so concluded that only savagery had lasted long enough to have selected those races of man whose instinctive endowment best fit its requirements. And clearly those instincts that best fit men for savagery were the parental bent and the instinct of workmanship.[51] Thus Veblen's argument for the universality of these instincts rests on his evolutionary theses that psycho-biological types are relatively stable, that savagery selected the present races of man because they were well fitted to survive its rigors, that none of the other periods of his social evolutionary scheme had lasted long enough to play this selective role, and that no changes in environmental conditions since the ice age had been severe enough to produce large scale mutations in the instinctive endowment then selected.

There is a further consequence of this doctrine. If the present races of man were selected by their fitness to the savage culture, and if human nature is as inflexible as Veblen believed, it follows then as the cultures under which men live depart progressively from the savage original, the fit between culture and human nature must become ever worse. Cultural evolution may therefore create a social environment to which man is so maladapted that his only alternatives are extinction or mutation. Veblen did not say this was the present situation, but this consequence of his position helps to explain his pessimism about the future.[52]

Veblen repeatedly attacked classical economics for being what he termed a taxonomic science and called for an economics which would be "an evolutionary science." What was it that Veblen wanted? Clearly, he wanted a science focused on the process of change and which analyzed it in terms of causality conceived as invariable sequence. This meant not only banishing final causes, but interpreting efficient cause as sequences of change in which each part of the process is the result of all that has gone before. Applied to human culture, Veblen said:

> The growth of culture is a cumulative sequence of habituation, and the ways and means of it are the habitual response of human nature to exigencies that vary incontinently, cumulatively, but with something of a consistent sequence in the cumulative variations that so go forward—incontinently, because each new move creates a new situation which induces a further new variation in the habitual manner of response; cumulatively, because each new situation is a variation of what has gone before and embodies as causal factors all that has been affected by what went before; consistently, because the underlying traits of human nature (propensities, aptitudes and what not) by force of which the response takes place, and on the ground of which the habituation takes effect, remain substantially unchanged.[53]

Understanding of the growth of human culture is not to be found in tools or weapons or machines but in men.

> The changes that take place in the mechanical contrivances are an expression of changes in the human factor. Changes in the material facts breed further change only through the human factor. It is in the human material that the continuity of development is to be looked for; and it is here, therefore, that the motor forces of the process of economic development must be studied.[54]

Man provides both the continuity in the process and the change. It is the instinctive nature of man which is the constant, at least over the period of recorded history, and that instinctive endowment has not changed since the glacial age. Change therefore is to be found in habits, and particularly in habits of thought. Veblen used the term habit in a very broad sense to include learned ways of acting, such as driving a car, and learned ways of thinking, which include not only methods of thought, but also beliefs. As Veblen argued in the passage quoted above, men respond to exigencies of their environment which constantly change. Thus old habits of belief are challenged by new data resulting from the changed situation in which men act, and they must constantly readjust their beliefs to conform to the dynamic reality they confront.[55]

A habit, of course, characterizes an individual at a particular time, but when habits are widely shared and become established within a group, Veblen called them institutions. Thus for Veblen institutions were not organizations or objects but habits or complexes of habits. For example, when Veblen said that private property was an institution, he referred not to the objects owned, but to the set of established beliefs constituting prescriptive rights and duties, by which the objects are made to be property. Institutions then are shared established beliefs, and as beliefs change so institutions change.[56]

The aggregate of our beliefs constitute our knowledge. The term knowledge is usually restricted to those beliefs that are true, but if it is extended to include all of our beliefs that we think are true, it will fairly match what Veblen regarded as the totality of our habits of thought. This body of habits changes over time; they are cumulative, having been created by our predecessors over many generations, and constitute the starting point for each new inquiry, and they are conservative, since we seek to make our knowledge consistent and new beliefs which contradict established beliefs are likely to be rejected. Habits of thought also define the world for action because we plan and execute action in terms of the environment as we believe it to be. As institutions are beliefs which are shared and established in the group, the history of institutions is really the history of knowledge.

Veblen was no idealist; he probably was a materialist. Certainly, he seemed to have regarded human beings as biochemical entities, and he rejected religion outright. The primacy he gave to ideas and beliefs as factors in cultural history had nothing to do with any theory of mindstuff or world spirit. Veblen was interested in causal processes, and in his view causal processes in the history of culture centered on human instincts and habits. A change in the natural or the social environment could produce effects only through changing the behavior of men, and that meant either changing instincts or changing habits. Instincts are the basic motivational factors, but instincts change only by being contaminated, and the contamination involves habits. It is therefore to habits, and primarily to habits of thought, that one must look to understand cultural change.

It is in terms of this theory of human nature and cultural evolution that one must interpret Veblen's economics. While a full treatment of his economics is impossible here, the point can be established by considering one of the most basic themes of his economic writings, the conflict between industry and business. By industry, Veblen meant the production and distribution of materially serviceable objects, that is, of material objects which serve the instinctive ends of man. As the aim of the parental bent is the material welfare of the community at large, serviceable objects will be those providing nutrition, shelter, heat, clothing, comfort, and similar basic needs. When Veblen talked about production and distribution in the industrial sense he referred only to the physical processes involved in producing and distributing such goods. The production of corn means the biochemical process of growing corn in a field; the production of a table means the physical process of turning wood into a table. Similarly, distribution means the physical processes of moving goods from the point of production to the consumer. Industrial processes do not involve money or ownership; they are the purely physical (or biochemical) processes of creating a serviceable object from raw material and transporting it to the person who will consume it. As Veblen said repeatedly, the processes of industry were those of efficient causality only.[57]

Such a definition of industry seems bizarre because we at once ask what values would impel men to produce and distribute goods if no monetary gain were involved. Veblen's answer was values defined by generic instincts. If men really value the material welfare of the community at large, and efficiency, they will carry out the processes Veblen called industrial without there being any need for pecuniary values to be involved. Assuming that men really do have instincts of the sort Veblen claimed they had, the value problem is solved without the introduction of pecuniary values, and the whole pecuniary structure is irrelevant to the production and distribution of materially serviceable goods.

What then is business? In Veblen's view, business was concerned, not with the production and distribution of serviceable goods, but with the exchange of goods. What happens in a business exchange is an exchange of the ownership of goods; exchange value is the value something has as an object of ownership.[58] And the ends served by ownership—in Veblen's sense of ownership as a prescriptive right—were emulative ends, that is, ends which arise from the contamination of the instincts rather than from pure instincts.[59] Production in the business sense means the production of pecuniary values rather than serviceable goods, and distribution means the distribution of income. Business is not of course independent of industry, for business exchange requires goods to be exchanged and the making of goods is an industrial activity, but the production of pecuniary values bears a highly variable relation to industrial production. Thus while there are situations in which pecuniary gain will be maximized by increasing industrial production, there are also cases where the opposite is true. In the classic overproduction case, pecuniary gain is maximized by reducing the output of goods. But of course overproduction here refers to business production only. People may be dying for want of the goods in question, yet if the price of the goods is deemed too low from the standpoint of the businessmen who control the process, the situation is described as overproduction. Business then involves the manipulation of the industrial process for the purpose of maximizing the pecuniary gains of those who own the means of production and distribution. And the values underlying this desire to maximize pecuniary gains are emulative values, and so derive from the contamination of the instincts.[60]

If the history of culture is the history of knowledge then both the development and the conflict of business and industry should be explicable in these terms. That this is true for industry is quite clear. Economists take the factors of production to be land, labor, and capital. Veblen rejected this triad as the factors of production in industry, but he substituted a triad of his own which is roughly comparable. What corresponds to land in his scheme is the material environment, indeed, Veblen defined industrial production as the turning of the material environment to account for man's use. The material environment, Veblen held, had been roughly constant throughout man's recorded history, and it cannot, therefore, be a dynamic feature.[61]

Corresponding to capital for Veblen was the state of the industrial arts, that is, the knowledge of science and technology held by the community at a given time. It was not tools or equipment, which may be thought of as capital goods, but the knowledge upon which they are based and which informs their use which is industrial capital. Thus in savagery, the loss of all the tools used in production would be unimportant because they were so simple that they could be easily replaced, but the loss of the technological knowledge underlying the tools would be fatal. The industrial arts, which are habits of thought, are the dynamic factor in industrial production because as that knowledge grows so does man's command of his material environment.[62] What corresponds to labor in this scheme is the community at large. The application of the industrial arts to the material environment is done by the community as a whole. Further, it is the community which is the carrier of the industrial arts, because the amount of knowledge involved is always far too great for any one individual.[63] Industrial development therefore depends upon the community, the material environment, and the industrial arts, with the industrial arts, or scientific and technological knowledge, as the key dynamic factor.

Business also depends upon habits of thought, but in a more complex sense since contamination is involved here. In his early writings, Veblen made emulation the key value of the pecuniary culture, and in *The Theory of The Leisure Class* he described its origin as follows:

> As a matter of selective necessity, man is an agent. He is, in his own apprehension, a center of unfolding impulsive activity—"teleological" activity. He is an agent seeking in every act the accomplishment of some concrete, objective, impersonal end. By force of his being such an agent he is possessed of a taste for effective work and a distaste for futile effort. He has a sense of the merit of serviceability or efficiency and of the demerit of futility, waste, or incapacity. This aptitude or propensity may be called the instinct of workmanship. Wherever the circumstances or traditions of life lead to an habitual comparison of one person with another in point of efficiency, the instinct of workmanship works out in an emulative or invidious comparison of persons.... The result is that the instinct of workmanship works out in an emulative demonstration of force.[64]

After the publication of *The Theory of The Leisure Class* the importance attached to emulation rapidly decreased and Veblen increasingly stressed animism as the basis of the pecuniary culture. The reason is not that emulation ceases to be important but that Veblen came to see it as a product of animism and therefore took animism as the basic factor. The animistic origin of emulation is evident in the above passage, for emulation arises from the invidious comparison of individuals with respect to efficiency or force. This of course involves the imputation to the individual of causal efficacy; the individual sees himself as the cause of his actions and achievements. But Veblen denied this status to the individual. In his analysis the individual's actions were the result of his instincts and habits. But as instincts were part of the race's inheritance carried by the community at large, so too the habits, or knowledge, which make the individual effective as an agent were part of the cultural heritage of knowledge which was created and transmitted by the community at large. Neither with respect to instinct nor knowledge (ends or means) therefore can the individual be regarded as independent or autonomous. He is an agent in the sense that the hammer is an agent in the driving of the nail, not in the sense of a prime mover who initiates his own course of action. The invidious comparison which underlies emulation is thus based upon an erroneous imputation of causal efficacy in which the individual's subjective sense of himself as an agent is taken for true, thereby misconstruing the actual nature of the process.[65]

Very much the same analysis applied to ownership. Veblen held that ownership originated in barbarism where booty served as a sign of individual prowess, and was continued in the commercial phase of the pecuniary culture where wealth similarly served as a sign of individual force. As in the case of emulation, there was a mistaken imputation of causal efficacy to the individual. Furthermore, the motive underlying ownership was emulation, and the desire to excel in invidious comparisons of individual efficacy so that the institution of ownership was animistic both with respect to its foundation and its use.[66]

It is at this point that one can see how radically Veblen differed from writers such as James and Dewey. In Veblen's view it was the group—the community—that was important in understanding sociocultural change, not the individual. It was the group that carried the gene pool which determined the instincts or motives of its members, and it was the group that created and transmitted the habits that provided the means for their fulfillment. Individuals are just particular combinations of instincts and habits, and their behavior is explained by their twin heritage. There is no significant role for human freedom, if indeed there is any such thing. A causal explanation of social evolution is for Veblen an explanation in terms of the instincts and habits of the group. All self-regarding motives arise from a failure to grasp this basic truth, for all of them arrogate to the individual the causal efficacy which the individual derives from the group. By their animistic imputation of causal efficacy to the individual, a ground is provided for invidious comparison either among individuals or between individuals and the group, and so for self-enhancement at the expense of others. All egotism, all doctrines of economic competition and natural rights, were for Veblen products of the animistic contamination of the instinct of workmanship. Veblen thus derived all the selfish motives of human nature from the altruistic ones through contamination, that is, through the false imputation of causal autonomy to objects which are in reality parts of a mechanical process.

These considerations should make it clear why Veblen believed that the machine discipline had the capacity to subvert the pecuniary culture. The machine process he held to be a strictly mechanical process based on causality as invariable sequence. Those who work with the machine process must come to understand it and so become accustomed to thinking in terms of such mechanical processes. But if this mode of analysis is turned upon the pecuniary culture, it will reveal the animistic character of the whole activity. From Veblen's point of view, the entire pecuniary culture is a system of reasoned make believe, and once recognized as such, he believed, those institutions on which it depended, such as ownership, would lose their credibility.[67]

Veblen's theory is not one that leads to happy endings. Even if industry triumphed and the pecuniary culture was swept away, there was no guarantee that this outcome would be beneficial for mankind. In Veblen's view, man's instinctive endowment dated from the late glacial era and man was best adapted to savagery—a culture in which animism was prevalent. The evolution of culture meant an ever widening disparity between man's latest culture and that to which he was originally adapted. Veblen saw signs in the America of his day of a reaction against the machine process and the notion of impersonal causal sequence, and he thought it entirely possible that industrial culture would not be congenial enough to man's instinctual nature to permit a satisfactory adjustment. Moreover, there was no reason to believe that the state of the industrial arts had reached perfection, and its further development might well make the machine order obsolete and replace it with some other economic order, the discipline of which would work to undermine the plausibility of just such causal analyses as that written by Veblen.[68] As Veblen rejected a teleological reading of evolution and with it the notion of progress, there was no guarantee that the races of man would prosper. As he put it on the eve of World War I:

History records more frequent and more spectacular instances of the triumph of imbecile institutions over life and culture than of peoples who have by force of instinctive insight saved themselves alive out of a desperately precarious institutional situation, such, for instance, as now faces the peoples of Christendom.[69]

Notes

1. Morton White, *Social Thought in* America (New York: Viking, 1949), 3-10.
2. Cf., Seymour Melman, *Profits Without Production* (Philadelphia: University of Pennsylvania Press, 1987).
3. Joseph Dorfman, *The Economic Mind in American Civilization* (New York: Viking, 1949), III, 438.
4. Joseph Dorfman, *Thorstein Veblen and His America* (New York: Viking, 1947), Chaps. 3-5.
5. Thorstein Veblen, "Kant's Critique of Judgment" in Thorstein Veblen, *Essays in Our Changing Order,* ed. Leon Ardzrooni (New York: Viking, 1945), 175-193. This volume of essays will be referred to hereafter as *ECO.*
6. Ibid., 175.
7. Ibid., 179-180.
8. Ibid., 180-181.
9. J. D. McFarland, *Kant's Concept of Teleology* (Edinburgh: University of Edinburgh Press, 1970).
10. Veblen, "Kant's Critique," 181.
11. Ibid., 192.
12. Ibid., 186. Cf. Stanley Matthew Daugert, *The Philosophy of Thorstein Veblen* (New York: King's Crown Press, 1950), Chap. 1.
13. Thorstein Veblen, "Why is Economics Not An Evolutionary Science?" in *The Place of Science in Modern Civilization* (New York: Huebsch, 1919), 74. This volume of essays will be referred to hereafter as *PSMC.* "The Instinct of Workmanship and the Irksomeness of Labor" in *ECO,* 78-96; "The Place of Science in Modern Civilization" in *PSMC,* 5; "The Preconceptions of Economic Science III" in *PSMC,* 155ff
14. William McDougall, *An Introduction to Social Psychology* (London: Methuen and Co., 1908).
15. Ibid., 19.
16. Ibid., 19.
17. Ibid., 29.
18. Ibid., 26.
19. Ibid., 27-28.
20. Thorstein Veblen, *The Instinct of Workmanship* (New York: Viking, 1946).
21. Ibid., 12ff.
22. Ibid., 3.
23. Ibid., Chap. 1.
24. Ibid., 25ff.
25. Ibid., 86-88. Thorstein Veblen, "The Evolution of the Scientific Point of View.," in *PSMC,* 40f.

26. Veblen, The *Instinct of Workmanship*, 31ff.
27. Ibid., 53ff. "The Instinct of Workmanship" in *ECO*, 88.
28. Veblen, "Evolution of the Scientific Point" in *PSMC*, 38.
29. Veblen, "Place of Science" in *PSMC*, 5.
30. Veblen, *The Instinct of Workmanship,* 40-41.
31. *Ibid.*, 53.
32. Thorstein Veblen, *The Theory of the Leisure Class* (New York: Random House, 1934), 207.
33. Veblen, *The Instinct of Workmanship*, 52.
34. Ibid., 54f.
35. McDougall, *Social Psychology,* 62.
36. Ibid., 65.
37. William James, *The Principles of Psychology* (New York: Henry Holt and Co., 1910) II, 409.
38. Ibid., II, 422.
39. Lewis Henry Morgan, *Ancient Society* (New York: World Publishing Co., 1967). 3.
40. Ibid., Chaps. 1-2.
41. Thorstein Veblen, "On the Nature of Capital" in *PSMC,* 324ff.
42. Veblen, *The Instinct of Workmanship,* Ch. 3.
43. Ibid., 150.
44. Ibid., Chap. 4.
45. Ibid., 171-172, 202.
46. Ibid., Chap. 6.
47. Ibid., Chap 7.
48. Ibid., Chap. 1. On DeVries, see G. Allen, "Hugo DeVries and the Reception of the 'Mutation Theory,'" *Journal of the History of Biology.* 2:55-87 (1969).
49. Cf. Joseph Deniker. *The Races of Man* (Freeport: Books for Libraries Press, 1971), especially Chap 9.
50. Thorstein Veblen, "The Mutation Theory and The Blond Race" in *PSMC,* 457-476; "The Blond Race and The Aryan Culture" in *PSMC*, 477-496.
51. Veblen, *The Instinct of Workmanship,* 36.
52. Ibid., Chap. 7.
53. Thorstein Veblen, "The Limitations of Marginal Utility" in *PSMC*, 241-242.
54. Veblen, "Why Is Economics Not an Evolutionary Science?" in *PSMC*, 71-72.
55. Veblen, *The Instinct of Workmanship,* Chap. 2.
56. Thorstein Veblen, "The Beginnings of Ownership" in *ECO,* 32-49; "The Limitations of Marginal Utility" in *PSMC,* 241f; *The Instinct of Workmanship*, 151ff; "Why is Economics Not an Evolutionary Science?" in *PSMC,* 74ff; "Evolution of the Scientific Point of View" in *PSMC,* 38-39.
57. Thorstein Veblen, *The Vested Interests and the Common Man* (New York: Huebsch. 1920), 55; "On the Nature of Capital" in *PSMC, *324-351; Thorstein Veblen, *Absentee Ownership* (New York: Viking, 1945), 126; Thorstein Veblen, *The Theory of Business Enterprise* (New York: Charles Scribners. 1935), Chap. 2.
58. Thorstein Veblen, "The Preconceptions of Economic Science II" in *PSMC,* 142; "Industrial and Pecuniary Employments" in *PSMC,* 296-298, 311; "On the Nature of Capital II" in *PSMC,* 352; *The Theory of Business Enterprise,* Chaps. 3-4.
59. Veblen, "Industrial and Pecuniary Employments" in *PSMC,* 299.
60. Ibid., *The Instinct of Workmanship,* Chap. 5; *The Theory of Business Enterprise,* 214ff.
61. Veblen, *Absentee Ownership,* 125-126; "Why is Economics Not an Evolutionary Science?" in *PSMC,* 71.

62.   Veblen, "On the Nature of Capital" in *PSMC*, 324-386; "Professor Clark's Economics" in *PSMC*, 185.
63.   Veblen, *The Instinct of Workmanship*, 141; "On the Nature of Capital" in *PSMC*, 325-326.
64.   Veblen, *The Theory of the Leisure Class*, 15-16.
65.   Veblen, *The Instinct of Workmanship*, 103, 138ff: "The Beginnings of Ownership" in *ECO*, 33ff.
66.   Veblen, *The Theory of the Leisure Class*, 22ff, 53ff; 'The Beginnings of Ownership" in *ECO*, 32-49.
67.   Veblen, *The Instinct of Workmanship*, 318, 333; "Industrial and Pecuniary Employments" in *PSMC*, 314ff.
68.   Veblen, *The Instinct of Workmanship*, Chap. 7.
69.   Ibid., 25.

14

The Nature of Peace

Warren J. Samuels

Thorstein Veblen was a brilliant, seminal, and skeptical analyst of American culture and the U.S. social, political, and economic system. His analyses of status emulation and its accompanying conspicuous consumption, the nature of the business enterprise and the corporate system, the preconceptions of economic science, and *inter alia* the critical differences between evolutionary and non-evolutionary science, between teleological and matter-of-fact thought and between production-oriented and pecuniary-oriented business decision making, made him a giant among social theorists and pragmatic philosophers.

Veblen did not examine only domestic phenomena and developments. In two major studies, *Imperial Germany and the Industrial Revolution*, published in 1915, and *The Nature of Peace*, published in 1917 and reissued in this volume, Veblen turned his inquisitive and critical mind to the subjects of war and peace.[1] In these volumes Veblen expounded upon key questions. One was the causes and consequences of war, with respect to which Veblen discussed the nation-state system; the psychology of nationalism, including war as a consequence of socialization and patriotism; and the fundamental differences between the predatory dynastic state and the live-and-let-live modern liberal democratic state, modified by recognition of the existence of predatory vestiges in modern states. Another key question had to do with the respective possibilities for peace and war consequent to technological, predatory, and pecuniary forces, including the sources and practices of imperialism and the common man as an object of manipulation. The foregoing led Veblen to consider the prospects for reformation of the nation-state system and, therefore, for peace. In some respects, such as his cosmopolitanism and affirmation of free trade, Veblen was quite orthodox. In other respects, however, such as his treatment of war as a non-aberrational phenomenon laden with causes and consequences endogenous to both the nation-state and economic systems, and his dispassionate and skeptical treatment of conventional beliefs, he was quite iconoclastic and heterodox.

In order to appreciate Veblen's specific ideas on war and peace, one has to see them against the background of his total approach to social science. First, for Veblen, the economy is not an independent, self-subsistent sphere isolated in practice from the rest of society. Such may, or may not, be useful for mechanistic theorizing and model building. In reality, however, the economy is what it is and operates the way it does because of its connections with the total social system. In one sense, the economy is one interacting subprocess of the total social system. In another, the conception of "the economy" is only an abstraction of certain aspects or parts of the total social system. In both senses, the economy is driven by factors and forces normally not included within their conception of the economy by mainstream, orthodox economists.

Second, for Veblen both the economy and the total social system of which it is, however conceptualized, one part, continually undergo systemic and structural/institutional transformation. His economics is explicitly intended to be an evolutionary economics, evolutionary in the nonteleological Darwinian sense.

Third, "institutions" for Veblen are ingrained habits of thought. For him, although individuals are socialized in the ways and mindsets of the society in which they are born and raised, the social world does not dictate its own conception. Society is socially constructed in two senses: (1) its actual organization and structure are produced by human beings, not by nature; and (2) our conception of society is manufactured by us. Social evolution is very much, according to Veblen, a matter of changing habits of thought. Apropos of individuals, whatever their genetic endowment and constraints, behavior is also, indeed largely, a function of socialization; socially inculcated habit is more important than hereditary human nature.

Fourth, for Veblen the phenomenon of war is neither an exogenously imposed irrational aberration nor a technical matter of the allocation of resources to military production (the "economics of war"). War is a complex topic with roots in the nature of social systems and the nation-state system.

Fifth, Veblen has a similar view of imperialism. Moreover, for Veblen no clear-cut, fine distinction exists between the so-called "political" and "economic" interpretations or theories of imperialism. According to the former, imperialism is a function of the machinations of domestic politicians using nationalist sentiments and patriotism (with which they too may be imbued) to achieve their own advancement. According to the latter, imperialism is a function of the profit-seeking schemes of businesses transported abroad. According to the former, trade follows the flag; according to the latter, the flag follows trade. For most objective analysts, the basic facts—as distinct from both the rationalizations and theories—of imperialism are rather straightforward. The facts, however, submit to different theories, the political and the economic; and advocates of each theory are able to interpret the basic facts from their own perspective. For Veblen, however, both war and imperialism emanate from the total social, political, and economic nexus of a nation and its place in the total nation-state system; imperialism is simultaneously both political and economic. Indeed, the designations of "political" and "economic" are matters of selective perception and specification. Still, because Veblen includes substantially all of the explanatory lines of reasoning found in the political and economic theories, it is possible to interpret him in terms of one or the other.

But *The Nature of Peace* is not about imperialism, it is about war; and the origins of war, which include those normally included in the origins of imperialism, go beyond those of imperialism. *The Nature of Peace* contains both a theory of politics and a theory of economics in regard to war, and while one can concentrate on one or the other, it would not do justice to Veblen's arguments to do so.

Before turning to the main text, let us glance at Veblen's Preface. Here Veblen acknowledges the source of his title: Immanuel Kant's *Perpetual Peace* (*Zum ewigen Frieden*) (1805). In Veblen's view, however, though each favors peace over war, the orientations of their respective books are different. For Veblen, "To Kant the quest of an enduring peace presented itself as an intrinsic human duty, rather than a promising enterprise." For Kant "there runs a tenacious persuasion that in the end, the regime of peace at large will be installed. Not as a deliberate achievement of human wisdom," Veblen relates, "so much as a work of Nature the Designer of things—*Natura daedala rerum*" (p. vii). Such teleology is not congenial to Veblen's way of thinking, however: "*Natura daedala rerum* is no longer allowed to go on her own recognizances, without divulging the ways and means of her workmanship" (p. viii). His own approach, he says, is one which "in Kant's time still lay over the horizon of the future" (p. viii). Veblen's approach is at once empirical, instrumental, and matter-of-fact. The quest of perpetual peace, he tells us, is a matter of the question, "What are the terms on which peace at large may hopefully be installed and maintained?" especially "within the calculable future" (p. viii). Peace is for Veblen a matter not of grand transcendent forces and design but of conditions, some of which are propitious and others inhibitive if not prohibitive.

The book has seven chapters. In the first, introductory chapter, "On the State and Its Relations to War and Peace," Veblen argues that war is not a matter of the Order of Nature. War is a matter of the predatory behavior of dynastic states in a nation-state system in which individuals are subjects owing allegiance to their monarch rather than citizens with rights against the state and in which dynastic ambition and whim govern international relations. But predatory behavior is a mark "of a particular species of governments, and not characteristic of the genus of governmental establishments at large. "These powers," Veblen writes, "answer to an acquired bias, not to an underlying trait of human nature; a matter of habit, not of heredity" (p. 11). As for the habits, they are a function, to no small degree, of socialization in predatory, dynastic states and the nation-state system of which each is a member.

Yet, says Veblen, for a couple of centuries a movement—both "a drift of popular sentiment, and indeed something of a deliberate endeavour" (p. 14)—has existed with the objective of rendering states both "harmless and helpless" (p. 14). "The movement in question is known to history as the Liberal, Rationalistic, Humanitarian, or Individualistic department. Its ideal, when formulated, is spoken of as the System of Natural Rights; and its goal in the way of a national establishment has been well characterized by its critics as the Police State, or the Night-Watchman State" (p. 14). Veblen points to what may be either an irony or a choice-theoretic predicament or both. The rise of the idea of such a limited state has coincided with great advances in the technology of transport and communication in the nineteenth century. But this new technology, so far from conducing to peaceful commerce, "has enabled closer and more coercive control to be exercised over larger areas, and at the same time enabled a more massive aggregate of warlike force to strike more effectively at a greater distance" (p. 15).

Ideals of *laissez-faire* and of Natural Liberty (his capitalization) have been finessed by the predatory exigencies of dynastic states in the nation-state system. In the nineteenth century, England was the residence of such liberal thinking; but it was also a most successful empire-building nation. Now comes competition from a Prussianized Germany with *its* combination of "enterprising force and fraud" (p. 20).

As for popular sentiment, it cordially supports even aggressive war. "Any politician who succeeds in embroiling his country in a war, however nefarious, becomes a popular hero and is reputed a wise and righteous statesman, at least," Veblen remarks with a hint of sarcasm, "for the time being" (p. 22).

Veblen speculates that "there are two main lines of motivation by which the spiritual forces of any Christian nation [more irony if not sarcasm] may so be mobilised for warlike adventure: (1) The preservation or furtherance of the community's material interests, real or fancied, and (2) vindication of the national honour. To these should perhaps be added a third, the advancement and perpetuation of the nation's 'Culture'; that is to say, of its habitual scheme of use and wont" (p. 23).

Apropos of the pursuit of material interests, Veblen examines not only the aggregate of predation by one country against another but the internal distributions of costs and benefits. Some of what he says is common to economists but some is a good bit more radical:

> To safeguard these commercial interests, as well as property-holdings of the nation's citizens in foreign parts, the nation maintains naval, military, consular and diplomatic establishments, at the common expense. The total gains derivable from these commercial and investment interests abroad, under favorable circumstances, will never by any chance equal the cost of the governmental apparatus installed to further and safeguard them. These gains, such as they are, go to the investors and businessmen engaged in these enterprises; while the costs incident to the adventure are borne almost wholly by the common man, who gets no gain from it all. Commonly, as in the case of a protective tariff or a preferential navigation law, the cost to the common man is altogether out of proportion to the gain which accrues to the businessmen for whose benefit he carries the burden. The only other class, besides the preferentially favored businessmen, who derive any material benefit from this arrangement is that of the office-holders who take care of this governmental traffic and draw something in the way of salaries and perquisites; and whose cost is defrayed by the common man, who remains an outsider in all but the payment of the bills. The common man is proud and glad to bear this burden for the benefit of his wealthier neighbors, and he does so with the singular conviction that in some occult manner he profits by it. All this is incredible, but it is everyday fact (p. 26).[2]

The occult is invoked by Veblen in regard to national honour: "The national honour, in short," he writes, "moves in the realm of magic, and touches the frontiers of religion" (p. 29).

Chapter II, "On the Nature and Uses of Patriotism," is pure Veblen in its combination of objectivity and skepticism, if not cynicism. "Patriotism may be defined," he says, "as a sense of partisan solidarity in respect of prestige" (p. 31). "The patriotic spirit is a spirit of emulation" (p. 33); "it lives on invidious comparison, and works out in mutual hindrance and jealousy between nations" (p. 38). More than that, politicians have "designs to make use of the popular patriotic fervor" (p. 35) for their own ends; indeed, "Among English-speaking peoples much is to be gained by showing that the path of patriotic glory is at the same time the way of equal-handed justice under the rule of free institutions" (p. 35). "But," he later adds, "in one way or another it is necessary to set up the conviction that the promptings of patriotic ambition have the sanction of moral necessity" (p. 37).

Veblen takes up the issue of whether patriotism is a hereditary trait, "an inborn impulsive propensity," or a product of habituation (p. 41). The ubiquity and strength of patriotism seem fundamental but Veblen is less sure of that than that "under modern conditions the patriotic animus is wholly a disserviceable trait in the spiritual endowment of" European peoples (p. 46). Veblen's celebrated way with words is evident in his treatment of the main issue:

> All this, of course, is intended to apply only so far as it goes. It must not be taken as intending to say any least word in derogation of those high qualities that inspire the patriotic citizen.... No doubt, it is in all these respects deserving of all the esteem and encomiums that fall to its share.... It is evidence of the ubiquitous, intimate and ineradicable presence of this quality in human nature; all the more since it continues to be held in the highest esteem in spite of the fact that a modicum of reflection should make its disserviceability plain to the meanest understanding. No higher praise of moral excellence, and no profounder test of loyalty, can be asked than this current unreserved commendation of a virtue that makes invariably for damage and discomfort. The virtuous impulse must be deep-seated and indefeasible that drives men incontinently to do good that evil may come of it. "Though He slay me, yet will I trust in Him." (P. 47)

Yet, if patriotism is a deep-rooted impulse, what sets it (and not other propensities) in motion, as it were, are certain institutions. Institutions can be predatory or pacific; patriotism can be directed to predatory or benign objectives. Not only institutions but technology can open to people opportunity for non-predatory advancement about which one can take patriotic pride; patriotic devotion can have an "intrinsic value as a genial and generous trait of human nature" (p. 54). However, technology combined with invidious comparison can reinforce both domestic and international predation. The propensities to predation so dominant in barbarous times continue into the present, and the common man—"so constituted that he, mysteriously, takes pride in these things that concern him not" (p. 57)—becomes the cost-bearing instrument of aggressive interests in whose service patriotism is enlisted.

On the one hand, "the national honour comes to be confounded in popular apprehension with the prestige of these personages who have the keeping of it" (p. 59). On the other hand,

> the common defense of any given nation becomes a detail of the competitive struggle between rival nationalities animated with a common spirit of patriotic enterprise and led by authorities constituted for this competitive purpose.

Except as a broad basis of patriotic devotion, and except under the direction of an ambitious governmental establishment, no serious international aggression is to be had. The common defense, therefore, is to be taken as a remedy for evils arising out of the working of the patriotic spirit that animates mankind, as brought to bear under a discretionary authority. (P. 61)

As for national material welfare, it "is to the purpose only in so far as it conduces to political success, which is always a question of warlike success in the last resort" (p. 64).

Patriotism is like government itself; each is an instrument available to whomever can control and put it to use. While the "patriotic animus is an invidious sentiment of joint prestige" (p. 67), Veblen summarizes a major argument in these words: "The chief material use of patriotism is its use to a limited number of persons in their quest of private gain" (p. x).

Shortly before the close of chapter II, Veblen maintains that the "pacifist argument on the economic futility of national ambitions" is not sufficient to "put out of the way...an argument showing that it [an hereditary bent of human nature] has its disutilities. So with the patriotic animus; it is a factor to be counted with, rather than to be exorcised" (p. 73). And it is to be counted in relation to the institutional system in which it appears and which gives it direction, presently a structure comprised of capitalism and the nation-state system:

> So that the chief material use of the patriotic bent in modern populations, therefore, appears to be its use to a limited class of persons engaged in foreign trade, or in business

that comes in competition with foreign industry....[and] has also the secondary and more sinister effect of dividing the nation on lines of rivalry setting up irreconcilable claims and ambitions...[all of which] falls in with the schemes of militant statesmen, and further reacts on the freedom and personal fortunes of the common man. (Pp. 75–76)

Returning to a theme noted early in this introduction, it should be clear that Veblen has developed both a theory of the state and a theory of the economy, both a theory of the economic sources of war and a theory of the political sources of war—in each respect a theory of war as an institution and as a function of institutions. His hope is that the conditions of peace and the terms of its perpetuation are affirmative.

Chapter III is entitled "On the Conditions of a Lasting Peace." The analysis is conducted with three players: Germany and, quite presciently, Japan, and the English-speaking nations. The first two are the modern models of the predatory dynastic state; the latter are not without predatory elements but generally are thought to have better things to do than to initiate war with their neighbors. The former "may safely be counted on spontaneously to take the offensive"; the latter "will fight on provocation" (p. x). Veblen's argument is summarized, in part, by his statement that "War [is] not a question of equity but of opportunity" (p. x).

The argument is this: Peace will have to be kept by and between peoples who are patriots. The chances of peace are a function of forces maintaining "a patriotic nation in an unstable equilibrium of peace for the time being" (p. 78). As of 1917, Germany and Japan are "bent in effect on a disturbance of the peace,—with a view to advance the cause of their own dominion" (p. 79). They are dynastic states with imperial designs; neither "'desires' war; but both are bent on dominion, and as the dominion aimed at is not to be had except by fighting for it, both in effect are incorrigibly bent on warlike enterprise" (p. 82). Their imperial enterprise is thus "the chief circumstance bearing on the chances of peace" (p. 83). If peace is to be achieved, the national ambition of the hitherto dynastic state must be changed and under conditions in which peacetime is not a lull enabling preparation for war (p. 87).

Peace, especially a lasting peace, requires the slow evolution of habits and institutions which involve peoples and nations in activities other than national aggrandizement. Such institutions cannot be developed overnight by design:

an institution is an historical growth, with just so much of a character of permanence and continuity of transmission as is given it by the circumstances out of which it has grown. Any institution is a product of habit, or perhaps more accurately it is a body of habits of thought bearing on a given line of conduct, which prevails with such generality and uniformity throughout the group as to have become a matter of common sense.

Such an article of institutional furniture is an outcome of usage, not of reflection or deliberate choice; and it has consequently a character of self-legitimation, so that it stands in the accredited scheme of things as intrinsically right and good, and not merely as a shrewdly chosen expedient *ad interim*. (P. 91)

The need is to change the social and political institutions in which patriotism hitherto has been captured and driven by the dynastic, warlike animus. That this is difficult to accomplish is underscored by the fact that "[h]abituation to personal subjection and subservience under the rigorous and protracted discipline of standardised service and fealty has continued" (p. 97) to support "a coalescence of unimpaired feudal fealty to a personal master and a full-blown sense of national solidarity" (p. 99) and inures people to predatory policies. To this point Europe has had "a differential in point of cultural maturing, due to a differential in the rate of progression through that sequence of institutional phases through which the civilised peoples of Europe, jointly and severally, have been led by force of circumstance" (p. 100). A lasting peace will have, therefore, to await the further development and especially the spread of a non-predatory way of life. People will continue to be patriotic, at least to a degree; they will respond to aggression. But the popular temper will be "of the defensive order; perhaps of an unnecessarily enthusiastic defensive order, but after all in such a frame of mind as leaves them willing to let well enough alone, to live and let live" (p. 105). The "decisive difference between those peoples whose patriotic affections center about the fortunes of an impersonal commonwealth and those in whom is superadded a fervent aspiration for dynastic ascendency" is that "[t]he latter may be counted on to break the peace when a promising opportunity offers" (p. 105)—and, of course, to work to create those opportunities.

The difference at bottom is the presence or absence of the dynastic state (p. 112). Veblen is not blind to predatory impulses from non-dynastic modern states. Their animus is largely to live and let live but predation and dominion are not unknown. He is not categorically juxtaposing the modern state of English-speaking peoples to the militarist regimes of Germany and Japan. But he is affirming that, in point of peace and especially a lasting peace, the existence of non-dynastic modern states is conducive to peace and that of predatory dynastic states is not. Until, therefore, all states are pacific, "the peace of the world would be conditioned on the inability of the dynastic State to break it" (p. 116).

Chapter IV, "Peace Without Honor," considers the unattractive but logically relevant possibility of achieving peace by submitting to the rule of German, and Japanese, dynastic establishment, as an alternative to "peace through elimination of these enterprising Powers" (p. 118). From the standpoint of 1998, one hopes that Germany, reunified after a half-century of partition, and Japan, the protagonists in World War Two, have been transformed and will eschew predatory militaristic aggression, except perhaps military actions under the aegis of the United Nations or the North Atlantic Treaty Organization (NATO). But that is only a possibility for Veblen. Here he considers submission, or "peace without honor."

Here Veblen considers the alternatives open to the dominating power in treating those who have submitted to them. The Imperial establishment will practice a benefit-cost regimen which should preclude "unadvised excesses" in the long run (p. 121) and be considerate if not humane (p. 124). But the calculations, such as they are and such as they lead to, will be undertaken by the dominating power, not those who have more or less voluntarily submitted themselves in hope of peace. The latter have made a calculation as well, and they may have miscalculated the benefits of submission and the "cost of disabling and eliminating the warlike Power whose dominion is feared" (pp. 132–133). Moreover, the psychology of nationalism and of patriotism is a major factor in the identification and weighing of the costs and benefits of war.

At this point in chapter IV Veblen pauses to make a subtle point. He argues that bellicose patriotism "is not of the essence of human life; that it is of the nature of habit, induced by circumstances in the past and handed on by tradition and institutional arrangements into the present" (p. 142). The decay of bellicose patriotism would result from "an habituation to unconditional peace and security; in other words, in the absence of provocation, rather than a coercive training away from the bellicose temper" (p. 142). In the case of a people's voluntary submission it is altogether possible that such bellicose national ambition would be "positively bred out of them by the stern repression of all such aspirations under the autocratic rule of their alien masters" (p. 144). More than that, after further discussion of various benefit-cost considerations, Veblen points out that "with the coalescence of these nations under one paramount control" (p. 149), even the emulative and predatory propensities of the resulting central establishment may decline.

Thus far Veblen has considered "the underlying community as a whole, with no attempt to discriminate between the divergent interests of the different classes and conditions of men that go to make up any modern community" (p. 150). Here Veblen is principally interested in the two classes that made up the population, "those who own the country's wealth, and those who do not," the latter "often spoken of as The Common Man" (p. 151). Veblen's judgment is that "it may well be doubted if this common man has anything to apprehend in the way of added hardship or loss of creature comforts under the contemplated régime of Imperial tutelage" (p. 153) after submission to the dynastic state. In democratic countries, Veblen argues, "public policy is guided primarily by considerations of business expediency, and the administration, as well as the legislative power, is in the hands of businessmen" (p. 156). The general ground of "the business system" is that "afforded by the principle of 'charging what the traffic will bear'" (p. 157). The position of labor in such a system, discussed at length by Veblen, is one of abuse if not downright exploitation, as the costs borne by labor do not have meaning for their employers. However, in "the modern economic system where a sufficiently ruthless outside authority, not actuated by a primary regard for the pecuniary interests of the employers, might conceivably with good effect enforce a more economical consumption of the country's man-power" (p. 165). One suspects that should Veblen have come to know the treatment of labor under Nazi Germany, Japan in conquered lands, and the Soviet Union, he might have handled this differently. But his analysis is a logical exercise of possibilities, and neither conjectural history nor prediction.

His conclusion, again, is that

By and large, and taking the matter naively at the simple face value of the material gain or loss involved, it should seem something of an idle question to the common man whether his collective affairs are to be managed by a home-bred line of businessmen and their successive filial generations of gentlemen, with a view to accelerate the velocity and increase the volume of competitive gain and competitive spending, on the one hand, or by an alien line of officials, equally aloof from his common interests, and managing affairs with a view to the usufruct of his productive powers in furtherance of the Imperial dominion. (Pp. 166–167)

It should be noted that the treatment of labor is not a matter of personal moral defects on behalf of either ruling class, the business-men or the imperial rulers. They too operate within and "are help-less under the exigencies" of the regnant system (p. 172).

So the calculations depend upon who is conducting them, the extraneous foreign power or the nation's business community. Veblen finds it "difficult to see on what grounds of self-interest such an Imperial government could consent to tolerate the continued man-agement of these underlying nations' industries on business prin-ciples, that is to say on the principle of the maximum pecuniary gain to the businesslike managers" (pp. 174–175). What Veblen perhaps does not fully acknowledge is the practice of superordinate powers reaching some form of accommodation with local subordinate pow-ers, thereby recruiting their compliance and support. Veblen feels, however, that "a contented, well-fed, and not wantonly over-worked populace is a valuable asset" to the imperial power, to which extent "the material interest of the common man would seem to coincide with that of the Imperial establishment" as "class privileges and dis-crimination would be greatly abated if not altogether discontinued" (p. 175). In any event, all such calculations, in the event of uncondi-tional surrender, are a function of such variables as the class distri-bution of wealth and imperial culture and policy.

Chapter V, "Peace and Neutrality," reverses the argument of the preceding chapter by introducing non-material considerations. Veblen begins the chapter by summarizing the argument to this point, cen-tering on the presumed better treatment of the common man by new masters than the old:

> Considered simply on the face of the tangible material interests involved, the choice of the common man in these premises should seem very much of a foregone conclusion, if he could persuade himself to a sane and perspicuous consideration of these statisti-cally apparent merits of the case alone. It is at least safely to be presumed that he has nothing to lose, in a material way, and there is reason to look for some slight gain in creature comforts and in security of life and limb, consequent upon the elimination, or at least the partial disestablishment, of pecuniary necessity as the sole bond and criterion of use and wont in economic concerns. (P. 178)

"But," he goes on, "man lives not by bread alone" (p. 178). In democratic nations, personal liberty, not creature comforts, is the ultimate end "in the pursuit of which...material means find their ulterior ground of valuation" (p. 179). The ideals of liberty are not homogeneous and will be compromised, decreasingly, by the dynastic spirit. The latter is because of the cumulative habituation of people, even in the hitherto predatory dynastic states, to democratic values on the basis of modern experience is gradually replacing subservience to dynastic ambitions. "Inchoate insubordination" (p. 192) shows itself increasingly. The "discipline of life by the methods of modern trade and industry" (p. 194) works against both the continuation of predatory dynastic states and voluntary subordination. Agencies of conservatism operate but are gradually eroded:

> The modern industrial occupation, the modern technology, and that modern empirical science that runs so close to the frontiers of technology, all work at cross purposes with the received preconceptions of the nationalist order; and in a more pronounced degree they are at cross purposes with that dynastic order of preconceptions that converges on Imperial dominion. (P. 197)

Repeated exposure to modern work and industry will gradually weaken the grip of the "spiritual virtues of national prestige and dynastic primacy" (p. 198). Thus is self-interest redefined; socialization changes with industrial system. The predatory dynastic state is increasingly defeated by modern economic sociology.

Veblen's case continues to be Germany. Some of his reasoning seems in retrospect, after World War Two, to have been wishful thinking, or at least thinking along lines not substantially realized until late in the twentieth century. But the economic sociology seems correct, if the implicit dating is questionable. Thus, "peace by submission under an alien dynasty...is presumably not a practicable solution" (p. 203) as had earlier appeared.

The measures to be taken to the perpetuation of peace among pacific nations, Veblen says, are "simple and obvious...and... are largely of a negative character" (p. 205). They center on "the neutralisation of all those human relations out of which international grievances are wont to arise...so much of these relations as the patriotic self-conceit and credulity of these peoples will permit" (p. 205). Some of the motives to be neutralized are economic, others are political. A centerpiece is free trade, "the beginning of wisdom as touches the perpetuation of peace," the first effects of which would be "wider and more intricately interlocking trade relations" and "a further specialisation and mutual dependence of industry,...which would mean, in terms of international comity, a lessened readiness for warlike operations all around" (p. 207). It "is plain," Veblen writes, "that the peace will be secure in direct proportion to the measure in which national discrimination and prestige are allowed to pass into nothingness and be forgot" (p. 217).

In the first volume reissued in this series, Frank W. Taussig put forth a major argument for capitalism: "Better that we should have Napoleons of industry than the blood-guilty Napoleons of history."[3] (Adam Smith had earlier called attention to the civilizing effects of commerce.) Veblen was, to put it mildly, not all that pleased with hierarchical capitalism as it emerged, especially with the "Napoleons of industry," but his economic sociology identifies how the transition to a large extent takes place—and may over time reform hierarchical capitalism itself. It is a slow, complex and neither preordained nor smooth process, but it is a powerful one. Democratic industrial regimes come to be moved by interests other than the warlike ones. These developments leave them handicapped in the event of predatory attack, handicapped but not defenseless. World War Two is again a relevant consideration, not least because *inter alia* Germany and Japan were persuaded, through war, not peaceably, "to let [their] unoffending neighbors live their own life according to their own light" (p. 232).

In chapter VI, entitled "Elimination of the Unfit," Veblen further tackles the combination of psychological, political, and economic factors involved in the transition to a world of peace. These factors include the defanging of nationalism and patriotism, the formation of a "league of pacific nations," the democratization of Germany and Japan as well as the further maturation/modernization of Great Britain and the United States. The general principle, as it were, is that "War is to be avoided by a policy of avoidance" (p. 281)— which includes the social construction of conditions conducive to peace and not war.

The imperial powers will have to be included in the league of pacific nations if they are to be educated with the live-and-let-live policy and if the league is to succeed (p. 237): "Without the definitive collapse of the Imperial power no pacific league of nations can come to anything much more than armistice" (p. 239). Recognizing the historical impact of domestic social structure and politics on predatory national policy, Veblen argues that "The people of the quondam Imperial nations must come into the league on a footing of formal equality with the rest. This they can not do without the virtual abdi-

cation of their dynastic governmental establishments and a consequent shift to a democratic form of organisation, and a formal abrogation of class privileges" (p. 241). Personal "loyal abnegation in
the presence of [royal and noble] authority" and its attendant nationalism and warlike patriotism must be aborted (p. 242). The "common man [must] get used to thinking that the vested interests and
the sacred rights of gentility are so much ado about nothing" (p.
252). National military establishments of all nations must no longer
be the domain of a warrior or gentlemen class (pp. 245ff). Moreover, "The league...must be in a position to enforce peace by over-
mastering force, and to anticipate any move at cross purposes with
the security of the pacific nations" (p. 238).

All this requires a league policy of unconditional surrender, "which
could be accomplished only by the absolute and irretrievable defeat
of these Powers as they now stand" (p. 243). Veblen advances a
somewhat detailed program, one element of which is "Cancelment
of the public debt, of the Empire and of its members—creditors of
the Empire being accounted accessory to the culpable enterprise of
the Imperial government" (p. 271).[4]

But more than defeat is required; so is transformation: "a lasting
peace is possible on no other terms than the disestablishment of the
Imperial dynasty and the abrogation of all feudalistic remnants of
privilege in the Fatherland and its allies, together with the reduction
of those countries to the status of commonwealths made up of un-
graded men" (p. 258).

But all this may also require a defanging of capitalism itself, in all
countries, if the Napoleons of industry are to neither become domestic tyrants nor lead to the blood-thirsty Napoleons of history.
Veblen believes that "The motives that work out through...national
spirit, by use of...patriotic ardor, fall under two heads: dynastic ambition, and business enterprise" (p. 283). "[N]either the one nor the
other," he feels, "comprises anything that is of the slightest material
benefit to the community at large" (p. 283). "The common man...who
gathers nothing but privation and anxiety from the owners' discretionary sabotage, may conceivably stand to lose his preconception
that the vested rights of ownership are the cornerstone of his life,
liberty and pursuit of happiness" (pp. 254–255). The common man
should learn "to distrust the conduct of affairs by his betters, and...to
trust his own class to do what is necessary and to leave undone what
is not"; in such ways "his deference to his betters is likely to suffer a

decline, such as should show itself in a somewhat unguarded recourse to democratic ways and means" (pp. 256–257). Business, as a "kept class" (pp. 288, 289), must lose its privileged status—including its protective tariff (p. 294 and passim).

The pacification of capitalism involves the transformation if not termination of all colonial systems (pp. 258ff) as well as free trade. What is wanted is a world in which there is neither colonial policy nor inducement to the acquisition of colonies (pp. 261–262) and no pursuit of economic advantage in a manner conducive to international jealousy, discrimination, grievance and possible eventual aggression (pp. 262, 276–277).

Veblen's final chapter is entitled "Peace and the Price System." The first parts examine different conceptions of peace and the psychological effects of war but are principally concerned with the effect of the machine process on political preconceptions, not least those of military valor and other values. The conclusion is both paradoxical and ominous for the dynastic state:

> The dynastic State is apparently caught in a dilemma. The necessary preparation for warlike enterprise on the modern plan can apparently be counted on, in the long run, to disintegrate the foundations of the dynastic State...[to] induce a decay of those preconceptions in which dynastic government and national ambitions have their ground. Continued addiction to this modern scheme of industrial life should in time eventuate in a decay of militant nationalism, with a consequent lapse of warlike enterprise. (Pp. 311–312, 314)

Veblen then turns again to "the discrepancy in fact between those who own the country's wealth and those who do not," which be believes "is presently to come to an issue" (p. 315). Veblen's total, anthropological analysis incorporates an evolutionary process in which power relations, including conflicts over property and other interests, are central. But, he points out, "The standard theories of economic science have assumed the rights of property and contract as axiomatic premises and ultimate terms of analysis" (p. 317). For Veblen, superior social power succeeds in having its interests vested as property rights and, correlatively, the ideology of Western civilization interprets the income accruing to property owners as due to their "productivity," whereas in fact it is due to a combination of property power and modern technology. For example, "Invested capital yields income because it enjoys the usufruct of the community's technological knowledge; it has an effectual monopoly of this usufruct because this machine technology requires large material appliances with which to do its work" (p. 322). The age of handicraft industry is past; now the age of machine technology and business power reigns, abetted and institutionalized by the system of property and the ideology which treats property relations as ontological givens. Bourgeois power has replaced feudal power.

But this system will be subject to change, once the perpetuation of peace is assured. Veblen points to "the prospective frame of mind of that unblest mass of the population who will have opportunity to present their proposals when peace at large shall have put national interests out of their preferential place in men's regard" (p. 324). The common man will take a matter-of-fact attitude toward domestic social, political, and industrial issues, no longer letting them be swamped by nationalist and patriotic sentiments. Modern developments, therefore, augur changes within both the predatory dynastic and pacific modern states.

However, "So long as the price system rules, that is to say so long as industry is managed on investment for a profit, there is no escaping [the] necessity of adjusting the processes of industry to the requirements of a remunerative price" (p. 325). Such necessity conflicts with the demands of the common man for greater participation in polity and economy and with the demands of peace itself. One possible result is a "shift back to the old familiar ground of international hostilities; undertaken partly to put down civil disturbances in given countries, partly by the more archaic, or conservative, peoples to safeguard the institutions of the received law and order against inroads from the side of the iconoclastic ones," that is, between "those who stand on their ancient rights of exploitation and mastery, and those who are unwilling longer to submit" (p. 330). But all results depend upon the impact of the market on firms in the matter of the "balance in terms of price" (p. 340). From Veblen's point of view, the alternatives are two: "either the price-system and its attendant business enterprise will yield and pass out; or the pacific nations will conserve their pecuniary scheme of law and order at the cost of returning to a war footing and letting their owners preserve the rights of ownership by force of arms" (p. 366).

The regime of peace is a function, therefore, of the pacification of both the dynastic state and the modern state, the class struggle, the control of government by privileged business and other propertied interests, and the workings of the market. Among the necessary conditions of a lasting peace is the taking of precautions "beforehand to put out of the way as much as may be of those discrepancies of interest and sentiment between nations and between classes which make for dissension and eventual hostilities" (p. 367). War and warlike behavior are matters not only of psychology but of both politics and economics, that is to say, matters of the social system and structure as a whole. Protective tariffs are not aberrations, any more than is war itself.

This introduction was written during December 1997. It comes, that is to say, after two World Wars (*The Nature of Peace* was written in the midst of the first) and after the cold war, after the League of Nations and the United Nations, after the Gulf War, after a variety of ethnic pogroms ("ethnic cleansing"), and after countless other conflicts. More immediately relevant, the interpretation of those wars and institutions is also variable. The United Nations is, at least in part, an attempt to substitute talk and negotiation for war in the resolution of conflict, with the hope that war is no longer the *raison d'etré* of nations, or that nations are no longer so predominantly predatory toward their neighbors, a hope that may well be misplaced in many cases. But the United Nations (and other international institutions) are also the means by which some nations attempt to impose their will or agendas or self-images, even their economic theories, on other nations, including the use of force, with patriotism and nationalism still actively manipulated ingredients. The Gulf War (ostensibly over the Iraqi conquest of Kuwait) could be interpreted in numerous ways, including (to use Veblen's phraseology) material interests (oil), national honor, and contest over culture.

The combination of the post-World War Two division of Germany and a NATO inclusive of West Germany helped to modernize West Germany and to prepare it for the absorption of East Germany, after a half-century, after the dissolution of the Soviet satellite system in East Europe and of the Soviet Union itself. (Veblen does not fail to notice Russia as a threat to peace; possibly the Soviet experiment involved the education and modernization of Russia.)

Will training in industrial process and preoccupation with material life, rather than predatory values, lead to the tempering of capitalism, perhaps along the lines of liberal social democracy? Is this the continuation of the Enlightenment program? Is development of the international corporate system, as a rival to the nation-state system, a step in this process? Or a different form of Napoleons?

Three-quarters of a century after Veblen wrote this book we remain uncertain of the prospects of peace. That so much lip-service is given to "peace" is a step in the right direction but is insufficient ground for assuming the achievement and perpetuation of peace. As to understanding why that is so, Veblen's *The Nature of Peace* is a good place to begin. But the reader must be prepared to suspend the rationales and moral indignations promulgated and reinforced by the institutions of social control and communication in his or her nation. The reader must be prepared to follow Veblen along more putatively objective lines and not simply presume the justness of one or another military venture.

As with so much of Veblen's work, once one has read this 1917 work one will never look at questions of war and peace again in quite the same way.

Notes

1. Veblen's ideas on these subjects are discussed in detail in Jeff Biddle and Warren J. Samuels, "Thorstein Veblen on War and Peace," in Warren J. Samuels, Jeff Biddle, and Thomas W. Patchak-Schuster, *Economic Thought and Discourse in the 20th Century* (Brookfield, VT: Edward Elgar, 1993), pp. 87–157.
2. It is a function of patriotic propaganda to induce preferences for and perceptions of gain from military adventure.
3. Frank W. Taussig, *Inventors and Money Makers* (New Brunswick, NJ: Transaction Publishers, 1989 [1930]), p. 129.
4. Veblen's program, particularly in matters of reparation, but also with a view to his larger scheme for transformation, should be assessed, in part, in light of John Maynard Keynes's critical volume, *The Economic Consequences of the Peace* (1919).

15

The Place of Science in Modern Civilization

Warren J. Samuels

Thorstein Veblen's *The Place of Science In Modern Civilisation,* published in 1919 as a collection of previously published essays, is a major contribution by a writer who continues to command attention and respect almost three-quarters of a century later.

The first three decades of the twentieth century witnessed the work of three writers who, each in their own way, produced comprehensive theories of society. The theoretical systems of Max Weber, Vilfredo Pareto, and Veblen made substantive contributions to the fields of economics, sociology, political science, and psychology, as well as sociolinguistics, broadly defined. The list of their principal modern precursors is arguably small but distinguished: Giambattista Vico, Adam Smith, Henri de Saint-Simon, Auguste Comte, and Karl Marx. Besides their comprehensiveness, Weber, Pareto, and Marx emphasized the interdependence of society. Neither polity nor economy, nor general culture nor language, was self-contained, each had profound impact on the other; society is a set of interacting subsystems. Also, many of their substantive formulations and contributions were parallel. For example, Weber placed emphasis on modern rationalism, Pareto on logico-experimental knowledge, and Veblen on matter-of-fact habits of thought, each with modern science (and technology) as a corollary. They also stressed the fundamental, albeit partly derivative, importance of the modern state and, *inter alia,* what may be comprehended as the common interactive tripartite elements of their overall systems, power, knowledge, and psychology.

Veblen was heterodox, iconoclastic, sardonic, caustic, and satiric. He also was brilliant, penetrating, original, courageous, literarily dramatic, and unique, as well as intellectually distant, if not alienated from the world around him—a distance that may have been both a help and a hindrance for his thinking. Some of these characteristics he shared with Weber, others with Pareto, some with both.

The continuing relevance of the positive analytical work of Veblen, Weber, and Pareto, derives in part from the depth and breadth of their analysis, especially their work on fundamental matters, which makes it in many respects timeless. The continuing relevance of Veblen's critical work, directed with often devastating implications for both existing capitalist society and mainstream economic theory, as well as for Marxism and socialism in general, derives from both the penetration and range of the positive analysis on which it rests, and the arguable failure of both capitalist society and neoclassical theory to change in material respects in the years since Veblen wrote. The continuing relevance of Veblen's topics, and of his specific ideas, is manifest in such diverse contemporary areas as the continuing critique of mainstream economics, much of which is a series of footnotes to Veblen; to controversies over the relations of deduction and induction (and the status of efforts to produce truth, with or without a capital T) to belief systems and language; to disputes about the significance of business mergers and acquisitions, considered as portfolio investment (and not direct contributions to income in the GNP sense), as substitutes for real investment as a principal money-making activity; and *inter alia,* to questions about the historic meaning and status of socialism.

The first six essays of this volume comprise fundamental, systemic, positive contributions to the study of the preconceptions that drive thought and modern science, and the origins of those preconceptions.

The next nine essays represent applications of Veblen's thinking to the critique of both the work of other economists and capitalism in general. These essays also make independently valuable contributions of their own. Three essays, on industrial and pecuniary employments and on the nature of capital, present a fundamental component of Veblen's view of capitalism and its problems, and are of lasting interpretive and analytical value. These nine essays both express Veblen's point of view and identify the limits of the work of such writers as John Bates Clark, Gustav Schmoller, and Karl Marx considered from a positivist's point of view. That Clark was a leading mainstream economist, Schmoller a major historicist, and Marx, well, Marx, indicates something of the breadth and power of Veblen's theoretical position. The arguments of these critical essays are also manifestly applicable to all sorts of comparable present-day theorizing.

The final three essays, especially the last two, reflect, alas, the invidious eugenicism, yes, racism, common among social scientists of Veblen's era; except as examples of that genre, and of the associated conjectural history utilizing natural selection, they have no other permanent value.

The arguments of the first six chapters may be considered as a whole. Veblen argued that mankind pursued its intellectual efforts, at the deepest structural levels, along certain habits of thought and systems of preconceptions, or prepossessions. These habitualized and typically unrecognized and unchallenged preconceptions were derived from the practices of ordinary life, especially how people made a living and the institutional arrangements under which people lived. He argued there have been two principal habits of thought or systems of preconceptions, the animistic or teleological, and the matter-of-fact.

The *animistic or teleological* preconception typically tends to project a personalized conceptualization of ultimate design, reality, and purpose. It involved, as Veblen portrayed it, a combination of projection and ceremonial rationalization, and served both as a psychic balm and as social control functions. At its least animistic it is a taxonomic venture, but more typically it is teleological in its imputation of final causes and inevitability of results, both centering on some notion of the substantiality of reality preeminent to man, the latter even when, as in more modern times, creation is understood to be particularly dedicated to the welfare of mankind. Veblen wrote specifically about classical economics, but in terms applicable to all forms of teleological reasoning.

> The standpoint of the classical economists, in their higher or definitive syntheses and generalizations, may not inaptly be called the standpoint of ceremonial adequacy. The ultimate laws and principles which they formulated were laws of the normal or the natural, according to a preconception regarding the ends to which, in the nature of things, all things tend. In effect. this preconception imputes to things a tendency to work out what the instructed common sense of the time accepts as the adequate or worthy end of human effort. It is a projection of the accepted ideal of conduct. This ideal of conduct is made to serve as a canon of truth, to the extent that the investigator contents himself with an appeal to its legitimation for premises that run back of the facts with which he

is immediately dealing, for the "controlling principles" that are conceived intangibly to underlie the process discussed, and for the "tendencies" that run beyond the situation as it lies before him.[1]

In this context, even the notion of a trend in events imputes purpose to the sequence of events, investing the sequence with a discretionary, teleological character asserting itself as a constraint over all the steps in the sequences by which the supposed objective result is reached.[2] Not surprisingly, in works (such as Clark's) giving effect to this preconception, nuances of a beneficent end are present, as are also "provocations to homiletic discourse."[3] While overtly taxonomic, such analysis subsumes "its data under a rational scheme of categories which are presumed to make up the Order of Nature"[4] giving effect to a range of preconceptions having one metaphysical ground, that there is one right and beautiful definitive scheme of economic life, "to which the whole creation tends."[5] Earlier economists "were believers in a Providential order, or an order of Nature... conceived to work in an effective and just way toward the end which it tends; and in the economic field this objective end is the material welfare of mankind."[6] Even Adam Smith's economics, for all its matter-of-fact elements, is driven by a "preconception of a normal teleological order of procedure in the natural course" which "affects not only those features of theory where he is avowedly concerned with building up a normal scheme of the economic process. Through his normalizing the chief causal factor engaged in the process, it affects also his arguments from cause to effect."[7]

What is true of mainstream economics, according to Veblen, is also true of historicist economics, whether Marxian or non-Marxian. Thus Wilhelm Roscher's metaphysical postulates were "the common-sense, commonplace metaphysics afloat in educated German circles in the time of"[8] his youth, a Hegelian metaphysics "of a self-realising life process...of a spiritual nature...essentially active, self-determining, and unfolding] by inner necessity," for which "the laws of the cultural development with which the social sciences, in the Hegelian view, have to do are at one with the laws of the processes of the universe at large...."[9]

Moreover, "the universe at large is itself a self-unfolding life process, substantially of a spiritual character, of which the economic life process is but a phase and an aspect."[10] Veblen saw Marx as combining materialistic Hegelianism and English natural rights, reaching polemical conclusions which "run wholly on the ground afforded by the premises of that school" and whose "ideals of...propaganda are natural-rights ideals" especially that of the right of labor to the whole product of laborer.[11]

The *matter-of-fact* preconception is concerned with observable phenomena and material cause and effect studied in an impersonal and dispassionate way. The matter-of-fact preconception focuses on process rather than predetermined outcomes[12] which narrows "the range of discretionary, teleological action to the human agent alone"[13] and is concerned with "the questions of what men do and hovel and why they do it"[14] and comprehends causation "in an unbroken sequence of cumulative change."[15] It is these characteristics that have made for the primacy of science.[16]

A critical difference between the two types of preconceptions centers on the nature of social change. For Veblen the crux of the matter was that matter-of-factness had enabled a specifically Darwinian conception of change as an unfolding sequence without necessary ultimate meaning rather than one or another animistic or teleological conceptions. The Darwinian conception is of a "run of causation unfold[ing] itself in an unbroken sequence of cumulative change."[17] involving a process of natural or artificial human selection brought about, in part, through the exercise of human purpose and choice, one driven not by some transcendental predetermined end, but by the interaction of actors and forces under changing natural and social circumstances.

Post-Darwinian science, Veblen said, focused on the process of causation rather than "that consummation in which causal effect was once presumed to come to rest." It is "substantially a theory of the process of consecutive change, which is taken as a sequence of cumulative change, realized to be self-continuing or self-propagating and to have no final term.[18] The "questions of the class which occupy the modern sciences" are "questions of genesis, growth, variation, process (in short, questions of a dynamic import)."[19] understood in terms of open-ended cumulative causation. For economics to be an "evolutionary science, it "must be the theory of a process of cultural growth as determined by the economic interest, a theory of a cumulative sequence of economic institutions stated In terms of the process itself."[20]

Societies historically have been blends of both habits and thought, though increasingly the latter, which is the hallmark of modernity. Moreover, pragmatic considerations have always been present, even in societies that were substantially animistic. Modern science and technology exist in a mutually reinforcing relationship with the matter-of-fact habit of thought, though there are residues of teleological preconceptions In modern society. The history of economic theory is a history, accordingly, of both the continuing co-existence of teleology and matter-of-fact theorizing, and the gradual eclipse but not total elimination of the former. The "history of the science," he said, "shows a long and devious course of disintegrating animism."[21]

Preconceptions, the animistic-teleological, or the matter-of-fact doctrines, come into being as part of what amounts to Veblen's large-scale model of society which, unfortunately, was nowhere completely spelled out, though he insisted upon both the key roles of culture and the state of the industrial arts (technology) and the general inter-dependent nature of the system The elements of this model include human nature, the material environment, institutions, technology, general culture, and belief systems (predicated upon preconceptions). Varying formulations of this general model are given in different contexts. Preconceptions are the product of both the state of the industrial arts, and the habitualized practices to which they give rise, and the institutional structure under which the community lives. But the "state of the industrial arts is dependent on the traits of human nature, physical, intellectual, and spiritual, and on the character of the material environment."[23] Change in preconceptions "is closely correlated with an analogous change in institutions and habits of life, particularly with the changes which the modern era brings in industry and in the economic organisation of society."[24] In the modern era, "science and technology play into one another's hands."[25]

More generally,

> the canons of validity under whose guidance [the scientist] works are those imposed by the modern technology, through habituation to its requirements; and therefore his results are available for the technological purpose. His canons of validity are made for him by the cultural situation; they have habits of thought imposed on him by the scheme of life current in the community in which he lives; and under modern conditions this scheme of life is largely machine-made. In the modern culture, industry, industrial processes, and industrial products...have become the chief force in shaping men's habits of thought. Hence men have learned to think in the terms in which the technological processes act. This is particularly true of those men who by virtue of a peculiarly strong susceptibility in this direction become addicted to that habit of matter-of-fact inquiry that constitutes scientific research.[26]

A two-word summary is cumulative causation. "And so long as the machine process continues to hold its dominant place as a disciplinary factor in modern culture, so long must the spiritual and intellectual life of this cultural era maintain the character which the machine process gives it"[27]—though the predominance of the machine process is itself a dependent variable. Moreover, the "fabric of institutions intervenes between the material exigencies of life and the speculative scheme of things," in such a way that "habits of thought...reflect the habits of life embodied in the institutional structure of society" that "is a matter of law and custom, politics and religion, taste and morals...." and with respect to which "the speculative generalizations, the institutions of the realm of knowledge, are created in the image of...social institutions of status and personal force...."[28] In addition, practice is always pragmatic, but it is not always matter-of-fact; economic "change is always in the last resort a change in habits of thought."[29] The habits of thought formed in any one line of experience affect thought in any other;[30] varying combinations of disciplines of the mind produce different social results.[31] There is a strong technological determinism here, because it must be comprehended in terms of a much larger model, perhaps better expressed as conditionism "...under the Darwinian norm the question of whether and how far material exigencies control human conduct and cultural growth becomes a question of the share which these material exigencies have in shaping men's habits of thought...."[32]

In emphasizing the role of fundamental structuring preconceptions or habits of thought, Veblen emphasized the difference between the terms (language and discourse) in which people express their understanding of nature, society, and mankind, and the actual facts of the matter. As our preconceptions change, even conceptions of the Deity change.[33] What we perceive to be "the facts" are preconception laden. Phenomena do not define themselves, rather, meaning is imputed by the observer.[34] What happens cannot appear to us except on the ground or through the mediating and defining influence of some preconception or prepossession.[35]

The single most encompassing theme of this volume is the presence and discourse-forming role of preconceptions in the history of economic and other thought: The "ultimate term or ground of knowledge is always of a metaphysical character. It is something of a preconception, accepted uncritically. but applied in criticism and demonstration of all else...."[36] Veblen was thus one of the earliest writers to concern himself with the social construction of meaning, rather than with the absolute category of truth, and with the formation of knowledge or belief or both as a product of group life in particular institutional and cultural contexts.

Veblen was rather adroit with words, especially in his ability to foment tone and attitude. Consider the evocative power of the sentence, "The gallantries, the genteel inanities and devout imbecilities of mediaeval highlife would be insufferable even to the meanest and most romatic modern intelligence"[37]—evocative, to be sure, but at once both descriptive and judgmental. Consider, too, his use of dramatically unusual words to elicit a sense of the archaic, "If we are getting restless under the taxonomy of a monocotyledonous wage doctrine and a cryptogamic theory of interest, with involute, loculicidal, tomentous and moniliform variants, what is the cytoplasm, centrosome, or karyokinetic process to which we may turn, and in which we may find surcease from the metaphysics of normality and controlling principles?" The message was, however, not left implicit: "There is the economic life process still in great measure awaiting theoretical formulation."[38]

One literary or rhetorical device Veblen used throughout the volume was that of asserting what he took to be both true and desirable as if it were beyond dispute at the highest levels. When he wrote that "economics is helplessly behind the times, and unable to handle its subject-matter in a way to entitle it to standing as a modern science,"[39] in the opening paragraph of the essay on "Why is economics not an evolutionary science?," he was presuming as the basis of comparison a Darwinian conception of social process and an economic science modelled thereon as beyond cavil, as a given— whereas his own argument establishes the problematic character of such an eventuality. Still, he insisted, when deriding the economics of "normal cases," that "it is only a question of time when that (substantially animistic) habit of thought shall be displaced in the field of economic inquiry by that (substantially materialistic) habit of mind which seeks a comprehension of facts in terms of a cumulative sequence,"[40] to close the penultimate paragraph of the essay. Veblen argued that people, for the most part, uncritically accept and think in terms of preconceptions and habits of thought that have become a part of them through socialization or enculturation. Beliefs and facts are then system-specific. Veblen unquestionably affirmed and indeed lauded modern Darwinian or evolutionary science and the matter-of-fact preconception or habit of thought on which it rested.

Thus, for example:

> In a general way, the higher the culture, the greater the share of the mechanical preconception in shaping human thought and knowledge, since, in a general way, the stage of culture attained depends on the efficiency of industry.[41]

But he clearly and unequivocally also affirmed the preconceptional nature of matter-of-factness and cumulative causation (in which metaphysical respects teleological habits of thought are substantively, but not discursively different), the preconception or system-specificity of belief, the consequent normative status of belief, and the applicability of these ideas to his own thinking. All these points, especially the self-referential nature of his argument, are evident in following the extracts:

> [Modern science] will bring under inquiry such questions of knowledge as lie within its particular range of interest, and will seek answers to these questions only in terms that are consonant with the habits of thought current at the time.[42]

> The prime postulate of evolutionary science, the preconception constantly underlying the inquiry, is the notion of a cumulative causal sequence....[43]

> [The postulate of consecutive, cumulative changer is an unproven and unprovable postulate—that is to say. it is a metaphysical preconception....[44]

> ...The notion of causal continuity, as a premise of scientific generalisation, is an essentially metaphysical postulate.... Before anything can be said as to the orderliness of the sequence, a point of view must be chosen by the speculator, with respect to which the sequence in question does or does not fulfill this condition of orderliness, that is to say, with respect to which it is a sequence. The endeavor to avoid all metaphysical premises fails here as everywhere.[45]

It will surprise no one that Veblen's several critiques of mainstream economic theory and of capitalism are both derivative and expansive of the arguments so far summarized. Veblen's critique of orthodox theory included the following interrelated arguments or themes.

1. Economic theory has become increasingly matter-of-fact but inevitably continues to have teleological elements. In this respect, the economist is like other people: "He is a creature of habits and propensities given through the antecedents, hereditary and cultural, of which he is an outcome; and the habits of thought formed in any one line of experience affect his thinking in any other."[46]

2. Economic theory, as we have already seen, serves the function of ceremonial adequacy, that is, as a social control and also as a psychic balm.[47] As such it represents and replicates "in large part the point of view of the enlightened common sense of [the] time."[48] It is too ready to accept the ground of sufficient reason rather than insist on the ground of efficient cause.[49] It is also too useful for casting luster and re-enforcing vested interests.

3. The defect of economic theory lies not in its lack of factual realism, but in its failure to be evolutionary in the Darwinian manner, focusing on development in a self-generating process of cumulative causation and unfolding sequence encompassing all the variables found in Veblen's general model.

4. The foregoing defect is especially clearly manifest in orthodox theory's conception of man as an isolated, passive responder to external stimuli, and not as an effectively purposive economic agent participating in larger processes. Veblen's description of this conception has been, appropriately, widely quoted:

The hedonistic conception of man is that of a lightning calculator of pleasures and pains, who oscillates like a homogeneous globule of desire of happiness under the impulse of stimuli that shift him about the area, but leave him intact. He has neither antecedent nor consequent. He is an isolated, definitive human datum, in stable equilibrium except for the buffets of the impinging forces that displace him in one direction or another. Self-imposed in elemental space, he spins symmetrically about his own spiritual axis until the parallelogram of forces bears down upon him, whereupon he follows the line of the resultant. When the force of the impact is spent, he comes to rest, a self-contained globule of desire as before. Spiritually, the hedonistic man is not a prime mover. He is not the seat of a process of living, except in the sense that he is subject to a series of permutations enforced upon him by circumstances external and alien to him.[50]

As a corollary, Veblen argued that orthodox theory failed to consider the respects and means whereby culture and institutions, such as that of private property affect human action.

5. Orthodox theory maintains the fundamental presumption of capitalist society, that to have an income means that one has been productive, disregarding what Veblen considered to be fundamental, namely, the distinction between industrial and pecuniary pursuits, or between making goods and making moneyed In this respect Veblen was not prepared to assume, along with orthodox theorists, that any business adjustment or any action acquisitive of profit is presumptively instrumental of the welfare of mankind, or in his language to the serviceability of the community. As Veblen put it, "the classical theory of production is in good part a doctrine of investment in which the identity of production and pecuniary gain is taken for granted,"[52] an assumption he vehemently rejected.

In the essays that comprise this volume Veblen was not principally interested in analyzing capitalism. The argument of the three essays on industrial and pecuniary employments and on the nature of capital, however, present the core of what subsequently became a key thesis for Veblen and for those who follow in his analytical footsteps, that is, the just-mentioned distinction between industrial and pecuniary, between making goods and making money. The production of goods is only incidental and by no means necessary to the acquisition of income. To Veblenians, the distinction is amply manifest in corporate mergers and acquisitions, hostile or friendly, in which real capital assets merely change ownership, and activity is directed toward reaping money rewards without adding to the production of serviceable goods; portfolio manipulations do not constitute real investment.

In Veblen's view, returns on the ownership of capital from both tangible and intangible assets were due to the differential advantages accruing to the owners, advantages typically arising from their class position, or with the assistance of government, as through the law of property, advantages that enable the owners to engross, as he put it, part of the flow of income. This approach, it should be noted, rejected both the orthodox productivity and the Marxian exploitation paradigms in favor of what may be called the Veblen-Weber paradigm of appropriation, in which income (and wealth) is distributed on the basis of a complexly grounded meeting of forces in the political economy, without normative status, except insofar as ideology and general social control impute such status.

For Veblen, the capitalized value of assets is a function of their income-yielding capacity to their owner. In the case of tangible assets there is a presumption that the objects of wealth involved have at least some potential serviceability at large, since they serve materially productive work. In the case of intangible assets, which largely derive from the creation of pecuniary arrangements, there is no presumption that the objects of wealth involved have any serviceability at large, since they serve no materially productive work, but are only a differential advantage to the owner in the distribution of the industrial product. Serviceability and claims to income are two different matters.[53]

One final set of principal topics warrants attention. Veblen believed the economist must consider: (1) purposive and habitual action by individuals; (2) methodological individualist and methodological collectivist methodologies, and (3) deliberative and nondeliberative social control (the collective correlative to the first). Veblen is appropriately well known for his criticisms of hedonistic rationality (as above), but the reader will notice the several elements of this criticism. First, the individual is said to be heavily motivated by habit, custom, institutions, and status emulation. Second, the individual is said to have teleology or purposes of his or her own, however much these are socially generated or influenced. Veblen did not insist on either habit, purpose, or socialization alone, but acting in concert. His comprehension of the inevitability of the combination of methodological individualism and methodological collectivism is brilliantly expressed in the following excerpts:

> The growth and mutations of the institutional fabric are an outcome of the conduct of the individual members of the group, since it is out of the experience of the individuals, through the habituation of individuals, that institutions arise; and it is in this same experience that these institutions act to direct and define the aims and end of conduct. It is, of course, on individuals that the system of institutions imposes those conventional standards, ideals, and canons of conduct that make up the community's scheme of life. Scientific inquiry in this field, therefore, must deal with individual conduct and must formulate its theoretical results in terms of individual conduct. But such an inquiry can serve the purposes of a genetic theory only if and in so far as this individual conduct is attended to in those respects in which it counts toward habituation, and so toward change (or stability) of the institutional fabric, on the one hand, and in those respects in which it is prompted and guided by the received institutional conceptions and ideals on the other hand. The postulates of marginal utility, and the hedonistic preconceptions generally, fail at this point in that they confine the attention to such bearings of economic conduct as are conceived not to be conditioned by habitual standards and ideals and to have no effect in the way of habituation.[54]

> Nor is it conceived [by marginal utility economics] that the presence of this institutional element in men's economic relations in any degree affects or disguises the hedonistic calculus, or that its pecuniary conceptions and standards in any degree standardize, color, mitigate, or divert the hedonistic calculator from the direct and unhampered quest of the net sensuous gain. While the institution of property is included...it is allowed to have no force in shaping economic conduct, which is conceived to run its course to its hedonistic outcome as if no such institutional factor intervened between the impulse and its realization...presumed to give rise to no habitual or conventional canons of conduct or standards of valuation, no proximate ends, ideals, or aspirations.[55]

There are also several other matters that will be of interest to many readers. One is Veblen's treatment of pragmatism, where his views were not yet fully worked out or at least not fully stated. This is particularly noteworthy in light of his affirmation of the ubiquity of pragmatic behavior. Another was his participation in early controversies over the nature of capital, preludes to the modern capital controversy, extending to the deep question of the fundamental coherence of mainstream economic theory, a matter already raised by Veblen.

It should be obvious that Veblen's ideas and theories are subject to criticism. For all his incisive brilliance he may be wrong. Even where he is correct, the Paretian doctrine of the social utility of falsity (or the Marxian doctrine of false consciousness viewed in a non-Marxian manner) may pertain. A society may mislead itself, say, through animistic or teleological reasoning, but this may be instrumental to the operation of that society and its transformation into a more modern society. A few more or less representative criticisms follow.

First, when Veblen said that because of the pressure of modern industrial or technological exigencies "it is only a question of time when that (substantially animistic) habit of mind which proceeds on the notion of a definitive normality shall be displaced in the field of economic inquiry by that (substantially materialistic) habit of mind which seeks a comprehension of facts in terms of a cumulative sequence"[56] he was surely ignoring the psychic balm function of economics as well as the social control function that puts psychic balm solutions to additional effective use. Moreover, he has been empirically wrong: while the tendency which he lauds is present, it remains swamped by another set of preconceptions. Teleological ideology seems inevitable.

Second, Veblen argued that the emulative system with its struggle for economic respectability, on which capitalism rests, breeds discontent with the institution of private property and "is one of the causes, if not the chief cause, of the existing unrest and dissatisfaction with things as they are," indeed, "necessarily adverse to the existing industrial system of free competition."[57] Now Veblen was certainly correct that: "The outcome of modern industrial development has been, so far as concerns the present purpose, to intensify emulation and the jealousy that goes with emulation, and to focus the emulation and the jealousy on the possession and enjoyment of material goods."[58] But to one writing near the end of the twentieth century, rather than in 1892, when those words were published, it seems that while Veblen may be empirically correct in his interpretation of social discontent (notice that it is a very different interpretation from that of Sigmund Freud in his *Civilization and Its Discontents*), certainly there has been no diminution of status emulation, "the struggle to keep up appearances"[59] and its accompaniments in American society, nor does discontent with private property as an institution seem to have grown. This, of course, does not mean that the contradiction between emulation and private property that Veblen noted has not manifested itself in institutional change.

Third, Veblen distinguished between valuation, production, and distribution. He said that valuation was a pecuniary matter fundamentally related to acquisition, and thus distribution, and in this he was surely correct. He said also that "Ownership, no doubt, has its effect upon productive industry, and, indeed, its effect upon industry is very large,...but ownership is not itself primarily or immediately a contrivance for production.

Ownership directly touches the results of industry, and only indirectly the methods and processes of industry."[60] A conservative economist would emphasize that the security required for production is provided, willy nilly, by the institution of ownership, but my point is a different one. Consider Veblen's related argument that "Pecuniary capital is a matter of market values, while industrial capital is, in the last analysis, a matter of mechanical efficiency, or rather of mechanical effects not reducible to a common measure or a collective magnitude,"[61] and that "Capital pecuniarily considered rests on a basis of subjective value; capital industrially considered rests on material circumstances reducible to objective terms of mechanical, chemical and physiological effect."[62] The problem is not with the distinction but with its force: Industrial capital produces goods, but which goods? Somehow society has to determine whose interests—whose subjective valuations—are to count in determining the allocation of resources and the production of real goods and services. (For Veblen, technological change and resource allocation were influenced by pecuniary factors.)

This consideration is underscored by Veblen's very candid recognition, given his stress upon the state of industrial arts, that "technological proficiency is not of itself and intrinsically serviceable or disserviceable to mankind—it is only a means of efficiency for good or ill."[63] The question is, serviceable for whom? The owner or the community? And if the community, how are different and conflicting serviceabilities to be reconciled? Matter-of-factness, science, the machine process, and culture may be interpreted or evaluated differently. "Seen in certain lights, tested by certain standards, it is doubtless better; by other standards, worse."[64] The results of technology are not conclusively good.[65] Subjective, normative inputs are necessary.

Fourth, Veblen wrote in an essay published in 1906, that "It is not the Marxism of Marx, but the materialism of Darwin, which the socialists of today have adopted."[66] Granted the place of pragmatic adjustments in Marxian theory (abetted by its dialecticism) as well as practice, it does not seem that Marxists have become Darwinists. There continues to this day controversy within Marxism between the deterministic and the conditionistic interpretation of Marx's dialectical materialism, but neither the latter nor, certainly, the former are evidently Darwinian in the manner understood by Veblen.

Finally, we are entitled by Veblen's own argument to ask of him the same question which he in effect posed to other schools of thought: what is reality (and in what sense of "reality") and what is preconception? We must take seriously the self-referential character of his argument. Of the "cumulative process of development, and its complex and unstable outcome, that are to be the economist's subject-matter," he said[67] What is objective and what is subjective? What is a matter of preconception and what is independent of preconception? What is it, precisely, which produces that which is matter-of-fact? What putative status are we to ascribe to "knowledge"? These are serious questions; the answers are not self-evident, even after reading Veblen and especially after such writers as Richard Rorty, Mary Douglas, Peter Berger, Michel Foucault, and Jerome Brunner. Veblen's argument about preconceptions is truly for the ages; belief, even in Veblen, must be held with some sense of diffidence. But if Veblen's Darwinism is correct, then what of a society in which belief is in fact held with a sense of diffidence? After all, it is not too much to say that Veblenian ideas are part of the Darwinian process of cumulation variation and selection. That fact may be the greatest monument to Veblen—who, of course, did not have good things to say about such ceremonial fetishes as monuments.

Notes

1.   Thorstein Veblen, *The Place of Science in Modern Civilisation* (New York: B. W. Huebsch, 1919).
2.   Ibid., 157.
3.   Ibid., 188.
4.   Ibid., 191.
5.   Ibid., 230.
6.   Ibid., 280.
7.   Ibid., 129.
8.   Ibid., 258.
9.   Ibid., 259.
10.   Ibid., 260.
11.   Ibid., 411.
12.   Ibid., 158.
13.   Ibid., 179.
14.   Ibid., 312.
15.   Ibid., 16.
16.   Ibid., 24.
17.   Ibid., 16.

18.   Ibid., 37.
19.   Ibid., 192.
20.   Ibid., 77.
21.   Ibid., 64.
22.   Ibid., 10.
23.   Ibid., 349.
24.   Ibid., 12.
25.   Ibid., 17.
26.   Ibid., 17.
27.   Ibid., 30.
28.   Ibid., 44-45.
29.   Ibid., 75.
30.   Ibid., 79-80, 105.
31.   Ibid., 105.
32.   Ibid., 438.
33.   Ibid., 14.
34.   Ibid., 15.
35.   Ibid., 76.
36.   Ibid., 149.
37.   Ibid., 23.
38.   Ibid., 70.
39.   Ibid., 56.
40.   Ibid., 81.
41.   Ibid., 103-104.
42.   Ibid., 38.
43.   Ibid., 176.
44.   Ibid., 33.
45.   Ibid., 161-162.
46.   Ibid., 79-80.
47.   Ibid., 65-66.
48.   Ibid., 86 49
49.   Ibid., 237.
50.   Ibid., 73-74.
51.   Ibid., 122.
52.   Ibid., 140.
53.   Ibid., 364-366, 372.
54.   Ibid., 243.
55.   Ibid., 244-245.
56.   Ibid., 81.
57.   Ibid., 398.
58.   Ibid., 397.
59.   Ibid., 399.
60.   Ibid., 296.
61.   Ibid., 310.
62.   Ibid., 311.
63.   Ibid., 359.
64.   Ibid., 29-30.
65.   Ibid., 31.
66.   Ibid., 432.
67.   Ibid., 267.

16

Thorstein Veblen's Last Hurrah: Kept Classes, Vested Interests, and the Common Man

Irving Louis Horowitz

Thorstein Veblen has become an iconic figure. This is especially the case for institutional economists who would like to be sociologists, and sociologists who would like to think that they are not thoroughly ignorant of things economic. He is, in short, an intellectually accessible figure, if a somewhat marginalized one in professional and occupation terms. The minus of this adoration is that criticism is not something that Veblen has had much of these days. And nothing is more deadly than hagiography disguised as evaluation or biography. Opponents ignore him with the same dedication as proponents adore him. One bracing aspect of *The Vested Interests* is that in these briefer pieces, written for the literary crowd, Veblen comes through warts and all. To ignore the warts is to pay scant attention to the achievement of the work as such.

Each of these essays appeared initially in *Dial,* and appeared from October 1918 to January 1919 under the general caption, "The Modern Point of View and the New Order." They are modified only slightly and not necessarily for the better, for the book version. In turn, the magazine pieces were based on a series of lectures that Veblen delivered at Amherst College in May 1918. The sense of World War I coming to a close hangs heavy in the choice of themes in these essays. Veblen in a brief note appended to the book gives a succinct summary of the purpose of the lectures, then the articles, and finally the book. "The aim of these papers is to show how and, as far as may be, why a discrepancy has arisen in the course of time between those accepted principles of law and custom that underlie business enterprise and the businesslike management of industry, on the one hand, and the material conditions which have now been engendered by that new order of industry that took its rise in the late eighteenth century, on the other hand; together with some speculations on the civil and political difficulties set afoot by this discrepancy between business and industry."

Veblen is the sort of protean figure who derives his reputation from a curious admixture of brilliant global insights, generalizations that call us back to first principles, and personal asides that make us smile, but probably made his contemporaries more than a little angry with the object of his derision. In short, he is the quintessential essayist. He was not given to academic protocol, and I suspect that the strange group of "institutional economists" that now consider themselves Veblenians often do so for stylistic reasons. For to approach Veblen as a grand systems designer would be not only a waste, but also a cruel joke on Veblen himself. The thin line between intellectual creativity and literary license, a line that Veblen crisscrossed with careless abandon on more than one occasion, gives us pause to consider whether it is scientific rigor or novelistic aperçu that make someone memorable. My approach to *The Vested Interests* is to take at face value the arguments he presents—meaning empirical value—and see how it is that a figure of such contrariness as well as contradictions survives in our minds while lesser figures of a more earnest sort pass into the dustbin of intellectual history.

Thorstein Veblen is the great American example of an academic social scientist who was also a writer turned prophet. Nowhere is this better displayed than in *The Vested Interests*. He wrote eleven books (several of them derived from essays, in particular *The Vested Interests*). Many of the chapters of these books first appeared as random essays for popular journals aimed at a literate, bourgeois audience of the college-educated and the business-trained—in short the very people for whom Veblen exhibited little compassion—some might say, the least appreciation. Indeed, over the course of the century, Veblen seems to have been transmuted from an economist to a sociologist. As economics veered to quantitative analysis of partial systems, and sociology took up the claims of qualitative analysis of whole civilizations, to discuss Veblen in relation to American sociology from Giddings to Park seems far more sensible than any other option in the history of ideas.

The Vested Interests is the perfect indicator of these contradictory trends in the work and thought of Thorstein Veblen. He was radical in input, conservative in outcome; analytical in design, ideological in rhetoric; materialist in economic analysis, idealistic in his emphasis on law and custom as regulatory mechanisms of the management of society. Veblen was a socialist in his hopes for a business civilization, and a feudalist, to the point of being medieval, in his faith in industry, thrift, and integrity. These contradictions are inherent even in the title. The book is variously titled *The Vested Interests and the State of the Industrial Arts*—a rather clumsy title disguising in perfect Veblenian terms a lifelong concern over the quality of work and the workplace. But the alternate title, *The Vested Interests and the Common Man* speaks to a late blooming concern with the fate of blue-collar America. In short, Veblen offers his classic pose on social status, intertwined with a growing interest in economic class—or better yet, the political prospects of that class.

In this sense, Veblen's work, although following the close of World War I, does not so much reflect what Eric Hobsbawm refers to as the "short" twentieth century lasting from 1914 to 1989 (the fall of communism), so much as the last hurrah of the nineteenth century. His is a specifically radical voice in a world in which issues of gender barely rise above a whisper and in which those of race rise not at all. That so many readers of Veblen continue to be charmed by his rhetoric is as much a function of his quaint sense of what matters, as any cutting edge sensibility of the postwar world coming to grips with American problems as world problems. Indeed, one is hard put to find in Veblen a sense of the global context in which America was operating in the early 1920s. His world remained from start to finish a nineteenth-century world. The Great War was a "disturbance"; issues of national self-determination were derided as "the self-aggrandizement of each and several at the cost of the rest." Isolationism was the operative principle, the conservative principle, of this radical son of the Midwest. The world became an "incursion of ideas and considerations that are alien to the established liberal principles of human intercourse." The League of Nations, then very much on the postwar table, became for Veblen "a blurred afterimage of the divine right of kings." Veblen ended his panegyric with an observation that such efforts at international order disguised "national pretensions, wrangles, dominion, aggrandizement, chicanery, and ill-will." It was the new format for "the old familiar trading stock of the diplomatic brokers who do business in dynastic force and fraud, also called Realpolitik." While one may be somewhat embarrassed by the severity of Veblen's isolationism, the fact is that the League of Nations did little to preserve the peace and much to defend the commercial right of particular vested interests.

One argument Veblen adduces against prospects for some general interest to contain the "special interests" is the argument concerning the need for tariffs to support a national economy. For Veblen and "all adult persons of sound mind" the tariff is part and parcel of the price system itself, and hence the use of things like tariffs obstructs the growth of industry itself. No free marketer could have spoken with greater ferocity against the sabotage and the pettifogging special pleaders than this dedicated champion of socialism could! Consider Veblen's categorical assault on the idea of ethnicity or at least small nationhood. Those Czechs, Slovaks, Slovenes, Ruthenians, Ukrainians, Croats, Poles and "Polaks," those "miniscule Machiavellians" clamoring for "national establishments"—whose sole real object in nation building has no meaning in a time of peace—working at cross purposes with other ministates. These are hardly the conventional arguments of the conventional Left. He could not care less for nationalism or self-determination. For Veblen, nations organized for "collective offense and defense in peace and war" are entities quite at odds with social organizations created to advance a "supposed community race— essentially based on sympathies and sentiments of self-complacency within itself." We have in short, a man given to simplistic homiletics like "Live and Let Live" as an answer to the driving forces of the twentieth century.

But if Veblen's late essays were reducible to a series of dialectical polarities, then his continuing reputation as one of the great figures of the twentieth century would long ago have gone up in a puff of smoke. One reads Veblen as a social scientific gestalt—a panoramic vision of the industrial genesis of modernism corrupted by its moral blindness. We are at home with these contrasts, and so we can enjoy his essays without being encumbered by the initial audiences Veblen had in mind.

Veblen himself was unsure of the title. He calls it at first *The Vested Interests and the State of the Industrial Arts*. Later it becomes *The Vested Interests and the Common Man*. And to confuse matters further, it is given a wholly different title in parentheses: *The Modern*

Point of View and the New Order. I am taking the liberty of calling this slender volume of essays, *The Vested Interests*. In so doing, Veblen himself offers the best reason for such an abbreviation. In the chapter called "The Vested Interests" he simply claims that "all that industry which comes in under the dominant machine technology, that is to say all that fairly belongs in the new order of industry, is now governed by business men for business ends, in what is to be done and what is to be left undone" (p. 99). In that phrase is encapsulated Veblen's harsh empirical view of the vested interests combined with a moral disapproval of the artificial limits this class sets on civilization and its thirst for progress.

But such a vision was old hat, even in the 1920s. The decade between 1910 and 1920 witnessed the emergence of a native socialism in the form of Eugene Victor Debs of some moral force no less than electoral power. Veblen reflected this in his final essay for *The Vested Interests*, that is the chapter on "The Common Man." While the ruling classes are pilloried as a set of "kept classes," who have better circumstances but not better values no meaningful class analysis follows. The place of the ruling classes is simply "to consume the net product of the country's industry over cost and so prevent a glut of the market." They also give rise to a series of intermediary classes, "such as the clergy, the military, the courts, police, and legal professions and occupations." These "subsidiary and dependent vested interests" are more refracted than reflective. They survive and even thrive on the "good will" of the controlling vested interests. "By sentiment and habitual outlook they belong with the kept classes." Of course, this was a disturbing wrinkle in the moral purity of Veblen's argument. It rated the academy, that most despised entity that also carried the message of rebellion and revolt, as little more than a vassal of the ruling classes. How it came about that this particular sub-set of the ruling class (of which Veblen himself was a part) often gave voice to and articulated the needs of the "common man," was a task later taken up by the sociologists of knowledge like Karl Mannheim and social psychologists like C. Wright Mills. Veblen had little time or patience with giving the intermediary classes a role other than that of lapdog. In this, he was very much a child of the Marxian revolutionaries.

Veblen knew as much, he understood his formulation served as but a crude reductionism, a reminder of why he was being listened to in the first place. Thus an infrequent appearance, the common man makes an appearance on his own terms—not as a stepchild to the ruling classes, but as a class in its own right. It is true that the trade union movement, dominated by the American Federation of Labor (AFL), was not aware of the brewing divisions in labor's ranks that led to the birth of the militant Congress of Industrial Organizations, that was organized on an industry-wide rather than craft basis. Veblen still had a model in opposition to the AFL, namely the International Workers of the World (IWW). Veblen saw the working class as the vanguard of revolutionary action. The independent farmers were hardly to be counted upon as friends of the organized worker, and the intellectual or professional elites were too busily engaged in getting their own largess to worry about proletarianized tradesmen.

That left the proletariat as the only class willing to fight for something more that "something for nothing." Veblen refers to a "cleavage" brought about in the new order in business and industry. It turns out that a larger (95 percent) group suspiciously like Karl Marx's proletariat is waiting in the wings to restore a vibrant capitalism or at least its moral equivalent—a society of trade unionists who have nothing to lose but their assembly line. Veblen sees the "common man" in broad blue-collar terms: "somewhat irresponsible and unsteady in his aims and conduct." In the eyes of the guardians of law and order, he is "an undesirable citizen." The way into a glorious future is to convert this "lack of respect and affection of the vested interests" into advanced forms of trade unionism. The wobblies of the International Workers of the World are to become the model for "the new order."

What evidence such syndicalism displays in the past that can serve as evidence for a new higher blue-collar morality is not made clear by Veblen—any more than it was made clear by Sorel in France. The idea of class collaboration was anathema to both advocates of syndicalism as a new morality, and not just a new way to gain better wages, hours, and health conditions. What Veblen saw as the "modern era" was little more than a capitalism that was unreconstructed and unbridled. Non-economic issues such as psychological modes of increasing awareness of common goals between the vested interests and the working masses were never entertained by Veblen, even if the work of Elton Mayo and Frederick Roethlisberger was already well underway. In this, Veblen was part and parcel of the socialist as well as syndicalist tradition. The idea of vanguard parties, dictatorship of the proletariat and generally authoritarian modes of behavior were anathema to Veblen. Hence, at the end of the day, Veblen was left with a dilemma: an economic order that was unpalatable and unacceptable at the political level—an order coming into being unknown to him. The conservative moralist as revolutionary is what we are left with at the close of the volume. Little wonder that this effort at a positive solution to a quarter decade of criticism was not exactly a highlight of Veblen's career.

One can draw a line from *The Vested Interests* to C. Wright Mills' *Power Elite*. It is a line that starts with the idea of the virtual monopoly of wealth and authority of the business class to a near conspiracy to bend and shape all aspects of society in its narrow image. It is a world in which notions of political democracy are virtually absent, and in which the people are served by marginalized groups like the International Workers of the World. Veblen knew full well that the common man was not simply the bearer of all virtue. But in identifying commonness with farmers who cultivate their own land, and factory workers who organize their own unions, Veblen was caught in the trap of populism. He wanted a virtuous outcome based on this common man, but on inspection was compelled to recognize that such common men were envious to the point of imitation of the businessman. Veblen, like Mills after him, saw no prospect of political struggle, party participation, and voting patterns changing very much. Economic robbers must be fought with economic methods. As a result, the development of the New Deal and its allied varieties of liberalism were not anticipated by Veblen—for whom the Roaring '20s was indeed the epitome and outcome of bourgeois decadence. Even if Veblen is now seen more as sociologist than as economist, he shared one characteristic of his professional tribe: a belief in the supremacy of a business civilization over a liberal state.

Contributors

E. Digby Baltzell (1915-1996) was professor emeritus of sociology at the University of Pennsylvania. He also had served in various visiting professional roles at Princeton Theological Seminary and Harvard University. Baltzell was the author of *Puritan Boston and Quaker Philadelphia*; *The Protestant Establishment: Aristocracy and Caste in America*; and *Philadelphia Gentlemen: The Making of a National Upper Class*.

Daniel Bell is professor emeritus of sociology at Harvard University. His most recent work is *The Radical Right*, which he edited. Bell is also the author of *The End of Ideology*, *The Cultural Contradictions of Capitalism*, *The Winding Passage: Sociological Essays and Journeys*, and *The Social Sciences Since the Second World War*.

Ivar Berg is professor of sociology at the University of Pennsylvania. He is the author of *Industrial Society* and *Education and Jobs: The Great Training Robbery* and co-author of *Managers and Work Reform* and *Work and Industry: Structure, Markets, Processes*.

Scott R. Bowman is associate professor of political science at California State University, Los Angeles. He is the author of *The Modern Corporation* and *American Political Thought: Law, Power, and Ideology*.

Douglas F. Dowd was professor of economics at The Johns Hopkins University where he was Guggenheim Fellow. His writings include *Modern Economic Problems in Historical Perspective*, *America's Role in the World Economy*, *Step by Step*, *Thorstein Veblen: A Critical Reappraisal*, and numerous articles for scholarly journals and encyclopedias.

Irving Louis Horowitz is Hannah Arendt Distinguished Professor Emeritus of Sociology and Political Science at Rutgers University, where he also serves as chairman of the board of Transaction Publishers. His most recent work is *Behemoth: The History and Theory of Political Sociology.*

Max Lerner (1902-1992) was Distinguished Professor at the Graduate School of Human Behavior, United States International University at San Diego; and before that, University Professor of Social Theory at Brandeis University. Lerner is the author of several books, including *Thomas Jefferson: America's Philosopher-King; Magisterial Imagination: Six Masters of the Human Sciences; Tocqueville and American Civilization;* and *Ideas for the Ice Age: Studies in a Revolutionary Era.* He was also a syndicated columnist for the Los Angeles Times Syndicate and the *New York Post* over a forty-year time span.

Marion J. Levy, Jr. is Musgrave Distinguished Professor Emeritus of Sociology and International Affairs in the Woodrow Wilson School of Public and International Affairs at Princeton University. He is the author of *Modernization and the Structure of Societies* and *Maternal Influence.*

Otto G. Mayer is managing publisher of *Intereconomics: Review of International Trade and Development*, a publication of the Hamburg Institute of International Economics, a leading German think tank. Mayer has written widely on economic and social issues.

C. Wright Mills (1916-1962) was professor of sociology at Columbia University. At the time of his death, he had been credited with calling into question the whole structure of social and economic power in American society. His books *White Collar: The American Middle Classes, The Power Elite,* and *The Sociological Imagination* have become modern social science classics.

Wesley Clair Mitchell (1874-1948) held major teaching posts at the University of California and Columbia University. One of the most eminent U.S. economists of his day, Mitchell focused much of his research on the statistical investigation of business cycles. His two major works are *Business Cycles* and *Business Cycles: The Problem at Its Setting.*

Murray G. Murphey is professor of American Civilization at the University of Pennsylvania. He is the author of *The Development of Peirce's Philosophy*, co-author of *History of Philosophy in America* and co-editor of *Values and Value Theory in Twentieth-Century America*.

David Riesman is professor emeritus of sociology at Harvard University. He is the author of *Thorstein Veblen*, *Abundance for What*, *Constraint & Variety in American Education*, and *On Higher Education: The Academic Enterprise in an Era of Rising Student Consumerism*. Riesman (with others) wrote the sociology classic *Lonely Crowd: A Study of Changing American Character*.

Warren J. Samuels is professor of economics at Michigan State University. He is co-editor (with Steven G. Medema) of the Classics in Economics series for Transaction Publishers and a former editor of the *Journal of Economic Issues*. He is the author of *The Economy as a System of Power* and editor of *The Methodology of Economic Thought* and *The Chicago School of Political Economy*.

Thorstein Veblen (1857-1929) served as editor of the *Journal of Political Economy*, taught at Stanford University, and then spent a decade at the University of Chicago, never attaining a rank higher than assistant professor. He wrote a great many reviews, introducing major German, French, and English social scientists to American audiences. His major works include *The Theory of the Leisure Class*, *The Engineers and the Price System*, *The Place of Science in Modern Civilization*, *The Theory of Business Enterprise*, *The Higher Learning in America*, *The Instinct of Workmanship*, and *Absentee Ownership*.